IN THE ABSENCE OF SUN

IN THE ABSENCE OF SUN

HELIE LEE

A Korean

American Woman's

Promise to

Reunite

Three Lost

Generations of

Her Family

THREE RIVERS PRESS
NEW YORK

To my brothers and sisters in North Korea,

friendship and peace

Published by Three Rivers Press, New York, New York.
Member of the Crown Publishing Group, a division of Random House, Inc.
www.crownpublishing.com

THREE RIVERS PRESS and the Tugboat design are registered
trademarks of Random House, Inc.

Originally published in hardcover by Harmony Books, a member of the
Crown Publishing Group, New York, in 2002.

Printed in the United States of America

Design by Lauren Dong

Map illustration by Mark Stein Studio

Library of Congress Cataloging-in-Publication Data

Lee, Helie,
In the absence of sun: a Korean American woman's promise to reunite
three lost generations of her family/by Helie Lee.
1. Lee family.   2. Baek, Hongyong, 1912– —Family.   3. California—
Genealogy.   4. Korea (North)—Genealogy.   I. Title.
CT274.L44 I5 2002
979.4'.004957'00922—dc21   2002001680

ISBN 1-4000-8138-6

Acknowledgments

WHENEVER POSSIBLE I have maintained original names; however, some names, dates, and descriptions have been altered to protect the identities of those outstanding individuals who assisted my family. I am thankful for them.

I am thankful for my literary agent, Jennifer Rudolph Walsh, for finding the perfect home for my book.

I am thankful for my wise and gifted editors and their assistants, who have shown me only devotion and grace: Linda Loewenthal at Harmony Books, Rebecca Strong at Random House, Emily Stephens (assistant to Ms. Strong), and Cara Brozenich (assistant to Ms. Loewenthal).

I am thankful for all my friends who came to my rescue during times of stress and who have been a constant, loving support: Denise Railla, James "Bear" Ryu and *KoreAm Journal,* Charse Yun, Mary Connor, Stacy and Peter Pae, Debi Key, Jackie Kiang, Lee Ann Kim, Melanie Smith, the O'Connell clan in Gladstone, New Jersey, Brian and Lynn Arthurs, Jeannie Olander, John Song, Tom Michalak, Sara Harris, Sharline Chiang, Lily Siao Sugino, Ken Wada, John Cha, Steve Yoon, Michael and Arline O'Brien, Mariam Hammert, Diane Kneeland, Rosanne Katon-Walden and Richard Walden, Julie Goler, Linda Griffith, Jill Dove, Eva Wong, Esther Kimm Pak, Minju Pak, Darlene Hunt, Meg Brogan, Cynthia Yoo, and Peter Yum.

And always I give thanks for my family. Without them I would truly be lost and undernourished.

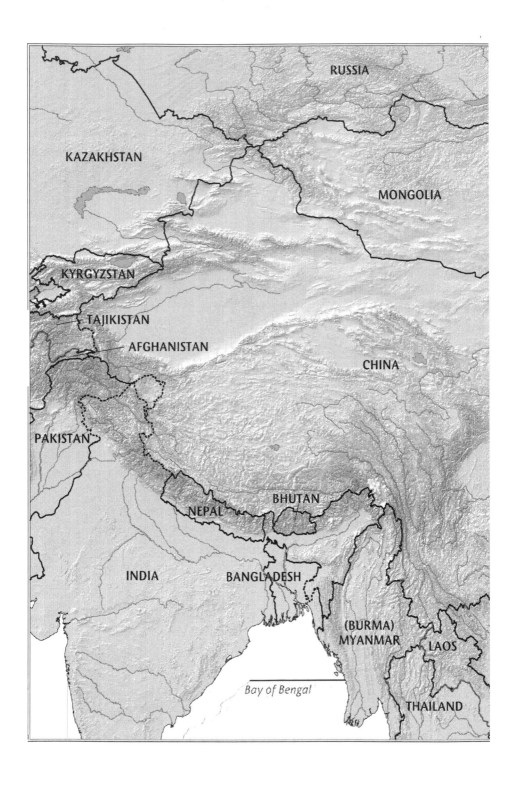

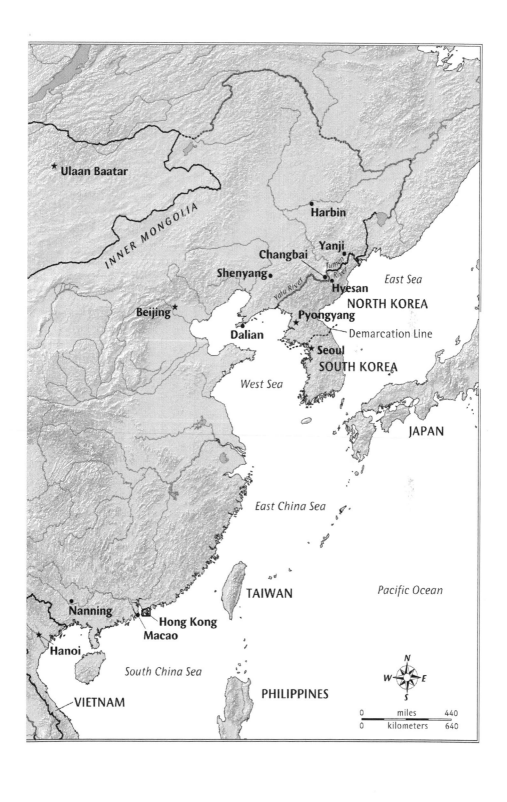

자유를 찾아서

SEEKING FREEDOM

어둠속
허허벌판에 깔아 논
바람의 여울목 자나서
갈망을 쫓아
큰 새 작은 새 모두 아홉
들켜도 괜찮은 나무에 앉아
서로 죽지를 비벼댄다

응어리로
얼어붙은 인내 가누지 못해
눈멀고 귀머거리로
반백년을 잠가 두었던
가슴앓이

이젠
싫건 울어라
노래가 아니면 어떠랴
그것이 자유인 것을 ...

Lee, Jae Hak

FAMILY TREE

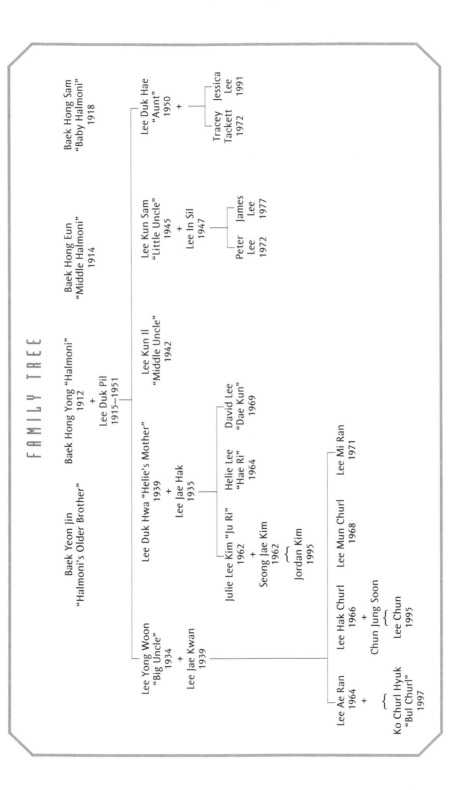

YALU

"Oh my God," I gasped.

I tried desperately to blink away the icy raindrops that the wind pelted against my face. An eerie fear crawled through my flesh as I stood on the Chinese side of the Yalu River, gazing across the murky water into one of the most closed-off and isolated countries in the world. I couldn't believe it. Even as my boots sank into the doughy mud, I had trouble coming to terms with the fact that I was actually standing there. Through the heavy layer of fog, I saw North Korea's sharp, mountainous landscape just across the watery border, which was about sixty yards wide and barely waist deep. The riverbank was strewn with rocks and stretched for about forty feet to the base of a tall stone wall. The wall didn't have floodlights or coiled razor wire along the top. It wasn't built to keep people from trying to get out; it was there to prevent the outside world from seeing all the decay, dirt, and disrepair just behind it. But the armed soldiers, posted every ten to fifteen yards along the rocky riverbank, would shoot down anyone who did try to escape over it and to the other side of the river.

I remained silent, terrified to speak, too scared to call out to the gnarled old man staggering toward the water. He reached the edge of the still, murky river and sagged with fatigue. Slowly he removed his droopy Lenin cap and worn tank-green Mao jacket, revealing a frame so bony I shuddered at the sight. As he washed in the freezing water, the dark, gaping holes of his eyes were fixed on me in a look of utter hopelessness: no food, no warm clothes, no future, no reason to live.

This was my uncle Lee Yong Woon.

I was torn between wanting this to be real and wanting to be somewhere else entirely. Below my feet it felt like the muddy earth was giving way. Turning away, I buried my face between my knees, put my head down on my arms, and began to cry, too. The tears came slowly at first, but they gathered fury fast and I broke down completely. My breath came in ragged gasps. At that moment, I wanted to click my heels three times and be transported back to my apartment in West Hollywood, curled close in my boyfriend's warmth. But the wretchedness that seeped into my soul tainted the memory of my happy, comfortable life back home. I was suddenly filled with guilt for the warm clothes I was wearing, for all the food I had wasted, and for the freedom I had taken for granted. If only I could have given my uncle my protective jacket, or at the very least called out to him. He was so close. But the presence of the soldiers, poised to shoot, froze my feet and silenced the words in my mouth.

God, please, please, help him, I thought, praying for a miracle. Like Moses, who parted the Red Sea with a wave of his wooden staff and saved his people from the tyrannical pharaoh, I wanted God to perform such a miracle and unite my people in the country where I was born.

I waited and waited in agonizing silence. But nothing happened. Where are you, God? Where are you? Damn it! Why are you letting this happen? I demanded.

A coldness that was not from the rain sank into my flesh. I felt absolutely deserted, and my faith cracked.

I couldn't stand the oppressive silence and feeling of helplessness any longer. Inside I was about to implode. I needed to pass on a message from Halmoni, my grandmother, to my uncle, her son. It was a message that we had traveled so far and waited so many years to deliver, and all at once, before I even knew what I was doing, my mouth jerked open and the words came croaking out.

"Halmoni has never stopped searching for you, Big Uncle. She's never forgotten you!" I shouted in my American-accented Korean. I quickly clamped my lips together in anticipation of a ricochet of bullets.

That was what Halmoni wanted him to know. She had never stopped searching for him. Her aged body had held on to life in hopes of finding him someday. And that had been my promise to her—to help her find her missing son, and when we did, I would take her to him.

I cranked up my hearing to draw in my uncle's voice, but he only wiped his eyes in acknowledgment. He wouldn't, couldn't, speak. Seeing him weep, his whole body quivering, I began to cry again. My tears became indistinguishable from the raindrops and flowed down my face, one after another, each leaving a burning trail on my cheeks. I was crying for him. I was also crying for Halmoni, who had mourned the absence of her son for over forty-seven years. And now that we had found him, a narrow river made so dense and impenetrable by clashing politics still separated them.

I was not prepared for the kind of despair and insane fear I felt that day. My wizened old uncle looked nothing like the sweet-faced teenager in the faded photograph that Halmoni kept pressed between the pages of her Bible. That day at the Yalu River, staring helplessly into his terrorized face, I hadn't fully realized what a dangerous thing I had done the year before. I had placed him and his family in danger. By including details of my uncle's life in a book, I had alerted North Korea's enigmatic leadership to the identity of my relatives in a nation where it was better to remain invisible.

The book began simply as a wish to discover my roots through my maternal grandmother. I was four years old and my sister, Julie, was six when we left South Korea in 1968. My parents sold everything to pay for our airfare to Montreal, Canada. I instantly liked our new home. It was the first time I had slept in a bed with legs, my own bed, and eaten sweet jelly-filled croissants. However, my parents kept gazing toward America's promise. As a young soldier, my father had watched John Wayne and Elvis Presley movies and was determined to get to America. A year later, in 1969, after the birth of my brother, David, our family of five finally landed in sunny Los Angeles, California. My father got a job as an electrical engineer for General Telephone Electric, and my mother sewed garments in a factory. They worked long, grueling hours, six days a week, and were eventually able to afford a house in the San Fernando Valley, where there were plenty of bagel shops and only one Chinese restaurant. My parents moved us to the Valley so my siblings and I could learn and speak English like a *miguk-saram*—like a white American. They didn't want us to confuse our *r*'s and *l*'s and *v*'s and *b*'s as they did, something they felt would cripple our chances of success. My father told us that in America, if we studied hard and got into a good university, then we could become a Ph.D., diplomat, or whatever else we wanted to be. In America, there were no limits, even for girls. I believed him, and in my fierce desire to fit in with the kids at school I wanted to be white. I bleached and permed and tortured my black hair, tanned my yellow skin, and Scotch-taped my eyes to crease the lids. I even taught myself how to sing

"Hava Nagilah," to ska dance to the Police, and to like cottage cheese. I was determined. I hated being labeled "Oriental." I hated people thinking we ate dog like the ragged refugees did on the television show *M*A*S*H*.

My parents' and Halmoni's stubborn refusal to integrate annoyed and confused me. Just the mention of a Korean kid earning a perfect SAT score, learning of a Korean winning a Ping-Pong championship, or seeing a Hyundai on the road would ignite their pride. I found myself wondering what was so great about being an identifiable minority. What was so great about being Korean? Why wouldn't they let go of the past? So at the age of twenty-four, I decided to return to my birthplace, something I had sworn up and down I'd never do. My parents were thrilled. They prayed fervently to Jesus that I'd come back triumphantly with a picture bridegroom. That was the furthest thing from my mind as I packed my Levi's 501 jeans and a framed photo of my blond boyfriend.

The moment I cleared customs at Seoul's Kimpo International Airport and walked through the double glass doors, I was engulfed by second, third, and fourth cousins, who eagerly welcomed me into their homes. From them, I was fed Halmoni's legendary past, from her childhood days in her father's house in Pyongyang to running a prosperous opium business in China, defying the communists, and surviving the Korean War. Halmoni was no longer the strange, clueless silver-haired woman who couldn't even operate a microwave oven or remote control. Halmoni was a warrior.

When I returned to the States a year and a half later, I was filled with an overwhelming, insatiable thirst to find out more about Halmoni's past. It was during this time that I first heard the name Lee Yong Woon. All my life I had assumed Halmoni had four children, my mother being the eldest. They never spoke about this missing family member until I started prying deeper, asking more questions. Through their choked sobs I learned that Yong Woon was the only one out of Halmoni's five children who hadn't made it out of North Korea during the war.

The family had just returned to Pyongyang after living in China for six years. They had retreated there in 1939 to escape Japan's ruthless occupation of Korea. The Japanese tried to strip away everything that was Korean—the language, the culture, and even our names. With Japan's surrender at the end of World War II, Halmoni's family eagerly rushed back home only to discover that their newly liberated peninsula had been divided along the 38th parallel. U.S. troops marched into the area south of the arbitrary line, and Soviet troops marched into the North, where Halmoni's family lived. To head its regime in the North, the Soviet Union appointed Kim Il Sung, a guerrilla commander who had initially fought the Japanese in China, then spent the last years of World War II in Manchurian training camps commanded by the Soviet army.

The division was only supposed to be a temporary solution for the previously Japanese-held territory, but over time the two regimes became increasingly opposed politically. On June 25, 1950, civil war erupted after long-simmering clashes and tension boiled over. The Soviet-backed Democratic People's Republic of Korea (DPRK) invaded the U.S.-backed Republic of Korea (ROK) in an attempt to reunify the country by force. As a result, the United States, South Korea, and fifteen other nations under the flag of the United Nations waged war.

North Korean forces lost ground and manpower quickly. The soldiers ripped through the countryside, abducting new recruits to replace the dead and the injured. Halmoni refused to sacrifice her husband and sixteen-year-old son Yong Woon to the communists. The communists had persecuted them for converting to Christianity and for being rich landowners. Instead she urged her men to flee to the South, while she stayed behind with her four younger children, her youngest just a newborn. When the police discovered the men had fled, they beat her brutally and threw her into prison. For several weeks Halmoni was locked up in a cold cell crammed with women before they finally released her.

When she returned home, she waited nervously for the war to end and for her husband and son to return. However, the bombs kept blasting the capital city of Pyongyang. Halmoni could wait no longer. She strapped the infant to her back, held her six- and nine-year-old boys by the hand, and had her thirteen-year-old daughter cling to her long skirt. During the height of UN air assaults in late November 1950, they joined the mass exodus of refugees shambling south. They dodged bombs and low-flying B-29 planes strafing the ground. On frostbitten feet, they walked against the icy wind, past exhaustion. Then on Christmas Eve, almost four weeks after they began their perilous journey, they finally reached the capital of South Korea, only to find out that the Chinese People's Volunteer Army had joined the bloody battle with North Korea. Chinese troops poured across the Yalu River and slashed at UN and ROK forces, heading directly for Seoul.

Once again, Halmoni and her weary children headed farther down to the tip of the Korean peninsula, to the port city of Pusan. It was the only southern city that had not been invaded by the communists. In Pusan, Halmoni joyfully found her husband among the throng of refugees searching for separated family members. She never found her eldest son.

Dead? Alive? No one knew. The last she had heard of him was that he had been captured by North Korean troops along with two of his friends just north of the 38th parallel. One of the friends had managed to escape to the South and found Halmoni in Pusan.

When the Korean Armistice Agreement was signed on July 27, 1953, to temporarily stall the bloody three-year fighting, Halmoni tried desperately to track down her son's whereabouts. But in the aftermath of the war, the ideological and political lines between the North and South didn't soften. They became violently opposed, and the cold war intensified. North Korea became one of the most isolated societies in the world. Kim Il Sung created a tightly closed, centrally controlled regime in the North, while the South eventually developed into an economic powerhouse.

Still, Halmoni would not give up her search. She diligently wrote letters to ambassadors and missionaries, went on South Korean television, and repeatedly applied for a tourist visa to North Korea. When all her efforts failed, she prayed for reunification between the two Koreas. Every morning at dawn and every evening before she went to sleep, she would kneel and pray for an hour or two, sometimes longer. Reunification never came.

It wasn't until 1991, forty-one years later, when I sat down at my computer and began writing about Halmoni's history, that the past came crashing down on the streets of the present and a letter arrived from North Korea resurrecting my uncle's ghost. The letter was addressed to Little Uncle, Halmoni's youngest and third son, Kun Sam. He had taken over Halmoni's search after she was hospitalized in 1988 for surgery to remove two golf-ball-sized kidney stones. The unexpected letter was written by Yong Woon Uncle's eldest daughter, Ae Ran, who was just a few months older than myself. The flimsy, yellowed sheets of paper were sealed in a coarse white envelope emblazoned with the emblem of the Workers' Party—the hammer and sickle, and the pen—in blood-red ink.

1991, June 4

DEAR LITTLE UNCLE,

How are you? On behalf of the Lee family I write this letter to an uncle whom I have never met, wondering how you are doing, what you look like, whether you are fine.

My name is Ae Ran, the oldest daughter of your big brother, Lee Yong

Woon. I understand you have been searching so long for him even in your dreams. Do you remember him clearly?

Time flies as swiftly as stream water. When you and my father were separated forty-one years ago, you both were very young. Now you are in your fifties with lots of gray hair.

I am twenty-eight years old. I was not born at the time when the tragic separation took place. My parents did not know if you had survived or not. They were deeply moved with the news that you are alive and all are well. If you were not in a country far away across the Pacific Ocean, we would run to you with wide-open arms and embrace you tightly. If there were no American barbarians, there would be a chance for you brothers to meet. Thinking of all the years of missed brotherhood fills our hearts with sadness.

I have strong feelings about the nature of the war. The country was divided into South and North, but the worst thing to happen to humankind was the enforced separation of the family. Though it left our land divided into two parts, the passion to search for our family never ended.

My siblings and I grew up not knowing that we even had a grandmother, uncles, aunts, and cousins. Now we know. I am sure that you, American uncle, have a big family by now. Ours consists of six members: father, mother, two younger brothers, a younger sister, and myself. My father is a trainer in the Revolutionary Construction Unit. My mother is a cook. I work for the Department of Food Quality Control as a quality controller. My younger brother, Hak Churl, twenty-six, is a student of Bochunbo Engineering College. My youngest brother, Mun Churl, twenty-four, is completing his military service in the North Korean People's Army. My youngest sister, Mi Ran, twenty-one, works as a volunteer for the visitors' field trip. Thus we are serving and doing our best for the country.

You know all about us, now it is your turn to let us know all about your life in America. I count every minute waiting anxiously for your letter to arrive. I hope it will be full of exciting news about the family. Please try to visit us in North Korea. I'm sure that it will be a great experience for you to step on the soil of the forbidden fatherland.

We never imagined you were still alive, much less in a big country like America. When the time to meet arrives, I would love to embrace you. Though we have never met, I feel very close to you because we share the same flesh. Flesh is a bond of fate. They say blood is thicker than water. I now agree. A family should not be divided under any circumstances. Nor the country.

There are endless questions, worries and concerns about the family.

Whenever I think of your dear faces in America, I can hardly sleep or work. Ashes fill my heart with such pain knowing you have a difficult and hard life in a foreign country.

I cannot go on writing.

Please take care. I wish everyone a bright future! I close my letter now, with love from all of us.

> *Your niece,*
> *Ae Ran in North Korea,*
> *the nearest and the farthest*

Korea remains in between war and peace. It has neither.

선동민주주의련련인공화
소 례선서 련물 동 39 반구
운 룡

JOURNEY ONE

I

April 18, 1997

We were on our way!

Three generations of us—my father, Halmoni, and I—were going to China to redeem the past. Soon we'd be in Yanji, a city in China's Jilian Province. Siberia was to the north, Chinese Inner Mongolia to the west, and North Korea just to the south. Westerners rarely ventured to this remote northeastern region. It was way off the beaten track. We had to change planes twice, and at last we embarked on our third and final leg of the journey.

It was unbelievable. After forty-seven years of separation, Halmoni was on her way to reunite with her son, Yong Woon. Ever since we had discovered that he was still alive in North Korea, I had not thought that a reunion would be possible. No one did. North Korea had been one of the most impenetrable and hostile nations in the world since the collapse of the Soviet Union and since the reforms in Cuba and China. Hardly anyone went in, and rarely did they go out. We prayed for a miracle.

A month before our journey began, a Korean Chinese man named Choi Soon Man phoned my parents from China, collect. He had lifted the phone number off one of our letterheads, which Yong Woon Uncle had shown him. He offered to smuggle Yong Woon Uncle across the North Korea–China border and bring him to his home in Yanji to visit with Halmoni, then sneak him back before the authorities discovered he was missing. Apparently, this man had befriended Yong Woon Uncle several years previously during one of his business trips to North Korea. He knew intimate facts about Halmoni that only Yong Woon Uncle could have revealed to him.

My family was stunned, and for days we pondered his outrageous offer.

Then we unanimously decided it was now or never. Halmoni couldn't wait any longer. Time was running out. Halmoni was a month shy of turning eighty-five (in Korean years she would be eighty-six, because a child was considered to be one at birth). Twice she had been hospitalized. Twice we had almost lost her. It was sheer force of will and her overwhelming desire to embrace her son one final time that made her rise from the hospital bed. And it was this same willpower and desire that was sustaining her during the long and exhausting journey from Los Angeles to Seoul to Beijing and finally to Yanji.

I had visited this remote area before during my travels through Asia to "find myself." That had been almost ten years before. So much had happened in my life as a result. After I returned to the States, I felt myself being steered toward a future I had never imagined. I began to write. Up until that point, I hadn't even known I could write. And as Halmoni's powerful stories moved through me, I was able to reflect on the delusional self-image I had crafted for myself. I could feel my true self emerging, rising. I no longer wished to be what I was not—white. This ignited a newfound awareness and excitement. With the publication of my book on the odyssey of Halmoni's life, I began to tour college campuses across the country, lecturing and promoting my heritage. My parents were very proud of me, but they worried about my untraditional lifestyle and advancing age. To them, marriage and family were everything, and they pressured me to walk down the aisle with my current boyfriend, Steven, before my thirty-third birthday. Steven was my parents' dream come true. He wore a suit and tie to the office every day, and he was a Korean-born American. Unfortunately, he lived in Hong Kong. The distance didn't allow Steven to be a constant presence in my life. To be totally honest, the distance and this trip to Yanji gave me time away from him to sort out my feelings.

Could I be happy living in Asia and being a banker's wife? I asked myself for the millionth time as I sank further into the cramped economy-class seat, trying to find a comfortable position.

Halmoni was sitting next to me. She had removed her clunky gray orthopedic shoes, and her eyelids, sunken into puckered cups, were shut. Her oversized gold-rimmed glasses had slid low on her bridgeless nose. They rested mostly on her pale cheeks, and her short permed silver hair, which she never combed back or confined with pins, fanned out onto the blue fabric of the seat back. Over the last few years, Halmoni had slowed down considerably, and her body no longer functioned perfectly—the muscles on her arms and legs were more shriveled, and she couldn't always control her bladder. However, her mind was as sharp as a knife's edge, and she looked marvelous. For a while I watched her. She seemed to be sleeping, but I knew she wasn't. Her mind was miles away. Ever since we had received Ae Ran's letter, she kept plunging into that well of memory.

After that initial contact in 1991, Halmoni once again applied for a visa, inspired by the news that North Korea was permitting war-torn families to reunite. It was because North Korea was desperate. The country was in a serious state of famine, worse than the 1988 Ethiopian crisis during which a million people died. Extreme winters, massive floods, and their corrupt and dysfunctional government system plagued the nation. Almost the entire population of twenty-four million was enduring severe hunger.

As Halmoni anxiously awaited for her visa to be approved, our families were permitted to exchange a few more letters.

1991, June 20

SEEKING MY BELOVED MOTHER,

Mother!!? Is this a dream? Are you real? It seems like a dream to me!! It has been forty-one years.

Mother, I write while holding back my tears. How did you manage to raise four children in a foreign country of materialism? There the mountains and waters are different; cultures and traditions are different; and skin colors are different.

After being separated from everyone, I was well taken care of by the country. Upon serving my country, I started a family and eventually relocated to Hyesan City. All four of my children have received scholarships to attend college. Now they are working. Therefore, I am living in paradise where everybody looks at me with envy. Our family is doing very well today, but I look forward to tomorrow's brighter days of our nation's resurrection, its reunification.

The nation teaches that regardless of your ideology and religion, people should contribute to the nation's reunification, each according to their means, with their minds, authority, or money. I sincerely wish that you, Mother, will also contribute to the reunification project so your name may be honored later by our children.

Mother, you are now eighty, but in my fifties I too have frost over my head. Mother, I wish to see you before I die. My wife and I wish to bow before you. You haven't even seen my children yet. They yearn to see you and bow before you, too.

Come at least once to the homeland, Mother, and see today's reality. Witness our family's life as it really is.

Mother, always be safe and let us talk once we meet. I am signing off now. Be well.

From your son,
Yong Woon

August 10, 1991

Dearest son,

Truly I felt the pain of my heart being torn out while reading your letters and seeing your pictures. I cannot bear to imagine how you survived all those years alone.

The last forty-one years are regretful. We did not desert you. After your father fled with the men and you went off with the students, we could not wait in our home any longer for your return. The bombs rained down on the city.

After forty-one years, I hear that you live, and it hits me like a dream. I am thankful for God's mercy. I have lived to eighty in hopes of seeing my dearest son, daughter-in-law, and grandchildren. As soon as possible, I will go there.

Your father passed away forty-one years ago, shortly after we found each other in the South. He died when we were refugees in Yech'on on December 29 on the lunar calendar. On my own I managed to raise your two younger brothers and two younger sisters wonderfully. Thanks are due to God. Duk Hwa studied English at Korea University; Kun Il majored in music composition at Suhrabul Art School and now is conducting a church choir; Kun Sam studied engineering at Hangyang University; and Duk Hae did not complete her college education, instead marrying when I left her behind in Korea with your aunts to join Duk Hwa in America.

Let us meet and talk about our forty-one years of mournful separation. Not a single day has gone by when I do not think of you with tears in my eyes.

Now I cry more imagining my little boy wandering around weeping, thinking his family had abandoned him.

This feels like a dream.

Stay well.

From,
Mother

August 16, 1991

DEAR OLDER BROTHER WITH AFFECTION AND REVERENCE, WHOM I LONG TO SEE,

I have a lump in my throat and I am lost for words.

So much time has gone by, so many changes. They say ten years can put new faces even on mountains and rivers. We could not bring ourselves to believe the initial letter from your daughter. Then when your letter came we were convinced. We wept till dawn. The two pictures you sent propelled us back to our youth and touched us deeply.

We used to live in Pyongyang. How is it that you are in Hyesan City now? No matter, though. I am only grateful that you are all well and everyone is healthy.

Over the years, we have all emigrated to America. Our two younger brothers and younger sister have settled down quite nicely with families of their own. As for my own family, we have been here the longest, over twenty-five years. My husband, who is the same age as you, is retired from General Telephone Electric, where he worked as an electrical engineer for twenty years. Our elder daughter, Ju Ri (Julie), twenty-nine, is an optometrist at a hospital. Our second daughter, Hae Ri (Helie), twenty-six, works at a television studio, and our youngest child, Dae Kun (David), twenty-two, is a third-year college student.

Our two aunts from our mother's side are also living here with their children.

I am sending you our photographs for now until we can meet in the flesh. Though we are far apart, we are one blood, one family.

Please stay well and live a full life until our two Koreas reunite.

I wish you all peace and calmness.

I remain,
Duk Hwa,
your younger sister

1991, November 4

To my respected grandmother whom I miss,

We received your letter, Grandmother, and beloved Grandfather's picture.

Having read your sweet words, I felt as though you were somewhere near and that I could run to you whenever I desired, as if I could share all the stories of our big and small worlds. However once I returned to my senses, I saw only in front of me the vast distance of America's continent.

Grandmother, when we didn't know if you lived or died, the thing we desired the most was confirmation. Now that you exist, there are no words to describe my longing heart. It cannot be measured to the highest sky or the deepest ocean. The sky has its limits and the ocean has its shores, yet our longing has no end.

My younger brother, Hak Churl, is currently attending his second year in college. He was awarded padded clothes and a student's uniform from school. Then comes Mun Churl, the youngest brother; he is in the Chosŏn Army Corps. After he completes his service, we'll send him to college. Lastly, there's my younger sister, Mi Ran, who works as a telephone operator. And I have graduated from college.

We are living well with no worries, but thinking about our flesh and blood living in such a faraway land, we cannot sleep. Imagining you suffering in somebody's else's land, we are unable to eat.

Grandmother, never give up, and live strong until the day we meet. I'll count the days until I can look upon your healthy smile. Picture a bright tomorrow and believe it is not too far off. A day may feel like a thousand years, but it will pass and the day of our dramatic reunion will happen.

Be well. Reply with pictures.

> *From faraway in the homeland,*
> *your granddaughter, Ae Ran,*
> *who loves her grandmother*

April 3, 1992

Dear Older Brother's couple,

Owing to Mother's sincere prayers, we recently completed the visitation applications to Pyongyang. Greatly concerned about Mother's health due to her advanced age, our family has decided to avoid the winter and apply for a spring trip. We requested May, but we must wait to see if the papers will be approved. And as soon as they're processed, Mother will visit you. The two other people accompanying her will be my husband and my second daughter, Hae Ri. Although we all wish to go to you, we must postpone our trips due to work and family responsibilities.

Here in America, every holiday, fifty family members gather together and, each wearing our traditional clothing, we feast on Korean food, so we won't feel so lonely about living in a foreign country. And each year, Mother has missed your absence. But now none of us are tormented with wondering any longer. We are incredibly fortunate, though we are miles apart. At least we can communicate. Let us cling to the hope that we shall all meet one day.

Mother, in spite of her age, continues to do good deeds for strangers and our church. Every Wednesday and Sunday, she and her younger sisters prepare kimchi and home-cooked meals for the entire congregation. Because of her many efforts, she is praised and respected and was honored with the Mother of the Year Award.

Next month she will be celebrating her eightieth birthday. We are planning to throw a big party, but she might refuse due to your absence. Our hearts are heavy watching her wearing away. This is the main reason why we have delayed her visit. I hope you understand.

Knowing this first meeting with you may be her last, my heart aches with pain. All I wish is that it will be a wonderful reunion which the memories will last her for the remainder of her life.

There is a song that all Koreans sing called "Our Dream Is Reunification." Older Brother, until that time stay in good health and live long. We here in this faraway land will also wait until the day we can all meet.

May God's blessing be upon your household. Look forward to the day Mother will come to you.

From Duk Hwa,
who misses you

Each poetic letter received from North Korea was saturated with emotional propaganda, and they left a lingering impression of what life must have been like behind the iron curtain. It was shocking how little they knew about the outside world. Our relatives believed we lived a suffering existence in America while their country awarded them padded clothes and uniforms. They blamed the American "barbarians" for our continued separation.

Halmoni and my family always wrote back with a cautious hand. For everyone's protection, they exposed very little of our privileged lives in America. They wrote about reunification and spring while becoming increasingly alarmed by the bittersweet testimonies from people who had made the trek inside North Korea and who told of extreme slum conditions and malnutrition. A friend of my parents returned wearing only a trench coat and shoes. Seeing his emaciated mother living in a crumbling shack infested with lice, sleeping under a threadbare blanket, he had left her his luggage, clothes, watch, and even underwear.

Halmoni became desperate to get to North Korea. The months kept passing, and another year was gone. Our entire family prepared a massive care package filled with jackets, long underwear, medicine, and dried foods. Then in 1993, the doors slammed shut. No more visas were issued. It seemed that North Korea had become upset with the stories and the bad press that were circulating at the time. They probably didn't want the world to know about the slums and poverty. In a socialist society, they weren't supposed to exist.

Heartbroken, Halmoni succumbed to pneumonia and had to be hospitalized. She looked so fragile and sallow with all the machines pumping her body full of fluids and oxygen. As I kept watch by her bedside, I could tell she was ready to give up. But I wasn't ready to let go of her yet. I wanted her to hold on to life, to fight. So I did what I had to do. I coiled my right pinkie around hers and promised her the impossible.

Sometimes the impossible becomes possible.

As soon as the plane cut through the dark clouds and dropped down over the unlit city of Yanji, Halmoni became alert. She sat right up, one knee propped up close to her chest. Her shapeless dress climbed high on her thighs, showing the hem of her long underwear, tucked securely inside thick tangerine-toned knee-high stockings.

Reaching for her hand, I wrapped mine inside her warm palm and asked in Korean, "What's the first thing you want to say to Big Uncle when you see him?"

Halmoni's small eyes met mine. Even though they had lost most of their lashes and brightness, they were penetrating. "My first words? My first words? I haven't thought about it." She paused. She was looking past me. Then, in a softer but firm voice, Halmoni said, "I want him to know that his mother has never stopped thinking about him. Tell him, tell him, 'You were a brave boy to have survived this long alone.' I even became an American citizen at the age of eighty, because they said it'd be easier to get a visa to go see him, but that never happened. Remember, I voted for President Bushi and you didn't want me to."

"I remember," I laughed. "Does this mean you're an American person now?"

"No. I'm Korean, but America is my home. Home is where my family lives. I'd like to be buried in America."

"Grandfather's buried in South Korea. Wouldn't you want to be with him?"

"It's only bones, and there isn't much left of him, just a leg and a few ribs."

"Gross." I used the American expression.

"What 'gro-shi'?" She giggled, her dentures clicking. "I saw it when we moved your grandfather to a better gravesite."

"Did you ever think of remarrying?"

"One man was enough for me," Halmoni joked, but I knew how much she had loved my grandfather. Then suddenly her mood became more solemn. "Omona," she sighed. "Oh my."

"Are you okay?" I asked.

Halmoni wiped her eyes with a rough cocktail napkin. "Inside I'm thinking about the recent pictures the Reds allowed Yong Woon to send me. His face is withered and troubled. He's the same age as your father, yet he looks as old as me. He has gray hair like mine. Your father only has a few strands."

We both stared at my father sitting across the aisle, busily double-checking our customs and immunization cards. It was hard to believe that they were born only a few months apart. They were both sixty-two in Western years. Though Yong Woon Uncle had more hair in the photographs and my father's had thinned on top, my father's moon-round face bore only a few laugh lines at the far edges of his eyes; his skin was well preserved and richly tanned from hours on the golf course. Also, he didn't dress like other Korean men his age. He looked modern and stylish in his stone-washed jeans, pale blue button-down Polo shirt, and triple-striped Adidas tennis shoes—a gift I had given him years ago, which he wore loyally.

My father and I had volunteered to take Halmoni to China. We were the only ones in my family not constrained by a job or the responsibility of small children. After twenty years at GTE, my father had retired early, at the age of fifty-five, to help out my mother at her growing garment factory in downtown Los Angeles. Every day he'd drive her to and from work, do the payroll, answer the mail, unclog the toilets—whatever needed to be done so that she could manage the business. Other men ostracized him for being my mother's glorified secretary, but he didn't see it that way. Her success was his success. They shared everything and worked well together, and it allowed him to have more time to play golf, to travel, and to write poetry—his true passion.

Growing up, we didn't have a lot of material things, but in each room of our house we had a television set—prizes won by my father's poetry. He poured his feelings into poems because it was hard for him to express affection otherwise. He was trained not to show too much emotion. He never called me endearing names like "honey" or "sweetheart" or told me that he loved me. The way he did it was by changing the oil in my car, by supporting my mother's business, and by escorting Halmoni to China.

We braced ourselves for the cold as we stepped out of the plane. A sharp breeze whipped my long black hair. Here the plane wasn't tethered to the gate by a jetway. Through the saffron-colored haze it was difficult to see the steep stairs descending to the tarmac below. My father went down the creaky steps first, toting Halmoni's imitation Louis Vuitton purse. He positioned himself directly in front of Halmoni in case she fell. I was behind her, gripping her soft, pillowy waist as she went down sideways. Once we made it to the tarmac, we followed the other rushing passengers through a rusty gate that resembled prison bars. On the other side of the bars was a chaotic parking lot. Gypsy cabdrivers, standing in a cloud of cigarette smoke, vied aggressively for our attention. They surrounded us, grabbing at my platinum jacket and silver man's watch and at Halmoni's pink angora cardigan. I tried to shield her with my five-foot-five, 110-pound frame, but there were too many hands clawing and pulling at us.

"Let go," I snapped, pushing them away.

When they heard my English words, they heckled them back at me. "Ret ko! Ret ko!"

Suddenly a burly, energetic woman with shoulder-length hair, hotcombed into curls, elbowed her way through. She was holding up a cardboard sign with my father's name written in *hangul*, Korean script. When my father identified himself as Lee Jae Hak, the burly woman shooed the crowd away with her sign. At that moment, two more men swarmed us. They were talking so loudly in their singsong Korean, I thought their voices would knock me over.

The senior man greeted my father the Western way by offering his brown, rugged hand, palm almost up. He chattered and pumped my father's hand with such enthusiasm, it was as if they'd been friends for many years. I wanted him to settle down and speak slower. His North Korean accent, flared with Chinese intonations, made it difficult to follow the rapid-fire words. I did manage, however, to catch the introductions. The senior man introduced himself as Choi Soon Man—the family name came first, the way it was done in Korea. Choi Soon Man was a strongly built man of about fifty-five with thick slicked-back hair, parted on the side, and a goofy, jovial expression. The burly woman with the hot-combed curls was his wife. Choi Soon Man referred to her as his "house person," not offering her name. It took me a second to figure out that "house person" meant wife and not maid. In this part of the world women and men were identified by their roles and relationships. The younger man was their son-in-law. He was a big, broad-shouldered guy with an easy, athletic stride. He stood a head taller than my father. In fact, the people here were taller than the average South Korean, Japanese, or Pacific Islanders by three or four inches. It must have been because of the cold, rough terrain and the whole Darwinian theory—survival of the fittest.

"Where is my son?" Halmoni wanted to know, her words direct and to the point.

"My house person and I will leave first thing in the morning to fetch him," Choi Soon Man told her.

I looked over at Halmoni's fallen face. A frown ridged her forehead. "Why isn't he here already? Didn't you let him know his mother was coming?" she questioned, echoing my thoughts.

"We just wanted to make certain you were definitely coming before we sneak him out of North Chosŏn."

Disappointed, Halmoni said nothing more as the six of us and our one huge accordion suitcase squeezed into the son-in-law's compact car, borrowed from his workplace.

Getting out of the parking lot was a safety hazard. Cars heading in different directions clogged the single exit. The son-in-law cranked the steering wheel and made a tight circle over faded white lines, and suddenly we were on the gravel road. We drove in darkness. There weren't any street lamps nor any flashing neon lights off shops to light our path, but the son-in-law didn't have any problems finding his way along the bumpy, potholed asphalt. Through the cracked window, a chilly breeze rushed in. I picked up the scent of rust and dirt and heard the rustle of empty tin cans banging.

The son-in-law pulled the car into what looked like a demolition site. He parked next to a seven-story matchbox-shaped concrete building surrounded by trenches and mounds of dirt. He lived in one of the apartment units on the fifth floor. No elevator. Only broken bricks and twisted steel cables.

"Dad, I think it's better if we take Halmoni to a hotel." I expressed myself in English so as not to offend our excited hosts.

The son-in-law, reading the concern on my face, volunteered his muscular back. "I'll carry her," he replied in his soft but raspy baritone.

"I've come this far. I can make it the rest of the way on my own feet," Halmoni insisted, taking hold of the railing.

She moved up the stairs. The rest of the procession followed from behind, matching her pace. She was going pretty fast at first, but at the third floor she swerved around the corner drunkenly. Her body hugged the paint-chipped railing. She began to rely on her arms more to pull herself forward, her eyes glancing up to see how much farther she had to go. She tripped slightly on one step but caught herself on the next. Sweat poured off her and she was breathing hard by the time we made it to the apartment. Halmoni paused in front of the door, half upright, to pump air into her lungs.

Choi Soon Man's daughter, Song Wol, answered the door in faded bib overalls that encased her round, pregnant belly. She couldn't have been more than twenty years old. The skin on her face was porcelain smooth, and she wore her hair long and straight with a curtain of short bangs. But the expression on her face was that of a much older, responsible woman.

Song Wol bowed us in, then helped Halmoni take off her shoes. The apartment was a tiny whitewashed studio. It consisted of a very small bathroom with a Western toilet, a small kitchen, and small living quarters. A queen-size bed took up most of the room. The only other pieces of furniture were a thirty-six-inch Sony color television set and a lumpy mock-leather sofa. Tacked on the wall above the sofa was a large laminated map of the world, with China at the center. It was caked with dust and marked with fingerprints. On the opposite wall, there was a ten-by-fourteen framed photo of a young couple in their traditional ceremonial wedding *hanboks*. In the picture, Song Wol had on a red silk jeweled crown, tilted forward, and a jade married woman's hairpin inserted through the coiled bun at the base of her head. The groom wore a stiff black cap with wings. They were an attractive couple, but their faces looked so grim. It had to do with an old wives' tale that warned against the bride and groom from smiling on their wedding day lest their firstborn child be a girl.

Halmoni asked to lie down. The challenging feat of climbing the stairs had sapped her last bit of energy. I became instantly concerned and was ready to rush her to a hospital.

"Are you ill?" I asked.

"I'm fine. You eat something." She yawned. It was just like her to think of me.

Song Wol kindly laid Halmoni on the bed and draped her with a large powder-blue beach towel as a blanket. Red hand towels covered the hard seed-filled pillows.

I sat on the lumpy brown sofa beside my father. Our hosts sat on square cushions on the floor, smiling up at us and talking. In no matter of time, my father was able to decipher their thick accents. He conversed freely with them, and I was able to follow along better. I learned a few basic facts about the people who lived in this region. About forty percent of the population was ethnic Korean. Choi Soon Man's parents, like many of the Koreans, had moved here between 1910 and 1945 to escape Japanese oppression during its occupation of Korea. They called themselves Chosŏn, using part of the Korean name for North Korea, Chosŏn Inmin Konghwaguk. Chosŏn was also the earliest name given to the Korean kingdom. We referred to ourselves as Hanguk Saram, "a Korean person," from the name for the Republic of Korea (Taehan Min-Guk). The Western name Korea comes from the Koryo dynasty, 918–1392.

These Chosŏn people spoke and wrote Chinese, but they held on to their Korean identity and traditional ways, and the Chinese government allowed them a degree of autonomy. The Chosŏn, unlike the Tibetans, enjoyed the right to some political control over their own areas and were given certain concessions and exemptions.

One concession was that they were permitted to have two children per family rather than the one child per family mandatory for the Chinese. Another exemption allowed Choi Soon Man to become an entrepreneur. He smuggled Chinese-made goods—clothes, shoes, socks, dried herbs, and rice—into North Korea, where he traded them on the black market for valuable antiques. He sold the antiques for a very large profit to wealthy Chinese and Japanese buyers. Sometimes he just sold his merchandise on the black market for ten times the original price due to the desperate shortage of consumer goods. The most coveted currency and effective bribe in North Korea was the U.S. dollar.

"Does your eldest daughter, Ju Ri, have any children yet?" Song Wol's mother inquired in her singsong voice.

"A son," my father replied.

"Isn't she an eye doctor?"

"Yes, she did my glasses." My father removed his gold frames and held them out in front of his eyes.

"It's useful to have a doctor in the family. How old is your son now? Is he still a student at a university? How are Halmoni's second and youngest sons, Kun Il and Kun Sam, doing? It's a shame about Kun Sam's automobile business going bankrupt." Choi Soon Man clucked his tongue against the roof of his mouth in sympathy as he fished in his shirt pocket for a cigarette. His fingers dug deep until he pulled one out and put it to his lips. "At least Hae Ri's mother's garment factory is doing well."

They knew so much about our lives and asked so many personal questions that it was discomfiting, even though I was used to it—Koreans would bluntly ask within the first few minutes after being introduced where you'd gone to college, what you did for a living, whether you went to church, how old you were, whether or not you were married, and if not, why.

Song Wol's mother asked the dreaded question. "Is Hae Ri married?"

"We're hoping soon," my father answered, then turned and glared at me. His look was loaded with guilt and pleading.

At that, Choi Soon Man clucked his tongue again. "She should be married already with a house full of sons of her own."

I was about to come to my own defense when my father steered the conversation back to the purpose of our trip. He asked if the famine in North Korea was as bad as the recent headlines and reports claimed. "Has my brother-in-law's family been eating?" he asked more precisely.

"They only earn about twenty-thousand won [about U.S. $22] a month, which used to be enough to survive on with the help of government food rations. These days, rations don't come for months if they come at all," Choi Soon Man informed us, leaving the cigarette in his mouth as he spoke. The fiery tip bobbed with the words.

"Then how are they living? What are they eating?" I questioned.

They all swiveled their heads over to my father for a translation. It was incredibly frustrating. I knew the power of language. It could flirt, tango, cry, do just about anything. But while I spoke serviceable Korean, it had a Valley

Girl accent and style. I counted on my listeners to adjust their ears and mentally reconjugate incorrect verb stem endings. Also, I made up words if I couldn't recall the right ones. When I was growing up, my parents conversed in Korean and my siblings and I responded in English, so I understood more than I could speak. Halmoni was the only person I felt comfortable bringing out my Korean with, simply because I had no choice. She spoke no English.

"Hae Ri wants to know how they have managed to stay alive," my father explained.

"They're living merely because they're not dead," Choi Soon Man replied matter-of-factly, then added, "It's the thought of their family in America that keeps them going. You're the source of their energy. People like them, who were sent to live in the harsh countryside, are the lowest class. The privileged get to live in Pyongyang, where they have modern houses, medical facilities, and special schools."

Song Wol's mother continued, "We do as much as we can for them. We save food, package it in large bags, and send it over. Your two nieces and two nephews are wearing all our old clothing. There, people go without socks and underwear during the winters. I've seen so many homeless people, and children skinny as sticks. People are dropping dead in the streets, really. In some of the worst-stricken areas, I even heard rumors that when someone dies, the family will keep the body in the house until it begins to rot or else neighbors will dig it up and eat it. Being a Chosŏn person myself, it's devastating to see our own people suffer like that."

"We're very grateful for your kindness," my father replied, and sighed heavily.

"It's nothing. They're just like our own family," insisted Choi Soon Man.

I decided to try again. "How did you find our phone number in America?" I blurted out, projecting my voice as if that would help.

Choi Soon Man nodded, understanding. "Once we became friendly with your uncle, he showed us your pictures and letters. When I saw the phone number printed on top of the letterhead, I decided to call you. And now here you are." He beamed. "We're the only ones that know about you. If anyone reports to the authorities that they've contacted you without going through the proper channels, they could get into big trouble."

Feeling a bit more confident, I asked, "What happened to Big Uncle after he was caught?"

Everyone threw me another funny look.

My father came to my assistance once more. "She's asking what happened to him after he was captured by North Korean troops at the beginning of the war. We suspect he must have been imprisoned, since he married so late."

"Ah, I got it," Choi Soon Man laughed. In that bawdy, openmouthed laugh, I could hear every cigarette he had ever smoked. "When he was captured, he begged for his life, and since he was so young-looking, they let him live. He was sentenced to a juvenile detention center for several years. When he was released he joined some gangs to survive until he was drafted into the army. In North Chosŏn, all men have to register for the draft at the age of fourteen. The typical draft age is seventeen, and they don't usually get out till around twenty-six. Once you're in you're in. They don't even let you out to get married or visit your family. That's why they all marry late over there." He paused, thought for a moment, then warned, "North Chosŏn is heavily militarized. It's dangerous to get them upset. They're crazy people who've been trained to handle weapons."

My brain wouldn't slow down. I thought of a dozen questions at once, but I let them fall away for the night. Instead, I pooled and savored the information in my mind. A deep and almost radiant elation filled me. I couldn't sleep. Finally, after six years of living with half answers that ate at every holiday, every celebration, every family gathering, I was now learning what had really happened to Halmoni's son.

II

Through drowsy eyes I watched Halmoni's silhouette as she knelt on the bed, her interlaced fingers placed on the pillow in prayer. The warm light from a small lamp fell onto her smooth-skinned hands, hands that were the source of her immense power and faith. For almost five decades, Halmoni had been healing people with an ancient bruising technique she learned in China. She called it *ch'iryo,* which in Korean translated as "medical treatment" or "cure." By slapping and pinching or scraping the flesh with the edge of a spoon, *ch'iryo* cleansed the blood. It was a very painful treatment, but people kept bringing her their sores, swollen joints, and internal illnesses. And while her strong hands moved steadily over their bodies, bruising the flesh, her all-glowing and apparent confidence would convince them that the world had been created in six days and that Jesus Christ was the Savior. My relationship with God was more private and definitely a more pleasurable experience, and I didn't feel compelled to convert anyone.

Once Halmoni was done praying, she jiggled me awake, then she woke my father, who was asleep on the floor covered with a giant doilylike blanket. It was only six in the morning. I never got out of bed before ten, but this morning I was willing to get up. My hipbones felt bruised and all my joints stiff from the board-hard mattress I shared with Halmoni. The simple act of getting out of bed and dressing was agony. As I was putting on some makeup, Choi Soon Man and his wife, daughter, and son-in-law arrived back at the apartment, wearing the previous day's clothes. They had left in the middle of the night. There just wasn't enough room to accommodate us all even if everyone slept shoulder to shoulder on the bed and floor.

Immediately Song Wol and her mother retreated into the closet-sized kitchen. I thought it was best if I didn't offer to help. Unlike Halmoni and my mother, I was a lousy cook, and I rebelled against learning because I associated cooking with my resentment toward the mounting pressure to get married.

I watched the women through the glass window cut into the middle of the wall that separated the kitchen from the living quarters. Song Wol's mother rinsed the vegetables in the twelve-inch sink with an old-fashioned tap, running only cold water. Then she carved out pieces of pork and fried them in a wok on the portable gas burner. As the pork sizzled and crackled, she confidently tossed in a pinch of something and a handful of something else. I could smell the food. My mouth instantly watered at the recognition of *kimchi*. The spicy dish is unique and essential to the Korean diet, and is served at every meal. *Kimchi* comes in a variety of pickled vegetables blended with garlic, red pepper, ginger, scallions, turnip, radishes, and oysters or anchovies, then fermented. Many people living in the country still fermented their *kimchi* by burying it in large earthen jars in the ground.

Song Wol was dishing cabbage *kimchi* out onto a saucer she had washed in a plastic tub with just a rag, no dish soap. Then she carried the *kimchi* and the rest of the dripping dishes and chopsticks out into the living area. She set them on a low yellow lacquered table that had been brought in from the kitchen and would be taken away when everyone was done.

Breakfast was served. Everything was communal eating. Plates of fried pork with jelly-like pine mushroom, eggs sautéed in leeks, raw green chili peppers and inch-thick scallions, and stew bubbling in a Crock-Pot were heaped onto the small table.

Song Wol reappeared once again from the kitchen hugging a large glass jug of colorless homemade liquor with jujubes, pine nuts, some kind of twigs I couldn't identify, and a huge ginseng root. The ginseng root looked like a little fat headless man with its thick pinkish trunk and arms and legs. It even had a navel and penis. Ginseng is supposed to be stiff with yang (male) energy as well as an aphrodisiac.

Song Wol wobbled over to where her father sat munching on a raw scallion. Kneeling in front of him, she carefully poured him the liquor, using two hands. Koreans always use two hands when giving or receiving objects to a person of higher status or age to show respect. No two people are equal. A clear hierarchy exists in the family. Even twins are unequal; the firstborn must be addressed as "big brother" or "older sister" and the marginally younger sibling as "younger brother" or "little sister."

Song Wol then filled my father's glass in the same manner.

Halmoni turned from her food and glanced at my father disapprovingly.

"It's so early," my father said to Choi Soon Man hesitantly.

"Nonsense. This is good for your life. It's medicinal," Choi Soon Man declared.

I watched in amazement as he snatched up a whole toad from the pot and popped the creature into his mouth, complete with bones, eyeballs, and webbed feet, which he then chased down with a drink.

"Here's one for Hae Ri. The belly's full of eggs." Song Wol's mother plopped a large bloated toad onto my saucer. When it hit the saucer, the slimy elastic skin around the belly fell back, exposing a purple sack of eggs. I tried to convince myself it was caviar, but my eyes weren't fooled. I couldn't take my gaze off the dead toad. It just lay there faceup, spread-eagled.

"Yeah, that's a good one." My father nodded, delighted. He wasn't squeamish at all. He copied Choi Soon Man and chased down a toad with a conservative sip from his drink. By his pinched facial expression I could tell it was potent.

"Go on." Choi Soon Man chuckled as he picked up another one with his chopsticks and shoved it into his mouth, then threw back another shot. Sweat dripped off his brow.

Not wanting to offend our hosts, I amputated a leg and delicately placed it between my teeth, lips peeled way back. I chewed and swallowed with effort. The texture was rubbery, but it tasted better than I thought—similar to garlic chicken.

Song Wol's mother scanned me appraisingly as I tried to eat. "Your frame is too narrow. I'm afraid if a gust of wind blows, it'll snap you in half."

"American women are always dieting. It's a big business, helping people lose weight," my father commented.

"*Ayeeyah.* You can make money doing anything in America, unlike here. It's a dream of ours to go to America," she sighed as she refilled her husband's glass.

Choi Soon Man lifted his shot glass to his mouth and swigged down the entire shot, letting out a burp of well-being. A trickle of alcohol slipped down his lips. He slurped it up and went on to explain that they would ride the public bus into Changbai, located right on the northern bank of the Yalu River. Hyesan City, where Yong Woon Uncle's family lived, was on the other side. The ride would take approximately fifteen, maybe twenty-five hours, depending on road conditions. They would smuggle Yong Woon Uncle across the river, dress him, then take the bus back to Yanji. Mother and son could visit for one night, then they'd escort him back before his absence was noticed.

"Are you sure this is safe?" My father suddenly sounded uncertain.

"Don't worry," Choi Soon Man said in an amused tone. "Like I said on the phone, North Chosŏn people sneak over all the time to scavenge for food. If you bribe the border guards with a cigarette, some liquor, whatever, they'll let you go. You just can't go with your entire family or they'll know you're trying to escape."

"The drive is so long," I commented. Impatience was one of my chief characteristics. "Isn't there a train or plane you can take?"

"No, they don't reach that area. It's not a favorite tourist spot. There is a faster way, though. We could rent a private car," Song Wol's mother offered. "But it's a bit expensive for people like us."

"How much?" my father inquired.

Choi Soon Man scratched his tussled head. "About three thousand five hundred yuan, I think."

I calculated in my head—one dollar was worth about 8.6 yuan, making the price of the private car around four hundred dollars. Switching to English, I turned to my father. "It's worth it."

"So much-e money," he returned in English.

It *was* a lot of money for them. The son-in-law held a respectable government post inspecting identification cards but made only sixty dollars a month, which was about the average salary in China.

"This is no time to be cheap, Dad. We can afford it." I spoke in English. "Making Halmoni wait another forty hours, maybe longer, is just too cruel."

I could see my father's thoughts churning. As he thought he took another swallow of liquor. He swallowed so long it surprised me. Finally he consented to the nonnegotiable price. On his go-ahead, the son-in-law made a single phone call, and a caterpillar-green Mitsubishi Jeep with tan seats turned up an hour later. There was no paperwork or other formalities. No insurance or *tojang*—the sticky red name seal. Nothing other than mutual trust between us and the owner of the Jeep, who would be the driver. I was informed that he was considered quite an eligible bachelor due to his yearly earnings, even though he was short and his eyes were too small.

"Since the car has so much room, it'd be nice if Hae Ri could come along. She'll be able to take pictures of the Changbai Mountains," Choi Soon Man said whimsically, pulling up his socks and getting ready to leave.

I definitely wanted to check out the watery border between China and North Korea for myself. I had seen the other border—the demarcation line, which sliced Korea in half near the 38th parallel. It was just north of the metropolitan city of Seoul. My fingers had gripped the high chain-link fence, topped with coils of razor wire. The demarcation line was also known as the demilitarized zone (DMZ). The name was a misnomer. The 2½-mile-wide strip of land, stretching 150 miles across the waist of the peninsula, was the most dangerous and heavily armed border in the world. Watchtowers, land mines, trip wires, searchlights, and giant loudspeakers used to shout out inflammatory propaganda were erected on both sides. But what made the DMZ so scary was that it was all that separated the 1.1 million North Korean troops from 660,000 South Korean and 37,000 American troops. At any time another bloody battle could erupt.

"I'll go," I answered excitedly.

My father crossed his arms, his face a sculpture of fatherly concern. "I don't think that's a good idea. Halmoni needs you," he said, reaching for excuses.

"No one needs to watch me." Halmoni sat up, smoothing back her hair.

"Our daughter can keep Halmoni company," Song Wol's mother said, offering a simple solution.

"Hae Ri will be fine." Choi Soon Man casually laughed off my father's protectiveness, refilling both their glasses. "You should come, too. It'll be fun."

My father, fearing for my safety, joined the carpool. Counting the driver and son-in-law, six would be going. I questioned if there would be enough room to accommodate Yong Woon Uncle on the ride back. Choi Soon Man assured me it was no problem to squeeze in an additional body, but our mammoth care package would have to wait till a later trip.

I grabbed my sporty shoulder bag and shoved in some clothes, a journal, a tape recorder, and a camera.

"Pray for us, Halmoni." I hugged her tightly.

Smiling, she said, "I always have. It's all I do."

The neighborhood looked like it was trying to rebuild itself after a bomb had been dropped. In some areas construction of boxy three- to five-story concrete apartment buildings was under way on top of demolished buildings, the sites not fully cleared of debris and broken bricks. The unwanted rubbish was simply moved onto the potholed dirt streets that bore no signs of trees, grass, or flowers. There were a few leafless shrubs clinging to life here and there, but they looked like obstructions that needed to be uprooted.

As we turned onto what in these parts qualified as a main road, an overcrowded bus screamed across our path. Luckily there wasn't an accident. Our driver calmly jammed on the brakes and tooted the horn; then, as if nothing had happened, he drove on. We passed by numerous little restaurants and shops with hand-painted signs written in both Chinese and *hangul*. There were almost no private cars, just buses, taxis, and bicycles carrying all sorts of items. A woman pedaled hard next to us. Behind her, she drew a cart of steaming tofu in wooden canisters stacked high like building blocks. Someone else was transporting a live pig in a wicker basket strapped to the rear rack of a bicycle, and a large cabinet was being balanced precariously on bamboo poles between two bicycles.

Farther south, blue pickup trucks loaded with black coal for sale were parked side by side in front of an open farmer's market that smelled of steamed bread, herbs, and dust. It was barely eight A.M., yet more and more chattering people crammed the already crowded little booths and stalls that lined both sides of the street. Food was abundant here. Everywhere were chicken cages, oil jars, pails of ingredients and spices, and large wicker baskets filled with white rice, golden wheat, yellow soybeans, and other colorful grains. Leafy vegetables were displayed on mats on the ground. Women in booths, wearing white doctor's caps and robes, sold dozens of varieties of *kimchi* and marinated dried squid from plastic buckets of all sizes.

Most of the sellers and shoppers were women. As the women bargained and perused, the men lingered in cafés and loitered on the streets as if they had all the time in the world. At a busy intersection, a row of ten pool tables was dragged out onto the sidewalk to keep the men busy. Those who weren't shooting pool squatted on their heels, observing and smoking and spitting, occasionally talking, rarely smiling. Nearby the pool tables were young children jumping up and down on a jumbo-size trampoline that looked like a gigantic henhouse. The children's high-pitched laughter almost seemed out of place like the leafless scrubs.

It didn't take us long to leave the city limits. Just outside of Yanji, the road was blocked by guardrails and uniformed guards doing checks and collecting tolls. We had to pay a small fee in exchange for a paper ticket, which we then handed off to another uniformed guard sitting in a second booth, just six yards away, waiting to collect the ticket. We drove through without incident. The lethargic guards waved us by after a quick glance inside the Jeep and a few words. We would have to be extra cautious on the way back with a temporary North Korean defector in the car.

Soon we were ascending a winding road into rural countryside. As far as my eyes could see in every direction were open space and luscious green and yellow pastures. Beyond the pastures were rolling hills, each one shaped differently than the others. Scattered along the undulating landscape, thatched mud huts were built facing the south and the sun. At intervals there were small groups of huts clustered together that came closer to the road. Jagged fences sectioned off the individual huts. The fences were constructed out of brittle tree branches that had been spiked into the earth. The crooked branches, resembling dried bones, cast threatening shadows on the ground. Every now and then, my eyes would catch a colorful surprise. Aqua-blue or emerald-green gated archways, painted with lucky symbols, occasionally marked the entranceway to a hut. The symbols were usually red-and-gold Chinese characters or a caricature of a plump male child.

There was hardly any traffic to be seen on the rutted one-lane road. Ours was the only car. Everything else on the road was blue pickup trucks and three-wheeled microtractors transporting produce and people. Sometimes we had to slow down for cows browsing, big-eyed oxen grazing, sheep dropping smelly pellets of dung, and groups of women with creased, leathery faces marching toward the flooded paddies, which looked like shiny mirrors. They were all carrying primitive hoes and sickles slung over their strong shoulders. The oddest sight, however, was a pretty young woman on a scooter puttering along. She was wearing white pressed slacks, a bright bubble-gum-pink blazer, white patent leather pumps, and large round sunglasses. I couldn't figure her out. The last town we passed was at least two hours back. She couldn't have been from one of the primitive mud hut villages. They didn't have plumbing, much less electricity to plug in an iron to press her white slacks.

But my mind couldn't hold that thought. I had a terrible headache. The road was like corduroy, and every few yards the wheels would ram into a bump or ditch and I'd bounce hard and smack my head against the thinly padded ceiling. As much as I wanted to complain, I knew the ride and cramped conditions were harder on my father, who was sitting on my left in the backseat. He looked rumpled and battered. I tried to give him some space, but my body kept slamming into his. I was envious of Song Wol's mother, sitting to my right. She had nodded off, her head forward, lolling side to side. Choi Soon Man was also fast asleep in the back storage space, curled up like a baby, his knees wedged against his chest. The son-in-law, being the largest, sat comfortably strapped into the front passenger seat.

Five grueling hours into our ride, halfway to Changbai, we came upon a sign warning us to stop. The road was blocked by another checkpoint. The fire-engine-red structure was hauntingly isolated on the overgrown road. Paying the toll, we were once again waved through.

From there we left the countryside and the land became wild and beautiful, with huge pine trees that grew to a hundred feet tall. Emerging from the dense pine forest like skyscrapers were the dramatically shaped jagged peaks of the Changbai Shan (Changbai Mountains). The moment I saw the towering mountain range draped with bluish snow, I fell completely under its spell. There was a kind of hush in the air, as if time had stopped, and I felt a sense of awe at being on the legendary mountains that ran northeast to southwest along the China–North Korea border for about 620 miles.

At the highest peak, nine thousand feet above sea level, was a two-million-year-old lake inside a volcanic crater almost eight miles in circumference. The Chinese called this Lake Tianchi (Heavenly Lake). The Koreans had always called it Chonji (Lake of Heaven) and the mountain Paektusan (White Head Mountain) because the main peak was covered year round by snow. Paektusan was the sacred, legendary birthplace of the Korean nation. The mythology claimed that the God of the Heavens had a young son named Hwan Ung. The boy wished to live in the human world to help mankind. Hwan Ung's father granted his wish and sent him to Paektusan. Hwan Ung later transformed a bear into a woman and married her. Their child, Tan Gun, born in the year 2333 B.C., became the first human king of the Korean peninsula. Tan Gun set up his capital at Pyongyang and called his kingdom Chosŏn.

South Korea had never officially recognized North Korea's border with China, which now straddled the mountain, and so in South Korea's national anthem, the words declared, "Until the East Sea's waves are dry, until Paektusan worn away, God watch over our land forever. Our Korea will live ten thousand years."

The Chinese feared that a unified Korea would attempt to reclaim the mountain, causing them to lose the substantial revenue brought in by the South Korean and Japanese tourists who flock to Paektusan every year in great numbers. The tourists come between late June and September, when it's possible to reach the summit. Otherwise the only way up is by snowmobile, which seemed highly dangerous even in April. The higher the road swung up, the more the temperature dropped. In the heated Jeep our breaths steamed around our heads. The sun couldn't penetrate to us as we passed under the snow-covered canopy of branches. Shivering, I asked the driver to crank up the heat, but he wouldn't risk overtaxing the engine. We still had a great distance to cover, and there were no emergency road services to come rescue us in this wild forest, where rare tigers and leopards and other creatures roamed freely.

Finally, we started cruising downhill after I don't know how long. Traveling alongside the road was a fast-moving stream in a broad brown bed, lacy with ice at the edges. The water rushed with a majestic rhythm. Its timing clashed with the driver's tape of a female Chinese singer, belting out a faster disco beat. This stream was borne from high on top of the snowy mountains, and it fed into the Yalu River, which flowed southwest. The Tumen River curved to the northeast. These two rivers marked the natural boundary between China and North Korea.

We followed the stream down, often detouring, but always returning to the stream, our only landmark. Around eight in the evening, eleven and a half hours after we left Yanji, we passed through our third checkpoint and bounced into Changbai as the sky was turning grayish black. I could feel the dung-colored dust in my nose, in my mouth, and between my toes, and everything ached and was stiff as if I had been beaten. But the moment I heard Song Wol's mother suggest we go to the border to arrange for Yong Woon Uncle's crossing, I perked up.

The driver wended the car through a confusing maze of side streets that led to the twilight gravel trail near the Yalu River. The road was blocked by a fleet of blue trucks heading in the opposite direction with tons of giant logs. North Korea was selling off its precious forest on their side of Paektusan to buy corn from China. Seeing all those trucks suddenly made the famine more real.

Song Wol's mother instructed the driver to park behind a tall pile of garbage and crushed stones and shut off the engine and headlights. Everything became dark and silent except for the crinkling sound of sunflower seed shells and sticky pineapple rinds being crushed under my feet. I couldn't keep still. I was so excited to be here. When I heard the side door open, I spun around to see Song Wol's mother already standing. All I saw of her was her maroon jacket and orange shirt tucked into black pants. She told us to remain in the car while she and her husband walked the rest of the way to the edge of the river. Even though the darkness blinded any view, I wanted to join them. Reading my thoughts, my father grabbed my wrist. "Don't make trouble. Stay." He squeezed. I looked back at Song Wol's mother. Fighting all my urges to swing open the door, I remained seated, craning my neck out the window. I strained my hearing to follow their footsteps. The footsteps stopped, and I caught Song Wol's mother's muffled voice hollering. I could tell she was using her hands as a megaphone to guide her voice.

"Hello! Hello! You by the water, you know us, don't you? It's Song Wol's mother."

"Yah," a faint, faint voice called back.

"Go to the house of Lee Ae Ran and fetch the people inside. We will reward you the next time we cross to do business."

The faint voice didn't respond again.

We waited for what seemed equivalent to a whole day before another faint voice floated across the river. "Yah."

"Who's there?" Choi Soon Man inquired.

"Ae Ran's mother."

My heart was thumping at three times its normal rate. It was Yong Woon Uncle's wife, my aunt.

"Halmoni is here with Duk Hwa's husband and second daughter, Hae Ri," Song Wol's mother called. She waited, but there was no reply. "Ae Ran's mother, did you hear me? I said Halmoni is here."

"Yah," came my aunt's thin, hoarse voice. "Halmoni?"

"Yah. Bring the entire family to this exact location tomorrow morning at seven. Bring them to greet your relatives. Understand?"

"Yah. Seven. Thank you, thank you."

The footsteps quickly shuffled back toward us.

"Did you hear her?" the couple asked excitedly, rubbing the chill from their faces.

"Yes," I nodded. It was really amazing. After almost fifty years of separation, they still shared the same language. Hearing them speak, I realized Korea's people were still one.

"What if others heard you?" my father asked worried.

"That shouldn't matter." Choi Soon Man shrugged nonchalantly. "They all want something in return. Like that woman at the river—she knows I'll pay her for her services, because my name's well known in the town. When they see me coming they all rush over as if I'm an important man."

"Can't Big Uncle come over now?" I asked impatiently.

"No, his house is farther up the hill. It's about an hour's walk away. Over there, there aren't any cars or taxis or buses or phones to call him to come. What luck that Ae Ran's mother happened to be at Ae Ran's house."

"How close is her house to the river?" I asked.

"Very close. Three or four rows of houses down."

If only we had known they lived so close to the border, I lamented to myself, we would have brought Halmoni years ago, when she was physically stronger.

Before it got too late, we drove back up onto the road in search of a place to sleep. The main stretch of street in Changbai didn't extend more than two hundred yards, but it was alive with activity and excitement. People were out, enjoying the changing season. Makeshift tent restaurants festooned with colorful Christmas lights set up tables and stools right out on the street. They roasted dried lizards and sparrows over rusty grills crackling with amber and blue flames. A group of old men were gathered around a lamp playing mah-jongg, a Chinese game of tiles. In front of a bank, a late-model television set, with artificial wooden side paneling, had been converted into a karaoke display screen. The twangy, reedy music could be heard from a block's radius. A crowd of wanna-be nightclub singers anxiously waited for their names to be summoned by the woman who owned the television.

A little farther on was an outdoor arcade with electric rifle shooting games. Whenever a player hit a bull's-eye, lights winked and bells sounded loudly, drowning out the karaoke singers. One game in particular caught my interest. The targets were caricatures of Hitler, Mussolini, Mao, and Stalin, all of whom qualified among the twentieth century's most despotic murderers. China had really changed. A few years ago a game like this would have been banned and the owner sent to a reeducation camp.

We parked in front of a *yogwan*—an inexpensive inn—tucked away in a narrow alley. Carefully I stepped out, then down, lowering myself gently on the steady earth. My head and bottom were so sore, I could barely walk straight. I wobbled like Halmoni behind the others into the faceless concrete building. The *yogwan* was dim and drafty and completely empty of any furniture or decoration. A mousy girl with barely pubescent features appeared through a faded mustard-colored curtain strung up with nails. She wore a long skirt that reached all the way to the floor and a blouse with darts that made room for future breasts. As she checked us in, her face displayed the same responsible expression that Song Wol wore.

To get to our rooms, the mousy girl directed us through what looked like a common kitchen/washing area. The floor of coarsely polished granite was drenched, and the white plaster had fallen away from several places in the wall.

Song Wol's mother and I took the first room. It was an empty cubicle with a three-foot-high floor. Rolled bedding was propped against the wall.

Copying Song Wol's mother, I unzipped my boots and climbed onto the high platform. Heat cleaved to the yellow lacquered paper floor like the *ondol* floors in older Korean homes, where underground flues ran the heat from the kitchen stove to the room. You could boil *kimchi* stew, steam fish, and heat the floor all at the same time.

I tugged on the long string that dangled from the ceiling to switch on the light. The exposed electric bulb buzzed as if it was about to blow. In fact, I almost hoped it would, because the room appeared a hundred times worse in the harsh lighting. The bald walls were scuffed, a third of the *ondol* floor was charred, and the place smelled of dead cigarettes and something else . . . some kind of rotting sweet fruit.

I struggled to pry open the sliding window. It wouldn't budge. It had come off its track, now covered with crunchy insect carcasses. I decided to leave it alone and get ready for bed. I remained in my jeans, striped turtleneck, and socks. Song Wol's mother stripped down to her tan thermal underwear, then rolled out the thickly padded mattress, the *yo*. It was saturated with a hundred different body odors that filled my nose and mouth. I had to force myself to lie down on the rank *yo*.

Yawning, Song Wol's mother reached across and drew a heavy blanket over me that smelled even worse. I nearly vomited.

"Your family's different from other South Chosŏn people we've met," she said. Her sandpapery hand touched me tenderly on the arm. "You never complain about the conditions. For most foreigners, nothing is ever good enough for them. They put down the way we live. I know it's not much, but we get by. You're good people."

I feigned a pleasant smile when what I really wanted was to throw off the blanket and scratch my head, because it felt as though a company of teeny bugs was touring my scalp. Then all of a sudden I heard a scurrying in the ceiling. It sounded like rats scratching the thin wood with their sharp claws, right above our heads. I bit down on my lower lip to hold back the little scream that threatened to emerge from my throat.

III

It shocked me that I wasn't dead in the morning. As I slept, the *ondol* floor got so hot, my body roasted. Song Wol's mother didn't seem to mind the roasting. She slept soundly through the entire night. At a quarter to six, I couldn't bear the heat any longer, and my bladder was pressing. I rose quietly and went searching for the outhouse. I headed out the back door into the courtyard. The air was misty gray and filled with ash and sand from coal-burning stoves, and it was piercing cold. The temperature must have dropped twenty degrees during the night.

A huge, muscular black dog was sniffing around the bottom of the outhouse. Seconds later, it rushed at me, barking and snarling. I flattened against the wall, frozen. Run or be mauled? I couldn't decide. My mind was still cloudy from just having woken up. Then, from upstairs, a rough female voice commanded the growling beast back to his shack.

I raced inside the protection of the outhouse and latched the door. Through the cracks in the splintered boards, I could see slivers of the dog mashing his nose between his legs and his white fangs chewing his privates. All at once, the pungent stench from below enveloped me, and suddenly I had this crazy urge to look down. The instant I saw the mound of brown human excrement, I became ill and teetered off balance. I had to quickly turn my gaze upward to the sky before I lost my footing on the two warped planks, spread ten inches apart. Don't you dare fall, Helie, I warned myself.

I searched around for the roll of toilet paper. There wasn't any. Great. I checked all my pockets and found a small square of coarse pink tissue Song Wol's mother had given me. Finishing my business, I zipped up my jeans, busted out of the stall in one quick, fluid action, and ran back inside.

Hot water was being boiled on the stove for guests to wash themselves and fill thermoses for tea. I was thrilled. The skin on my face was suffocating from all the dust and ash. I didn't even want to imagine what it was doing to my lungs. No wonder people hawked up mucus as if it were a national sport. The sound they made as they cleared their entire chest cavity and sent a lump of thick, slimy mucus flying across the air and onto the ground was stomach-turning, to say the least.

My father showed me what to do. He ladled the seething water out of the cast-iron pot, then poured it into a dented bronze tub on the floor. He squatted down on his heels with the tub between his spread knees and began to wash his face, the back of his neck, and lower arms. When he was finished he dumped the dirty water right onto the floor and the water drained into a hole. Then my father refilled the tub for me. The water smelled strongly of pork and felt greasy. I decided only to splash my hands. It felt cleaner not to wash up.

Song Wol's mother was awake by the time I slipped back into the room. She was crouched over writing a lengthy note, her left arm blocking my view. I watched as she copied it onto a second sheet without pausing to explain, then a third. She wrapped each one separately around smooth stones. The stones were then wrapped with blue plastic and tied with string. I stared at the three stones arranged on the yellow floor in a straight line, curious to know what was written. When Song Wol's mother exited the room, I quickly unraveled the original, took a photo of the message because I wasn't able to read *hangul*, and then rewrapped and carefully arranged the stones just the way she had left them. Next, I extracted the Sony Walkman recorder from my bag. For Halmoni and my mother, I wanted to record every detail. I planned to capture Yong Woon Uncle's image and voice on film and tape, so they would be able to keep his memory long after he returned to North Korea. I prepared the recorder with a blank cassette tape and threaded the microphone cord inside my jacket. The tiny silver head clipped perfectly into the top button slit. No one would suspect anything. The technology around here was years behind.

At five to seven, the sky a heavier misty gray, everyone languidly climbed into the Jeep. The driver put the Jeep into gear, and slowly we pulled away from the *yogwan*. He took the same route as the night before and parked behind the same pile of garbage and crushed stone.

This time my father and I were allowed to accompany the couple the rest of the way to the riverbank. Our presence would confirm to our relatives that Halmoni was indeed in China, and then arrangements could be made for Yong Woon Uncle to cross the river at night.

When my father popped open his door, the cold air and the foul odor of sewage and outhouses rushed in. I got out and shut the door behind me. White wisps of breath streamed out in front of my face. I bit my lips so the others wouldn't hear my teeth chattering.

I seemed to be the only one who was revved up. I forced myself to slow down to match the others as we walked along a dirt footpath. In the early morning light it was not a pretty sight. Running down the center of the footpath was a narrow, unsightly gully filled with sewage heading toward the river. The footpath led us through fascinating little labyrinthine alleys that formed a tight miniature grid of walled courtyards and passageways. Walls roughly built from loose bricks, boards, sticks, and mud merged into squat single-story homes overflowing with several generations of family. Several women, up early, squatted in open doorways doing their morning chores. One woman was shelling hard-boiled eggs. Another woman was washing dishes in a plastic scarlet tub. A grandmother was supporting a little boy as he straddled the gully, dumping his bowels. His white bottom stuck out from his pants, which were split along the crotch so he didn't have to take them off. I stepped around them, watching carefully where I placed my feet next.

As we drew closer to the river, there was a strange chorus of rhythmic beating floating in the air. I couldn't interpret or place it. It made my heart pound faster and harder against my chest, and I could feel the blood rushing through my veins. I broke ranks and increased my pace. Shock widened my eyes. My mouth dropped open.

"Oh my God," I gasped. "Oh my God," I heard myself say again.

There it was, right in front of me. The border. I couldn't believe it. I had imagined the Yalu River to be treacherous and miles wide. It was absolutely still and only about sixty yards wide. In other sections it was even narrower. Across the water was the riverbank, strewn with rocks. It stretched for about forty feet to where a tall stone wall was erected. The wall screened off the rows of homes that fronted the river. All I could make out were thin, rusty chimney pipes rising from behind the wall. Most of them were empty of smoke, even though the morning was freezing. But the wall wasn't high enough to conceal the taller buildings and factories made of gray concrete. They were cracked and stained black from ash and dirt mixed with rain. They reminded me of old headstones in a neglected cemetery. Everything was dead.

Through the grayish blue mist, I saw the vague outline of a chain of rugged mountains looming in the backdrop. They were sharp, rough, and beautiful, but completely stripped of trees and vegetation, which probably had been used as firewood.

The beating of unfamiliar drums I had heard as we came up was in fact the sound of women doing their laundry. Women stooped on both sides of the dark, calm river, beat out the dirt from their clothes with short wooden bats against flat boulders. The women on the China side were well equipped for the cold. They wore protective rubber gloves all the way up to their elbows and colorful windbreakers to shield them against the icy water. The North Korean women were inadequately covered in dark, muted clothing and were gloveless. Some had gray rags draped over their heads instead of hats and hoods.

"Over there." Song Wol's mother pointed a little farther down.

I spotted three women standing some distance apart from each other. The eldest woman, my aunt, stood erect in an ash-colored Mao pantsuit with the high mandarin collar. Over her left eye was a white patch. Mi Ran, the younger daughter, was at the foot of the river, leaning on a closed umbrella. Her hair was tied in a single ponytail, and she wore a woolly green blazer. A few feet behind them, Ae Ran sat on her legs, which were folded underneath her. Her body was slumped, her arms limp at her sides. She had on black leggings, a flimsy black jacket, and a black scarf wrapped over her head and pulled tight over her mouth like a mask. I squinted to better see their faces, but I couldn't make out any of their features.

As I scanned the area for Yong Woon Uncle, I caught sight of armed soldiers patrolling the rocky riverbank. The soldiers, suited in green uniforms and red-trimmed hats with wide brims, toted long rifles swung over their narrow shoulders. I froze when one of them barked at a woman, squatting over her wash. She had called across to a man standing on our side. The soldier's harsh voice became increasingly brutal as his rifle threateningly sliced the air above her head like a sword. "Why have you come out here!" he barked louder at the woman, but she kept her face down the whole time, enduring his assault. "Take your wash and get out of here." He slammed the butt of his rifle into her back; she jerked forward, then hurried away.

I was filled with fear. It flowed like molten lava through my arms and legs, and it made my breath stop.

"Hae Ri. Hae Ri's father." Song Wol's mother twirled her hand over us.

I almost yelled at her to stop. She was jeopardizing everyone's safety.

"Hello," acknowledged my aunt.

I didn't respond; neither did my father. We both stood like marble people.

"Go on, it's okay. The soldiers have already been paid off," Choi Soon Man assured us. "They're the first things that must be taken care of, or your family wouldn't be able to talk, just like that woman."

I wasn't convinced. My forehead was bathed in cold sweat.

"Uncle, I don't see Halmoni," Mi Ran called out.

"Ah, she waits in Yanji. She's too elderly to make this long a journey by car. She so badly wants to meet you all," replied my father, his voice strained. "Where is your father?"

"He should be on his way," informed my aunt, then went on to tell us that Ae Ran had had a son seven days before.

No wonder Ae Ran was slumped on the rocks and looked so weary. How had she managed to give life to a child when there wasn't enough food? I worried about the condition of her baby. Was he normal? Was he fully developed?

"Poor Ae Ran. She's really a very smart girl, smartest of all the children, but such bad luck with men. She's been married three times, and this third husband of hers is also useless. He beats her when he's drunk," relayed Song Wol's mother candidly. Her words lingered inside my head. I tried to shake them loose, but they only burned deeper into my chest, because I felt the closest to Ae Ran. Ever since we had received her first letter six years earlier, I thought a lot about her. Her writing was so passionate and heart-wrenching. I remember holding the flimsy sheets of paper for a long time, thinking we were the same age.

"I've waited so long to see your faces. Hae Ri, at last we meet," Ae Ran called out weakly, her voice terribly sad.

There was much I wanted to share with her, exchange all the emotions I was feeling. But I was all choked up, and I lost the Korean words I needed. It was impossible to retrieve even the simple ones I had heard all my life at this crucial moment. My level of frustration was maddening. What shot out of my mouth was "Sorry, I can't speak Korean too well."

"It's because she speaks Chinese. She doesn't know the Chosŏn language very well. She can understand everything, though," Choi Soon Man told them, then quickly turned to me and said in a heavy whisper, "It's not okay to be American here. If it's discovered that you flew all this way, your presence will stir a commotion."

That was the first time I heard caution in his voice. In a strange way it was more comforting than their calm reassurance.

Song Wol's mother motioned to my aunt and cousin to walk to where the river meandered into a grove of scrubby trees. I watched out of the corner of my eye as my aunt and Mi Ran strolled away in the indicated direction and disappeared. I knew what they were up to. Choi Soon Man planned to toss the wrapped stones across; I had seen him practicing earlier. He'd picked up a round stone and swung it, but it landed short and the river swallowed it with a loud plop. The second one had skimmed over the dull brown surface, skipping several times before it sliced out of sight.

"Did Aunt come with you?" Ae Ran asked, inquiring about my mother.

"She couldn't make it," my father answered. His lips were blue from the cold.

My mother was the only one in my family who hadn't returned to Asia since we left in 1968. She insisted she couldn't take the time off from managing her company. I knew the truth, though. It was the memories that kept her away. Memories didn't end even if you got rid of all the photographs and stopped speaking the person's name.

While we waited for Choi Soon Man, Song Wol's mother, my aunt, and Mi Ran to reappear, a drop of water fell from the cluster of gray clouds, darker and denser now. At first I mistook it for a small fragment of sand, but then more raindrops trickled down, one right after another, landing on our heads. A thick layer of white fog hung over everything. It was eerie. I felt like I was viewing North Korea through a veil.

By the time the four of them returned, the temperature had dropped still further and the sky opened up more to let more cold rain fall. The chill seeped through my high-tech insulated jacket and into my bones. I was freezing. I didn't do well in weather that was below seventy, having spent most of my life in sunny southern California. I didn't even own a pair of gloves. My unprotected fingers were practically glued together, and my feet were numb from the damp chill of the ground below. I tried to blow air into my cupped hands and stomp my feet to get the circulation going again, but it was useless. My hands and feet were lost to me. They had detached themselves from the rest of my body.

"Mi Ran's got the note," Song Wol's mother whispered excitedly.

All of a sudden, a soldier ordered my aunt, Mi Ran, and Ae Ran to crouch down low and be quiet. Another soldier was coming on duty. Song Wol's mother motioned for us to do the same. We stayed crouched down for some time until the new soldier marched away and the danger passed temporarily. Swirling his fingers around his mouth, Choi Soon Man signed that we could begin our dialogue again.

My father and I remained motionless, petrified.

Song Wŏl's mother was the first one to test the tightrope of safety again. "Ae Ran's mother, go see what's keeping Ae Ran's father," she said. My aunt scurried over to the tall wall, climbed a set of steps cut into the wall, then vanished.

"Is Hae Ri married?" Ae Ran asked.

"Hae Ri hasn't married yet," my father announced.

"Hae Ri, you should get married. You're very pretty," she complimented.

"We'll match her up with a Chosŏn man." Choi Soon Man beamed, rocking forward and back on his heels, his hands propped on his square hips. For an instant, everyone forgot what surrounded us and they were lost in laughter. I lifted my face up to the sky in comic disbelief. The rain pelted my face. I couldn't believe we were discussing my unmarried status when there were soldiers with rifles within range. I felt like announcing that I had a man and that I wasn't a virgin so they'd put away their laughter, but my lips and gums were frozen.

"What's happening?" The sharpness of Choi Soon Man's tone caused me to jerk my head forward just in time to see two soldiers roughly haul Mi Ran away by each arm. Evidently they had seen her catch the stone.

"Where are they taking her?" My words came out mumbled. I could hardly open my mouth.

"No English." Choi Soon Man hushed me.

I clamped my numb lips shut. I hadn't meant to speak English, but it was as natural as breathing for me.

"Maybe the soldiers want another bribe? Mi Ran's a smart girl—she'll know what to do. She'll give them something to drink or eat. The soldiers are hungry, too. Hunger drives even the saints to thievery." It was clear that Choi Soon Man was reaching for some kind of explanation for why they had taken Mi Ran.

"*Omona.*" Song Wŏl's mother kneaded her hands and paced between her husband and me.

The constant noise of hard paddles thrashing wet clothes—*smack, whack. smack-smack-whack*—suddenly sounded identical to human flesh being pummeled. It became unbearable. My body jerked convulsively as we waited for Mi Ran to return unharmed.

"He's here," someone called out in a hushed, raspy voice. I caught the call. In one quick motion, I stood tall and pivoted to face the southern banks again.

A young male, my cousin Mun Churl, waded toward the water. He went right up to it and took off his shoes—he wore no socks—and rolled up his pant legs. He started washing his feet and picking under his toenails. He waved cautiously, then quickly returned to his task.

"He's here," my father sang out in the same hushed manner.

My eyes raked the rocky banks once more. I saw him, an old man staggering forward. He looked nothing like the picture of the vivacious teenager Halmoni kept tucked in her Bible.

"He's here," everyone whispered together, as if our collective calls could pull him steadily closer, helping him place his feet securely on the rocks so he wouldn't fall and crack open his head.

Yong Woon Uncle wore a droopy green Lenin cap, dull green slacks, and a dull green Mao jacket, which was wide open to expose a soiled thermal shirt. His face I could see more clearly, better than the others', because there was no meat underneath the sallow skin. His face looked as if it had been carved, with hollow cheeks and dark, gaping holes for eyes and mouth.

As he feebly crouched down over the wet pebbles, I jerked forward, stretching out my arms, as if I could catch him. I watched Yong Woon Uncle strip off his jacket and cap. His hair was gray and spiky, and his narrow torso and arms were bonier than I had realized. His thinness verged painfully on the grotesque. Never in my life had I ever witnessed the ravages of starvation. Pushing up his thermal sleeves, he began to wash his face and neck in the ice cold water, not wanting to draw attention to himself. Yong Woon Uncle's dark, sunken eyes seemed to be staring at me personally. My heart contracted as if someone's hand had grasped it, seeing the awful combination of despair, terror, and hopelessness in his eyes.

I shuddered. If this was a bad dream, I was ready to wake up in my cozy apartment in West Hollywood, snuggled close to my boyfriend. The mere thought filled me with guilt. My mind raced. I wanted to do something for my uncle, for them.

Behind me, I heard my father's broken sobs. His head was bowed and his shoulders sagged. He sounded like a wounded animal with its foot mangled in a trap. I had never seen my father cry before. Only once, when I was a little girl, had I even heard him sob. After everyone had gone to bed, he cried alone in the living room for his widowed mother who had passed away in Korea. Hearing my father's strangled sobs now shook me as it had when I was little, and I sank to the ground. I buried my face between my knees and put my head down on my arms and cried. I couldn't stop the tears from rising. They gushed out.

I wanted to ask God why. I started to pray, but I was so shaken I couldn't even put my request into words. God, please, please help. I begged inside my head for some kind of miracle, rubbing my hands together as if rubbing a magic lantern. I looked up at the clouds that hung overhead, hoping to see a burst of sunlight come through a tear in the clouds and set alive the river, the landscape, and fuse together the divided country. I waited in agonizing silence for God to perform a miracle.

Time seemed to stand still. Every second was an eternity.

Nothing happened.

I couldn't stand God's passivity. Where are you, God? Where are you, damn it! Why aren't you helping him?

The silence wound around me, tighter and tighter, until the veins on the sides of my neck bulged.

My faith cracked.

I couldn't stand my silence, my helplessness, and suddenly I felt this overwhelming need to tell Yong Woon Uncle something, the most important thing. All at once, before I even knew what I was doing, my mouth jerked open.

"Halmoni has never stopped searching for you, Big Uncle. She's never forgotten you!" I hollered over the water. I quickly clamped my mouth shut and strained to hear the sound of my uncle's voice, but even after the soldiers walked a considerable distance away he didn't speak. He just kept wiping his eyes. Seeing him weep, my eyes filled with tears again. He was so close. I wanted to give him my jacket, as if a single jacket could protect him.

Then I saw Yong Woon Uncle strain to straighten himself. He was waving good-bye with his limp cap and turned his narrow back to us. He was walking away. I sprang to my feet. Why was he leaving? I struggled to maintain control as I watched him move farther away, pain and helplessness in my heart.

Gritting my teeth, I reached into my bag, frantically searching for the camera. Finding it, I pulled it out and snapped several pictures, my index finger pressing and pressing as fast as the camera set up the next shot. I could hear the whir of the automatic winder. My father was trying to work the video camera, but his hands were shaking and he couldn't focus the picture on the tiny screen. I grabbed the video camera from him, but suddenly Song Wol's mother's high-pitched voice made me stop what I was doing. "They're coming after you. Both of you, go, go back to the car," she urged.

Not knowing what was going on, my father and I rushed off the riverbank as fast as we could without running, but the trail of mud splattered by our shoes made it appear like we were. I couldn't pick up my feet. My jeans were sodden and heavy with moisture. It felt like I was walking under water. Close behind us, someone shouted indistinguishable Mandarin words, and clomping boots chased after us. A tidal wave of adrenaline coursed through my veins as I remembered the microphone clipped to my jacket.

The clomping boots cut in front of our path.

We halted.

A man with a pockmarked face and a weight lifter's build asserted something in Mandarin. His green police uniform shirt was sloppily tucked into unmatching navy blue civilian pants rolled up to show his thick calves.

"We don't speak Chinese. We're Chosŏn," my father replied calmly.

The policeman frowned, then easily switched to Korean. "Hand over your camera," he said threateningly, and ordered me forward with a sharp gesture. When I didn't oblige, the policeman grabbed my arm with his right hand. The grip was so powerful that I winced.

"Here, take it!" My father cut in between us and handed over his video camera. My arm was suddenly released.

The policeman weighed the video camera in his palm, high in the air, then he walked it around in front of the faces of the locals who had formed a circle around us to witness a potential scene. My father and I were trapped in the middle of the tight knot.

The policeman leered at me. His mouth set in a hard line. "You're not allowed to take pictures of the border. It's espionage."

"I didn't," I denied with pure conviction in Korean, digging my heels in the ground. I was unwilling to have the film confiscated. It was the only proof I had of Yong Woon Uncle's existence, and I wasn't about to surrender it.

"Someone said they saw you."

"I didn't," I said again.

"Who saw this woman use this? Who saw this woman take a picture?" the policeman called to the crowd, making his authority felt.

There was no reply.

"Come with me!" he said with more intensity. He was taking my father and me to the police station.

"There are no signs that say filming is prohibited here. My daughter and I were merely sightseeing," my father tried to explain.

I was afraid, but I forced myself to look directly and frankly at the policeman. This made him angrier. Remembering I wasn't in America, I immediately lowered my eyes demurely and softened my posture. "Really, I didn't take a picture. I tried but the camera was broken," I flirted in my silkiest voice, avoiding my father's bewildered stare. I was embarrassed that he was seeing me in action. Keeping my profile to him, I placed a hand lightly on the policeman's arm and smiled my most seductive, good-Korean-female smile with my lips sealed together so not to show my teeth. I smiled and maintained the contact long enough for him to become flustered.

"It's not me," he said, the meanness in his voice gone. "I would let you take them, but it's not my choice. There are watchtowers behind us, on top of the hill, and across the way, monitoring all activities down at the river," he explained, motioning with his chin.

"Thank you for telling me. I didn't know." I touched him again, then smiled once more.

"You have to excuse my niece. She's not from around here. She's from Yanji." Choi Soon Man slipped through the barrier of bodies and offered the policeman a cigarette, chuckling good-naturedly. By luck, it turned out that Choi Soon Man somehow knew the policeman's father, and we were released.

As the two of them stood together smoking, the son-in-law whispered near my ear, "Let's go. I overheard the women mention your shoes."

Petrified of attracting any more attention to myself, I followed him through the crowd toward the Jeep. I tried to look casual, but I was conscious of every step, slip, and stumble my black platform boots made. By the time we reached the Jeep my legs were literally frozen with fear. I couldn't control them, and I collapsed on top of the hood. I had to use my arms to pull myself inside.

Once back at the *yogwan,* I excused myself and drifted into the solitude of my warm cubicle. Shutting the thin plywood door, I peeled off my jacket and boots and sat against the wall. My temples throbbed as my body began to thaw. Even with the pain in my head, I could still hear the haunting pounding, slapping, and whacking. I jammed my fists against my burning ears and shut my eyes. Visions flashed inside my lids as if I were watching a movie on a theater screen. I saw the Berlin Wall being torn down, the eastern bloc being dismantled, KFC in Beijing serving up coleslaw behind Tiananmen Square, all superimposed over Korea's slashed peninsula. Korea's fate might have been decided by the leaders of the United States, Great Britain, and the former Soviet Union after World War II, but I believe it was the Korean leaders who kept the so-called demilitarized zone in place, the country broken, because of colossal stubbornness masquerading as righteous ideology.

I sat a long while, staring at my scuffed, muddy boots, trying to get a grip on everything that had happened.

⤳

I awoke to absolute silence and the room shades darker. My tongue was parched and swollen, and stuck to the roof of my mouth. Concentrating hard on the thought of *kimchi,* I got the saliva going, and it provided temporary relief. I needed water. Zipping on my boots, I trudged into the common area. My father was pacing the entranceway. His hands were shoved deep down in his front pockets with worry. When he turned his head over his shoulder to greet me, he gave me a peculiar look. In the glass window, I caught my strange reflection. The tears and rain on my face had smeared the dirt into streaks. Using the end of my sleeve and spit, I rubbed away the grime. As I pressed my face up to the glass for a closer inspection, I saw the couple and son-in-law approaching the *yogwan.* They didn't speak, merely signaled with a series of glances for my father and me to follow them into a room.

Once inside, Song Wol's mother reported that Mi Ran had been released. The soldiers had interrogated her for a while, asking who we were, asking if we were South Korean. She denied knowing us but said Choi Soon Man was her uncle and that he had thrown her father's medicine. When they demanded she show them the medicine, she cleverly convinced them that the river had swallowed it up.

The news concerning Yong Woon Uncle wasn't good, though. The shock of seeing us had caused his blood pressure to rise, and he had passed out. His family wanted us to wait till the morning, hoping he'd regain consciousness. All they could do in the meantime was watch and wait. There wasn't any medicine they could give him. There wasn't a hospital in Hyesan or in the nearby towns, or an ambulance or car or bus to transport him to where there was one. Even if they somehow managed to get him to a hospital, patients died of the most minor illnesses, as the hospitals had no medicine or supplies. Song Wol's mother told us that doctors operated with bare hands because there was no money to buy surgical gloves. Her own sister had bled to death in one of their hospitals two years ago.

"A single pill works miracles over there because their bodies aren't used to medicines. Pitiful." She clucked her tongue.

"Why can't we buy some here and throw it over?" I suggested, my throat hoarse with thirst.

"It's too dark. They'd never be able to find it. They don't have flashlights."

"We should just go back tonight," my father muttered, moving his hands from his pockets to his collar. He seemed to slip further inside his beige leather jacket.

"Father, let's wait as they suggest." I spoke to him in Korean. It felt odd, and even to my own ears my accent sounded totally off.

My father shook his head slowly. "Hae Ri, you're not thinking clearly. He's really sick."

"What about Halmoni? You need to think of her," I cried, switching back to English because I didn't want the others to know what I was saying. In this society, children, even adults, especially daughters, didn't talk back to their father. Here I was expected to know my place and hold my tongue. I strained to keep my composure and voice calm. "I'll go back and get her. If we drive carefully, she'll be able to make it here. It'll take twice as long, but that doesn't matter."

He came back at me, also in English, looking at me severely. "You not care if Halmoni die?"

I let out a whoosh of breath. "She's waited too long for this one chance, and no one has the right to take it away from her." It felt like I was fighting for Halmoni's life. I wanted to shake my father hard and scream at him to put away his fears. But even in rage, I wouldn't disgrace him.

"You think it good for Halmoni come, see guns, not be able talk, just cry?"

"At least she gets to see him."

Sensing the tension, Choi Soon Man suggested we let Halmoni decide. I agreed immediately, but my father was hesitant because we were both certain she would side with me. Finally, he begrudgingly consented. He made the call from the private phone of the *yogwan*'s owner, upstairs. My father's voice was tight with emotion. We all listened with heavy hearts as he informed Halmoni of her son's frail health. "All right, that's what we'll do, Mother." He hung up.

"What did she say?" I asked excitedly.

"She didn't even hesitate. She wants us to return to Yanji. She said she didn't search all these years, travel this far, to cause her son's death."

My hope crumbled.

"If only Ae Ran's father had some courage, it would have been so simple. His fear is the biggest danger. In that family, the men are soft-minded and the women are the strong ones. It's strange," Choi Soon Man said. "Yes, it's better we go. All this shock could result in a stroke."

I begged them to let us at least say good-bye so Yong Woon Uncle's family wouldn't wait for us in the morning. My father pondered, rocking ever so slowly forward and back on his feet, then nodded.

With that, we all got into the Jeep and drove to a different spot near the river as a precaution. The light was almost gone and there was no moon, no stars. Raindrops slid down my face like tears as I stumbled over rocks and debris toward the river with the others. In the gloom, the river was an absence rather than a presence. It was dark and quiet. The taller buildings behind the stone wall were dark and quiet. Hardly any lights glowed from the windows. Only one spot on a hill, farther down to my left, was lit. A high-wattage floodlight illuminated a bronze monument of the North Korean flag. The monument was at least five stories tall, and it appeared almost heavenly. Around the base were smaller figures of people holding the pole and marching the flag to socialist glory. The people didn't look big enough to hold up the reputation of the flag.

At the foot of the river, Choi Soon Man attempted to summon someone from the other side. I bent my ears and neck with reverence, listening for a response. No one answered for a long time, then shadowy figures appeared on top of the rock wall. Choi Soon Man hollered at the strangers to go fetch the people at Ae Ran's house.

"They're dead," a voice shrieked back. "They're dead."

My hands rushed to my mouth, blocking a moan. Had we caused this?

"Who's speaking?" Choi Soon Man demanded.

Childish giggles burst through the darkness, and relief flushed through my body all the way to the very ends of my fingertips. I let out my trapped breath and gulped in the thick air. My head felt dizzy.

A throaty grown-up voice, barely audible, called out from the other side. Choi Soon Man, with his bionic hearing, recognized the woman. Promising liquor for her husband, he sent her off to do his bidding. I could barely make out her silhouette dashing across the top of the wall. It was difficult to distinguish her bamboo-thin body from the thin rows of chimney pipes peeking over the wall.

This was all so surreal, with the blackness descending and the illuminated flag on the hill. Stooping down, I grabbed a handful of wet gravel and held it. I wanted to feel how real it was, feel how close we had come, how far we had traveled, only to have it end up this way. I couldn't help imagining what life would have been like if Yong Woon Uncle had made it out during the mass exodus with the rest of our family. Everything would have been different.

"Uncle." Another voice rang out clearly. An electric current coursed through me as I recognized it as Ae Ran's. My unblinking eyes searched for her, but it was pitch-dark now. It felt like a thick wool blanket had been pulled down over my face. No matter how hard I strained my eyes, I couldn't see if she was standing on the wall or down near the water.

"Ae Ran, we're leaving tonight," my father called back, his shoulders up against the chill.

"Please, wait. We'll carry him over tomorrow night. Just give him some time to rest."

"It's better if we go."

"Please don't leave us." Ae Ran's plea was brittle with desperation.

"We must."

"Ae Ran older sister," I yelled out to her.

She didn't answer.

"Yah, go." It was my aunt's voice.

"Stay well." My wish for them was feeble and useless, I knew. What I really wanted to tell them was to swim across, to leave that horrible and frightening place.

Cupping my hands to my mouth, I shouted even louder, "Stay well!" Still Ae Ran wouldn't respond. I frantically turned to my father, choking on my words. "Tell her for me in Korean, Dad. Explain to her we don't want to leave them. Say the right thing so she'll understand."

Suddenly a flash of white light cut the black sky. The light bounced around—it was a pair of headlights speeding toward the place where Ae Ran and my aunt's voices were coming from. Then the high beams popped on, and I saw their hunched figures quickly skittering away from the light. Rushing over to the driver's seat, I flicked the Jeep's high beams on my father. He stood tall and waved both arms over his head. "In peace we shall meet," he cried, expressing the hope of millions of war-torn families.

No other sound or light came from the North Korean side.

Doors slammed all around me like the sound of bullets. I shivered with pent-up terror. My father misinterpreted my shuddering and tried to cover me with his jacket. I wished I could make sense of the world we were leaving, but it was beyond my understanding. I knew I could never begin to fathom how really grim life must have been for my uncle and his family over there. Wasn't socialism and communism conceived to create a perfect society by abolishing injustices and implementing equal opportunities for all? Instead, those political doctrines would forever be associated with obscene suffering and suppression because of people like Kim Il Sung, who had hooked themselves onto the movement and ruthlessly built personality cults centered on themselves.

I felt sick at heart as we drove away.

Thirteen hours later, the countryside started giving way to more houses and shops. We had driven nonstop, and we rolled into Yanji as a faint pinkish-gray blush oozed up ahead of the sun.

Sluggishly, I lugged my camera bag up the five flights of stairs to where Halmoni waited. I only half noticed the blur of an old man doing his t'ai chi exercise on one of the landings. All my focus was on what was ahead, and my legs struggled up each step. I had failed to keep my promise to Halmoni. The recording and undeveloped photos were all I had to offer her. It was a lame consolation.

A calm smile was stretched across Halmoni's face, accentuating the wrinkles around her eyes, as she received us. She had on the same blue satin pajamas she'd been wearing when we left days earlier. I looked at her for a moment that seemed longer than the entire trip back. I wanted to tell Halmoni how sorry I was.

Halmoni took the recorder and held it. She screwed up her eyes as if a bright light had been shined in them, and pressed the cold plastic against her ear. Her wedding band seemed more golden against the beaten-up black recorder. Even with the volume cranked full blast, Ae Ran's, Mi Ran's, and my aunt's voices were faint. Halmoni listened, her mouth a thin, pained line. A single silent tear squeezed out. The opaque drop glistened as it slipped down her cheek excruciatingly slowly, lingering as though it wanted to drag her skin along with it. The tear stopped at her lip, refusing to move farther, then it dropped and hit her satin top.

"Halmoni . . . Halmoni." I called her name twice before she turned toward me. Her expression was vague. "We'll try again," I said with conviction throbbing through my voice, but in the back of my mind I wasn't sure if she had another year.

Halmoni took in what I said for a long while, then exhaled loudly as if she had been holding her breath. "What he has I could fix so easily," she said sorrowfully.

Her words gave me an inspiration. I suggested that Halmoni teach Song Wol's mother ch'iryo. Once she learned the technique, she could enter North

Korea with a travel certificate granted to Chosŏn Chinese citizens and treat Yong Woon Uncle. Halmoni's eyes glistened with new energy. "I can do that. I'll stay here and train her for as long as it takes," she answered right away.

"I'll stay with you," I volunteered. As much as I wanted to soak in a porcelain bathtub with perfumed oils and sleep in a regular bed with springs, I knew the ordeal of getting on and off planes was too difficult for Halmoni to manage alone.

"You two can't stay here. Our flight leaves tomorrow," my father reminded us, spoiling our excitement.

"This is another chance. We can make him well," I said in English, annoyed. I was too tired to remain composed, and I could hear the anger in my voice, an anger that had been there since the day before.

"It's better for us to go back and think bigger," he said cautiously, hinting at something. "Maybe we can get them all out permanently. Is that possible?" He turned to Choi Soon Man.

"It's been done," Choi Soon Man answered as his daughter poured him a cupful of medicinal liquor. He tossed all of it into his mouth, then put the cup firmly on the floor. "Ahhh, leave it to me, I can do it. I'll plan it for January or February, when the river's frozen. Then all they have to do is walk across the ice."

"I'm still staying to teach Song Wol's mother," Halmoni insisted. She couldn't think past her son's illness.

IV

The following day, my father prepared to leave for the airport alone. I could tell he was concerned about leaving Halmoni and me behind, but he knew it was a lost cause. Our minds were made up. When his packing was all taken care of, he pulled out a big roll of hundred-dollar bills. My father counted the money, his fingers nimble. He dealt one thousand dollars into Choi Soon Man's palm to deliver to Yong Woon Uncle and an additional two thousand to our host family for their hospitality. He gave Halmoni two hundred in case of an emergency. To me he gave a quick one-armed hug. It was as sweet as it was awkward. I could tell he wanted to say something. I saw it on his face and in his stance, just as he must have in mine. Instead he rummaged through his fanny pack and produced an international calling card. He insisted I take it even though I already had one. I slipped it into my pocket to ease his mind.

"As soon as Halmoni meets Big Uncle, send him back right away," he urged.

"I know, Dad. We'll be fine," I assured him in English.

"All right. You be careful."

After my father was gone, Halmoni and I relocated to Choi Soon Man's home. It was in a slum settlement of small brick houses heaped one upon another, hidden away and blocked in behind more walls. The foul, fetid gullies running down the center of the footpaths made it impossible to maneuver the car to the front gate of the house. Choi Soon Man had to lead us by foot over the slimy gullies, past dirt gardens and the communal squat toilets, which were a line of concrete slits in a hut. The hut reeked with accumulated ammonia gases that burned my eyes.

Choi Soon Man's house was off a side alley from the toilets. It was a small white-plaster and brick house with a red clay roof. Smoke streamed out warmly and enticingly from a tall chimney stained with soot. The front door and the two windows that flanked it were painted aqua. The windows were covered with plastic to prevent the chill and dust from seeping in. Beneath the farthest window was a rusty bicycle parked against the wall.

Choi Soon Man's mouth was all scrunched up in a smile as he showed us in with a wide sweep of his hand, a gesture of all-encompassing ownership. The door creaked on its hinges as it opened unwillingly. As soon as I stepped inside, it felt as though I had walked backward in time, into the pages of an old Korean novel. Brown earthenware jars, high as my waist, were stacked along the wall, and a large black pot was built into the floor for cooking. Before the potbellied stove was a wooden hatch that led to the coal-burning oven in the basement. A plain old faucet jutted out from the side of the wall with a short hose attached to it to drain the constantly dripping water into a tall basin from where people drank. The room was almost empty of furniture. A large cupboard and a teak cabinet stood at the far end of the room. Inside the cabinet, piled in colorful bundles, were the silk-lined *yo* mattresses and blankets that would be brought out at night.

"Mother, we have company!" Choi Soon Man announced.

At his call, the hatch was flung open and out popped the head of an old woman. Her face was broad and worn smooth, and she wore her iron-gray hair coiled into a tight bun at the back of her head.

"Who's there?" The grandmother screwed up her eyes to get us into focus. Seeing she had company, she began setting out fish and meat. Then with her strong stout arms she lifted the heavy iron lid to the pot. Steam curled upward and around her bent head as she smashed a peeled potato into the cooking rice using a wooden spoon. When the rice was done cooking, she had us sit around a low plastic-topped table. She stood to attention over Halmoni like a one-woman guard of honor while Halmoni ate. Over the next days, the grandmother listened in respectful silence as Halmoni spent long hours preaching about Jesus Christ and training Song Wol's mother. In less than a week Choi Soon Man and his wife were ready to depart for North Korea and Halmoni had converted the entire Choi family to Christianity.

Halmoni became physically and spiritually drained. All she wanted to do was sleep until the couple returned with her son. I did, however, manage to get Halmoni to record an audio message for Yong Woon Uncle. Hearing her beautiful voice and uncensored thoughts would inspire him to health along with the *ch'iryo* and Tylenol.

I clipped the silver microphone on her blue satin pajama top. Halmoni sat still for me to make the necessary adjustments. Her hands were calmly clasped in her lap. Years ago I had used the same recording equipment to record her oral history, but she hadn't been familiar with the equipment and constantly fumbled at the thin, snaky wire dangling down her front, linking her like an umbilical cord to the small black recorder.

When I cued her to begin, Halmoni bowed her head and closed her eyes in deep meditation, then proceeded.

"I'm very grateful for this opportunity to tell you what has so long been trapped in my heart. We have been separated a lifetime. Knowing you are hungry, we traveled this far, prepared so carefully a package. *Ayeegoo,* how much you have suffered. I'm going insane with heartache. Whenever I recall back to that night you fled our home in Pyongyang, my entire body shakes. I pray always to God, our Father, to please allow me to see you. I plead for a way.

"This kind man and his wife will try once more to bring you to me. I wait for you. Though I want to speak now, want to speak, want to speak . . . I . . . am . . . unable." Her words broke up into pinched sobs. Her entire body shook. Then came silence. She remained quiet for a very long time.

Wiping her face with a wadded tissue, she started anew in a stronger, composed manner. "I shall do whatever it takes to get you all out of that place of darkness. I have set my heart on this. Now that I've found you, I will not lose you again. All you children prepare for this day and stay well. Until we meet, stay together and be brave. Whatever it takes, do not leave behind one person. When you cross over, all must come together."

Halmoni wearily opened her small eyes and gazed up at me. "Finished." She blew her nose on the tissue.

I kept the ninety-minute tape going. "Tell Big Uncle something about Grandfather. I'm sure he wants to know what happened to his father," I encouraged her.

Halmoni pondered for a moment, then clasped her fingers, bowed her head, shut her eyes, and resumed. "Your father liked to drink, liked to play, wasted good money on pretty *kisaengs* [professional female entertainers] in China. All that changed once we moved back to Pyongyang after the Japanese surrendered. Remember? *Omona.* Your father, who was used to only the richest foods, was not accustomed to hardship, and he became ill while we struggled to make a life for ourselves in Yech'on during the war. So alone . . . alone, I raised the children. When we meet we shall tell each other all that we have endured and we shall weep together." She stopped talking, but her mouth remained open as if she intended to say more. After a while, her eyes, red and shiny with tears, turned to me, but it wasn't only to me she was speaking. "I don't wish to do this anymore. I have so much to say, but how can I say it all? I have it all in my head. Why didn't he keep going? Why didn't you keep going? You should have crossed over to the South and not waited for your mother in Haeju. If you had kept going, the Reds wouldn't have captured you. For a man he's too soft. Turn this off." Her fingers clawed at the microphone.

"For Big Un—"

"I told you he'll be here soon." Her expression turned unnaturally hard.

I unhooked the microphone, and the hardness in her face faded. I handed over the tape, the Walkman, and extra batteries to Song Wol's mother. I instructed her to give it all to them to keep. Then I pulled out a Chanel lip gloss compact for Ae Ran. I knew lip gloss was a silly gift for people who were starving, but I wanted Ae Ran to feel good about herself after giving birth. I wanted her to feel beautiful amid all the ugliness and her abusive marriage.

Five days after the couple left, the call we were waiting for finally came in around eight in the evening from Changbai. Choi Soon Man informed us that his wife had crossed over alone and treated Yong Woon Uncle, but he was still too frail to make the journey to Yanji. There would be no reunion. A letter was being driven to us instead. It was supposed to arrive the following night.

I leaned in toward Halmoni, thinking I would see tears of disappointment streaking her face. But her expression was blank. "Hae Ri, take me home."

"What about the letter?" I touched her hand, which had always been warm and quick to respond, but the flesh was cold.

"Have them mail it."

"What if it gets lost in the mail? We should wait."

"It's just a letter."

I looked at her, stunned. She sounded like she was giving up. That made me spring to my feet. "Get dressed," I told her. "I'm taking you to the river."

Halmoni shook her bowed head. "I'm too old to survive the ride."

I looked at her again, my expression suddenly harsh, intent. Where was all the doubt coming from? Halmoni was the female warrior. Fear had never stopped her before, and certainly not age. She had outlived Joseph Stalin, Mao Zedong, and Kim Il Sung, who was born the same year as she was. Kim

Il Sung's reign of power lasted almost half a century, throughout the terms of six South Korean presidents and nine American presidents, until he died at the age of eighty-two. Yet Halmoni had outlived him.

"Come on, stand up, I'll take you right now. Let's go." I tugged at her sleeve.

"What's the use? My eyes are weak even with glasses. It's too painful imagining him standing so near and not being able to see him clearly. Will my ears be able to hear him call out to his mother? We both might drop dead right there from all the surging regrets. Then what will become of our families? *Ayeegoo,*" she sighed with such despair. She fell silent. After a while she said suddenly, "I have to stay alive and go to Seoul, where I can earn money for his freedom. I have to go there right away. I can make a lot of money in Seoul. Many of my patients are successful people." She glanced at me with genuine excitement.

Seeing her radiance return, my lips curled up into a smile. "Let's wait for the letter. It's just one more day," I urged.

Halmoni looked pensive, but after some more coaxing she finally agreed to wait.

The letter never arrived. Only a messenger came to the house early the next morning, informing us the delivery truck had broken down. It would be delayed another day. Something didn't feel right, and I became restless. I decided we should leave that afternoon.

With me balancing the camera bag on one shoulder and holding Halmoni's upper arm with both hands, we made our way across the tarmac to the plane. The other passengers cut in front of us, rushing and shoving, and I had to fight to keep the stampede away from Halmoni, swinging my bag for interference. I was panting by the time we ascended the unsteady stairs. I checked our seat numbers and realized they were all the way in the rear. Unwilling to make Halmoni walk the remaining distance, I sat her in the first row, reserved for the crew. I prepared myself for a confrontation, but none developed. Seeing Halmoni's hanging jaw and haggard-looking face, the flight attendant merely instructed us to fasten our seatbelts.

In Beijing, we had to transfer planes because there were no direct flights from Yanji to Seoul. While we were waiting, I picked up the *China Daily,* an English-language newspaper. There was a story on the South Korean and

North Korean Red Cross negotiations for food aid. It was being held in Beijing just as we were leaving China.

In celebration of the talks, I bought myself a desperately needed cup of coffee. The instant coffee automatically came heavy with creamer and sugar. I took my time sipping it, letting the tan liquid ooze down the back of my throat. After the third sip, my body jolted to a state of alert, having been deprived of caffeine for so long. Immediately my mood lifted, and the buzz sustained me all the way to South Korea.

The descent into Kimpo International Airport was a tricky maneuver. The approach had to be exact, the North Korean aerial frontier was only a few minutes' jet time away from Kimpo and the approach route passed a few miles from the Blue House, the South Korean presidential residence. So any airplane that strayed too far north of the route could appear to an unsophisticated radar operator to be a North Korean terrorist on its way to attack the Blue House. It had happened to a Northwest Airlines jet, which nearly got shot down by the South Korean air force.

But our pilots did their job with smooth efficiency, and we screeched to a halt at Kimpo on time. An hour later Halmoni and I were in a taxi. After spending sixteen days in northeastern China, I experienced culture shock in the capital city of Seoul. I couldn't get over all the greenery and hundreds upon hundreds of gleaming shops selling all the paraphernalia of an advanced society, all the familiar icons of mercantilism and materialism—Gucci, fast food, HDTV, expensive cars. There were more cars than usual on the smooth, paved highway because we had arrived on a holiday weekend, celebrating Children's Day. Traffic was backed up around the metropolitan area and was almost at a standstill along the mighty Han River, which bisected the city from east to west. On each side of the river were parks and tall buildings. People took pleasure cruises and windsurfed on the water. The tents that used to serve drinks and snacks along the banks were gone, banned in the city. They were relics from the past when Seoul was nothing but a bombed-out place with long lines of shambling refugees and smoking tanks. Those reminders had no place in modern Korea, especially in Seoul, which is the center of the nation, the heart of the country. The city is constantly under construction and changing shape rapidly to accommodate its growing population of over eleven million.

The only constant fixtures are the ancient palaces and regal gates that were once a part of a ten-mile stone-and-earth wall built around the old city. Of the five remaining gates, the two largest gates are Tongdaemun (Great East Gate) and Namdaemun (Great South Gate). To me, these gates were a symbol of Korea's struggle for survival against impossible odds. Korea's four-thousand-year-plus recorded history was a turbulent saga of a small nation sandwiched between powerful neighbors—Chinese, Mongol, Russian, and Japanese. In the twentieth century alone, the capital had been invaded and occupied by no less than four foreign armies. Nevertheless, it has preserved its own unique character and cultural identity. Still, despite Seoul's impression of power and prosperity and comfort, the Korean War is not over. It's woven into the social fabric of the country. The army is omnipresent, and every man has to serve a two-year stint. Four times a year, around the middle of the month, the government stages *minbangwi hullyon,* civil defense drills. When the sirens blow, cars must pull over to the side of the road, and everyone has to take shelter in the nearest available doorway. The roads must be clear for twenty minutes until the all-clear signal is given. The purpose of these drills is to keep the civilians prepared should the communists invade again, as they did in June 1950.

The taxi dropped us off at the Shilla Hotel. Built on a small rise, it was famous for its traditional elegance and first-class service. My boyfriend, Steven, had phoned ahead and had prearranged everything for us. He was incredibly generous and reliable that way. All I had to do was sign my name. I signed both my English and Korean names, unwilling to deny one identity over the other, even if it was only a signature.

A well-dressed woman followed us to the elevators almost at a run. When she caught up to us, she bowed and smiled. "Are you Baek Hong Yong Halmoni?" she gasped timidly.

I wasn't surprised. Wherever Halmoni went, she constantly ran into old friends and people she had treated years ago. I just hoped the woman didn't want a treatment right then and there. Halmoni could never turn away an ailing person.

The woman's gaze widened as she turned toward me. "You must be the granddaughter. I enjoyed your book very much. Do you mind if I get a picture with you and Halmoni?"

I flushed at her recognition, but Halmoni wasn't a bit affected by her new celebrity status. We let her snap as many pictures as she wanted.

Once we got into our room, all I wanted was a moment to appreciate my return to the elevated world of beds with legs, sit-down toilets, massaging showerheads, and freshly cut flowers. I moved toward the vase of roses. It seemed as though I hadn't seen a flower in all of China. I was mesmerized by its soft pink petals and sweet fragrance.

Halmoni cut the moment short. She put me to work, shoving into my hand a tattered phone book held tightly together by several rubber bands. She wanted me to contact her patients. As I snapped off the rubber bands, the phone rang and I answered it, thinking it was Steven. A male voice asked if I was Baek Hong Yong's granddaughter, the author. When I gave him a tired confirmation, he revealed that my father had sent him to speak with us about my book. He referred to my father as Lee Teacher, using the respectful form of addressing people with titles. The voice said that he wished to meet us in the lounge downstairs.

That was the last thing I wanted to do. I was done posing for photographs and interviews. Right before we flew to China, my South Korean publisher had taken me on the publicity rounds. We had visited almost every major newspaper, magazine, and broadcasting station in Seoul.

The voice became insistent when I declined. Realizing he wasn't going away, I left it up to Halmoni, who was already lying in the bed with her arms and legs crossed at the ankles as if she were napping.

Halmoni rose. She slowly pushed herself up to a sitting position, willing to do her duty for the success of her granddaughter's career. Guiltily I helped her squeeze her swollen feet back into the gray orthopedic shoes, then rushed into the bathroom to freshen my makeup and tie back my oily hair in a ponytail.

A sharp-featured man with high, blunt cheekbones, hooded eyelids, and thin lips approached us as we walked out of the elevator. He was of medium height and had broad shoulders, and he was somewhere in his mid to late forties. His face was clean-shaven, but his heavy pelt of blue-black hair, lightly iced with silver, was untrimmed and wild. He wore a dark leisure suit, a white sport shirt with a collar, and buffed dress shoes. The suit and shirt didn't fit his broad shoulders too well.

Rather than interview us, the man launched directly into a serious discussion as soon as we sat down in the lounge. He lowered his deep, gravelly voice to a conspiratorial whisper. "The recent Korean publication of Lee Hae Ri-ssi's book," he said, applying the courteous honorific ending to my name, "has endangered the lives of Lee Yong Woon-ssi's family in North Korea."

For a moment I had to process his words. When I took in the meaning, a dull ache started in my chest, and I began to squeeze the arms of the chair. I grabbed them so tightly, the muscles on my forearms were on fire and stood out like rope beneath the skin. But the rest of me remained rigidly still, overwhelmed by his arrogance and callousness. Who did he think he was? He didn't know me. I glared at him, but his eyes wouldn't lock on to my face. They kept stealing glances about the room. I wanted to snap at him, but in the most secret region of my heart I knew what he said was true. When I was staring across the Yalu River into North Korea the thought had flashed through my mind that the book and publicity could have endangered my family, but I had pushed it away. I didn't want to think about it. I didn't want to admit it.

"Halmoni, Lee Teacher and I met before he flew back to America last week. He asked me to assist your son because I've spent the last fifteen years traveling back and forth from northeastern China. I know the area well. It'll be extremely dangerous, but I think it can be done with careful planning. I came here tonight to get your consent before I accept the job as guide."

That was how he referred to himself—as a "guide." He didn't use his real name.

I swallowed hard. I tried my best to put aside my intense feelings of guilt and worry and concentrate on his words, on what he had offered up to us.

"You don't have to bother. We know a man who's getting them out once the river is frozen over," Halmoni returned flatly.

The guide scooted forward in his chair. I could tell that he wasn't sure if she had grasped the import of his words. "Your son doesn't have that kind of time. It's imperative you get them out soon. The North Korean Secret Service no doubt already knows you've made contact at the river. That wasn't good. By going there, you seriously placed their lives in danger," he said crisply.

"We barely spoke. He didn't cross—"

The guide cut off my words, still not looking up at me. "Yes, but you've plastered Lee Yong Woon-ssi's picture and real name on a book sold all over South Korea and America. The wide publicizing of your family's story makes Pyongyang look bad. That's the deadly difference. Halmoni, Lee Teacher agreed that May or June is the best time to move them out, before they're relocated and lost forever."

"It has to be in the winter," she objected, clicking her dentures.

"Winter is the worst time. They have to pass over high mountain ranges.

If they have to escape by foot through the snow, they're dead. That region is extremely cold. Even the thickest fur coats can't protect them."

A chill ran down my spine, remembering the icy cold and the snowmelt-fed river. Choi Soon Man had been so casual about the journey that I didn't even consider the possibility of the car running out of gas or getting stuck in the snow.

"My son can't walk in the water. The blood will rush to his head and he'll drown."

"The river's the narrowest between Hyesan and Changbai, and it's only knee deep in that area this time of year. The river's the easiest part of the escape. All he has to do is walk a few yards."

Halmoni shook her head, and deep crinkles formed at the corners of her eyes. "No, we have to wait till January or February."

"Halmoni, I've been asked to rescue many families before, but I turned them down. Either the people were situated too far from the river border or there were just too many of them. In your son's case, their location is good and there are only seven total. Their situation is the best of the worst."

"Why are you doing this for us? What do you want?" Halmoni shot at him.

The guide glanced down at his hands and cleared his throat. Then he looked up. "I, too, had a father and older brother in North Korea. My mother brought my older sister and me to Seoul right before the war. My father and older brother promised to join us in a few weeks. Weeks stretched into almost fifty years. A few years ago, I finally made secret contact with them, but they're located too deep inside. From the moment of escape, you only have about five hours before the police discover a whole family is missing. Armed soldiers in jeeps will be dispatched, and they'll chase after the defectors, even into China. I couldn't help my family, but I can help yours, Halmoni. It's your decision. Do you want your son and his family out?"

"Of course." She thrust her chin up. "I want them out, but I can wait a little longer. I don't want to lose him now."

"Just to verify his condition, I'll send one of my aides to his house," the guide told us. "My aide will need something to identify himself as a messenger from you, Halmoni. Do you have any personal items that Lee Yong Woon-ssi would know belonged to his mother?"

I thought of the photos of Yong Woon Uncle that Halmoni kept in her Bible. I contemplated whether we should give them to him. He did say my father had sent him to meet us. How else would he have known about our trip to the river and our plans to get the family out of North Korea? More than anything I desperately wanted to believe that he could save them. "Upstairs we have photos," I finally said.

In our room, the guide crept along the perimeter for an awkward while until Halmoni motioned him to sit. "Yes," he said, still standing, his hands clasped in front of him. He tentatively moved closer when I pulled out the well-worn leather-bound Bible and carefully spread out on the desk three photos of our North Korean family and a letter. To the collection, I added my own picture of Halmoni at her eightieth birthday party. She was dressed up in her finest pink *hanbok*. The long, billowing skirt was worn high up and tied just under the arms. The shortened jacket had curved sleeves and a narrow white V-shaped collar, and tied in front with an asymmetric bow. Shimmering in her silk *hanbok*, Halmoni was leaning into a tall three-tier cake to blow out the candles.

The guide looked at the photographs. "Halmoni, does your son recognize your face?" he asked.

"He knows." She was offended.

He selected the birthday photo and one of Yong Woon Uncle and his wife sitting cross-legged on a green lawn, framed so that there was too much sky above their heads. The guide also requested the letter from North Korea. Not wanting to give him the original, I made a copy on the hotel's machine. He then beckoned Halmoni to sit down on the straight-back chair at the desk. He instructed her to write what he dictated on the back of her birthday photo: *Lee Yong Woon, the person who carries this letter you must listen to very carefully. Mother 97.5.3.*

The guide hovered over Halmoni's shoulder as she slowly drew the Korean letters. Her hand was no longer steady. The lines turned out spidery. It took her a long time to finish, but it was perfectly legible.

"How much will your services cost?" she wanted to know as she placed the pen down on the desk.

"Don't worry yourself. I don't do this for profit, but you will have to pay for their transportation and expenses and other guides along the journey."

"Will it be a lot?" she pressed.

Before he could respond, there was a knock. The guide stopped what he was doing and craned his head in the direction of the door. He signaled me to ask who it was as he shrank back into a concealing corner. The person on the other side of the door identified himself as Elder Kim, the husband of Halmoni's older brother's granddaughter. I let him in. He had come to escort

Halmoni to his house, which was also a *ch'iryo* clinic. I wanted her to come home with me the following day, but Halmoni was determined to do as she said. She was going to stay in Seoul and earn money for her son's freedom.

The guide didn't budge from the corner. From where he hid, he bowed deeply to Halmoni, then requested a few more minutes with me downstairs. I agreed but stalled for time. I needed a moment with Halmoni in private.

Once he was gone and the door shut, I drew a chair close to Halmoni, sitting in it. I knew she didn't like or trust the man. That was understandable. He had an unpleasant, sour personality and a superior attitude. He was the kind of guy who probably didn't get along with anyone.

"That person knows too much," she whispered so softly I could barely make out her words. "Tell him to go away. Didn't you see his eyes? He wants something. Why else would he risk getting killed? He couldn't even save his own father and older brother. Why did your father have to tell him our plans? He should have left things as they were. Your big uncle's family will be okay now that we sent the money. I even bought them five bags of rice, soy sauce, and red pepper paste."

"What? You bought them rice?" My voice was sharper than intended. "Halmoni, did Choi Soon Man take the money Father gave you?"

"He didn't take it. I gave it to him. I'm Yong Woon's mother. I wanted to be the one to buy my son food."

"That little snake," I cursed in English. My father had given Choi Soon Man enough to purchase a second house in Yanji. I moved my chair even closer to Halmoni. My head was so bent forward that my nose almost met hers. "Think very, very carefully. This guide has people, cars, and maps. He knows a lot. Choi Soon Man acts too casual, and he drinks too much. He can get our family and himself killed."

"If it's that dangerous, we should let them be. Sending rice is enough."

"That's not enough. They're dying," I said tersely, verging on disrespect.

"I pray that reunification will come before that happens."

"It may not come for a long time. The time is now."

"You don't understand. I pray every day. Don't worry yourself," she said.

I nearly flinched. Of course I worried. The guide had plainly said it was my book that had placed Yong Woon Uncle's family in danger. "Halmoni, you weren't there. You didn't see them. I'll never be able to forget." Their images and the choking fear stayed with me.

Halmoni shook her head, sighing. I waited patiently, letting her think this out. After a long agonizing while she stopped moaning, paused, then said as she rose to her feet, "All right, I'll do whatever you say, but you speak to that person carefully."

I threw my arms around her shoulders for a second, trying to postpone parting. It hurt to release my hold and see her go. "Go well," I called after her, then forced myself to divert my attention. I had to meet the guide downstairs before it got too late. The last thing I wanted to do was get on his bad side. There was something all too cool about him, but if he could do everything he claimed, he'd be useful to us.

I found the guide seated in a tucked-away corner in the lounge bar, away from the large windows that overlooked the manicured garden. The room had been dimmed for the evening, white candles flickered on each table, and a live five-piece band was playing. The band wasn't very good. Their selections were exclusively sappy American love ballads, normally reserved for elevators.

The guide didn't rise as I took the seat opposite from him. He barely lifted his eyes off the copied letter he was scanning. A cigarette was jammed between his thumb and middle finger, lit end turned inward and protectively cupped by the palm, almost as if he wanted to conceal the ember. I sat quietly sipping espresso as he read through to the end without comment, then flicked back to the beginning to check and underline a paragraph here and there with a blue felt-tip pen. He double-underlined certain portions. Once that was all done, he replaced the cap and took a slow, long drag on his cigarette. The dense smoke swirling around his head made his eyes squint.

"This letter . . . this letter is a fake. I'm certain Choi Soon Man forged it, possibly without your uncle's knowledge," the guide started, then stopped and asked me if I understood Korean. I guess it was because I hadn't said more than a few words since meeting him.

"Yes," I said, and started to explain that I understood almost everything, and when I didn't understand, I was smart enough to fill in the blanks. He curtly waved me into silence and began to read the letter out loud, his voice dropping. I followed along even though *hangul* script read like Sanskrit to me.

1996, December 23

SEEKING MOTHER WHOM I WISH TO SEE ALIVE,
I still cannot believe that it has been forty-six years, years of grievances and sufferings. How long will this tragedy go on?
In the last letter, I mentioned that I received your check. I think it is better if you send the checks to a person named Choi Soon Man in China and

make it out to his name. He will then send me the money. Soon Man is like a younger brother. He does business with North Chosŏn. He trusted me with two hundred thousand won to start a business and we were able to scrape by. Unfortunately, while my wife was hospitalized due to her eye surgery, our house was robbed and everything taken. Yet, Soon Man younger brother, bless his soul, gave us ten thousand won worth of goods so we may begin anew. Mother, I ask you to speak to my younger siblings to send me five thousand American dollars. Then I can pay off my debt and have three thousand American dollars to start a new business. Three thousand American dollars isn't enough to operate anything big, but at least I'll be able to sell some miscellaneous goods at the outdoor market. The motherland does not recommend doing such work, but without it there is no way anyone can survive.

If you can help Soon Man younger brother get to America, he will expunge me from my debts. Ask the younger siblings to help him out in any way possible.

Mother, I am a sheep dumped and lost in a thorn bush, taken away from his mother's bosom. For the grace of God, please send five thousand American dollars to this poor sheep. The situation in our motherland is beyond description. The inflation is so high that it reaches the sky. The government has cut down rations from little to none for the last three years. It has been especially hard this year since we suffered a big flood and all the harvest crops and houses were swept away. In addition, the American government is putting enormous pressure on us economically. Thus, the situation here is completely desperate. Our living conditions are horrible.

I guess I will stop here, Mother. This year is almost over and the New Year is dawning. I want you to stay firm and strong like those seasonless pine trees and don't lose hope. You shall see your son alive in your lifetime.

From your eldest son,
Yong Woon

The guide was rolling the glowing ash of the cigarette against a full ashtray, methodically tapping it. He let it burn near to nothing before he pressed it out and lit a fresh one. "This kind of letter would never be allowed out of North Korea. It's treason. It's a death letter."

"It was smuggled out and mailed from China," I told him.

"Still, every North Korean always feels that his life is threatened. They've developed an animal instinct of survival. No matter how close of a friend one is, one would never entrust another with a letter that reveals national secrets such as financial difficulties. One has to mention how fabulous the country is prospering and ridiculous things like 'our Great Leader Father,' 'Kim Il Sung is a god in the flesh,' 'Socialism is the best.' That's pretty much all they can write. And here—read—it refers to God," the guide pointed out. Then all of a sudden he held up a pack of 88's, a Korean brand of cigarettes, and asked, after the fact, "Do you mind if I smoke?"

"No," I said, looking around and hoping for a No Smoking sign. There was none. Smoking was the lifestyle here.

The guide continued, "People have been shot for lesser things. But they're not killed right away. Ten shots are fired. First the kneecaps, arms, here, here, here, side of the neck, then lastly in the head. And if one member of the family is sentenced, the entire family, including children and grandparents, are sentenced as well and sent away to one of the dozen or so concentration camps."

The news was shocking. All of Korea was roughly the size of Pennsylvania and New York put together, and yet, I had just discovered, North Korea had a dozen concentration camps, possibly more. "Really?" was the most intelligent, clever thing that I could come up with, because my heart was racing with fear, secondhand nicotine, and caffeine.

"Let's suppose I'm Choi Soon Man and I know Lee Yong Woon-ssi has a family in America that in my eyes is wealthy. I'll use it for my own benefit," the guide said, then paused. "You understand?"

"Yes," I answered, meeting his gaze.

The guide swiftly turned his eyes back to the letter. "Tell your father I require three things before we go ahead with this project. First, I need Halmoni's consent. Second, I need your big uncle's consent. And lastly, it must be understood that this project is executed solely by Lee Hae Ri-ssi's family. I'm not a family member, so I'm in no position to make a family decision. I'm a stranger. I'm just here to help." He folded the letter and slid it back to me across the coffee table. "Let's review. Who's making the decision?"

"My family is."

"Who am I?"

"A helpful stranger."

The guide looked as if he couldn't figure out if I was making fun of him. I didn't bother to help him out. I wanted to leave. He had given me a lot to think about, more than I needed. And the more I thought, the more unbearable the tension in my neck became.

I couldn't unpack, shower, or go to sleep that night. I just lay on my back in bed and stared up at the ceiling, cursing my stupidity. Why had I used Yong Woon Uncle's real name in my book? Why had I included Ae Ran's letter at the end? To be honest, in the back of my mind circulated the stories I had heard of secret agents, of espionage, of brainwashing, but for some reason none of it had seemed to pertain to my family. It had never occurred to me that what I was writing was unsafe. Other people had written about North Korea. If I had known the whole story, I wouldn't have included the letter and real names, but the fact was, I hadn't known about the concentration camps, the killings. I thought I could do some good by drawing attention to the plight of war torn families. Instead I had led the authorities right to my family.

V

Sometime between staring at the ceiling and sunrise, I decided to delay my return to Los Angeles and go spend some time with my boyfriend, Steven, in Hong Kong. I gave myself a perfunctory wash, forgoing a very badly needed shower, then checked out of the hotel. I was back at Kimpo International Airport by seven A.M. On the way to my gate, I toured the magazine stand. A tall stack of my books was being sold. And there, on the cover, was a clear black-and-white photo of Yong Woon Uncle in his Lenin cap and Mao jacket with the high mandarin collar. It had been taken during better times. The uniform was clean and pressed, and his face looked years younger, but so sorrowful. Seeing the photo made the tension in my neck return as I boarded my flight.

Sitting back in the seat, I tried to relax my body. I tried to clear my mind of everything except Steven's long, angular face and sexy slanted eyes. Just knowing I'd be seeing him soon suddenly had a calming effect on me, and I liked it. I needed it. For the first time I felt a rightness about my relationship that I hadn't felt before.

I had met Steven my junior year at UCLA. I kept him at a friendly distance, because I had resolved not to marry a Korean man. Since I was a teenager, Korean guys had harassed me for not bowing my head and conforming to their sexist demands, calling me demeaning names like "unnatural" or "banana." White guys never judged me for not being interested in marriage at the age of twenty-five or for wanting a career. They weren't turned off by ambitious women. Rather, they seemed to affirm my intelligence.

But none of my relationships with white men ever lasted. All the things that in the beginning impressed my blond boyfriends about me later began to bother them. They tired of eating sticky rice all the time and complained about *kimchi* breath. They felt crowded when I began each sentence with "we" and "us." I was mystified. My parents, who were my constant role models, were rarely apart. They shared everything and worked as a well-functioning unit.

I kept wondering what was wrong with them, until someone painfully pointed out that I was the problem. While I lectured to young Korean American students, "Be proud. Embrace your heritage," I hadn't fully embraced my own identity. I still gravitated toward men who looked like Brad Pitt instead of Chow Yun-Fat. My attraction was based on race rather than a man's character. Worst of all, I had rejected the group of men that my dear and proud father belonged to. For him and everything he had done for me, I decided to give Asian men a try.

It was right after my thirtieth birthday. I had just buried another relationship with a long-haired musician when Steven called from Hong Kong. By the end of our phone conversation, he had cajoled me into visiting him. I didn't make the trip till a year and a half later. It took me that long to gather up the courage.

As soon as I got off the plane, Steven courted and wooed me as I hadn't been courted before, with compliments and gifts and exquisite manners. He brought me out of my isolation. He showed me how to have fun, to laugh at myself once in a while, and to feel something I'd never felt before with another man: *jung* (an affinity). It instantly bonded us. We skipped over the whole dating phase and moved right into being a familiar couple. We finished off each other's sentences and dipped our spoons into the same soup bowl. Without my having to go off into a long diatribe about Korean history, cuisine, or family duty, he understood me perfectly. We talked endlessly about a future together, but when he actually proposed I became speechless. Joy and dread intermingled. In Asia, I didn't feel I could be myself. I couldn't be outspoken, independent, and career-focused in the same way I was in America. I questioned whether I could be happy living there and being an investment banker's wife. So I took some time to be on my own. It was at the Yalu River that I realized how precious family was and how quickly everything and everyone you love could all slip away. And I felt changed.

Having made the decision to marry Steven, I was filled with excitement. I decided I couldn't wait until my next planned trip to tell him. I had to see him before returning home. As I arrived in Hong Kong, my heart quickened, then missed a beat as the plane skimmed daringly low over terraced rooftops before landing on the runway flung far out into the ocean. Hong Kong, with its bay, hills, and tangled mass of gigantic skyscrapers, reminded me so much of Manhattan, except most of the people were Asian. It was hard to believe that at the beginning of the nineteenth century Hong Kong was basically a rocky and mountainous island.

At Kai Tak Airport, I ran through the terminal building, along the carpeted corridor to immigration. The place looked more like a parade than an airport. Red, blue, and yellow triangle flags proclaiming Welcome 97, Celebrate 97, and Hong Kong 97 fluttered overhead. Great Britain was handing its richest colony back to China on July 1.

Once I cleared customs, I sprinted through the crowd like an Olympic champion, dove under the red velvet rope, and slid into the backseat of a cab. The taxi cruised on the left side of the road, hugging the white line too closely, as we headed for the Hong Kong Island side. Immediately I caught that energizing but disturbing scent in the air. It wasn't exhaust fumes or food or the salty harbor. When I first visited Hong Kong and smelled it, I couldn't pinpoint it. Then as I became familiar with this place, I realized it was wealth. There was no escaping the obscene abundance. It glittered from shop windows crammed with gold, jade, and diamonds. It gleamed off Mercedes-Benzes and Rolls-Royces. It was advertised on double-decker buses, the sides of buildings, men's ties, and women's handbags. It was sobering to think that the cost of one Gucci bag, one pair of Prada boots, could save a life in North Korea.

We went up the winding path to Magazine Gap Road, which led to the Peak—the tallest mountain on the island. A kid had spray-painted in big crimson letters MTV Rules on one of the gigantic pillars supporting an overhead expressway ramp.

Steven's building was just beyond the pillars. His flat occupied the entire fifth floor. It was a huge place, enormous by Hong Kong standards. Steven had picked it out so I could have a room of my own and we could entertain.

I let myself in with a duplicate key. The second I stepped across the threshold Steven's Filipino housekeeper ran out from the kitchen. She was puzzled because I had arrived with only one small carry-on bag. Usually I came with a set of matching luggage, prepared to nest for several weeks. To her horror, I undressed right in front of her, handing over all my clothing except for my flowered underwear and bra. I gave instructions to stuff it all in a trash bag and throw it away, but then instantly changed my mind, remembering the threadbare rags my relatives had worn.

I headed straight for the master bathroom. I stood dumb with surprise before the mirror. Every inch of me looked travel-stained, and my skin itched. My arms and calves were covered with large red insect bites, and my hair was stuck together in strings and ropes. I scratched my head with both hands, moving my whole scalp back and forth. I examined the gray paste of sweat and dandruff lodged under my fingernails. I didn't even want to think about what I must smell like. Disgusted, I cranked the water, making it hotter than I thought I could ever stand, then eased under the showerhead with a long drawn-out sigh of pleasure. It felt decadent to lather up my hair with sweet-smelling shampoo and massage the fragrance into my scalp. When that was all done, I used a scrub cloth to exfoliate layers of dead skin until clear, smooth skin shone through.

Clean and feeling human again, I went to the closet. Everything was lined up and in perfect order. I grabbed a sapphire terry-cloth robe from the top shelf, careful not to disturb the other clothes.

Wrapped in the oversized robe, I strolled barefoot through the apartment, finger-combing the snarls out of my hair. I inspected everything as if for the first time. In the bedroom was a wrought-iron crown bed with a canopy frame looped with yards of white gauze that trailed on the floor at the four corners. At the foot of the bed was a large, ornate bench with a blue-and-red silk cushion. Other than a pear-shaped porcelain vase and an ivy plant, the decoration was spare. The windows were without curtains, and the walls had no pictures.

I sat on the bench. The hard cushion wasn't comfortable at all, so I moved into the living room. I snuggled into the soft chaise longue after trying out the various chairs and sofas. The living room was a mixture of Chinese and Korean antiques and rich hand-woven Persian rugs. The upright Kenwood piano where Steven liked to release his work-related stress by playing the theme song from the movie *Somewhere in Time* was the only American item.

Stretching my arms straight ahead, I examined the lean muscles. They ached, I thought, from the effort of constantly willing Halmoni my energy as I supported her on my arm. Lying back down on the chaise, I stared out the row of big picture windows. The view was fantastic. It overlooked all of Hong Kong, onto Kowloon across the harbor, and onto the ferries carting passengers back and forth across the water. I witnessed the fiery sun slowly descending and impaling itself on a spearlike skyscraper, then completely slipping away into darkness. But the darkness sparkled with the colorful flickering lights that seeped upward from this ever-awake city.

Close to eight, I heard the sound of keys jingling. I rushed to the front door and threw my arms around Steven's shoulders. Momentarily stunned, he stood erect and stiff. His dark brows, which usually stood close together, lifted and opened wide. He was wearing one of his immaculate navy blue suits with a snow-white dress shirt, and his neatly trimmed hair was flawlessly blow-dried back from his temples. He smelled so familiar. Inhaling him deeply, I clung to him even more tightly. I could feel the steady and reliable beat of his heart. When I felt his hands slide around me underneath the robe, my skin melted into his, seamless, and my bones remolded themselves to fit against his.

The next day, an uneasiness grew inside me. Every now and then I'd turn deliberately to observe Steven. I couldn't figure out if he also had changed or if it was just me. He seemed the same, yet somehow different. He had felt nearer to me when I was far away in China. When I started to tell him about my decision to accept his proposal, his mind seemed elsewhere, and it silenced the words on my lips.

I scolded myself for being so sensitive. Steven had the number two position in one of the most successful brokerage houses in Hong Kong. He was an important man. His business was by nature extremely preoccupying. The Dow Jones ticked in his heart, and his pulse rate went up and down with the volatile market. I knew this. I knew it, but still I was troubled. I couldn't shake this new sense of insecurity. Instead, I tried to make myself more attentive and attractive. As the week wore on, I went out of my way to decorate the flat with flowers and baskets and curtains and photographs. I made sure the meals were properly prepared. I traded my sleek trendy outfits and dressed more conservatively in Chanel outfits he had bought me. But for all my effort, I'd only get monosyllabic responses and polite smiles in response to my conversation on those rare nights he wasn't working late. On other nights he hit a racquetball against a wall with a pack of overgrown boys rather than face my searching eyes.

I could barely contain my emotions by the time the weekend rolled around. Even then Steven wasn't available. He went to work early Saturday morning and came in late, bleary and smelling of liquor, then stumbled off to an oblivious sleep. I was furious. My anger flooded through my body. I could feel it coursing through my veins. When I was finally able to close my eyes and fall asleep, I was awakened by strange sounds coming from the next room. I reached over to wake Steven, but he wasn't in bed.

My mind raced.

I sat up and put my feet on the cold floorboards. Cautiously, I opened the door and followed the sounds. They increased in volume as I got closer to the adjoining room. I slowly glanced in.

Steven was lying on the sofa wearing only the bottom half of a pair of black silk pajamas, a cigarette between his fingers. He was completely absorbed in a kung fu movie on television. Bathed in the flickering light and cigarette smoke, he looked even more withdrawn.

I walked past him, around the sofa, my eyes and movements very provocative. As upset as I was with him, I wanted to slip inside his skin and bury myself in his heart. But Steven wasn't interested in what I was offering. His eyes stayed glued to the television. Suddenly, I burst out laughing. I couldn't believe it had come to this. I, Helie Lee, with all my feminist proclamations, was scheming like a temptress to lure a man. I laughed a high, hiccuping laugh until the tears poured down my cheeks.

Steven held me. He held me as long as I needed him to, but his touch was distant. I didn't understand what was wrong. I couldn't stop crying.

"What's happened?" I asked him.

Steven didn't respond.

I moved above him. My hair fell in curtains around his head. I wanted it to stay that way, to exclude the outside world while I stared into his eyes to search for the truth. In them, I found the same piercing intensity that had cut through the protective layer around my heart. Also I could see that on the inside he was full of despair and conflict. "Tell me," I pleaded.

"I'm finally able to admit to myself," he said tightly. "I'm finally able to admit to myself that you're not happy here."

"I'm happy," I said, my heart pounding with dread, my mouth dry. "I can live here. I want to live here with you. That's what I've been trying to tell you ever since I arrived, but you've been so busy. I'm ready to get married," I said.

Steven pulled away and stood erect. He had one arm across his chest, his hand tucked under the other arm. His movements were awkward and serious as he paced in the narrow aisle between the television and scarlet chest. I didn't understand why he was being so cold, why he was being so distant. All at once it dawned on me that this might not be about me. I looked at him. Was there another woman? It killed me to ask, because I wasn't prepared to hear the wrong answer. But I had to know. "Is there someone else?" The question sailed from my mouth with a long stream of breath.

There was a long pause. Steven said with infinite care, "There's no one else. I've never loved anyone as much as you." Tears trickled down his face like oil. The sight shocked me. Until that moment, I had assumed Steven was as incapable of crying as he was of failing in business.

Steven continued, but it sounded like he was talking to himself. "I've also come to realize something about myself," he said.

Suddenly I didn't want him to go on.

"You've seen my family. My father's expression of love for our family was by providing for us financially. That's all, and my mother accepted it. She took care of the house. You expect more than I can offer." He squared his shoulders and lit another cigarette, visibly working to calm himself. "I've worked hard to climb to the position that I'm at. My goal is to be one of the richest and most powerful bankers in Asia, but I can't do it if I'm distracted. For the first time in the five years since I've been here, I actually contemplated moving back to the States so I could spend more time with you. I even thought about retiring. Loving you distracts me." His voice trailed off as he stared into space.

For Steven to even think about returning to the States confirmed his love for me. His hatred and bitterness toward America and Western ways was deep. Steven's family had immigrated to the States when he was twelve years old. Because he couldn't speak English, he was tormented as a child growing up in Orange Country, California—the land of conservative white Republicans. He was called "Jap," "gook," and "Hop Sing." He hated America the most for the demise of his family. It pained him to see his father lose his dignity breaking his back peddling sodas and cigarettes, and his parents' marriage crumble over his older sisters' Western liberalism.

"I'd never ask you to retire. You're good at what you do," I said.

Steven tipped his head back to examine me. His jaw hardened. "Helie, do you really know what I do for a living?"

"Yes, of course."

"What? What do I do?"

"You authorize the sale of bonds for your company," I rattled off easily, having been quizzed on this question multiple times.

"But you find it boring, don't you?"

"No." I gave the expected answer.

"Just admit it. You find what your unemployed artsy ex-boyfriends did more interesting, don't you?"

"No!"

"I'm proud of what I do, and I'm damn good at it." A hot and bitter rage leaped to life in his dark eyes.

"Steven, why are you acting like this?" I asked, and in my voice I heard as much hurt as I heard fear.

"Helie, you're more than a housewife. I can't marry you," he blurted out.

I snapped away from him and bent over at the waist as if just stunned by a blow. It was worse than if he had hit me. More tears sprang to my eyes, and I felt my mouth tremble with the hurt and loss. I couldn't hear what he was saying after that. My neck went hot, and my breath felt short. While on the plane coming to Hong Kong, I had pictured this moment, and it wasn't supposed to turn out like this. He was supposed to get down on one knee and pledge love, devotion, and permanence.

Lightning flashed across the sky. Powerful gusts sent the rain horizontal against the windows with such force, I thought the glass might crack. What time was it? I reached for the small clock on the bedside table and peered closely at the black face: six forty-five. Steven was already in the bathroom going about his morning routine. When he came out fifteen minutes later, he was shaved and dressed. He was meticulous about shaving, blow-drying, gelling his hair, and selecting a suit for the day. He wore only solid-color, single-breasted, three-button suits, impeccably tailored to size, with either a starched white or powder-blue shirt with cuff links. And he only wore one brand of ties: Hermès. It was simple, no hassles.

I complicated his life.

Steven said something as he collected his watch and leather briefcase, but I wasn't thinking of his words. I was searching for a touch of emotion, the faintest glow. When I attempted to rise from the great wrought-iron bed, still wishing he'd draw me in close and whisper "I love you," my arms and legs began to shake. I fell back on the pillows.

"We'll talk later if you want," he said absently, his face still closed. He put his hand on my shoulder and gave me a gentle squeeze, but he didn't kiss me. It was the first time that he had left me without doing so. I fought the pain and tears as hard as I could, so he wouldn't see them.

With all my might, I willed him back, keeping my eyes fixed on the door after he had gone. God, make him realize he made a mistake. Make him come back now. I began to count. One . . . two . . . three . . . I counted all the way up to one hundred, but Steven never reappeared. He used to be able to sense my thoughts—but not anymore. I knew it was time to go. I wondered if Steven would be relieved to discover my side of the closet empty. Would he cry again? I wanted him to cry hard, strangled barks of pain, but I knew Steven. He wouldn't allow himself to be that vulnerable again.

My bags all packed, I was ready to walk out of the flat. I stopped a foot away from the front door. For a moment, I stood there, staring at the door like someone who had just run into a brick wall. I needed something. I needed something of Steven's to carry away with me, not because I'd forget him, but to help me let him go.

I began searching for anything, an item. In the bathroom, on the back of the door, the dress shirt Steven had worn the previous day was hanging on the hook. I brought the shirt close to my nose and slowly breathed in the masculine scent of Shiseido aftershave through the starched cotton.

I tossed the dress shirt into my bag, then turned my back to the flat and pulled the door shut.

VI

May 11, 1997

When the shuttle turned off Santa Monica Boulevard and pulled up to my street, I saw the Royal Gardens apartment complex with its six-foot-high wrought-iron gates, large French windows, and cherub molding. The quaint two-story complex had been home for almost three years. The courtyard was filled with my neighbors—"the boys"—tanning in their tighty-whities and toasting each other with iced margaritas. Their cheerful greetings halted my footsteps. I was expecting things to be different, people to look more serious, act more serious, but there was nothing different. People still smiled, tanned, and drank margaritas.

My apartment was in the left corner of the U-shaped structure, at the rear of the courtyard. I shoved the door open and stepped in. The air was stagnant. My roommate, Tiffani, had taken up residence at her new man's place across town. I was all alone among the stark white walls and white floors. There were no flowers in the vases, no pretty, fresh smells, no happy signs that people cared.

Aimlessly, I wandered around the living room and dining area, touching things, opening and closing closets and drawers, searching for clues that I belonged here. I did this for a while before slowly easing to the answering machine. The red light was winking. I played the messages half hoping, half expecting to hear his voice. But none was from him.

My heart sank.

I fought an insane impulse to call him, and ran into the kitchen. I took out a bottle of wine. I didn't check the color or what vintage it was. Opening it, I took the bottle and a glass back into the living room and dumped myself onto the couch. My hands shook as I poured a huge drink and gulped it down. I could hardly taste the wine, but that didn't matter. I needed the alcohol to ease the pain. It worked for a while, but then around four in the morning unwelcome thoughts about Steven floated in, and all the rage and grief and shame I was feeling settled at the pit of my stomach. I doubled over as a sharp, furious cramp wrenched my whole body. I was blinded with sweat and pain and fear. That night my period began. The blood was so heavy and dark, I felt that something inside me had died.

I slept for most of the next three days. I could have slept longer, but the phone rang and rang, rattling the quiet apartment. Foggy and dazed, I swam to it. I picked up the receiver, still clinging to the crazy hope it might be him. When I opened my dry mouth, no words came out at first. Then I heard a slow and hollow voice that wasn't mine say, "Haaa-low."

"Why you not call home?" my father asked. His words came to me dully, as if he were speaking through a rag over his mouth.

"Uuuhh," I groaned, burrowing more deeply into the couch. I was upset at him for waking me up from my coma in the middle of the day. I wasn't ready to emerge from my depression. It was safe. It protected me.

My father was saying something about an important meeting that evening with the guide and that I should be there.

I didn't feel up to it, but I knew I couldn't avoid people forever, especially my parents. When I tried to stand, I felt weak and woozy. It took everything I had in me to shower, get dressed, and repair my face. I looked better once I was all done. The contours and rosy highlights on my cheeks and lips made me look more alive, but I couldn't hide the fact that there was a great void behind my eyes. I had seen it before in the eyes of the homeless and badly wounded. It would have been better if I cried, broke things, and then moved on. I felt nothing. Inside me, something had closed off. The only thing I was aware of was the slow, spongy thudding of my heart and the expansion and collapse of my lungs, but even those sensations were dulled.

I was the first one to arrive at Dragon Restaurant at six o'clock. It was located next to a minimart, just off the crowded corner of Olympic and Vermont Avenues in Koreatown. I walked in a dreamlike detachment from the cocoon of my parked car to the entrance. The room was not too crowded, but the mirrored walls gave the illusion of more space, more customers.

In a strange, faraway voice I requested a large table. It was the longest sentence I had said for a while. The waitress ushered me around an elevated fish tank with a crab gliding through the murky water to a table next to the mirror. I sat with my back to my reflection and my face to the entrance. I spotted my mother under the archway right away, because she always walked into a room, any room, with so much confidence. Her short permed and teased hair was pushed behind her ears, and her round face was shiny from too much moisturizer. She had on a leisure outfit of bold colors that her factory manufactured. She favored primary colors, no indecisive pinks or wan lavenders.

My mother had wanted to be a doctor. Even at the age of eleven, as the war raged around her, she was determined to continue her education. Without Halmoni's knowledge, my mother secretly carried her schoolbooks underneath her shirt during their exodus to the South. She held on to them through the air raids and along the icy, mountainous trail. For weeks she stumbled along on frozen feet and an empty belly beside her younger siblings and Halmoni. But when Halmoni could no longer carry the weight of the baby strapped to her back, my mother surrendered her schoolbooks, her dreams, and carried her younger sister.

In the South, Halmoni struggled to eke out a living for her children. She could barely afford to feed them, much less pay for their schooling. So, my mother hitchhiked a ride on a cabbage truck to seek out her father's friends, who admired her courage and gave her money for her tuition. My mother studied diligently and was eventually accepted into Korea University, one of the top-ranked colleges in South Korea. When she declared her major in medicine, her professors strongly discouraged her from pursuing an unrealistic career. They advised her to study home economics, get married, and fulfill her duty to her widowed mother. There just weren't that many options for women back then in Korea.

When our family immigrated to America, my mother had fewer job options because of the language barrier, but she was determined to find work. She wanted to earn money for her children's college education. In America, she thought, there were no limits.

So she taught herself how to operate an electric Singer sewing machine by sewing straight lines on scraps of material. When she became proficient, she asked my father to teach her how to drive our blue Mustang. Each morning after she dropped him off at the office and us children at school, she'd drive downtown to the garment district. No one wanted to hire an inexperienced young mother whose entire English repertoire consisted of "Hello" and "Thank you." But she wouldn't give up. She kept visiting all the factories until someone was willing to give her a chance. The man who hired her was the first black person my mother had ever met. He was kind and patient, and when he saw that she fell below her daily quota, he allowed her to take the work home.

I remembered her spending long nights isolated in our dark, unventilated garage sewing away, only to emerge on Sundays for church. One day my mother came up with an idea. She began to contract out her work to other Korean women who couldn't drive a car but knew how to sew better than she did. Soon she had women all over the city working for her. That was how she became a contractor. With my father by her side and a second mortgage taken out on our small Santa Monica house, she opened her own company, called Lily's, which grew to employ more than a hundred employees.

My parents worked harder than ever. My father shared the household duties during the weeknights. He shopped, cooked, vacuumed, and made sure we children did our homework and washed our feet before bed. On the weekends he helped my mother at the factory. They sacrificed their youth so that my siblings and I could move to a big house in the San Fernando Valley, attend the best public schools, and become doctors.

I felt like I owed them so much. Marrying Steven would have been redemption for all the heartache I'd given them and the fact that I didn't become a doctor. It would have made them extremely happy. I had failed them. Failure was synonymous with catastrophe. I couldn't face my mother as she took the seat to my right. I avoided her diagnostic eyes, which never missed anything. She knew instantly when I wasn't taking care of myself, forgetting to eat, forgetting to pray. I guarded myself as much as possible, but I could feel her sharp eyes reading the side of my face, my posture, and the black pantsuit I wore. I managed through a pure effort of will to hold myself erect, because I was afraid if I shifted my vertebrae one centimeter off alignment, I'd topple to the floor.

"Where's Dad?" I asked.

"Your daddy's parking the car. Only Kun Sam Uncle is coming. Duk Hae Aunt has to pick up Jessica from the baby-sitter's," she answered. "How is Steven?" she wanted to know, throwing me instantly off alignment.

"Fine." I just couldn't tell her—the shame was too great. "What about Kun Il Uncle? Does he know what's happened?" I asked to distract her.

My mother shook her head. She was quiet for a moment, her eyes reflective. "This is tragic. Halmoni has three sons, and her life turns out like this. One son's trapped in North Korea. The second son, who is here, doesn't want to be found. And the last son can't financially help her at all now. The responsibility falls on your daddy and me."

Kun Il Uncle, Halmoni's second son, at the age of fifty-five had run away to the East Coast. He just couldn't get his life together when almost everyone else in our family had succeeded in living up to America's promise. It was because he had succumbed to Halmoni's pressure to give up his music career in Seoul and join the rest of the family in Los Angeles. After he traded in his guitar for a passport, he failed in every business venture and had three wives leave him.

Kun Sam Uncle, Halmoni's youngest son, had a less tragic fate. He had a wife and two sons and owned a very prosperous business of importing recycled Japanese engines at a low cost and reselling them for a profit in America. When the Japanese yen grew powerful and the American dollar deflated in value, Kun Sam Uncle was no longer able to import the engines, and eventually his business went bankrupt. He lost everything except his family.

"I'm so angry that I was born a woman. I should have been born the son. If I were a man, somehow I would have kept the family together," said my mother.

The raw anguish in her voice made me feel such enormous sympathy for her that I wanted to wrap my arms around her, but I was afraid I would disintegrate if I did. So I busied myself by pouring tea into the small porcelain cups. As I put the cup to my lips and took a sip, Kun Sam Uncle arrived wearing a brown tweed suit that was too heavy for the weather. It had been a while since I'd seen him. Bankruptcy had taken its physical toll. He had grown leaner and darker and had developed an unpredictable facial twitch accompanied by nasal and guttural sounds. What was sadder was that he had lost a lot of his presence.

"Did you hear? Two families, twelve members total, defected by fishing boat on May ninth. There was even an old woman and a two-year-old baby. They sailed the boat across the inter-Korea sea boundary, where a South Korean navy ship picked them up," Kun Sam Uncle said in a hushed voice. "The Seoul authorities believe they were assisted, since South Korean–made instant noodles, cigarette packs, and a cell phone were found on board."

"Maybe this guide was involved in that case?" my mother speculated hopefully.

"I didn't even know there were people who did this kind of work," Kun Sam Uncle sniffed.

Glancing up, I saw my father cross the room to where we were seated. A frown creased his tanned brow. "We need to decide yes or no before the guide gets here," he warned us. "He came all this way to receive our answer in person and to meet our family."

"First we have to listen and watch him very carefully to see if we can trust him," my mother said calmly. Unlike myself, she was the kind that kept her eyes wide open to the world and her feet planted firmly on the ground. "I wouldn't have even agreed to meet him if he didn't come highly recommended by your daddy's friend," she revealed.

My curiosity was piqued. "What friend?"

"You don't need to know that."

"Who?" I pressed, my voice stronger this time.

"We got the connection because of your book." She smiled.

I was curiously unsettled, but I backed off the subject for the moment. My mother was asking me if I believed that Choi Soon Man had given Yong Woon Uncle the thousand dollars. "That was a lot of money by Chinese standards. It would have been better if you gave Choi Soon Man a few hundred dollars, then more after you had proof that they delivered the money. Now that he's received that much for only letting you see Big Uncle, he might demand we pay a greater sum later."

"Why are you thinking the worst of him? His family's done so much for us," my father said curtly.

Remembering, I handed over the letter the guide had marked up with a blue felt-tip pen and the photograph I had taken of the note that Song Wol's mother had wrapped around the stone and thrown across the Yalu River.

My father read it out loud:

AE RAN'S FATHER,
Upon our phone call, Halmoni, Hae Ri, Hae Ri's father, three people came on the eighteenth and arrived at my house. I brought them here. Halmoni is too aged to come out, but Hae Ri and her father are with us now, so come and greet them. Halmoni's only wish is to meet her son and daughter-in-law once more before she passes away.

AE RAN,
Bring your father out. We have a car so we can take him to my house where Halmoni waits. Try your hardest to bring him across.

And one more thing—tell them about us. Although we weren't much of a help to you, tell them we were. Tell them it's very difficult to survive in China, so we can go to America. I already told them it's hard here.

Discard the letter.

I leaned back in the chair, catching my father's look. He didn't say anything, but the lines around his eyes deepened and the corners of his mouth curled downward.

"We should still be friendly with Choi Soon Man and act as if the plans are still on for the winter. Cutting off communication will only make him suspicious. Who knows what he might do then?" Kun Sam Uncle warned.

"Kun Sam's right. Everything goes in vain if we earn their hatred," my father said in a flat, somber voice. He stopped speaking as his eyes focused on the other side of the restaurant, and we all followed his gaze. The place had quickly filled up. Through the open door I could see the guide striding toward us. His blue-black hair was tousled; his casual attire was smart-looking but noticeably crumpled. A slight smile twisted his lips, but his eyebrows were crimped in a seriously unhappy expression. He kept his eyes at half-mast.

We all stood up. The men shook hands and bowed. I faked a smile at him, my lips never parting, just turning up at the corners. The guide didn't offer his hand to me or bend his head in the slightest movement of recognition.

"I'm the third son," Kun Sam Uncle introduced himself.

"I'm the second eldest and the first daughter," said my mother, bowing her head, but she studied him with eyes that were full of caution.

After the formalities were satisfied, everyone chatted for a moment about inconsequential things while we waited for a private room upstairs. At first, the nonplused hostess informed us that all the rooms were reserved. My mother thanked her, then strode up to the owner and kindly demanded service. We got our room.

The space was very small—a king-size bed could have easily taken up all of it—but it seated five people comfortably around the round table. The guide sat between my father and Kun Sam Uncle. My mother and I sat across from them. My mother ordered seven dishes immediately from memory. The service was pretty fast. The waitress arrived within fifteen minutes with plates of food arrayed along her arm.

Kun Sam Uncle jumped in once the waitress had left us to attend to other customers. "Let's get to the issue," he said with a cough.

The guide delicately laid his plastic chopsticks across the top of his plate, then cleared his throat. "I flew here to receive, in person, your family's decision concerning this project. I return to Seoul tomorrow and then immediately on to China if you decide to go ahead with everything." He spoke in a low voice, sounding impressive, but he filtered his words through his fingers in a strangely feminine gesture.

"How much will everything cost?" my father asked.

"Nothing's concrete, but I've priced the boat at around thirty, forty thousand. That's about five thousand American dollars per head."

"So expensive!" my father exclaimed. We were all stunned by the amount at first, but when we thought about the lives we would save, it didn't seem outrageous at all. In fact, it was gross to think a life was only worth a measly five thousand dollars.

The guide's tone remained constant as he went on. "It's a rough estimation. I'll go and see if I can negotiate a lower price for you. Although this is a life-and-death escape, you don't want to be taken. But I must tell you it's very hard to secure a boat. You have to check out several crucial factors: what type of boat it is, when it will come in from sea, where it anchors, whether your relatives will board directly or whether a smaller boat will take them to it, how many tons the boat carries, the estimated time of arrival, and whether it can sail beyond the North Korea sea boundary."

"How long will this entire mission take?" my father inquired in the same low voice.

"Once I get to Changbai, I might have to stay there five, maybe ten days maximum. It's now mid-May. I'm shooting for the end of June."

"That soon?" Kun Sam Uncle's eyebrows froze into lopsided arches.

"Once contact is made with Lee Yong Woon-ssi and he agrees, that's the time to go in. At that point, everything has to happen quickly. You must be very careful, because you don't want to arouse suspicion among the neighbors. They all watch each other very closely. That's how it is over there."

"Why not take them to the South Korean embassy in China?" Kun Sam Uncle sniffed. He didn't stop with all the nervous sounds and twitches.

"Once that route's taken, your family will be doomed. To maintain international peace, ambassadors send refugees back to the North, knowing they'll be disposed of. The media doesn't report such news though. High-profile defectors are always accepted, like Hwang Jang Yop, who was a longtime member of the inner circle and the highest-ranking official ever to defect. He's still holed up in the South Korean consulate in Beijing. He's been there since February twelfth. Hae Ri-ssi's book will be considered, but there's a chance your family won't be accepted as political refugees."

I couldn't believe it. How could it be that embassies would turn away refugees, including children?

"Then shouldn't we bring them to America?" asked my father.

"Getting your family into South Korea will be relatively easier. After Hong Kong is handed over, on July first, the South Korean government will accept all North Koreans attempting to defect by sea, because Hong Kong will no longer be a means of escape. Also, the South Korean government has a refugee program all set up. Once you get them into the country, they'll be well taken care of and it won't be such a cultural shock. I'll assist you as much as I can. I'll give you contacts and names of people who can be your drivers and guides through China. They'll help your family get identification cards, and keep them out of sight. I can even introduce you to some Chinese officials for your protection, but I can't make any decisions for you. The plans must be made and executed by your family." The guide paused, blinked at the ceiling. "I'm just a helpful stranger. Understand?"

"Yes," my father responded for our group.

"Therefore, all the expenses must be paid by your family," the guide finished.

My mother spoke up at this point. She had been very quiet up till now, just sitting, her left hand resting easily in front of her on the linen-draped table. "What you're suggesting has only a fifty-fifty chance of success. But we have to go forward."

I was amazed that she didn't question him closely and had agreed so easily. I guess my mother, like myself, was grasping for any shred of hope, and this person offered us just that.

The guide lowered his hand, no longer filtering his words through his fingers. "You're absolutely sure you want to go ahead with this project?" he enunciated clearly, glancing toward my father and Kun Sam Uncle.

"Yes," my parents answered in unison.

"Then from here on you must be very careful. You mustn't tell anyone about this project. Don't underestimate the power of Pyongyang. Even in America there are many North Korean spies." The guide paused. One more thing. I think it might be helpful to have Lee Hae Ri-ssi present when I negotiate the boat price. If she shows up with her book, the people with the boat will be certain this is a real North Korean family and not a trap. Her presence may even get you a better deal."

My parents and Kun Sam Uncle glanced at me. There was an instant of silence. I could see the sudden tension in their bodies. "Sure?" they asked all at once.

The guide nodded. "How old is she?" He didn't address me directly, but rather threw out the question to my family.

The others burst into uncomfortable laughter.

I grimaced. I felt as limp as the cooked noodle on my plate. I wanted to slither under the table and disappear completely.

"Thirty-two in American age. In August, she'll be thirty-three, so in Korean age she'll be thirty-four." My father once again gave up my personal information.

"A woman should be married and have a child by a certain age," Kun Sam Uncle interjected in a scolding tone.

"I would like to introduce someone to Lee Hae Ri-ssi in our country who holds a very high position." I couldn't believe the guide wanted to play matchmaker. He was the last person on this planet I wanted setting me up.

"That's not the problem. Plenty of outstanding bachelors have proposed to her already, but she's rejected them all," my father explained, then went on to brag, "Even in high school she was very popular. She was a cheerleader. You know how hard it is to be one? You have to be extremely active and the entire student body has to vote for you."

My face turned hot, and I sat rigid with temper, both arms crossed firmly over my chest. I hated it when he brought up my cheerleading days. I'd achieved more since then. Pompoms and a husband weren't a measure of my worth. I would prove to them and everyone else that I could make it on my own, that I was my own person with my own identity. I didn't want to be a man. I was better.

"I can do it," I said, looking at my mother, then at my father.

They exchanged glances. They were scared.

"I can do it," I said again, feeling stronger.

After a long silence, my mother spoke. "I think she deserves to go. If it wasn't for Hae Ri's book, we wouldn't be meeting here today, planning all this."

It was decided.

선동민주주의련예인공화
5 혜선서 련붕 동 39반구

운 룡

JOURNEY TWO

VII

May 28, 1997

The mission became the center of everything I did. I thought of nothing else. After two weeks of being on standby, the guide's cryptic call finally came in. By that time, I felt stronger and focused. For some curious reason I wasn't scared. My only reservation was that I would have to spend time with the guide alone. There was an uneasiness in every muscle of his body, especially those hooded eyes that never really looked directly at anyone.

I told myself to forget about it and concentrate only on the task of packing efficiently. I borrowed a friend's high-tech backpack used by serious mountain climbers. At first, I looked in horror at the complexity of adjustable straps and clip-on extras, but once I mastered all the gadgets, I was able to adjust it perfectly to the length and width of my back. Shoulder and hip straps distributed the weight of the bag evenly so my spine wouldn't compress. I was enormously impressed.

Next, I searched the closet for proper travel clothes—something mainland Chinese–looking, or what I thought could make me pass as a native. I stared into the closet for a while before picking out everyday brown tapered J. Crew trousers, a short-sleeve cream knit shirt, and a nondescript black jacket with a zip-away hood and monster pockets to hide things. All that remained was selecting the right footwear. No platform boots this time. Inspecting all the pairs of shoes lining the back wall, I chose the least conspicuous one: durable maroon loafers with chunky inch-and-a-half heels.

Done dressing, I wrote out checks for all my household bills, prepaid June's and July's rent just in case, and copied down phone numbers that I might need. As I flipped to the back of my day planner, a white business card fell out. It belonged to one of ABC's anchorwomen in San Diego. I had met Lee Ann Kim when her broadcasting station did a spot on my book. She wasn't just a pretty ex-model-turned-anchor reading the TelePrompTer. She was actually a good reporter, and I instantly had liked and trusted her. Staring at the card, an idea came to me. I slapped the card, face up, on the nightstand and dialed the number. The receptionist connected me.

"Hey, grrrl. How's it goin'?" Lee Ann said with a girl-from-the-hood drawl.

I explained the situation as briefly as I could without exposing too much.

"That's amazing. If you guys pull it off, I'll get it on the air," she said.

"Be careful who you tell. Nothing can be reported until everyone's out," I cautioned. As a last resort, if we had to, I figured we could exploit the media to pressure the South Korean government to give my family asylum.

"Are you taking a video camera?"

"I wasn't planning on it," I said, remembering the incident at the border.

"Take one. Get a lot of footage. Most people have never been to that part of the world. It'll help your story if they can see it. Seeing is believing."

She'd convinced me. "All right, I'll do it."

"Good luck, Helie."

An uneasy feeling came over me after I hung up with Lee Ann. I hoped I had done the right thing. As I switched on my laptop and downloaded news articles, reports, and essays on North Korea and China off the Internet, I mentally ran through a checklist of things that needed to be taken care of before I left. I went through the list several times. When every last item was crossed off, I got into my car and drove to Laurel Canyon, climbing the hill through the serpentine pass, speeding onto the 101 on-ramp, eager to get this journey on the road. The whole hazy San Fernando Valley stretched northwest beside me. To the east was the mighty spur of the San Gabriel Mountains. I cut past all kinds of faster, larger cars in my little black VW, jumping lanes, changing freeways, speeding toward my parents' house in La Crescenta.

The house was the largest one on the block. It had three mammoth pine trees in the front yard and an imposing wooden door. My parents had only moved here two years earlier from the Valley. It didn't feel like home. It was too new and too big. The size gave the false impression of wealth. My parents were actually in debt. They were paying off someone else's mistake. In good faith, they had cosigned on a box-making factory for an elder at their church. Their friend secretly filed for bankruptcy and fled the country, leaving my parents to deal with threatening bill collectors and slick lawyers. It angered me to see them taken advantage of, but they didn't see it that way. It was a part of their Christian faith to give charity and practice forgiveness.

Using my key, I let myself in. As soon as I walked through the door, Halmoni's two younger sisters hurried into the foyer. Middle Halmoni dragged her bottom on the marble floor and reached up her brown-spotted hand to grip mine. A huge, unrestrained smile was stretched across her wrinkly, pockmarked face. It amazed me that she still possessed a wonderful childlike spirit even after everything she'd been through. At the age of four, Middle Halmoni was crippled by polio and wasn't able to feed or relieve herself. Knowing that there would be no future for a crippled girl in Korea at that time, her mother carried her outside to the courtyard and placed her on top of a large stone wheat grinder to die. For several days she was abandoned there, but she refused to die. Finally, her mother carried her back inside the house.

Baby Halmoni, on the other hand, always looked so hard. She walked around with a scowl on her face and her shoulders permanently hunched forward. It was because she had outlived her three children. Her son was killed in a car accident when he was only fourteen, and her two daughters died of illnesses. The sadness of their early deaths had turned Baby Halmoni into a fearful woman.

"Hae Ri, you've done a good job, good job." They praised me for the pains I'd taken. Their excitement and laughter were closely mixed with sorrow.

My mother came right up behind them, her house slippers slapping loudly against her stockinged feet. She was wearing a crisp red-white-and-blue flag bib apron advertising a local Korean real estate agent.

The three of them hovered around me like moths as I kicked off my loafers. They ushered me to the dining table. The table was literally groaning under the weight of all the lavish dishes my mother had prepared. Feeding me was one of the ways my halmonis and mother demonstrated their love. I wasn't hungry, but I filled up a plate anyway.

Most of my extended family was gathered in the den. People were seated side by side on the oversized Western couches, on the thick gray carpeting, and on spare chairs brought in from the living room. The chairs were gaudy Louis XIV knockoffs bought in Koreatown. They clashed perfectly with the rest of the décor—a mismatch of Korean artwork, a wall-to-wall entertainment center, and Jesus Christ memorabilia. Calendars and paintings of a white Christ bleeding on the cross and having his last meal were hung up between hand-sewn silk screens and hand-brushed poetry my father had composed. Golden plaques awarded to my parents for their tireless service to their church were propped along the seven-foot-long bar, which was also a shrine of framed photographs dedicated to my two-year-old nephew, Jordan.

I sat down on the floor and put my plate on the large oak coffee table. Jordan and my little cousin Jessica, Duk Hae Aunt's five-year-old daughter, flopped down on my lap. They settled themselves as I dealt out the glossy photographs taken at the Yalu River. Yong Woon Uncle was only a dark speck. In my frenzied haste, I didn't have time to zoom in or focus. It all had happened so fast.

"Did Halmoni get to see him?" Baby Halmoni brought a photo close to her eyes.

"You met him, right?"

"How did he look?"

"What did North Korea look like?"

They were all staring at me and clucking their tongues. I tried to sort out the multitude of questions flooding me in both Korean and English. The questions triggered the memories of that day at the Yalu River, and the feelings hit me again with tremendous force. I felt the coldness, the misery, the absolute sense of helplessness, and no God coming to the rescue.

When my father settled everyone down, I was grateful for the relief. He handed me the Korean version of my book and a plane ticket with the return date left open. He then revealed a letter from Ae Ran, the letter that was never delivered to us in Yanji.

1997, April 29

To Grandmother whom I long to see,

I feel like this is a dream. The frustration is too great knowing Grandmother is so near yet I cannot go to her. The fact that she traveled so far to Yanji and we sit here helpless feels like the sky and the earth are stuck together. What shall I do? If I hadn't had the baby just days ago, I would have gone immediately to you myself.

Since the dramatic meeting with Uncle and Hae Ri across the river, we pass the days with tears. We were so stunned by the unexpected visit we weren't able to do anything. Unfortunately due to Father's high blood pressure, we haven't told him Grandmother still waits for him in Yanji. Though this is heartbreaking, it's better to wait till winter. We must keep him well till winter when we may all meet again.

Song Wŏl's mother and father have enormously good hearts. We help each other as if we're real brothers and sisters. Tragically, they've filed bankruptcy trying to do business with Chosŏn. Can you assist them a bit, Grandmother?

It's painful to think Grandmother will be returning with no fruit after having journeyed such a far distance. Grandmother, blame me for not sending Father across, but once I regain my strength I'll find a way to get him to you.

Father later told us that he wasn't able to hear what Uncle and Hae Ri were saying to him. All he could do was weep and wash his face in the river. We all cried hearing his story.

The goods Song Wŏl's mother brought:

Women's long underwear	*5*
Men's long underwear	*6*
Blouses	*5*
Panties	*3*
Socks	*4*
Slip	*1*
Red underwear	*1*
Towels	*2*
Undershirt	*1*
Cold medicine bottles	*3*
Watches	*2*
Pants	*2*
Lipstick	*1*
Rice	*5 sacks*
Money	*$1,000*

Additional milk powder, socks, fabric for a suit, underwear, etc., were received.

I looked at the papers and the words my father's voice had caressed gently, wondering if Ae Ran had actually written it, or Choi Soon Man and his wife. My mother also doubted its authenticity. "When you see Big Uncle, show him this letter," she instructed. "But first ask him to name all three *halmonis* and his younger siblings' names in order of birth."

"That's too easy. Compare his face to this picture." My father pointed to the black-and-white photo of Yong Woon Uncle on the book cover. I didn't notice it before, but on Yong Woon Uncle's jacket, over his heart, was a button-size badge of Kim Il Sung.

My mother took the book and fingered the picture. "When I stare at this middle-aged man, I don't see my older brother's face. He could be my older brother, but I can't be sure. I remember him at sixteen. Hae Ri, ask him things about our family. It's up to you to identify him."

Startled, I went blank. So much was in my head that nothing was. I forced my mind to work. Mentally, I raced through the avalanche of stories from my book, recalling the final hour Halmoni had spent with her son.

"Come back to me unharmed, I beg you. I will be here waiting," she'd promised him, wanting so desperately to cradle him in her protective arms. At sixteen, he was considered a man even though he was too young to shave. All she could do was caress him with her eyes as he prepared to flee to the South. After he had vanished into the night, Halmoni left the gate open for a long time. Never in her worst nightmares did she ever imagine she would have to say good-bye to her firstborn son. She wanted to lash out at the futility and unfairness of a war that took its greatest toll on innocent lives.

"What if I'm wrong? Halmoni should be the one to identify him," I said, panicked. For the first time I was experiencing second thoughts. I wanted to tell my mother that I had changed my mind.

Understanding, my mother smiled. Her smile was full of confidence, and it said, I know you can do it. "Halmoni will only slow you down. Once you're all safely in South Korea, she'll reunite with them there. That's why we've kept her at Elder Kim's house in Seoul. Here, this will help you." My mother opened her brown leather wallet and carefully slid out an aged head shot of a man in his late twenties with a crew cut. He was handsomely dressed in a tailor-made pinstriped blazer, sweater vest, button-down shirt, and tie. His dark unblinking pupils, under thick eyebrows, stared back at me.

"This is one of the few pictures that survived the war. If this man is really my older brother, he'll recognize our father."

I stuffed the snapshot in my passport for safekeeping. "Would you like to record a video message to Big Uncle?" I asked.

Excited, my mother scooted to the edge of the couch, straightening her back. She clasped her hands together and placed them lightly on her lap, as Halmoni had done. She stared directly into the lens. "I will pray every day and night for you to meet Hae Ri in China. When you meet her, see her as if she were me. I would have liked to have gone myself and brought Mother, but it's much too dangerous to expose her so frequently. She waits for you in Seoul. I will meet you through pictures in China and greet you in person in South Korea. I wish you all well. Take care." Pause. "OK. *Finishi.*"

She placed her hands on my shoulders, and her black eyes bore into me. Her expression was suddenly intense. "Bring everyone. Don't leave one person behind." She drew me into her arms and embraced me tightly, pressing her cheek next to mine. I could feel the weight of her arms dragging down my shoulders.

My mouth went dry thinking about what she had said. The tragedy must not be repeated.

Ten-thirty. It was time to go.

As everyone wished me good-bye, my younger brother, David, walked in three hours late, sweaty from band rehearsal. His long blue hair was concealed under a black baseball cap. I caught my parents flashing him a stern look. It was loaded with disappointment at his lifestyle. They relentlessly harangued him to give up his drums, go back to college, and pursue a respectable career because he carried the family name—a torch only a son could bear. Usually I'd defend my brother by reminding my parents of Kun Il Uncle's fate, but I stayed out of it this time because I had too much on my mind already, and so did my parents. As they drove me to the airport, the midnight drive was filled with suspense and speculation. I kept wondering if our North Korean family had all crossed over yet or if they were just about to. I couldn't stop thinking about it—couldn't stop imagining them trudging through the cold, murky water.

"We're here," my father announced, pulling the car up to the curb in front of the Tom Bradley Terminal Building at Los Angeles International Airport.

I shoved the back door open and jumped out. While my father parked the car, my mother and I walked with our fingers knitted together to the Korean Air counter. Boarding time had been pushed back, and the new departure time was one-forty in the morning. I decided to treat myself and cash in mileage points for an upgrade to business class. It was going to be a long flight. The backpack was already feeling a bit burdensome. But I didn't want to check it and risk losing it. Most of it was camera equipment, blank tapes, and research material. I had packed very little clothing for myself. The stuff I did bring along was for my relatives to change into, including infant clothes for Ae Ran's baby. I made a mental note to remove the DKNY and other American designer tags before distributing the items.

Through the throng of noisy people, I saw my father quickly weaving through the crowd. He was winded by the time he reached us, and he looked so scared. "When you get to China, don't move around. Stay hidden as much as possible. An American lady will stir attention."

"I'll be fine," I said as confidently as I could for my parents' benefit. "I'll be fine," I said a second time to reassure myself as I walked alone to my gate.

Just after one, we started boarding the plane. Tired and agitated, passengers rushed for the barrier, which only allowed one body through at a time. Once settled into a comfortable business-class seat on the upper deck, I extracted the pile of papers, which was about four inches thick, and put it on my lap. I accelerated through the printed reports and news articles from Yahoo's Web site.

First I read up on the city of Dalian, where I was going. Dalian bordered the West Sea and Bohai Sea in the south region of Liaoning Province, which was in the southern part of northeast China. Due to its ice-free port, the Russians set up a trading center in Dalian during the nineteenth century but lost it to the Japanese in their 1904–5 war. The most recent information I could find on the harbor, unfortunately, dated back to 1992. All it said was that it was China's biggest shipbuilding center and it handled 67.37 million tons of cargo. That information did me no good.

I moved on to the notes about North Korea. I needed to understand exactly what kind of force I would be dealing with. The information was overwhelming and almost unbelievable. I read about all sorts of human rights abuses under the one-man dictatorship of Kim Il Sung, even three years after his death.

Kim Il Sung's party controlled the people from cradle to grave. The party decided the profession and work of everyone. It decided where someone could live and at which house, and monitored all their activities. It was illegal to travel within the country; only official trips were permitted. Even then, a person had to secure a travel order from his workplace and then report to the People's Committee of the city where he lived in order to get a travel certificate. When he arrived at his destination, he had to report to the local public security (police) office to get permission to stay there.

North Korea's surveillance network was watertight, and it was cited as being far stricter than the Nazi Gestapo. Every organization and workshop, regardless of how small or large, was under close watch by party members. Even at home people weren't free. Every village was organized into units of five households responsible for each other. If one household broke a law the other four would be punished as well. This created a society of snoopers and snitchers. Also, household teams were responsible for conducting study sessions, because deviation from their ideology was not tolerated. Every person, including young children, had to learn by heart and obey the Ten Principles. The North Korean Constitution stipulated citizens' freedoms to speak, assemble, and demonstrate, but in truth, freedom was simply a seven-letter word. People were free to do all those things as long as they supported and promoted the cult of their leader, Kim Il Sung and his son, Kim Jong Il.

Ko Young Hwan in his report "Human Rights Conditions in North Korea" listed the Ten Principles. They were: (1) all of society must be suffused with Kim Il Sung's revolutionary ideology; (2) Kim Il Sung must be upheld with unwavering loyalty; (3) Kim Il Sung's authority must be made absolute; (4) Kim Il Sung's revolutionary thought must be regarded as the people's belief and his instructions as the people's creed; (5) the principle of unconditionalism must be observed in carrying out Kim Il Sung's instructions; (6) the party's ideological unity and revolutionary solidarity, with Kim Il Sung at the center, must be strengthened; (7) party members must emulate Kim Il Sung, and thereby equip themselves with the same communist personality and revolutionary working methods as he has; (8) party members must thankfully keep the political life given to them by Kim Il Sung to themselves, and must return his political confidence in them with loyalty; (9) the entire party, nation, and armed forces must establish strict discipline to move in unity under the monolithic leadership of Kim Il Sung; and (10) the revolutionary task initiated by Kim Il Sung must be inherited and perfected by generation after generation.

The Ten Principles came with very specific guidelines. For example, Principle No. 3 went on to elaborate that "Kim Il Sung's portraits, plaster figures, statues, badges containing his pictures, publications carrying his pictures, paintings portraying his image, monuments or public notices containing his instructions and posters showing the Party's polices must be carefully handled and protected from being spoiled." As severe as this sounded, citizens obeyed it to the word.

In 1985, Burundi's ambassador to Beijing checked into the Botonggang Hotel in Pyongyang. When he unpacked his bags and saw that his shoes were flattened, he stuffed a sheet of newspaper into them. A bellboy reported the "crime" to the police because the newspaper contained Kim Il Sung's picture. The ambassador was accused of damaging the dignity of the Great Leader, nearly causing a diplomatic incident.

Even a child's innocent mistake was not exempt from punishment. In testimony from Ko Un Ki, a defector from the North, he mentioned an incident involving a three-year-old child. The parents had locked their child inside their apartment, as they did every day to go to work. While the parents were gone, inspectors checked each unit. In the couple's apartment, the inspectors found a Kim Il Sung booklet that was spoiled by the child's urine. The family was branded as disloyal elements and arrested.

The State Security Agency (secret police) has the power to arrest anyone at any time. In a report by Do Joon Ho, deputy managing editor of the *Chosŏn Ilbo,* a daily newspaper in Seoul, he listed twelve "prisoners' camps" throughout the country where people were sent. Each camp held some two hundred thousand inmates. Camps were encircled with two or three rows of barbedwire fences ten to thirteen feet high. Some portions of the fences were electrified and reinforced by minefields and various traps. Watchtowers, over twenty feet high, were set up at quarter-mile intervals. Sentries with German shepherds patrolled the grounds.

Within the camps, there were two different areas: the "ideological indoctrination area" for ordinary criminals and the "maximum security area" for serious criminals serving life sentences. Within each area, there was a family housing section and a section for unmarried men. Each household in the family section was given one blanket. Each adult was given a set of quilted clothes and a set of work clothes every three years. Work shoes were issued once every one and a half years and winter shoes every five years, but underwear and socks were never given. Unmarried inmates got no clothes and received less food per day, only 360 grams of corn with a little salt. Adults in the family section received 550 grams plus salt and some acorn paste. Rations were often reduced on the pretext of laziness.

In 1994, Amnesty International reported on a specific camp based on testimony from former inmates. This particular camp ran "a special district to incarcerate felons who have committed serious crimes. These prisoners are denied even food and other necessities, and therefore they are compelled to solve the food and clothing problems by themselves."

I read on voraciously even though I had reached a point where I was having trouble processing what I was reading and my weary eyes were punishing me for mistreating them. I had to read it all. I flipped back to the Ten

Principles and read about the violations of Principle No. 4. "In North Korea, if anyone is found to harbor foreign videotapes, foreign magazines, or even cassette tapes containing Beethoven's classics, he and his family members will be taken to an unknown place."

I slumped back in my seat. All my good intentions only kept placing my uncle's family in danger. If Beethoven was considered a crime, his music considered a harmful influence, then what about the tape recording of Halmoni I had sent over with Choi Soon Man? I tried to recall what Halmoni had said on the tape. I couldn't remember exactly if she mentioned something about defecting, but it seemed possible. The penalty would be severe.

Why hadn't Choi Soon Man warned me? Were they setting us up?

I had to be cautious like never before. I was up against an alien world that was extremely dangerous.

VIII

From the air, the port city of Dalian looked impressive. Sitting on the tip of the peninsula, it was surrounded by the sea on three sides, and the brilliant, colorful lights that sparkled from it reminded me of a postcard. Legend had it that the city was shaped like a tiger's head because a mermaid had flattened the animal into land as punishment for eating the fiancé of a beautiful girl. Tiger or not, I was ready to land. The twenty-eight hours of travel between Los Angeles and Dalian had been pure torment. As soon as the wheels of the plane thumped on the runway all I could think about was a place to lie down—preferably in the blissful comfort of a stationary bed.

Clearing immigration and customs, I walked numbly into the airport lobby. I copied how the people moved and kept the same blank expression on my face. The guide was standing beside a cracking column. I immediately felt relieved. He looked irritated. His cheeks were red, and his heavy-lidded eyes glared at me. He made no effort whatsoever to be friendly. No hellos, no "how was your trip," no welcoming smile. I wasn't accustomed to being treated so rudely, and I resented it.

"Don't talk. Don't look at anyone. Don't look around. Follow me." He flicked his orders at me, then grabbed my bag. I wouldn't let go of it, because I was sure he'd disapprove of the camera equipment. Luckily, I had dumped the reports in a trash can in Seoul as a precaution.

The guide and I struggled for a moment playing tug-of-war. Finally he snatched the bag out of my hands. Surprised by the heavy weight, he gave me a measured look, then swiftly averted his eyes and steered the backpack out of the airport as if he were being watched. I had to quicken my step to keep up with him.

At the taxi stand the guide waved me off to the side as he negotiated in Mandarin with a cab driver slouched down in his seat, smoking a cigarette.

They talked fast and the next thing I knew we were climbing in. The guide slid into the front passenger seat and I sat alone in the back, caged behind white-painted bars. I rolled down the window partway to avoid getting carsick from the cigarette smoke. The breeze settled my stomach and blew the smoke away from my burning eyes so I could focus again.

I had envisioned Dalian to be an exotic town of old China fraught with glowing red paper lanterns and rickshaws—a suitable setting for adventure. It was far from that, yet I wasn't disappointed. The city was a refreshing change from Yanji and Changbai. The sea air was clean, the temperature mild, and the wide paved streets were cosmopolitan. German cars, Kentucky Fried Chicken, girls in colorful miniskirts, and Western music blaring from boutiques gave the city an international flavor. There was a wonderful feeling of booming prosperity. In Dalian, it was obvious that China had transformed itself. The Red curtain had been raised and capitalism embraced. We passed by first-rate hotels and multistory shopping malls that were stocked with high-end imported goods.

When we reached the city center, we drove under a rainbow archway that said, in English, Welcome to Dalian, and on the back side Let Us Build a More Beautiful Dalian. As we circled the roundabout, I saw the most striking buildings in the Zhongshan Guangchang (Sun Yat-sen Square). The Bank of China was an old tsarist-era building capped with three green domes shaped like helmets. Next door, the People's Cultural Hall looked like a neoclassical palace built from huge blocks carved out of stone. The other stately colonial-era buildings had been converted to hotels, government offices, a theater, and kindergartens. All the buildings around the square faced into a manicured park with green grass and trees and street lamps. The park was alive with lots of fashionably dressed people enjoying themselves. It was a playground for young and old alike. Young men kicked around a Hacky Sack in a tight circle. Lovers lounged on the lawn beside their bikes. Older folks practiced ballroom dancing to ambient music. The scene was the picture of a model town—the way people should live.

Our hotel was just a few minutes' drive from the square. It was beside the scaffolding of an impressive construction site. The glass front of the two-tower hotel carried the name Furama, an upscale Japanese hotel chain.

The guide moved very briskly, threading his way between a long line of parked taxis bordering the hotel. As we drew nearer to the entrance, he stopped, turned on his heel, and faced me. His eyes betrayed some inner debate, and his dark eyebrows met in concentration. "Before we go in, I must ask you something," he said in a sedate voice. "There's a lot of security and police hanging around in the hotels. A single American woman traveling alone will attract too much attention. It's better to register together. You understand?"

I hesitated. Besides the fact that he made me incredibly nervous, it was drilled into my head that in Asian society men and women, especially single women, weren't supposed to mingle so intimately with each other. Trained by Confucian customs, they kept their distance. Confucianism set strict rules for proper behavior between people so as not to disturb the harmony of a household or society. The five most important relationships were between parent and child, ruler and subject, husband and wife, elder and younger, and friends. By friends, Confucius didn't mean boyfriends and girlfriends. According to his teachings, boys and girls should be separated from the age of seven.

My instincts told me to ask for separate rooms, but I needed to work with him, trust him, and not waste money.

"Yes, I understand," I said.

"If anyone questions you, you're my wife and we're on holiday from Seoul."

I had a sudden hysterical urge to laugh. My love life was turning out to be a tragicomedy—I had to come all the way to China to be proposed to by an assassin-faced, probably sexually frustrated middle-aged man with a dry-ice personality.

Having said that, the guide indicated for me to sit in the expansive atrium while he went to the registration desk. My clunky heels clicked on the gleaming marble as I made my way to one of the plush wing chairs that commanded a master view of the jewel-case lobby filled with tropical plants and expensive artifacts. Two women lifted their mascara-spiked eyes at me as they passed by. The younger one was decked out in black leather shorts with nylons and white patent-leather pumps. Her hair was parted and tied into two glossy braids like Pocahontas. The older woman with her was suited in a peach-colored blazer cinched tightly with a rhinestone belt. To top off the outfit, she had on a wide-brimmed Easter bonnet sprouting large silk flowers.

I felt underdressed in my earthy cotton clothes and hair hastily twisted up in a butterfly clip in the back. If I wanted to blend in, what I should have worn was something garish and reptilian instead of subdued. But I hadn't been expecting crystal chandeliers and expensive Oriental rugs, much less an

Easter parade. I had mentally prepared myself for a rugged existence. This was far from slumming it.

⌢

Our room was on the fifteenth floor. The guide inserted the card key into the door, and he let himself in first. In the short hallway, he stopped abruptly again, and I nearly barreled into him. I was shocked to see that there was only one king-size bed. However, the guide was so much more unnerved that I became calm inside.

He quickly dialed the front desk, and soon a bellhop wearing a crisp marching-band-type uniform ushered us to another room down the hall. He scurried ahead of us to open the door. We were bowed in. The guide bolted the door, then circled the modest space the way an animal might. He carefully inspected the telephone receiver and vents, then felt underneath the lacquered redwood chest and the round breakfast table pushed up against the window. When he was done, he told me to choose a bed. The twin beds were positioned barely two feet apart against one long mustard-colored padded headboard. I claimed the one next to the bathroom wall, closest to the door. Tentatively, the guide perched himself on the edge of the other bed, seeing if he could stand it. He shifted uneasily, as if his skin had shrunk to a less comfortable size.

I waited for him to fill me in on the mission. Instead, he helped himself to a Heineken from the minibar. He poured the beer from its cold green can into a glass, tilting it with the concentration of a chemist in his laboratory. Without offering me anything to drink, he then pulled out a cigarette and rolled it back and forth in his palm before lighting it. The sudden and awful smell of sulfur from the match filled the air. He curled his lips tightly around the white filter and took a long drag, holding the smoke in his lungs.

I couldn't wait anymore. I needed to know if my uncle's family had crossed over, and if so, where were they? I wasn't sure how to address this guide. It was improper to call an older Korean person by his first name, but I didn't know his anyway, so I was spared from making that mistake. Usually, if a man was only a few years older, I'd call him *o-bba* (older brother). If he were around my father's age, I'd address him as *ajossi* (uncle). I tried to guess his approximate age. I figured he must have been in his mid to late forties, making him too old to be my older brother, but "uncle" sounded too paternalistic, and I didn't want to give him that advantage. I decided not to call him anything and just keep on thinking of him as "the guide."

"What's happened so far?" I jumped right in.

"Tomorrow." He rubbed his head, dismissing me as if he felt I had no right to ask.

I figured I had the right to know everything and that he had an obligation to answer all my questions. "Have they all crossed?" I leaned in closer, my whole body a kind of insinuation.

"Have you been to China before?" he asked, sidestepping my question again.

I played along with his game in hopes that this would transform his unco-operative mood. Calmly, I listed in English all the countries that I had visited, then I added with emphasis, "By myself."

The guide pondered for a long time as I sat squarely on my side of the room with a false air of assurance. I forced myself not to reach up and play with my hair or fold my arms in discomfort.

I didn't think he'd say anything further, but finally he gruffly cleared his throat and measured his words out carefully. "There's been a delay. Upon delivering Halmoni's picture and note, your big uncle went into hiding for three days. Choi Soon Man, realizing he may lose his chance at making more money, sent him away. I'm sure of it. My messenger feared that Choi Soon Man would report him to the police, and so he escaped back to the China side. I arrived in Dalian on May seventeenth by boat from Inchon, and I made contact with a possible boat person for you. May eighteenth, I flew to Yanji, then drove on to Changbai. Hearing my man hadn't made contact yet, I sent three more people over—two Chosŏn brothers and one woman. They all crossed over at different points along the river at night." He stopped to pon-der again. I could tell he was judging me to see how much more of the plot to reveal.

"So then?" I prompted him.

"So finally on the twenty-eighth, we made contact. Ae Ran and your big uncle showed up at the river. After I bribed the North Korean border guards with cigarettes, we were able to talk for a moment. I told them I had to get back to Dalian, but that before June fourth they must send one member across to Changbai to speak with me. I think they'll do it even though they don't fully trust me. I mentioned nothing about escaping. That information must be passed face-to-face."

"You should deal with Ae Ran. She's the best choice. She's very sharp."

"It must be the father or a son. They have the authority to make decisions. If the daughter says 'Let's go,' and the father objects, this whole project is off.

His opinion as the head of the family matters the most. Now, recite to me what I told you so far."

"Why?"

"I want to see how much you understand."

My temper began to rise. He treated me as if I were an idiot. Taking a steadying breath, I curbed my anger and continued to play his patronizing game. "You came to China and met with the boat person. After that, you flew to Yanji, then to Changbai. You sent two men and one lady over at night. Big Uncle was so scared, he hid for three days. But finally you spoke to him and Ae Ran, telling them to send one person to Changbai before the fourth." I smiled triumphantly. I was totally impressed by my language skills. Spending all that time with Halmoni had really improved my Korean.

"You remember only thirty percent," the guide criticized. "I've told you more than even my own people."

"It's a problem if you can't trust your own people."

"They're good people, but when I do a project like this I can't trust anyone. They think they're bringing over only four people, who'll go to Shenyang and then return. At the last minute I'll add the others so they won't panic and think it's an impossible job. If they know the full plans, they'll demand more payment. Did you bring your book?"

I nodded, handing it over to him using both hands respectfully. What I really wanted to do was smack him over the head with it.

"This book will be your proof that your family's legit. Bring it to the meeting tomorrow. Remember, it's your job to bargain down the price of the boat. After the meeting I have to get back to Changbai. You fly back home. I'll call you when it's time to come back and identify the man as Halmoni's son."

My chin jutted. "Leave? I just got here." I had meant to sound tough, but it came out petulant because I was exhausted. I hadn't endured a twenty-eight-hour journey with two layovers—one of them being in Hong Kong, a painful place for me just then—to turn right around and go back simply because he ordered it. I refused to be dismissed.

"I'm going to Changbai," I stated.

"Why are you going?"

"Because I can help you."

"How?" demanded the guide. "Can you speak Mandarin or sneak into North Korea undetected? Do you know the roads through the Changbai Mountains? Are you a relative of the South Korean president? Are you married to a top Korean CIA agent?"

"You even said yourself that my big uncle doesn't trust you. He's seen me. He knows my face. He'll listen to me."

The guide's expression suggested that my reasoning was absurd and flimsy. "Your face is the problem. On both sides of the Yalu, they know you. When I was there, the Chosŏn people were still talking about the two foreign-looking relatives who came to meet their family. And if they're still talking about you, you can bet the North Korean Secret Service has heard about your meeting as well. You've made my job very dangerous."

I offered the video recording of my mother as a barter item. Careful not to expose the abundant supply of tapes, I brought out the palm-size video camera and played the message for him. My mother's shiny round face appeared clearly on the miniature monitor.

"This will be useful." He leaned forward, fondling the video camera.

I snatched it away from him. "I go with the camera."

The guide folded his arms in front of his chest. His expression was a cross between anger, confusion, and irritated tolerance. "Then go by yourself. I can't stop you if you want to risk your life, but you have no right to risk anyone else's. Your looks will attract too much attention. If the secret police discover what we're up to——" He stopped and with his right index finger pantomimed the slicing of his throat for dramatic effect.

"I'll cut my hair short and dress like a Chinese woman," I offered, then thought about rescinding my offer to part with my vanity.

"They'll still be able to tell you're a foreigner. You carry yourself like a Westerner."

I knew he was right. Even if I cut my hair and permed it, wore shorts with patent leather pumps, and donned a rhinestone belt, something in my eyes and the way my head was set above my shoulders would always give me away in Asia, always mark me as an outsider.

"I'm still going with you." I wouldn't give up.

"No, I work alone."

"For me, this isn't work."

For the first time, the guide looked full at me, into my eyes, and saw me looking back. He took a final puff of the cigarette, then smashed it out in a glass ashtray. He did that decisively, one jab and one grind, signaling the end of our discussion. "You look tired. I'll give you some time alone so you can do what you want. Think of the bathroom as yours to freely take a bath, wash your clothes, brush your hair." He squeezed his eyes almost shut, as if he were saying something delicate. "But stay away from the phone. Once you dial zero-zero for an international call, they automatically start recording downstairs. If the police suspect anything, they'll search our room. It's like that at all foreign hotels in China." He grabbed the card key from the desk and left.

He was the strangest, oddest character. I couldn't figure him out. I supposed if I tried really hard and looked beyond the lack of finesse, there was probably a heartbeat in there somewhere. There had to be. He couldn't have gotten involved with us for the money. The risks outweighed the maximum fee my family had agreed to pay.

Suddenly my fatigue engulfed me, and I almost fell as I lifted my backpack onto the bed. Summoning more strength, I rummaged in my bag for something to sleep in. I pulled out a large T-shirt and boxer shorts. If I had known I'd be rooming with a total stranger, I would have packed baggy flannel pajamas and pepper spray.

Changed, I half crawled, half slid into bed. I lay down gratefully on the medium-hard mattress. The joy of being able to stretch out full length and be still was euphoric, and I fell asleep effortlessly.

IX

In the morning I awoke totally refreshed. I slept better than I had since all this began. An extreme case of jet lag had done for me exactly what wine and melatonin couldn't.

The guide was still knocked out, but it was only six A.M. Quietly I gathered my clothes and retreated into the bathroom. I showered and dressed, then headed for the front door. As I pulled it open, the guide sprang up instantly, startling me. "Where are you going?" he croaked.

"Coffee," I said innocently.

He kicked off the blanket and walked right past me and out the door in his gray sweats. I trailed ten paces behind his hunched walk, not because of custom but to keep a safe distance from him. He was grumpier than ever, which I didn't think was possible. His temperament was as pleasant as a rotting tooth, and he looked like he had gone through the worst night of his life. His face was all bloated and flushed, and his bedraggled hair was a spiky disaster.

Passing the maître d' at the reservation podium, the guide staked out an isolated table in the corner and claimed it. As soon as we sat ourselves down, a slender waitress with large eyes came to take our order. She smiled prettily, but the reality of her smile was empty, with nothing behind it except boredom. I declined the international buffet and requested only coffee to rev up my blood. The waitress filled my cup to the brim with real coffee.

"*Shay-shay*," I said, thanking her in Mandarin. It was one of the few words I knew.

The guide began his morning meal with nicotine. After he was through smoking his first cigarette of the day, he got up and brought back a plate of watermelon cubes, cherry tomatoes, scrambled eggs, white toast, and cucumbers pickled in sweet vinegar. He picked the cherry tomatoes out and put them on one side of the plate, the watermelon on the other side. He then brought out his own tube of *koch'ujang* (a spicy red bean paste), which he smeared all over the toast like jam. I was riveted by the curious ritual unfolding on his plate. You can tell a lot about a person from observing his behavior rather than what he says or doesn't tell you about himself.

"*Shey-shey,*" the guide grumbled, his fork poised in the air.

I had no idea what he was thanking me for. "You're welcome," I replied.

"It's not *shay-shay*. It's *shey-shey,*" he corrected, then speared a tomato into his mouth. His Adam's apple jumped up and down when he swallowed.

I smiled my patient, obliging smile at him. I wasn't going to let his coarseness rattle me.

When he was finished consuming his odd breakfast, none of which he seemed to enjoy, he pushed up his sleeves and reached for another cigarette. There were livid red puncture marks on both his forearms. The marks were in the form of opposing arcs from teeth bites—front, sides, and molars.

"Who bit you?" I gasped.

"Dogs" was all the information he was willing to give up.

"Why did they bite you?"

"They bit me because they were mad."

"Why were they mad?" I imagined large, mean dogs with pointy fangs.

"How do I know why dogs get mad? Should I have asked them, 'Dogs, why are you mad at me?'"

"Did you see a doctor? You need shots."

The guide leaned back and studied me as if a new angle had suddenly brought me into focus. "I'll worry about myself. You take care of yourself. Don't make me be concerned about you. I can't tell if someone's sick, so monitor your own health. Eat, sleep, all that stuff."

His tone made me back off. I didn't know why he disliked me so much. Did my presence, my face, my voice, or all of the above aggravate him? What had I ever done to him?

Without saying anything else, the guide rose to go back to the room to await a call from our boat contact. It was amazing that two adults who had just recently met and who were planning a risky operation together couldn't find a single thing to say once we were alone in the room again. It was so quiet, almost too still to breathe that I wanted to make some kind of noise to fill up the huge, empty silence.

"So, am I going with you to Changbai?" I sneaked the question in, shattering the silence.

The guide combed his disheveled, overgrown hair with all ten fingers. "Look, you don't speak a word of Mandarin."

"I'll speak Korean."

"Even your Korean sounds like English. And you're a woman. It's a big inconvenience," he said in a flippant macho-man tone that told me he viewed my gender as being useless. So that was it. That was what he disliked about me. I suppressed the many comeback lines that were itching to leap off my tongue, waiting until the call finally came.

The guide flipped open his cell phone on the first ring. He let out a huge grunt, ending the call, then gave me last-minute instructions in a deep, urgent voice. "Two things I want you to say." He held up his left thumb, counting. "Tell them Halmoni and your family don't have much money." Next he flipped out his index finger. His hand formed a gun aimed at my temple. "Ask for their help. Nothing else. Keep it short. Wait for my cue to come downstairs with your book." He exited, leaving me the card key.

I prepared to plead for my relatives' lives. The responsibility was overwhelming. I had to pick so carefully the exact words. They couldn't sound pathetic or contrived. I didn't want to seem too forward or timid, but somewhere in between. I practiced speaking and looking serious standing in front of the mirror, but my face looked too happy. I couldn't control my nervous grin. I decided I needed a little armor to make myself appear more mature and formal-looking. Skillfully, I applied some makeup and neatly swept up my hair in the butterfly clip, letting a few strands dangle at the sides and back as enticement to do my will.

The hotel phone jangled on the nightstand. It was the guide summoning me. He wanted me to bring my passport as well. I became anxious. Without my passport, I couldn't leave the country. Reluctantly, I pulled it out, checking my image in the mirror one last time before descending downstairs. When I got off the elevator on the ground floor, I didn't see the guide. Spinning on my heels, I glanced around the entire area. On the second spin, I spotted the guide. He was sitting on the C-shaped landing overlooking the lobby with two men. They stopped what they had been saying and their eyes followed me as I climbed the flying stairway that curved up to the second story. Taking one step at a time, I felt very much like Cinderella being presented at the grand ball—but without the support of a sequined gown or a fairy godmother to protect me with her magic wand.

The boatmen stood up as I bowed my greeting, but the guide remained seated. The taller, slimmer man had a fresh, preppy look. He sported a blue-and-red nylon windbreaker over a white sweater with a large embroidered emblem. His partner was his physical opposite. He was stocky in frame, about my height, five foot five, bull-necked with a shaved flattop. He was wearing a shiny double-breasted gray pinstriped suit, an off-white silk shirt, a purple paisley tie, and large Bruce Lee sunglasses with iridescent blue lenses. The boatmen must have known I was Western because they both held out their right hand to me. The stocky man had solid gold rings at the base of each finger and a gold Rolex on his wrist. I shook their hands one at a time, gripping them a little longer than required so they could feel my sincerity through our touch.

The guide motioned me to sit next to him on the sofa, divided by a glass rectangular coffee table from the boatmen. I sat down very properly, my back as straight as I could make it, knees together, hands clasped. It felt like the guide and I were customers at a bank, asking for a hefty loan. I sat there, not sure what to do next. Then the guide reached for the book and my passport. He thumbed to the back and softly read out loud a short portion of Ae Ran's letter. Then for the emotional finale he read Halmoni's ending wish: "When I remember my life I feel so much, hurt so much, love so much. I am tired, very tired, but I am not ready to die just yet. The uncertainty of my child's fate keeps my heart from stopping." He gingerly closed the book, paused, then gave me a slight nudge as a signal.

It was my turn now. My words had to move them.

"Thank you for meeting with us. I came all this way to China for my *hal-moni,* because she's too old to come herself. She turned eighty-five this year. For her, I ask you to help us. If we could, we would gladly pay whatever price you're asking for your boat, but we can't. My parents' and uncles' businesses aren't doing well. Please understand. Will you help us? We can't do this without your boat." My voice splintered off and I was unable to speak further.

The stocky man lowered his sunglasses and looked at me. His eyes were clear gray and, I thought, anxious. "If it was up to me, I would charge you nothing. Unfortunately, it's not our boat. We're merely the middlemen. We'll try to arrange the fairest price for you, but this country is becoming materialistic," he said. His voice wasn't unpleasant, wasn't intimidating in any way.

I nodded, unsure if I should have said anything else. I wanted to. I wanted to start all over again. My choice of words hadn't been eloquent or persuasive enough. They hadn't had the power to make the men feel what I felt. But I didn't get a second chance. The meeting was over.

✦

Back in the room I learned that the boatmen were actually members of a Chosŏn gang. The Chosŏn gangs in this region were the toughest. They were also well organized and well connected. That was why they were able to do the kind of illegal, very lucrative business they did. Ten, twenty—whatever their percentage of forty thousand dollars, it was a lot of money in China. When I questioned the guide on how he was connected to the gangs, he admitted matter-of-factly that he used to be a gangster. But that was all he was willing to admit. My mind started to wander, and I wondered if he was now working for or connected with the South Korean government, or one of those underground fraternities, or some political organization. Or was he a revolutionary or urban legend hero or simply a mental case? Suddenly I remembered he had possession of my passport. I asked for it back.

"I gave it to them," the guide revealed in a neutral voice.

"Why did you do that? How am I supposed to go home?"

"So now you don't want to go to Changbai? You don't want me to get you a plane ticket?"

I couldn't read him. I couldn't tell if he was teasing me. "Are you playing with me?"

The guide's cigarette hand stopped on its way to his mouth and remained motionless. "Do you think I'm the kind of person who'd play with you?" He returned my question with a hostile question.

I leaned forward in the chair, my excitement showing. "Thank you," I said.

The guide folded his arms over his chest, at once self-conscious. "I don't want your gratitude. Just do as you're told."

My heart skipped with anticipation, eager to go. But the guide's aides, the two Chosŏn brothers, hadn't smuggled Yong Woon Uncle or anyone else across the river yet, and it was three days till June 4, North Korea's Victory of Bochunbo Battle Day, when Kim Il Sung's guerrilla army had defeated the Japanese at Bochunbo, a town near Paektusan. On that day, guards would be heavily posted along the border to make a show of power. A meeting would be impossible. If not by the fourth, the guide would have to leave the country and reenter with a new tourist visa. The thirty days allotted on his current visa were quickly expiring, and he didn't want to apply for an extension. It would attract attention to himself. He was counting on the Chosŏn brothers to stop stalling, but they kept exaggerating their hardship in hopes of extracting more money from the guide, from my family. The guide refused to give in to their game, though he expected me to play his. So we had to wait. We waited most of the day in the room. The hours of confinement chafed painfully. The guide passed the time chain-smoking and glowering up at the painted ceiling as if he were waiting for it to crack open. I could tell his mind was far away, because he was careless with his ashes. Just then he got up from his bed, startling me, and walked out. The thick smoke moved with him out of the room. As soon as the door shut and I was sure he wasn't standing in the corridor, I brought out the shoulder bag I had brought during my layover in Seoul. It was a durable blue bag with two front pockets and a flap. The nonsensical English words Go Top Exclusive Detail were embroidered across it.

I laid the bag, the hotel sewing kit, a tube sock, a razor, and the recording equipment on the tan carpet. I hadn't come prepared with a pocketknife, but I wasn't expecting to need one. Using the razor, I sliced open a small hole through one of the front pockets for the video camera lens. The loose threads I burned with a match. The burning fabric twisted and crackled. I then sewed a snug pocket out of the tube sock to hold the camera in place. Next, I made a tiny incision just underneath the handle on top of the bag and slipped the microphone head through the opening, clipping it securely into place. The cord was hidden behind the inner lining, where it hooked up to the camera. It was a rough but solid construction.

I tested out my amateur 007 creation in front of the bathroom mirror. It was tricky judging the point of focus—how much I needed to lean forward or shift my hip. After two attempts, I still ended up cutting off my head and shoulders. I was about to try again when I heard someone rapping at the door. Frantically I shoved the sewing kit underneath the bed and gathered the loose threads before opening the door.

"Were you smoking?" The guide sniffed the air.

"Oh, boy, you caught me. I'm a closet smoker," I said in English, acting guilty.

He caught my words but not the meaning. "Don't smoke in the closet. You'll cause a fire," he said strongly, then instructed me on how to safely hide all sensitive items in the ceiling vent in the bathroom. He had me climb on top of the toilet and lift the dusty grille as he directed from below. The grille came right off. It seemed like a very obvious hiding place to me, but it wasn't to my advantage to argue with him. Besides, I had agreed to follow all his silly instructions.

Replacing the grille, I jumped down to the floor, then went to stand by the guide. I glanced over his shoulder as he partially zipped my backpack and his bag closed and delicately positioned a tiny piece of torn paper on top. He did it so that if anyone sifted through our belongings while we were gone, we would know.

The guide marched swiftly out of the room, expecting me to follow him this time, which I did with my 007 bag slung over my shoulder. I had never noticed it before, but there was something very regal about the way he walked. I was becoming very curious about him. After all, I didn't know anything about this man, really—where he came from, how he managed to do what he did, what kind of people he was connected with besides Chosŏn gangsters. He was a mysterious person, always in the background, not wanting to be seen, seemingly suspicious of his own shadow. Never in my life had I encountered anyone like him before, even among the characters in the books I'd read or the eccentric people I'd worked with in the entertainment business.

Once we reached the front entrance of the hotel, we turned left. Taxis and three-wheeled pedicabs offered to take us where we needed, but the guide chose to walk. The uncrowded, wide streets made it easy and allowed me to admire the city's atmosphere. The combination of Russian, European, and Japanese architecture that survived from the colonial era gave the city a charm and worldly sophistication similar to that of Shanghai.

My heart was thumping by the time we were out of the area of the hotel. I found myself standing on an overpass. Dozens of train tracks converged and merged below the pass. In one direction the tracks curved left and disappeared behind a cluster of warehouses and buildings. In the other direction the tracks separated and widened and went on forever.

The harbor was just a short way down from the train tracks. I could smell the cool, salty breeze coming from that direction. All kinds of ships were anchored alongside the long piers that extended like fingers out from the wooden dock into the open sea. The ships ranged from rusty tugboats to medium-size steamers and grand white cruise ships. The smaller fishing boats and dinghies weren't tied along the piers but huddled closer to the harbor, seeking shelter from the wind.

I peered out at the deep blue water outside the harbor and swallowed. This was the place. Once my relatives crossed the Yalu River into China and made it this far to Dalian, all they had to do was get on a boat. The boat would take them across the Northern Limit Line, the maritime border separating the two Koreas, in the West Sea. As soon as they passed the borderline into the South, they'd attract the attention of a South Korean naval ship or coast guard vessel patrolling the area, and they'd be picked up.

Remembering I needed to get footage of everything, I discreetly turned on the video camera and lifted the flap to expose the lens. I panned the harbor without the guide's knowledge.

"What are you hungry for?" he asked.

"Korean food," I replied. The guide shot me a puzzled glance. I figured he'd been expecting me to say hamburgers or pizza.

The Korean restaurant was a few buildings down from our hotel, across from the China Dalian Ocean Shipping Agency. It was a medium-sized restaurant with flowered curtains and laminated menus. The aroma of garlic intermingled with the thick sweet smell of barbecue beef being grilled from charcoal pits built into the white tile tables. The fat spattering on the coals made popping sounds. My mouth watered instantly, and I realized I was starving. My insides growled with anticipation as small saucers of appetizers were dropped on our table. It felt wrong to be so hungry. I restrained myself from devouring all the food.

As I nibbled on marinated anchovies, the guide poured himself a glass of *soju,* a clear liquor, strong and cheap. He drained it. The muscles holding his jaw in place flexed as he bit on the raw liquor, then relaxed, and flexed again as though the muscles were being stimulated by jolts. I thought I almost saw a smile as he poured and drank again. After his third straight shot, he set down his glass with a startling click. A pink blush flooded his cheeks, and suddenly he was in a talkative mood. It wasn't exactly what I'd call a pleasant conversation. It was more of a one-sided critique, centered on me.

"Your career, it doesn't suit you. Because you left Korea when you were four and have been raised in Western society, you shouldn't write about Korean things anymore," he advised.

"Then what do you think I should do?"

"I can't answer that."

"But you know everything. Tell me, what kind of work do you think I should do?" I asked coldly.

"Why are you upset? I'm not angry with you. I was merely giving you an honest opinion," he grumbled into his shot glass. He sipped the liquor, trying to make it last. He gave up and downed the whole drink, then loudly signaled the waitress to bring a second bottle of *soju*. "By dividing your identity into two halves—Korean and American—you are neither. Don't hold on to Korea anymore."

"Oh, you think it's that simple, do you?" I snorted.

"Then marry someone white and make it easy for your children. They'll be complete Americans."

"No."

"In that case, come back to Korea, marry a Korean, live in Korea, and cut all ties with America."

"No!" He had no idea what he was talking about. He had no idea what it was like to be from one culture, looking the way we do, and growing up in another culture where people look totally different. Even if I wanted to choose one identity, others wouldn't let me. When I went to Korea, Koreans scolded me for not being Korean enough. In America, if I said I was American, people would persist and ask, "Where are you really from?" until I caved in and said Korea. The guide had no clue. I was so sick of him telling me what to do, what I shouldn't do, and what I did wrong. He was trying to control me, change me into his ideal image, probably because I made him uncomfortable. In his eyes I was contaminated. I wasn't pure. Deep down I knew this was why my relationship with Steven had ended. It had nothing to do with me distracting him from his goals or uprooting my life and moving to Hong Kong. Those were only excuses to cover up the real reason. Steven had an image of himself and what his ideal wife should be. She had to be virginal, quiet, properly dressed, respectfully subservient, and have no interest in a career of her own, like his mother. As hard as I tried to erase the lovers from my past and tame my Western-woman liberalism, I didn't fit into that mold. I would never fit into that mold. And now I knew that I would never again drive myself crazy with unhappiness just to please a man, any man.

"Keep your advice to yourself. I'm happy the way I am."

"*Ii-sh,* do what you want. I don't want to talk about your life anymore," he grunted, pouring.

"Fine. I never said you could talk about my life." I lurched to my feet, pushing the chair away from me, making an ugly scraping sound on the floor. My sudden movements startled the other diners, who glanced over at me, whispering, gesturing.

"Good, good, go." The guide waved me contemptuously away.

Some time much later, I was awakened by a loud series of bangs. Scrambling to my feet, I felt my way to the door and undid the locks. The door flew open and the light snapped on. I squinted in the brightness. The guide looked over my boxer shorts and T-shirt disapprovingly, then staggered and stumbled his way over to the refrigerator for a Heineken. Can in hand, he dropped into the armchair next to the window and poured the beer into a glass, surprisingly without spilling a drop. "Hae Ri, have a drink with me. Come on, come-onoverhere," he slurred, his lips wet with drink.

"Uncle, it's late," I said, returning to bed. I called him *ajossi* (uncle) to remind him of his senior age and of the boundaries he was supposed to maintain, but, more important, to sexually neuter him.

"*Ii-sh,* I thought American women like to have fun. Why, you're no fun at all. Someone should loosen you up."

The guide's boozy threat made the hairs on my arms prickle, and I squashed my face into the pillow. I lay there motionless. I heard the pop of another beer can. I wanted to kick myself for not going with my instincts. Rooming together was the worst possible idea. I should have objected. By consenting, it removed all respect and protection, but my realization had come too late. I began to shiver under the blanket. I suddenly feared for my safety, and this triggered an instinctive, self-preserving impulse to fight, run, escape.

"Do you know who I am?" he barked. "Everything you want, I do, but you don't show me the same consideration. You're selfish. That's what you are. Why won't you come over here and sit down and have a drink with me? Just one drink? Hey, I'm talking to you. You think you're too good to talk to me? Is that it? *Ii-sh,* no wonder you're still unmarried."

I went completely still. That remark quickly turned my fear into burning rage. I bolted out of bed and stood ramrod straight, loathing him. I wanted to reach out and slap the smirk off his shiny, drunken face and then kick him to the ground. "I told you not to talk about my life. It doesn't concern you. It has nothing to do with why we're here!" I hurled the English words at him.

"All I was trying to do was have a conversation with you, and you treat me this way." He swayed to his feet and would have toppled backward if the window hadn't been behind him. "Do you know who I am?" he barked louder at me.

"Screw you." I pulled on my pants roughly. My feet got stuck. I heaved them on with sheer force, then threw everything into the backpack. I dragged it out of the room to the elevator. The elevator wouldn't move fast enough. I stabbed at the down button, panicked that the guide might leap out and grab me. As soon as the doors slid open, I jumped in and hid in the corner. My right hand was pressed against my chest to ease the pain. It felt like I was having some kind of heart attack.

The lobby was completely empty of guests, and the cashier's counter was closed. The only people awake at three in the morning were the bellhops slumped over the concierge's podium and two female clerks at the registration counter. My hand trembled as I slid the American Express card on the polished counter.

The female clerks curiously eyed my disheveled dress and backpack with half a lacy bra hanging out the side. They gave me one of those glances that said to me that they knew something was cheap and dirty about me. They wouldn't give me a room without a passport. The women refused to break from the rules, quoting formalities from a manual. They were so focused and determined, I thought, that I could see why China had survived such a cataclysmic event as the Cultural Revolution.

Finally, after frantically pleading with them for an hour, I broke them down—and nearly broke down myself.

X

I was up half the night in my new room, dozing fitfully, then wide awake, reconstructing what had happened. I had stood up and fought back, but my sense of self-righteousness quickly evaporated, as I knew my uncle's family would suffer. I needed to approach the guide, without emotion, and smooth things over before he abandoned the mission or left me stranded in China without a passport. I waited for the milky gray sky to lighten before making the call but then realized it wasn't going to get any brighter. It was time. I picked up the receiver. I gripped it so tightly I bruised the bone at the base of my thumb. The guide answered after the first ring. His voice was icy and venomous. I tried my very best to sound friendly.

"Where are you?" he wanted to know.

"In another room." I kept my exact location a secret.

"Why?"

"Can we talk in the café downstairs?"

Long pause. We listened to each other breathe. "Talk here," he said.

The thought of being confined with him in that room again gave me butterflies in my stomach. I didn't want to be alone with him, but I consented. I had to. I needed him, and that gave him the power. I went, even though my instincts were screaming, Don't do it!

My courage came and went as I walked along the lung-colored corridor. At the guide's door, I made a last-minute adjustment, untucking my shirt and stretching out the material around my chest, then firmly knocked twice. The door barely opened and then shut in my face. I knocked again. The second time the door swung all the way open and I was able to step in. It was dark. I tried not to squint at the guide, who had retreated to the corner and was smoking. Behind him, a small lamp gave the only light. It formed an eerie silhouette over his body that prevented me from seeing his face, though I could feel his eyes staring me down. My skin squirmed and my legs weakened. After several excruciating minutes of silence, I heard him exhaling as he sent two streams of white smoke from his nostrils.

"You're a cold woman," he said.

I wanted to say that he understood nothing about me and never would, but then I collected myself. I needed him. If I lost my temper again, Yong Woon Uncle, Ae Ran, Halmoni, my mother, everyone would lose forever. Wait. Breathe. Count. Smile. I tried to think about the things I enjoyed doing, like taking a hot bath with scented lavender oil and candlelight, listening to beautiful music, watching my nephew play in the park, and taking long walks.

"You could have interpreted my actions two ways. One, you're in physical danger. Two, you could see that I'm a good person heavily burdened by my task. I've been stuck in China for fifteen days. I've been attacked by mad dogs. I've had to deal with Choi Soon Man and others. Now I also have to worry about you being killed or getting me killed. You chose to see the first; that's why you packed your bags and left. All you had to say to me was 'I know you're feeling tired and burdened. Please go to bed.' I would have gone straight to sleep."

"If I'd known how you were feeling, I would have stayed," I lied. Reasoning with him would have been useless. He was so self-centered and knew so little about women that he was incapable of seeing it from my perspective. He was taller than me and at least seventy pounds heavier. Any woman in her right mind would have done the same thing.

The guide shifted backward into the light. His eyes were terrifying. They were red and swollen with anger. "Couldn't you sense how I was feeling? It's in my expression, my shoulders, my movements. You thought you were in danger and stormed out of here. You thought I was that kind of man. That hurt my feelings and put me in a bad mood all night long."

Suddenly I realized what had happened. The guide used the Korean word *kibun* to refer to his mood and feelings. When a person's *kibun* was hurt, it caused him to lose face, which was much more than just his own shame. Sometimes it involved the family, and sometimes the entire country. I had to allow the guide to save his pride and dignity. It was important. In some extreme cases, I heard people even killed themselves if they had been made to feel ashamed or, worse, killed the person shaming them.

Burying my own pride and dignity, I agonizingly apologized for misjudging him and offered to leave China if that was what he desired. The guide didn't answer right away. The tip of his cigarette glowed red as he inhaled. He was considering my offer. After contemplating for what seemed like an age, his face softened a trace and he said, "If we go as friends, then I welcome you. If we're only business partners, it'll be easier for me to go on alone."

Friends? He wanted friendship? Under other circumstances I would have told him that there would never be friendship between us. I would never be friends with someone who treated me like a tree stump. Inside I screamed, Fake it, Helie! Get it over with or you'll be trapped here all day. Move your mouth.

"Then let's be friends," I murmured.

It felt like I had made a bargain with the devil, but I had to say it. What else could I do?

Dark gray clouds pressed down on the city. I could taste the moisture and ash in the air the moment the guide and I stepped out of the hotel with our bags. The clouds could bring with them a storm of heavy rain, thunder, and lightning. In this region, a storm could mean a typhoon. A typhoon would bring more heavy rains and spiraling winds that could blow away houses and people, leaving nothing but turmoil and destruction. I had an awful feeling, but I didn't want to think the unthinkable. I shut my mouth and thought only about getting to the airport on time. When we arrived, we discovered that our plane to Yanji had been delayed due to engine malfunction. No other explanation was given. We were shepherded into the waiting area, already crammed with hundreds of people. Every available yellow molded seat was taken. So the guide wiped a spot clean on the floor with a newspaper and folded his jacket into a square cushion for me to sit on. I settled into a comfortable cross-legged position, wondering why he was being considerate all of a sudden. It made me nervous.

For the first three hours, I entertained myself by letting my eyes cruise the duty-free glass cases stocked with Lancôme and L'Oréal cosmetics. After looking over all the feel-good products like royal jelly, ginseng, deer antlers, bear gallbladders, and other ground animal parts a dozen times, I became incredibly bored, although I wouldn't admit it. I sat quietly, trying to attract as little attention to myself as possible, while the guide went to go stretch his legs. When he returned, he was carrying three bowls of instant noodles. He gave me one and gave the third bowl to an elderly gentleman sitting next to us.

"Why are you being so nice?" I finally had to ask.

The guide crossed his eyes comically and the muscles around his mouth creased up a bit into a smile. "I've decided to change. The other day, I went a little crazy. Understand? No more fighting. I've changed my way of thinking," he said.

I didn't buy it. Not for all the tea in China. Not even if a hundred saints testified that he was a kinder, gentler man would I believe he had changed. The next time I did something or said something he didn't like, I'd see just how thin his layer of kindness was. I kept safely to myself as the hours clicked away without an update. The flapping departure board kept delaying our flight time. It wasn't until five in the evening, seven hours after we arrived at the airport, that a high-pitched female voice blared an announcement over the PA. The malfunction had been rectified. We were to board the same damaged plane. I wasn't reassured when I saw the small commuter plane on the tarmac, clean and in one piece. In my mind, it was still broken. But a desire to get to Yanji overshadowed my fear of the plane exploding in the air, so I boarded with the other dazed passengers.

My heart stalled for one prolonged beat, then kicked painfully inside my chest as the plane wobbled and rose shakily into the air. Only when the plane finally stabilized and we were cruising effortlessly was I able to relax slightly. The guide was asleep less than five minutes after takeoff, his head leaning back against the seat. I had never been this close to him before. I took this opportunity to get a good look at his face. It was long and lean with sharp angles, except for his hooded eyes. The skin on his face was unhealthily pale, and along his square jawline there were pockmarks—undoubtedly the result of an excess of male hormones in adolescence. I decided it wasn't a frightening face. Rather, it was mournful. There was something faraway and lonely about it.

When the flight attendant's voice shrieked through the compartment, advising us to prepare for landing, the guide's eyes popped right open. I quickly diverted my stare to his hands. They were shaking. He needed a nicotine hit badly.

"Be prepared to sleep in an inn. Make sure you sleep with all your clothes on, and wrap your head in a towel to prevent the worms from crawling inside," he warned, tucking his hands away under his armpits.

"No problem," I replied lightly, pretending not to be totally disgusted. I could feel the worms crawling on my scalp already.

Everything became chaotic the instant the wheels skidded on the ground. It rained luggage as passengers scurried to collect their belongings from the overhead bins. The guide had to body-block a passageway for me to slip out of my window seat into the aisle. We barely made it to the exit.

From the top of the steps, I saw the prisonlike gates at the end of the windy tarmac. I couldn't believe I was back in Yanji again. A month earlier, if someone had joked that I would see Halmoni's son at the Yalu River and then return alone to China to plan his family's defection, I wouldn't have believed them. Even as I was standing there again staring at the iron gates I could hardly believe all this was happening to me.

"Hurry up." The guide's voice brought me back.

I dragged my eyes back to him. I followed him down the steps, keeping my head low and my face shielded by my long bangs in case Choi Soon Man showed up. My eyes stayed glued to the guide's feet. I was so concentrated on them that I lost my footing on the second-to-last step, unbalanced by the heavy weight of the camera bag, and came crashing down. My only concern at that moment was the equipment, and as I was falling, I grabbed my bag instead of cushioning my fall with my hands, sacrificing both knees and a shoulder. I screamed. Hearing me, everyone stopped and stared. I struggled to get up, but the electrifying pain of hitting my funny bone against the concrete paralyzed me. All of a sudden two hands grabbed both my arms and hoisted me to a standing position. It was the guide's hands holding me up firmly.

"Are you okay?" he asked, looking shaken as well.

I could feel the blood oozing down my shins. The nerves in my legs pounded, and my whole being was focused on the pain. It stung so badly, but I tried not to show it. I was afraid if I shed one tear, the guide wasn't going to take me the rest of the way to Changbai. "I'm fine," I said as I wriggled out of his grasp and kept moving. I tried my best to ignore the fabric rubbing against the gashes every step I took.

"Remember to play your part. The secret police are scarier in this area. They'll be watching us," he whispered near my ear.

I nodded my response, unable to speak again.

A tall, stringy fellow in his mid-thirties, who reminded me of an Asian Napoleon with his lock of slick black hair falling across the forehead, came up to us with his stocky, cherubic-faced wife in tow. Her simple dark bob was parted in the middle and held tight to each side with oval barrettes. They were a strange-looking match. He was severe-looking, all arms and legs, whereas she was short, thick, and cuddly.

The guide called the man Jambbong, after a spicy Korean Chinese noodle dish that was a mixture of everything. The two of them interacted as if they knew each other very well, although neither of them nor Jambbong's wife acknowledged my presence as we got into Jambbong's red taxi, double-parked near the gate.

"Ah, I've missed you," said the guide affectionately, lighting up a cigarette.

"What am I, a woman?" Jambbong replied good-naturedly, shifting gears as he pressed down on the accelerator.

"Truly, I've missed you. I consider you my closest friend," the guide said, wounded.

"*Ayeeyah,* stop it already. We're drinking buddies," Jambbong chuckled.

I listened to the exchange, intrigued. Usually the guide wasn't this affectionate, keeping his emotions heavily guarded, but now it seeped out of him like honey. I almost felt sorry for him. Finally, when the guide was good and ready, he presented me like a trophy. "This is Lee Hae Ri. She's my *tai-tai,*" he told his friends.

"I'm not," I said impulsively. The word *tai-tai* left a raw, unpleasant taste on my tongue. In Hong Kong, I was told *tai-tai* referred to rich, spoiled housewives who passed all their time going to expensive hair salons and boutiques, spending their husbands' hard-earned money. I wanted these strangers to think better of me despite the guide's put-down; however, my outburst had just the opposite effect. It put a chill in the pungent car air. No one knew how to respond. All at once the guide cleared his throat and laughed, a crackling one-note sound that had a slightly crazed, cruel ring to it that said he'd deal with me later for not behaving in a more dignified, wifelike manner. The guide released another short, hard laugh and proceeded again with his sentimental reminiscing. Following his lead, the couple hastily picked up the conversation. They kept their eyes averted from me even after they dropped us off at a hotel for the night.

My anxieties lessened considerably as I saw the Daewoo Hotel instead of the worm-infested inn the guide promised. The brand-new stucco building was in the middle of a flattened dump. Upon entering the lobby, I immediately felt the guide's tension as I shadowed his footsteps past two uniformed guards standing near the registration desk. When I casually glanced around at them, their stone-hard faces stared me down as if I were guilty of something. They monitored our every move until we were able to escape into the elevator.

Once inside the wallpapered room, we both felt much better, more at ease—so much so the guide started to undress, forgetting for a moment that he wasn't alone. I watched with dreadful fascination, unable to look away, as he pulled out his shirt and tugged at his belt slightly to release the tongue from the buckle. When he finally noticed me standing there, staring, he pulled his shirt down past his hips. His cheeks turned fiery red. "This is why I work alone." He grabbed his toiletries and left the room.

When he was gone, I locked myself in the tile bathroom to examine the damage done to my legs. The left shin was pretty scraped up, and it looked like I was wearing blotchy red knee pads. There'd be scars.

I searched all the drawers for a first-aid kit. There wasn't one, just all the essential paraphernalia of the bath. I didn't dare call room service, paranoid the guide would find out. Instead I dabbed Vaseline onto the open cut to stop the bleeding—something I learned from watching *Rocky*.

XI

Dawn drew the guide up and onto his feet. I stayed in bed, not wanting to get up yet. It was chilly in the little room. From underneath the warm blanket I watched him wrap dull trinkets taken from the bathroom in a newspaper he had brought from Seoul. The cover story was of the two North Korean families that had escaped by fishing boat. The guide planned on showing the article to Yong Woon Uncle as proof that such a mission had been successfully executed. When he was through, he gave me strict instructions. He told me to prepare only one change of clothing and to wrap the items in plastic before putting them inside his leather duffel bag. Everything else would be stored at Jambbong's house. The guide made it very clear to me that he didn't want our clothes touching. Sometimes I'd almost forget how eccentric he was until he did something like this.

I got out of bed in my boxer shorts and T-shirt and went to my backpack. The guide averted his eyes. I donned slacks and a sweater, then did as he asked.

"Pack away the camera bag, too," he said, narrowing his eyes with sudden suspicion. "What are you up to? Why do you have so many tapes? I don't want you recording anything we do. None of it. And it's dangerous carrying around all that equipment. If you fall again and get caught with that stuff, you'll be suspected as a spy."

I felt exposed, thinking he must have gone through my things. What else had he inspected? "I'll pretend I'm a tourist. We're on a holiday from Seoul."

"No, you're a rugby ball."

"Excuse me?"

"Do you know what a rugby ball looks like? Is it round?"

I was in no mood to be teased, least of all by him. But I answered anyway, "Yes."

"No. It's shaped like an American football. When you kick it, it's very unpredictable. It can flop left or right or go straight. You're a rugby ball. Very unpredictable. When I think you should go this way, you pack your bags and go the opposite direction. That worries me because I have to know where you're going at all times."

What the guide didn't realize was that I watched him, too, with the expectation that he could do anything at any time.

"The camera bag goes with me." I wouldn't surrender it. I negotiated hard, as if my life depended on it. At last he agreed on a compromise, his compromise: the video camera, one blank tape, and one one-hour battery. I handed over the still camera, tape recorder, journal, and abundant supply of tapes and batteries to the guide with the rest of my belongings. When he left to deliver the goods to Jambbong's house, I pulled out three more tapes and a spare three-hour battery. I concealed the items inside the zippered collar of my jacket, where the hood was stored.

The first thing I did when we got outside was squint up at the sky. It had drizzled during the night, but the clouds weren't white and fluffy like headless sheep. They had grown huge and dark with ragged bases, and there was a heavy, sulky wetness in the air that hung around us like the aura of a migraine. I knew what was coming. The anticipation was almost worse than the actual event.

The guide said what I could not. "Even the heavens seem to be against us."

Jambbong and his wife were waiting out front for us in their red taxi. They were in the same outfits as the previous night. Jambbong's wife was slumped low in the backseat. I could tell she wasn't feeling well. She looked pasty, and her eyes were practically swollen shut. Even so, the guide was pleased to see her. Having another woman around would attract less attention than two men with one woman, he said. I suspected the real reason why the guide had asked her to join our group was to be my chaperone. I didn't mind as long as I got to go.

Jambbong started the car, gave the engine a few revs, and we were on our way. A pack of Yves Saint Laurent cigarettes slid back and forth on the cracked vinyl dashboard. On the way through town the guide wanted to exchange some money, so we stopped at the nearest intersection, where a group of middle-aged women milled around clutching dark shoulder bags slung across their chests. When Jambbong rolled down his window, the women rushed the car. The most aggressive woman positioned herself in front and stuck her weather-beaten face through the open window. In Mandarin, Jambbong tried to negotiate a high exchange rate for the guide's money. The woman chicken-scratched numbers onto a pad of paper, shaking her head in dismay, but once she saw the crisp, green stack of hundred-dollar bills, she dealt out the yuan into Jambbong's awaiting hand as though she were giving change at a drive-through.

From there, we left town at about seven-thirty. Just outside of Yanji, we came to the first checkpoint. Jambbong paid the toll and we were waved through without pause.

The ride on the one-lane rutted road wasn't as jarring as my previous journey on that route. The night's rain had softened the hard-packed dirt, making the tires turn more smoothly; unfortunately, a loss of speed was the trade-off. Miles clicked away, and the rolling hills seemed to stretch on forever. To pass the time, I looked for familiar landmarks. Some of the fenced villages and pastures we passed by looked familiar, but I couldn't be sure. Everything looked the same, except for the flat rice paddies that had been planted. The water glowed fluorescent green, as if lit from beneath like enormous swimming pools. Farmers, most of them women, waded through muddy paddies with their baggy pants rolled up to their knees, feet and legs bare. Where rice hadn't been planted yet, women were stooped over in fixed positions sowing seedling rice stocks in straight, even rows. The work looked backbreaking, and it was all done by hand. No agricultural machinery, except for the occasional tractor—full of workers catching a ride—were on the road.

By now we were in the lush green foothills of Changbai Shan, and we drove through folds of hills dense with pine trees. The air was crisp and damp and pine-scented, and there was a whole web of sounds. Hidden in one of the folds, surrounded by a canopy of forest, was a brick barn house with two huge barn doors painted blue. An awning was propped up in front of the barn to shade a makeshift café. Cans of mandarin orange juice called Sac Sac, beer, instant Maxim coffee, and Coca-Cola with white Chinese characters on the red can were displayed on a long plank table. Finding this café in the middle of nowhere was an unexpected and pleasant surprise, and I smiled and breathed in deeply the smell of pine-scented coffee as it was being mixed in Styrofoam cups. The woman preparing the drinks had a large rosy-cheeked boy, maybe as old as eight, propped on her hip. She and the boy greeted the guide and Jambbong as though they knew them.

When I requested my coffee black, the boy's mother looked at me as if I were uncouth and insisted I try it the proper way. She poured two heaping scoops of powdered creamer and sugar into my coffee.

Cuddling my cup, I got back into the taxi and we were off again. The hills quickly grew into higher ridges, and we started climbing into the steeper regions of Changbai Shan. I used to think of mountains as being indestructible and immutable, and that was why I was drawn to them and hiked them when things in my life became turbulent. But as we drove higher along the shoulder of Changbai Shan, the weather shifted wildly. One moment lens-shaped clouds became flattened and chiseled by the wind as they moved miles above us; then they'd become ragged and dark and descend lower and lower. At the highest point, the clouds leaned down all around us and touched the ground. They shrouded the road in a thick haze, making it almost impossible to see anything even with the headlights on. The fog got so thick that it hit the ground in droplets the size of dimes; more droplets rivered down the wind shield, and then a full-on storm slammed sheets of rain against the car, seeming to resent every mile we gained. Sealed inside, I felt we were watching a movie of a storm, real time compressed into minutes, with the sound turned up too loud. Suddenly, the roar of the rain eased to a dripping silence. Swirling sunshine came out and set alive the sky and forest, evaporating the clouds.

It was a humbling and awesome experience because it made me realize that with time the powerful forces of nature changed and shifted even the greatest mountains. Yet the balance of the forest wasn't upset. Any disturbance, no matter how small or how large, replenished the forest, and the plants and animals adapted. They sought new opportunities that were created from the death or growth of a tree or stream. That was how I used to be, but these days the slightest disturbance set me off.

That was how I wanted to be again.

Around seven that evening, just as the pale yolk of the sun began to dip beneath the jagged peaks, we drove through the third and final checkpoint, then followed the zigzagging course of the mountain stream down into Changbai. As soon as we came out of the mountain pass, the road suddenly made a sharp right and we were running parallel to the Yalu River on our left, elevated thirty feet above it. I could see that the river was swollen and running fast from the melting snow rushing down from the top of Changbai Shan. The water was breaking hard in white waves against the riverbed. For the first time, I was able to get a clear view of what was hidden behind the stone wall, what the North Korean leaders didn't want us to see. I was shocked at how decayed, cramped, and depressed everything looked. The rows and rows of single-story houses were packed closely together, utilizing every bit of land. Narrow dirt alleys ran between the leprous-looking houses barely held together by scraps of plywood, canvas, and tarp. Some of the houses were in an even greater state of disrepair, half collapsed, with only part of the roof left. Still, there seemed to be people living in them. I saw the blur of a person in a red sweater coming out of a crumbling home.

Just beyond the slum of houses were taller buildings in better condition, but not by much. The buildings were five, maybe seven stories tall and rectangular, with windows running across each floor, all uniform in height and design. They reminded me of shoeboxes with tiny air holes punched into them so the animals trapped inside wouldn't die of suffocation.

All this was set against the splendor of the sun-draped mountains. For a split second, the way the golden sunlight suddenly swirled down through the clouds, linking sky and mountains, made me think it was possible that there could be peace someday, that I'd live to see reunification. Then I saw the propaganda slogan. Like the Hollywood sign, a large white placard with *hangul* script was staked into the face of one of the barren mountains, which I was told proclaimed "Moving Forward Together! It was a taunting reminder of the poverty and soul-destroying squalor below. The news reports I read suggested that the North Korean leadership had no intention of moving forward or together with South Korea. The inter-Korea Red Cross talks in Beijing had broken down because of the North Korean delegates. They walked out when South Korea wouldn't give a specific advance pledge on how much aid it would ship, as the amount depended on citizens' donations. Also, the North made a demand that the sacks of rice not be labeled. They probably feared it would undermine their propaganda that the rest of the world was no better off than them. It was frustrating to read about the North Korean delegates casually playing with time while their people forged in fields trying to find rice stalks, empty pea pods, tree bark, or anything else to stave off hunger. The World Food Program (WFP) reported that the food shortage had become so intense in the improverished northern areas, where Yong Woon Uncle lived, that the provincial governments were even ordering citizens to dig up rocks, which could be traded for food.

The guide had Jambbong unload his wife and me the instant we drove into town. They dropped us off at the end of a worn hotel driveway. Camouflaged military jeeps were parked near the entrance, and the red People's Republic of China medallion, punctuated with five golden stars, was mounted above the door. It felt like they were turning us in at Communist Party headquarters.

"Keep her out of sight," the guide ordered Jambbong's wife.

"You'll send for me when my big uncle crosses over, right?" I asked quickly.

"Right," the guide assured, leaving me behind in a fog of exhaust fumes. He was going to spend the night at the Chosŏn brothers' house, down by the river, to put pressure on them to cooperate. We didn't have much time. The next day was June 4, North Korea's Victory of Bochunbo Battle Day. We had to meet with Yong Woon Uncle, tell him the plans for defection, get his agreement, and choreograph the escape. The escape depended on several factors: the changing of border guards, the darkness of the moon, and the water level. Nothing was definite, with many possibilities and unforeseen factors. One person, maybe two at a time, could cross daily. Maybe two groups of two might come over at different points of the river or all at once. Yong Woon Uncle would be floated across in an inner tube with someone pushing him from behind. The goal was to get everyone to Dalian before the seventeenth, when the guide's thirty-day tourist visa expired.

Jambbong's wife led me inside. My poor derriere felt permanently flattened and my joints creaked as I limped into the entrance hall. A locked glass case, to the left of the door, displayed a collage of pictures giving tribute to Kim Il Sung. In all the pictures the deceased leader was painted with a sunburst emanating from his head, adorned with colorful flowers, and accompanied by happy children wearing traditional *hanboks*. The happy children were made up to look like flawless porcelain dolls. Their lips and cheeks were rose-petal red and their lids shimmery blue.

Without glancing at anyone directly, I casually surveyed the rest of the interior. It was a gloomy, tomblike room that had been stripped of all its furniture. The lighting, which was more brown than illuminating, made the place seem colder inside than it was outside. When I looked up to admire the original crystal chandelier hanging down from the rain-stained ceiling, I caught sight of a young woman monitoring the hall from the second-story balcony. She was in her early twenties and wearing the standard tank-green uniform with her hair done in stout braids. I knew not to be deceived by her youth. The young ones were the most dangerous, the most fanatical, the jumpiest, the most eager to report on you.

Jambbong showed up ten minutes later without the guide. He checked into his own room while his wife and I shared another. The moment I saw our room, I felt squalid. The walls were nicotine-stained and streaked with black heel marks and handprints. The twin Western-style beds sagged severely and were missing legs—one bed was missing two of its knobby legs at the head, the other was missing three. When Jambbong's wife sat on the one-legged bed, it sagged even more and gave a loud metallic creak. The worst thing about the room was the badly scarred red carpet. Every inch of it was filthy and covered with thousands of cigarette burns. The burns looked like an army of tiny black invading cockroaches. Just glancing at the diseased carpet made my skin crawl and itch.

I told myself to get a grip, that I could deal with a little adversity. It was useless to demand particular standards of cleanliness when such luxuries were impossible. This was the way of life over here. I needed to stop making judgments and comparisons. When the couple offered to take me out for an evening meal, I was beyond thrilled. In China, a nation with a history of famine and the largest population in the world, food outranked even a direct order from the guide to keep me out of sight. I had to eat.

The restaurant the couple chose was two buildings over, on the same side of the street. Peering through the dust-curtained window, I saw that the place was totally empty, but Jambbong pulled open the blue weathered door any-way and we went inside. The first thing I noticed were the interesting deco-rations. Torn-off glossy calendar photos of Asian women were plastered on the main wall. Their hairstyles and clothes were from the late seventies— long and feathered like Farrah Fawcett's—and the photos were shot with a romantic, dreamy filter. On a separate wall was another calendar photo of an Asian woman in sharp focus with a sizzling red backdrop. She had on a black leather biker's hat and a black leather vest zipped low, revealing a generous cleavage, and she was straddling a motorcycle.

The three of us sat cross-legged on the heated *ondol* floor, which converted back to the cook's sleeping quarters in the evenings. The cook came out from the adjoining kitchen wearing a bloodstained apron. Memorizing our order, he went back to work. I saw him wipe a sharp saber knife and cleaver on his apron ceremoniously, then hack away at a carcass, leaving on the fat. The chopping was accompanied by cheerful humming. Soon the small room filled with the scent of a variety of spices put together, and the cook served the food with a flourish. A large stone crock of beef bubbling in soybean broth occupied most of the table. On a medium-size saucer was a stack of paper-thin yellow squares, which I mistook for napkins. It was actually pressed tofu, which was used like a tortilla to wrap food.

Following Jambbong's wife's example, I made a tofu wrap stuffed with chunks of meat from the stew and *kimchi*. The flavor of the meat exploded in my mouth—very strong, very rich, and with a background flavor of kidney. It was the best thing I'd eaten in China.

"Hae Ri-ssi, this house is famous for its dog," Jambbong's wife boasted with her mouth full.

"For what?" I looked down at my tofu wrap.

"Their dog is always fresh here. It's very good for your health." She giggled, patting her husband's stomach.

I reached for the tea and swigged a hearty gulp to get the taste out of my mouth. I managed to refrain from gagging. *Poshin-tang* (dog soup) was reputed—along with ginseng, snake stew, and powdered deer antler—to work wonders with a male's sexual performance. It would heighten sexual drive, erections would last longer, performances would be of a more virtuoso nature, and sperm would be more fertile. To me, on the other hand, dogs have always been our loyal companions. Growing up, it was imprinted into my head that we were supposed to take them on walks, play fetch the stick with them, and love them, not boil them in a soybean broth to enhance libido and stamina.

Unable to eat, I engaged the couple in conversation in hopes of gathering some facts about them. After the initial shyness, they started talking. She was a high school English teacher, but she wasn't fluent at all. She could only rattle off a few heavily accented phrases. He was a taxi driver whenever he wasn't working with the guide. The couple had been married for thirteen years, no children. Despite my open-mindedness, I still reacted as my parents would, finding it shocking that they didn't want to have children. Then I sensed it might not have been a choice. Maybe they couldn't have a child. According to Confucian teaching, having no children was one of the seven sins of women. Although rarely put into practice, a husband could divorce his wife if she bore no sons, disobeyed his parents, carried a hereditary disease, committed theft or adultery, was jealous, or even for excess chatter.

Even though Jambbong's wife was full of spunk and excess chatter, it was obvious Jambbong adored her just by the way he looked at her. This cherub-faced woman with her dimples and schoolgirl haircut had a rebel heart and had found a way to live here on her own terms, and I liked her very much for that. I actually liked them both very much.

"Because of her, I can't accompany my friends to hostess bars. None of the women will talk to me. They know my wife will beat them up." Jambbong's lips twitched.

Jambbong's wife slapped him flirtatiously on the back. "That's right, I will."

"You dare strike your husband?" He tried to sound threatening, but as hard as he tried, he couldn't maintain proper manly composure. His wife's high-pitched, squeaky giggles were contagious. I was limp with laughter and savored the feeling of relaxation. The feeling faded immediately when Jambbong confided that he knew Choi Soon Man.

"Are you friends?" I asked cautiously.

"Never." Jambbong talked as he poured himself some *soju*. "A relative of a pregnant North Choson woman who crossed over to Changbai asked Choi Soon Man to help him find her because she came in search of food to feed the baby she carried. The relative gave him some money to give her, but Choi Soon Man propositioned her instead. When she fought off his advances, he kicked her out onto the streets and kept the money. The relative came to me afterward. I had some people here search for her. She's being cared for now at someone's home until she has the baby."

"Are you sure it's him?" I asked, still wanting to give Choi Soon Man the benefit of the doubt.

"He's the one. That man's a scam artist. He'll do and say anything for money. One of his scams is to pretend to be a Christian so people from abroad will send him money because they think he's being persecuted for his religious beliefs."

Hearing that, I could hardly contain my anger. Choi Soon Man had deceived Halmoni. My thoughts started racing. An eye for an eye. Forget tolerance and compassion. I wanted to figure out a way to punish the bastard, set him up so that he'd be captured and thrown into one of North Korea's concentration camps. Then he'd know how much Halmoni had suffered.

Jambbong read my mind. "Don't worry too much. We're going to make certain he never pulls that again."

As we headed back to the hotel, we ran into the younger Choson brother. The young man stepped directly into our path and asked Jambbong what business he had with North Korea.

Jambbong's wife tugged on my arm to keep walking. We pretended to be on our own and walked straight ahead. We didn't turn in at the hotel. We continued past it, then ducked into a dark alley. Every couple of minutes Jambbong's wife checked to see if the coast was clear, but the two men were still talking in the open street. She decided we should return to our hotel before someone questioned us. Slipping her hand into the crook of my arm, we threaded our way through the back alleys and sneaked into our hotel. We waited in our room with only the bathroom light on. It felt closed and stuffy after leaving the cool outside air.

Sometime after midnight, Jambbong came knocking at our door. Hearing his hushed voice through the wood, his wife pulled him inside. His face was red with liquor. The younger Choson brother had dragged Jambbong to a *soju* house and tried to pry out of him who the two women were. Jambbong was concerned that if the Choson brothers found out that I was Lee Yong Woon's American niece, they'd make more financial demands, knowing I could afford to fly out to China.

All night and the next morning we didn't hear from the guide, and I was panicked that we might have jeopardized the mission. By the time two o'clock rolled around without even a call, I had Jambbong phone the Choson brothers' house. He put on a good act, pretending it was a great coincidence that the guide was in town at the same time. A moment later Jambbong was speaking to him. Using as few implicating words as possible, he briefly explained what had happened the night before. The phone call didn't last long.

"What did he say?" My question was loaded with worry.

"Everything's arranged. After sunset tonight, your big uncle will be brought over. When that happens, the guide will call me and I'll take you to the river." He was putting on his dress shoes to leave.

"Where are you going?" his wife asked.

"He said to buy Hae Ri some coffee."

I felt my face turn hot. I tried to cover my embarrassment. I didn't want them to get the wrong idea and think there was something romantic going on between the guide and me.

Jambbong promptly returned with some packets of Nescafé and a thermos of hot water.

"You didn't have to do that," I said, careful not to blush again.

"If I didn't, he'd chew off my head." He chuckled merrily.

Sipping Nescafé, the three of us stayed cooped up in the room watching a small flickering television—all the colors were wrong. There were only three channels to select from, one of them being a North Korean station whose programming consisted mostly of shows dedicated to spouting the superhuman achievements of Kim Il Sung. I was more absorbed in a report spotlighting an invention that heated cooking coals. The cylinder, made from tin, looked like something I'd seen on an infomercial late at night. The North Korean design was primitive and crude, but the way the reporter boasted, you'd think they had invented a nuclear generator.

I also watched with rapt attention a rerun of the previous year's singing competition. North Korean children painted like pretty rose-cheeked dolls fluttered around the stage in their short ruffled *hanboks,* singing. The only way I could accurately describe their animated facial expressions and dance choreography was by simply labeling it the dance of socialist glory. They sang and twirled and posed like happy communists moving forward together.

In the middle of the finals, I became anxious. Sunset was approaching. At any moment I expected the phone to ring. When the guide didn't call by seven, Jambbong phoned the house. The Chosŏn brothers' elderly mother informed us that the guide had stormed out of the house forty-five minutes earlier. My heart tightened with panic. Something must have gone terribly wrong for the guide to leave so abruptly. My head buzzed with thoughts that kept circling and circling, with nowhere to go.

Grabbing our belongings, Jambbong, his wife, and I left the hotel. We were practically running. We slipped through a fence, taking a shortcut down to the river. We stole up a soaked path that curled through a well-tended field of vegetables. The wet mud squelched underfoot as we ran through the fields. We ran as far as we dared toward the edge of the river.

Night was falling. A line of fiery red lit up the horizon, as if the city of Hyesan was on fire. About a half mile down, I could make out the place where I'd first laid my eyes on my uncle's family. On that exact spot, there must have been at least thirty large black dogs and a squad of armed border guards scattered along the edge of the rocky riverbank, putting on a display of force. Their shadows, lengthening across the ground as it grew darker, made them appear monstrously big and threatening. From where we stood I could hear shrill echoes of the dogs' cries as they struggled at the ends of their short leashes, sniffing the ground excitedly. It was as if they picked up the scent of prey and were anxious for the hunt. When they barked at the top of their lungs, my heart almost stopped.

"Let's go back. They're watching." Jambbong pointed to a sparkle on the crest of a mountain about a thousand vertical feet up. Curious, I turned on the video camera and poked the lens through the hole in my bag. I switched on the night setting for better visibility, then tilted the bag up the length of the peak and zoomed the superpowered telescopic lens. Through the viewfinder appeared a tiny surveillance station perched on top of the mountain. It was massed with enormous antennas. From that height, the spies could see north, south, east, and west. They could secretly survey people making contact or crossing below.

I slowly backed away from this frightening landscape.

Unable to find the guide, we drove around in the taxi, covering more ground. Jambbong drove through the streets crowded with people and shops and games. Through the window I spotted the guide coming around the corner. His face was covered with stubble and his clothing looked rumpled and stale. I had never been so glad to see him. At the same time I felt myself collapsing inside with a terrible sense of dread.

"Let's get out of town," the guide said, his voice hoarse and weak, as if he'd been shouting. He slid into the backseat beside me and sat staring straight ahead. Jambbong gunned the car and we lurched forward. He went around corners doing thirty in first with the transmission howling. Speed-shifting into fourth gear, the car thundered like a World War II bomber. We were going so fast, the taxi bounced over the corrugated road. I careened into the guide. My hand landed on his thigh and my head on his chest. Quickly I scooted back over to my side and clung to the door handle to hold myself in place.

Only when we were safely past the first checkpoint and the mountains rose around us did the guide finally turn toward me and hand me a letter. The letter was one sheet folded over twice. I examined the fragile recycled-looking paper in the pink moonlight. I knew instantly it was from North Korea. I had trouble opening it. My hands had become slick with sweat. Jambbong's wife kindly offered to read it to me. She held it up to the dim lighting. The writing was thick and hard, and the impressions of the words stood out on the back of the paper.

CONVEYING TO THE GUIDE,

I regret having caused you distress for such a long time. Living here has made us suspicious of all people and unexpected events.

Sir, it's our family's wish to reunite our father with Halmoni. We will go ahead with your plans and we will be ready to take action immediately.

Though it's dangerous, live or die, we ought to try. The last visit was too sudden and unexpected and we were unprepared. It was as if a thunderbolt came down from a clear sky and struck us with no warning. And we were exposed without security.

Sir, please go ahead with your arrangements. Lee Yong Woon, whom Baek Hong Yong Grandmother has been searching for, is for certain our father.

Words cannot express our gratitude for your journey.

Ae Ran, sending

I refolded the letter as best as I could and placed it inside my sock, then gazed at the guide's profile. "You met with her." I bit down on my lower lip, overwhelmed by opposing emotions.

"No, only your big uncle crossed over."

"Why didn't you send for me?" I was supposed to identify him. That was the purpose of me going to Changbai, why I had insisted.

"There was no time. At sunset they all came out to the river. I knew the officer in charge. It was incredible luck. He ordered his soldiers to turn their backs while the younger Chosŏn brother swam across with an inner tube and fetched your big uncle. The officer came across as well and we toasted with beer together near the water. For insurance I gave him a sack full of beer, cookies, and candies to take back. I spoke very briefly to your big uncle. He's been told the plans. Now he has to discuss it with his wife and children," the guide said, watching me.

I slumped back into the seat and turned away from him. My anger and frustration had tightened my heart so much, I couldn't ask any more questions. I was fighting tears with all my might. I didn't want to weep in front of the guide.

XII

The sun was creeping up into the eastern sky when we rolled back into Yanji. I squinted through the mud-splattered glass and saw the Daewoo Hotel again. Opening the door, I stuck my feet out to get my bearings, then eased myself up off the backseat. My brain felt stiff and cramped, like my body. One leg was asleep, but I managed to hobble along to my position. I knew the routine by now. I'd stand in the rear like a good *tai-tai* as the guide checked us in at the front desk. Once in our room, I stretched and wiggled to ease the large knot between my shoulders, then rolled my head around in a do-it-myself massage. Feeling a little relief, I aimed my behind toward the cushioned mattress and fell back with a sigh. I never imagined it could feel so pleasurable to be in a strange hotel room with its fragrance of cleaning products.

Monitoring the guide's mood, I gambled and went in for the questioning. "What was he like?" I asked, trying to sound casual, even though I was still very upset.

"I hate to say this." The guide exhaled the words along with a lungful of smoke. "Your big uncle isn't all there. And I've been told he's been drinking heavily, and when he drinks his favorite thing to do is talk. He leaks one thing and we're all dead. Why is he being so careless?"

"He's been through a lot," I said loyally. I was disappointed in the guide. For a man whose life depended on being observant, he couldn't see that Yong Woon Uncle was a broken spirit. The war, the separation from his family, his banishment to Hyesan, guards brandishing rifles at his back—any one of these things could break even the strongest person and make him lose his mind. I moved beyond the guide's insensitivity and asked if Yong Woon Uncle had received the money. I was told that Choi Soon Man had kept it. All he'd given them was a small amount of rice and some clothes. Knowing beyond any doubt that we had been betrayed was like being pushed off a plane without a parachute.

"From here on, the family's on standby. They move only when they hear the passwords. I did that in case Choi Soon Man or my own people try to sabotage this project. But they're not our biggest problem. There's a complication with your big uncle's family. Ae Ran's husband came back home after he heard you and your father visited. He suspects something's up and is now holding Ae Ran and their baby captive. At this point, your big uncle isn't sure who goes or stays. This makes their situation and our work dangerous because they're not united. I told him to be clear in his head how many people. It's imperative." The guide searched for another cigarette. He found an empty, crumpled pack and a battered blue lighter. He dug into another pocket but found nothing. A second and third time he checked the same pockets—still nothing. A frown creased his brow, and he went away.

The guide didn't return till midafternoon. Lying on my side in bed, I watched bleary-eyed as he prowled restlessly about the room. He did that for a while and then picked up his cell phone. When I heard the name Lee Yong Woon I immediately sat up and stared intently at the guide. "Take the palm of your hand and press the receiver right up to your ear so no words will escape to the people around you. Don't say anything, just answer yes or no. You understand?" The guide waited for the person on the other end to answer, then continued. "Listen carefully, memorize these passwords . . ."

The first was the rose of Sharon, South Korea's national flower. I couldn't hear the other two names because he mumbled too softly.

"All three flowers are summer flowers. Got it? . . . A man named Jambbong will be there tomorrow to instruct you on hand signals. After that you'll spend one more night at the house, get some food into you, then go back. Quickly gather your family and have a discussion. When you tell them the details, don't be shifty or else things won't work out. Lee Yong Woon-ssi, the plans go beyond China all the way to Halmoni. Even faced with torture or a gun to your head, you must be the only one with this information. Take it to your grave if you must. Understand? . . . Remember from this moment forward: Unless you're given the correct passwords, don't trust anyone. Guard your words and don't lose your courage."

The guide hung up.

I felt a thickening in my throat, a constriction across my chest. I was grabbing air with quick, short breaths, sitting up with my entire body compressed in an effort to control my temper, but my anger flared up red and blinding.

The bastard had lied to me. Yong Woon Uncle was still in Changbai, and I was deliberately being denied the chance to meet him. I hated the guide. I hated those heavy-lidded eyes of his that glared into me. I had had enough. The charade of being his friend was over. Caution went out the window. "You lied to me," I shouted in English.

"I didn't. I told the truth, but I wasn't totally honest."

"Why didn't you let me see him?"

"I told you there wasn't enough time."

"I don't believe you. I can't trust a word you say. You lied to me. Why? Why are you such a bastard? Are you like this to everyone or just me because I'm a woman and it's a big fat inconvenience to you?" My voice spiraled up and up.

The guide was outraged. His face was scarlet and his neck was all purple. Sweat dripped off his upper lip. "You, you only see one side of the hand and think only that is right. You pass judgment on my character based solely on how I treat you, a woman. Ever since you got here, I've suppressed my own will and opinions to make you happy. I eat carefully so as not to make offending sounds for your ears' sake. I sleep with my clothes on because of you. I roam the hallways of strange hotels for rest rooms so you can have your privacy."

"I didn't ask you to do all those things for me! Make all the sounds you want when you eat. Sleep naked. I don't give a damn what you do. All I ask is that you treat me like a human being. Would it kill you to talk to me nicely once in a while? Smile!" It felt great to strike back and not have to suck up to him, with his moods and insults.

"I didn't come all this way to China to receive etiquette lessons from Lee Hae Ri. Do you think that's why we're here?" He advanced nose first.

"Whatever." I turned away.

He spun me around by an arm. "I'm fine just the way I am. I've been fine. I don't ever plan on living in America. In Seoul, I don't have to think obsessively about how a woman is going to feel or react. It's not necessary. She just follows me."

I shoved him away in revulsion. "Lucky lady," I said, my voice heavy with sarcasm so there would be no misinterpretation.

"That's why so many couples divorce in America. American men say, 'Wow, you look lovely,' pull out your chair, open your door. It's all action. That's not our custom. And because I don't do those things for you, you think all Korean men are wild and impolite."

"No, not all Korean men, just you. You're rude." I kept using English in defiance.

The guide was about to fire off again, then abruptly turned away and went to the window. For a moment he stood with his back to me, hands braced on the windowsill, trying to pull himself together. When he turned around again and looked at me, it was a long, deliberate look. He pulled out a chair and motioned to it. I wouldn't accept his pathetic peace offer, if that was what it was. I could never be sure with him.

After a long, ringing silence he sat down on his bed, closing the distance between us. I readied myself for what might happen next. "Hae Ri-ssi," he said in a soft voice, reinstating the respectful ending to my name, "you're an extremely good-hearted and clever woman. I'm sorry if my actions hurt you, but everything I do, I do because it's necessary."

I was taken aback. I had never heard him speak so tenderly to me before. Right then I felt the anger run out of me, and the tension between us eased up. We both slumped back against our headboards like boxers at the end of a heated round.

Sometime in the middle of the night, I was slowly awakened by the presence of a body and the smell of liquor hovering over my bed. I kept my eyes pinched shut, afraid to open them. My heart pounded. Not again. I began to make all sorts of promises, swore I'd do a hundred good deeds if I got through the night. Before I was done listing all the things I was going to do, I sensed the footsteps receding.

In the morning, neither one of us mentioned him coming over to my bed. I would have if I thought he had any sexual designs on me, but I was sure that he didn't think of me in that way. It was just that we'd been confined together under the most unreal, threatening situation far away from home, and it made us both restless and jittery with tension. Even a blind person could see we were complete opposites. It wasn't due to generational differences, either. There was a vast cultural gap as wide as the demarcation line that separated the two Koreas. The guide was a relic of another century, when men wore topknots and wide-brimmed horsehair hats, and women were confined at home. In those days, women even in their own home weren't permitted to enter the *sarang bang* (meeting room). This room was furnished with a writing desk and bookshelves for study since the *yangban* (literati class) was expected to study the Confucian classics.

The *anbang* (inner quarters) was reserved for their use. The husband could enter this room, but no other male, since modesty ruled. This room was filled with beautiful wooden chests for linen and clothes. The designs on the chests were usually lucky symbols of dragons and a phoenix, and ideograms suggesting wealth, longevity, and happiness, although a married woman wasn't to expect domestic happiness or to share interests with her husband. As a wife, she accepted the fact that her husband would live a life separate from hers. His pleasures usually came from his male friends, whom he would entertain in his *sarang bang* with music and wine, or from beautiful *kisaengs* at teahouses. *Kisaengs* were trained from childhood in the art of singing, dancing, playing musical instruments, and companionship.

This made it difficult to be around the guide. But I was determined to flow with his mood swings, ride out his insults, and always come up smiling. This was the role I had to play, my duty to Halmoni.

I kept the peace all the way to the airport. We had to get back to Dalian for our final meeting with the gangster boatmen. Once again our plane was delayed. The guide went off and searched the premises for something to drink. He brought me back a cup of coffee—black, just the way I liked it—then reached into his front shirt pocket and handed me a red tin container of Tiger Balm.

"What's this for?" I asked

"Your bruises," he said. He did know everything.

It was a tender, small gesture that melted what was left of my hardened feelings. I accepted the balm and immediately rolled up my pants legs. My knees and shin still looked pretty bad. The purple color was more vibrant, but they didn't hurt so much anymore. I applied the balm gently to show my appreciation. The rubbing action generated heat that penetrated through the skin, and I was thoroughly enjoying myself.

Instead of looking pleased, the guide's face crinkled into a frown. "Don't do that here."

"Why?" I kept rubbing. It was addictive.

"You're always touching yourself. Touch yourself as much as you like in America, but in Asia don't do it in public—wait until you're alone. But even in your home, don't do it out in the open. Change your clothes, put on your makeup, brush your hair, rub on lotion quietly, without anyone's knowledge."

"Why should I have to hide in my own home?" I lightly slapped his shoulder.

He flinched. "What did I just tell you? Koreans don't like being touched."

"Then why did that grandmother over there touch that little boy's penis and the boy's mother just laughed?"

"Don't use that word!" He tried to smother his laughter.

"You mean *penis?*" I said again, teasing him. I knew I was being wicked and naughty, but there was something thrilling about saying something forbidden. And I just wanted him to laugh for once.

The guide was spared from continuing our conversation by a PA announcement telling us to board our plane.

We flew back to Dalian and checked into the Furama Hotel. The gangster boatmen arrived at our hotel just after us at four in the afternoon. I accompanied the guide to the meeting downstairs. The stocky gangster was dressed in a dusty blue sport coat over an open-collared white shirt and painfully bright royal blue slacks. He held my book in his hand, discussing something written in it with his partner. He glanced up immediately, as if our entry had activated some sensor within him. He smiled and came to me directly.

"Nice to see you again." He shook my hand firmly, lingering a bit.

"Hello," I said, smiling, bowing.

"You're wearing your hair down," he noted as he stepped behind me to offer a chair.

Once we were all seated around the coffee table, the stocky gangster asked if I would sign my book to him. His request seemed absurd. Here we were negotiating lives, and he wanted my autograph. I did what he asked. When I glanced up for a moment to ponder what I should write, I saw him looking at me. Seeing my eyes meet his, he blushed.

After I signed the book, the guide dismissed me back to our room.

Half an hour passed before the guide joined me upstairs. His facial expression gave away no clues as to the outcome of the meeting. "Come on, I'm taking you out." He held the door open for me. I followed him all the way outside onto the street. He stopped for a moment to admire the gold and red fading in the west, marking a close to a cool summer day. He was humming low in his throat, a playful Mozart-ish tune.

"So we got the boat?" I asked, knowing he wasn't willing to surrender any information unless I milked it out of him.

The guide suddenly stepped into my path and stretched his arms out to the side with an exaggerated sweep. Then he whispered excitedly, "Things turned out better than I ever expected. We got a Chinese navy ship."

"What about the fishing boat?"

"They're unreliable. Many times I've seen their old rusty engines shut down or explode as they're pulling out of the harbor, and they're closely watched by the Coast Guard for refugees and other illegal activities. Your family will sneak into a large container marked South Korea and will be lifted onto the ship. It'll be supplied with food, water, and blankets. When they wake up they'll be free, and it's all because of you."

I looked deeply into his eyes to see if he was being sarcastic.

"I'm being completely serious. You made this happen. You moved their hearts, and they secured the safest passage for your family."

"Really?" I beamed in spite of myself. At long last, I had done something right. I smiled even more broadly as we continued to make our way down the street. We walked all the way to the park at the center of Zhongshan Guangchang. The sound of music drifted in the air while voices and laughter murmured and rose. That night, Dalian seemed more enchanting to me as we watched a couple ballroom-dancing under soft yellow lamplight. They moved with sinuous grace. When the man swiftly spun his partner, her full-skirted pink dress, tightly cinched at the waist, billowed out, and it looked as if she might fly away if he released her hand. But he didn't let her go. His left hand clasped her hand, and his right arm wrapped around her slim waist, keeping her anchored to the ground as they swayed and dipped together.

As we watched them dance, the couple nodded and smiled at us, beckoning us to join them. I felt so swept up in their dance, I found myself looking over my shoulder to the guide hopefully.

He grinned. "Oh no, you're not getting me out there."

"Just one dance. It's good exercise." I surprised myself by genuinely wanting to dance with him.

"It's tiring just watching them. I get hungry. Come on, you haven't eaten anything all day. What do you feel like eating? French, Italian, Japanese, Chinese? I'll buy you whatever you want."

"Korean."

"For an American you sure love Korean food."

My voice shot high. "It's because I am!"

The guide laughed, genuinely and spontaneously. At that precise instant, I actually liked him. He suddenly looked more appealing.

We visited the same Korean restaurant with the flowered curtains. The place was energized. The guide chose a table near the back, away from the window and the live entertainment. I enjoyed the entertainment. The singer was a wanna-be Chosŏn Wayne Newton. He had badly dyed shoe-polish-black hair with Elvis lamb-chop sideburns and large gold-rimmed glasses. He launched into the theme song from the movie *Ghost* while a female keyboard player accompanied him. The keyboard player looked more like a boy than a girl, with her hair cropped short and wearing a plain white T-shirt and jeans. She looked out of place here but wouldn't stand out at all in West Hollywood or the West Village in New York City. As she played, she flirted with a dark, impish-faced waitress. The waitress flirted back. I was amazed by their boldness and sensuality.

The cashier called out loudly to the waitress to take our order. He noisily banged on the cash register to convey his displeasure to her. Promptly she skittered over to our table, ponytail swinging from side to side. Her shoes, flattened at the back, flapped against her heels. She smiled, bowing, and scribbled down the banquet of dishes the guide rolled off his tongue. The whole time she was stealing glances at the keyboard player, who smiled back at her, causing her to blush. The guide waited until he commanded her full attention before giving his final order. "A bowl of rice. Make sure it's served at the beginning of the meal." He then turned to me and said, "Hae Ri-ssi, you won't think badly of me if I drink *soju* tonight, will you?"

He asked with such humility that the waitress looked questioningly at me. I shook my head, not wanting him to lose face in front of her, even though it terrified me. Alcohol amplified his madness and unleashed his demons.

Our waitress came back at once with a bottle. The guide filled his clear shot glass and placed it far away from him. "I'm going to say this before I start drinking, because after I begin, don't listen to my words," he advised me, then handed back my passport before starting again. "Tomorrow I want you to go home. It'll take some time for your big uncle's family to get organized. Until then, there's nothing either one of us can do here."

"How much time?"

"It could be a few weeks. When everything's set, send your father with Halmoni to China. You don't come."

"Why? What did I do wrong?"

"Nothing. Nothing at all. However, you appear young and you're a single woman. That's the reality. Handing over money should be done by your father." He hesitated, seeing the waitress returning to our table with a heavy tray bearing small saucers containing cold cooked vegetables, marinated beef and fish, and a single serving of steaming white rice in a metal bowl. She

Halmoni in 1996, holding a picture of her long lost son. He's wearing a North Korean uniform. *Reprinted by permission of the* Los Angeles Daily News, *photo by: Michael O. Baker.*

A North Korean stamp
Helie purchased at the
airport in Dalian, China.

North Korean
currency.

Helie and her father in
Changbai, April 20, 1997.

Helie's father standing in front of
the Imperial City in Beijing. Above him
hangs a portrait of Mao.

Decayed homes in Hyesan, North Korea, where Helie's uncle lived.

Mun Churl squatting and Yong Woon Uncle standing as they gaze across the Yalu River at their family on the other side.

Halmoni at her eightieth birthday party held in Los Angeles. Her two younger sisters, Baby Halmoni and Middle Halmoni, sit beside her.

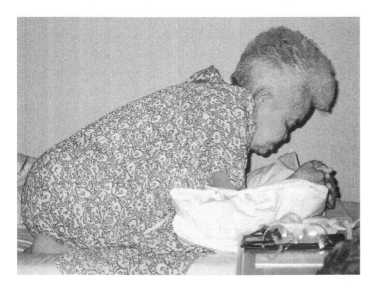

Halmoni praying in hotel room in Shenyang, China.

On the one-lane road to Changbai.

One of the checkpoints between Yanji and Changbai, where we had to pay a toll.

Halmoni reunited with her son, Ae Ran, and Hak Churl in Shenyang, China.

Helie's father throwing Hak Churl's son his first birthday party. Chun stands in front of the cake as his mother holds him.

Helie's mother, Halmoni, and Helie rushing to greet their North Korean relatives, Seoul, South Korea.

Ae Ran, Halmoni, and her son Yong Woon.

Helie's mother, Duk Hwa, tearfuly hugging her older brother, Yong Woon.

All nine North Korean defectors with Helie, her parents, and Halmoni in
Seoul, South Korea, after the reunion.

quickly unloaded everything, placing the rice in front of the guide, then scurried away with the tray tucked under her arm to another table.

The guide picked up the hot metal bowl with his bare hands and placed it gingerly before me. The sticky white grains were packed down tightly to create a snow-cone effect. A thread of steam came from it. The guide took the choicest morsel of sesame fish and laid it on the bed of rice. I stared down at it as if I'd never seen fish before. I needed a moment to recover.

"Hey, I want you to finish your rice. You always leave it half full. Rice is the blood and sweat of Koreans. You mustn't waste rice. It's life itself," he said, drawing the shot glass closer to him. His eyes were square on mine.

I tried to look away, but I couldn't pry my eyes from him. I saw something different in those eyes of his, a kind of goodness, a caring. I wondered what he was like when he wasn't saving lives. Was he simply a regular civilian? He had an entire life I knew almost nothing about except for a few remarks he'd made about his family. My mind drifted. Did he have a favorite color? Did he like to read? Had he ever been married?

"When this is all over, I'd like to hear more about your family, more about why you do what you do," I said.

"No." The guide recoiled, and his hands fell from his glass. "You can't cross the boundaries into my personal life."

"How come?"

"Because I love you."

Silence. All the noises in the restaurant receded, as if a wide space had opened around our table. The guide's eyes looked spent, as though he felt relieved at having said it. He gave me the sweetest and saddest smile at the same time, which made his brown eyes more brilliant.

"Ever since I first saw you come out of the elevator with Halmoni at the Shilla Hotel, I haven't been able to get your image out of my mind. When I asked your parents to send you here, I really didn't think they'd allow their unmarried daughter to come alone. When you did come, I kept asking myself if this is fate. I kept examining and reexamining all the factors: our age difference, differences in thinking and our lifestyles. I must decide if I will allow myself to love you or end it here." He paused for a long time, as if he was trying to decide. At last he said, "If I were ten years younger, I would ask you to marry me. Now it's impossible."

My eyes teared. He moved me more than I wanted to admit. I ached to reach out my hand and touch him, but I found that I couldn't approach him.

I wouldn't allow myself, so I sat soundless, twisting the paper napkin again and again until it was roughly the size of a quarter. It suddenly hit me why Steven had been a constant, overwhelming presence ever since I arrived in China. He and the guide shared the same sad, tormented eyes. I saw Steven growing old like the guide, fighting against his own self-isolation, but in the end powerless. Now that he wanted love, ached to grasp love, and possess it, it was too late for him.

"To you." The guide raised his glass. "Supreme of the supreme. That's what the Chinese mean by *tai-tai*. The husband may be the head of the household, but the wife is the supreme lady of the home." He drew in a deep breath, then tossed the *soju* into his mouth. He held it there a little while before swallowing. He didn't look at me as he did it.

I filled his empty shot glass, knowing that usually wives and daughters poured for their husbands and fathers. I did it to commemorate the ending of my position as his *tai-tai*.

"I'm sad. Tonight I must say farewell to my Hae Ri." The guide bowed his head humbly as he received my offering with both hands.

XIII

July 1, 1997

I arrived back in Los Angeles with Halmoni the same day Hong Kong was returned to China and China's back door slammed shut, eliminating a major transit point to freedom for North Korean refugees.

After dropping off Halmoni at my parents' house, I watched the festivities on the ten o'clock news, curled up in a rocker in my apartment. The hand-over ceremonies were a mix between the Olympic opening ceremonies and the Miss Universe pageant rather than a serious political exchange of power. Big-time Hollywood producers had been flown in to choreograph the whole event. However, the producers couldn't stop the rain from pouring down on Prince Charles's white captain's hat as he stood in front of the podium with dozens of microphones spearing up at his weak chin. In his stiff English accent he relinquished Britain's wealthiest colony. Images of visiting dignitaries from around the world, including America's own secretary of state, Madeleine Albright, flashed on the screen. I almost expected to see inserts of mainland Chinese shouting: "The queen is ousted! Long live the PRC!" But everything was kept nice and friendly.

When the news was over I stayed up watching Jerry Springer and David Letterman. I wanted to rest, but I was afraid to fall asleep, afraid the guide might slip into my dreams. I suppose if we had met under different circumstances and at the right time, it could have been nice to be with him, with someone who loved me. But we had gone beyond romantic love. It was all about need and power, and I didn't want that. If I had needs, I could satisfy them myself. "I don't need a man to make me happy. I don't need a man to complete me. I am complete. I am complete," I repeated to myself over and over again as my personalized mantra, trying to stay awake.

Without warning I slipped into a dream and was back in China. In the dream, Halmoni and I were hiding out with our North Korean family on a wet rooftop somewhere near Changbai. The chill and the rain sliced into our faces with knifelike sharpness. I tried to use my body to shield Halmoni as best as I could. I was soaked to the bone, but it wasn't the wind and rain that made me shiver. It was the sound of fierce, high-pitched voices arguing. Ae Ran and Mi Ran were bitterly fighting with a third woman. I didn't know who she was. Her face was blurred, as if her identity was being withheld from me. She was sobbing brokenly, begging them to let her return to North Korea. Ae Ran and Mi Ran were screeching, "You mustn't go back! You mustn't go back!" My sense of capture was so great that I couldn't take any more of their wailing screams and yelled at them to shut up. My roaring outburst triggered an alarm from the streets below. Shrill whistles blew and harsh searchlights swept across the rooftop in spasmodic crisscross patterns. The entire building was quaking. I could feel the thunder of dozens of combat boots stomping up the flights of stairs. I tried desperately to lift Halmoni, grasping her beneath the arms, but she was too heavy. Struggling against her weight, I tried dragging her. The footsteps and deep voices grew louder and closer. As the soldiers broke through the door, I woke up in a cold sweat, adrenaline pumping so fast that I was shaking from head to toe.

The nightmare seemed so real that it took me a full minute to realize that I was sitting in my own apartment and not on a rooftop in China. Even after I was aware of this, I was still shaking because the threads of the nightmare wouldn't go away. I desperately needed to talk to someone. Whom could I confide in? I couldn't tell anyone, not even my family. Especially not my family. I could never tell them about the guide's admission of love and my confused feelings about him. I didn't think they'd abandon the mission, but they'd try to stop me from being involved. I couldn't let that happen. I was already deeply involved emotionally, and things were becoming increasingly complicated.

The American FBI and the South Korean Central Intelligence Agency (KCIA) were both sniffing around. A special agent from the FBI left me several messages on my answering machine, wondering if I was back from my travels. Mark Oh had initially contacted me the year before, when my book was first published, to see if I had been contacted or harassed by any pro-Pyongyang fanatics. He'd showed me his badge, gun, and business card.

It was too much of a coincidence that he would be calling me now. I decided not to return his call right away, and I didn't tell my parents. They were already overwhelmed by a KCIA agent's unannounced visit to their garment factory in downtown Los Angeles. The KCIA agent had asked them all sorts of questions regarding Yong Woon Uncle and our April trip to the Yalu River. The KCIA was an agency that inspired real fear, more so than the American FBI and CIA. Even though they received their name from the American agency, the KCIA was said to be like the Soviet KGB in its unlimited power and cruelty.

Would they slap us down? My mind worked at high speed. How had they found out about us? I tried to think of all the possibilities. The only other person outside of my family who knew of the mission was the ABC reporter in San Diego. Who else knew? Did the American CIA? Was this in their jurisdiction? Would our U.S. citizenships be revoked?

Unsure of how to handle the situation, my father contacted the guide. At first the guide made him swear not to say a word, but then he later phoned back instructing us to meet with the KCIA agent to find out what threat the agency posed.

The meeting was set for three days after I arrived home. My father picked me up promptly at nine in the morning in his blue Toyota. The KCIA agent had chosen Denny's in Koreatown as our meeting place. My guess was that it was familiar. Denny's was a popular Korean hangout. It was one of the first U.S. franchises permitted to set up business in South Korea, along with Wendy's and Pizza Hut (which served *kimchi* pizza).

I walked into the brightly lit building ahead of my father and took in the surroundings. The place was classic diner—middle-aged loud waitresses in grease-stained uniforms a size too small, orange vinyl seats in the booths, wood-grained plastic laminate tables, and a long counter with round padded stools. The classic décor was capped by a scenic view of the crowded parking lot.

The man was already seated at a booth, studying the menu with a small frown, as if having a tough time choosing between the breakfast special and oatmeal. He didn't fit the stereotype of an intelligence agent. He had a plain face with a small mouth set in compressed lines and no scars, was medium height, and wore a matted brown suit with a plain yellow-and-green striped tie. I was expecting him to look more slick and agile, perhaps with aviator sunglasses, and not so businesslike and normal.

As soon as my father and I sat down, the agent introduced himself as

Special Agent Yoon and then pulled out a small pad of paper from inside his blazer. He started scribbling notes before anyone started talking. He had thick hands and impeccably clean fingernails. Special Agent Yoon was expecting us to give him a rapid, fact-filled summary.

"How did you hear about us?" I asked in English, dropping my voice.

"It's our business to know every activity that involves North Korea." He scribbled incessantly.

"It's unconscionable to abandon this mission at this late stage. Things are already in motion, and desperate people are depending on us," said my father.

"Can you help us?" I put in.

Special Agent Yoon glanced over his shoulder, as if someone might be listening. "You're asking us to get involved?" he returned in Korean. He refused to commit himself. He was being resistant.

I decided to apply a little pressure by using the ABC card. "I've been in contact with a reporter from ABC. They're going to broadcast our family's story," I told him, frosting the truth. I could see that the subject interested him—there was an almost imperceptible tightening of his brow before he disguised it beneath a haughty look.

My father's gaze locked on to mine. I cautioned him with my eyes. He understood what I was doing and played along. "The success of this mission can only help South Korea's image. All the negative publicity from the international press about the Red Cross talks makes our people look bad and heartless because we aren't bowing to the North's irrational demands."

"No broadcasting agency should report anything until we know the outcome." Special Agent Yoon ran his pen along his finger.

"Unfortunately, that's out of our control. ABC's definitely doing a story no matter what. It would be great for everyone if this has a happy ending," I said innocently.

"Who's the reporter?"

"I'd rather not say."

"What other networks or newspapers have you spoken to?" He knitted his eyebrows in a way that kept me on my guard. It was difficult to pinpoint exactly what was so menacing about that look, but I think it had to do with the way his eyebrows were so perfectly curved that they appeared plucked.

"I have many friends who are writers and journalists," I replied, stretching the truth.

"Who are they?"

"They're just people who are concerned about what's going on in North Korea."

Special Agent Yoon pondered for a moment, tapping his pen on his pad now. He permitted himself a brief smile. "I think I've heard everything I need to." He rose, picking up the bill for our coffees.

My father fought him for it. They went on for a while before Special Agent Yoon shoved it into his pants pocket, ending the battle. I watched him pay the bill at the counter and disappear around the corner to the parking lot. He was hard to read. If his agency intended to stop our mission, we needed solid leverage to force them to assist us. My father was thinking the same thing and came up with a daring idea. He contacted an old schoolmate who was an executive at the Seoul Broadcasting System (SBS) in South Korea. The friend excitedly offered us a deal we couldn't walk away from. If we allowed a small television crew to tape the escape, which would then be broadcast on their station, they'd use their finances and close government contacts to get Yong Woon Uncle's family safely out of China and into South Korea.

Suddenly I was energized, but I was very concerned about the guide and his reaction to a television crew following him around. It was imperative that he understood how much we needed SBS.

$$\smile$$

July 24, 1997

The guide met with the SBS director heading the documentary team in Seoul and agreed to let them shoot the escape under two conditions: one, nothing must be reported before everyone made it safely to South Korea; two, the names and faces of all the guides must be concealed. SBS agreed to both terms.

We were ready to go forward with the mission again when something unexpected came up. The next day, my parents, my older sister, Julie, and her son, Jordan, arrived at my apartment from opposite ends of town for an urgent meeting. Kun Sam Uncle and Duk Hae Aunt weren't able to make it, so the burden of decision rested on the four of us.

My father leaned back on my leaf-patterned couch with his sock-clad feet propped on the low coffee table. My mother sat right beside him and brought out a letter from her purse. She handled the sheets of paper delicately, holding them by the edges. "These letters are different from any others we've ever received. They express my big brother's true thoughts. His words aren't guarded because he wrote them during the time he hid in Changbai," she said, smoothing the papers out on her knees, careful not to tear them, then handed them to my father to read out loud.

1997, June 4

DEAR AGED MOTHER,

I learned that you had left for South Chosŏn, so I picked up a pen and started writing as I sit here in Changbai. Despite Brother-in-Law's friend's effort, my extreme cautiousness drove me to waste his precious time, and I am truly apologetic.

During this river crossing, two out of four men were swept away to their deaths. I too would have been lost if it weren't for the young lad, who risked his own life to save mine. I owe him my life.

Mother, what's so good about me that you crossed the wide Pacific Ocean? Now I finally realize the true meaning of love, which is deeper than sky and ocean. I do not deserve your love. I am an undutiful son who could not even fulfill my role as the eldest. I have done nothing but cast a shadow on your already gray mind. Because you did not even get to see me, I have once again cast a thicker shadow of misery when I could have lightened it. When I stood at one side of the river with Brother-in-Law and Hae Ri on the other, all I could do was sob.

Mother, at this time, I am free to tell you about my life. It is full of turns and twists. After I was separated from you, I formed the YMCA and the Anticommunist Corps. Because of my activities, I was sentenced to serve seventeen years in a juvenile prison for rehabilitation. After being released, I lived like a gypsy and wandered, then eventually started a family. In 1974, September, I was condemned to a life of exile in the mountains where streams are as long as time.

Mother, I was given detailed instructions from Brother-in-Law's friend. It wouldn't be much of a problem if I were alone without a wife, children, and grandchildren. For them, I must be cautious, thus I will wait for the right time.

Mother, take extra care of yourself and live long till the day your lifelong wish of meeting your eldest son comes true.

From your son,
Lee Yong Woon

BROTHER-IN-LAW AND HAE RI'S MOTHER,

I am concerned about Mother's well-being and wonder if she arrived home safely. Mother flew all the way over the Pacific Ocean with a big hope and was unable to see me. I am a bad son. Mother's love cannot be compared to even the sky or the ocean. As the eldest, I should be the one to say eat first, use this, have this, instead of being a burden to Mother, younger siblings, nieces and nephews.

By the time I finally crossed the river, Mother had already left for South Chosŏn and the friend had to leave Changbai, too, but I was able to communicate with him by telephone. He filled me with detailed instructions, which I am determined to follow if that is the family's wish. But I am not a single body. I have a wife, children, grandchildren, and a daughter-in-law to regard. I must be cautious. I witnessed with my own eyes two people beside me swept away to their deaths in the river.

Socialism is also devoted to the pursuit of wealth, and money is everything. With money you feel as though you have wings. There is a saying that money bears money. I know our escape will cost a fortune. This is my thought: I'd rather you send me the money so I may start a business on my own to support us. Please discuss this option with Mother and the rest of the family. But if it is Mother's only wish to see her eldest son, I will follow the friend's directions.

I wish you and everyone well.

No one moved, not even Jordan, who was snuggled peacefully in my mother's arms. Jordan was Halmoni's first great-grandchild to be born on American soil. For him, I thought we should keep going so his future wouldn't be burdened with the weight of the past.

"We have to give the guide an answer by five tonight. That's two hours from now," my father murmured, loosening his silk tie.

"What shall we do? Your big uncle is very scared. As he says, if it was just him alone escaping, it would be no problem, but he has a grandchild and a daughter-in-law to think about as well. He'd rather stay and have us give him the fifty thousand dollars instead, so they can live there. But in any case, he'll do as we say." My mother took the letters back and held them in her hand.

"I thought it was forty," said Julie.

"No, the total amount will be around fifty or sixty thousand. Forty thousand for the boat, and the rest will be used to pay the guide's aides, North Korean border guards, and others along the way that need to be bribed for their silence," said my father.

"Where are we getting all that cash?"

"SBS will help out some, but the rest we have to draw from the business."

"Even if we decide to give them the money, they can't stay there. They'll be found out eventually," I voiced.

"I agree with Helie," my father said, casting his vote.

We all turned and looked at my mother. The lines around her eyes crinkled as she thought deeply, rocking Jordan in soothing rhythm. He nuzzled against her and drifted off to sleep, sated with love. The silence lingered for a while as she studied the little grandson in her arms. "Okay," she finally said with a deep sigh, laying the letter on the coffee table.

"All right. Now we have to decide on who gets to come." My father moved the discussion along, glancing from time to time at his ticking watch. "There are six family members plus Ae Ran's baby. Her husband is cut. In the elder son's case, Hak Churl is still with his wife, but he's also very sick. Something to do with his liver. He could be a problem."

God, what if Hak Churl's wife comes and he doesn't make it? That possibility kept running through my head, recycling itself like an endless loop.

"What's his wife's name?" I asked. Suddenly her name was very important to me. By referring to her as just someone's wife, someone's possession, it made her seem less human, like cheap baggage that we could bring or discard. She wasn't baggage. She was a real person with parents and relatives and a life in North Korea, and we, who didn't even know her name, were deciding her fate.

"Name? We don't know. They just call her Daughter-in-Law," answered my father.

"What does Hak Churl want to do?" Julie inquired.

"Only Big Uncle, his wife, and Ae Ran know about the plans."

"They have to tell Hak Churl. It's his choice. But if he decides to stay behind because of his wife, none of them can come. They have to come all together," I reminded everyone.

"Do Hak Churl and his wife have any children?" Julie asked.

"I don't think so. The guide and Choi Soon Man didn't mention it," my father replied.

"Then Hak Churl's wife should stay. The marriage has to be severed.

That's the only way," advised Julie, her tone so certain and dispassionate. "Hak Churl should just leave and not tell her."

Startled, I stared at my sister. She was barely five foot three inches tall and soft-bodied, not physically tough at all, but her will was strong. You could see it in her large, expressive eyes and thick, dark eyebrows that dominated her face. Growing up as the eldest child, she always had to take on the role of the responsible and solid one, which left the door wide open for me to lose my head in the clouds. She took violin lessons and got straight A's so I could be a cheerleader and slide by with B's. She became an optometrist and married a nice Korean American guy, named Jae like my father, so I could spread my wings as an artist and ride the stars. I owed her so much, but she never kept count.

I told myself she didn't mean it. "You don't mean that, right?" I wanted her to say it.

"Ju Ri's right. If Hak Churl's wife comes, it's not good for her family. Because there's no baby involved, it's better to leave her behind," my mother said.

"Then for the rest of her life she'll be wondering why her husband abandoned her." I felt like I had to fight for her.

"We have to hurry," my father prompted us. "If our decision is yes, the guide wants me to fly out to Seoul tomorrow."

"Tomorrow? You're going?" I asked, deflated. I had hoped the guide would change his mind and request my assistance instead.

"To deliver the first payment of twenty thousand dollars. A man has to handle that."

"Why can't you wire the money?" Julie wanted to know.

"Because the guide wants to meet face-to-face to give me several secret passwords. Depending on the password, I'll know where he's going to take the family, so I can meet them after they cross the river."

"How do we know if Big Uncle's other two children want to come?" Julie threw out.

"They will. I saw Mi Ran and Mun Churl at the river," I assured.

My father pointed at his watch. The little hand was on the five and the big hand was exactly on the twelve. "All right, I'm going to tell the guide that our answer is yes, but all seven must come as a unit. If Hak Churl's wife wishes to join them and if the situation allows for it, he should bring her as well. We have to trust him, because at the crucial moment only he can determine what's best." My father spoke firmly.

He made the call.

Long after everyone had left, I was haunted by Hak Churl's wife's wretched predicament. Would Halmoni's years of suffering be reincarnated into this young woman? How could we ask her to leave her family behind in all that misery? My heart ached for her, because whatever decision she made, go or stay, she would never be at peace. What was her name?

선동 인 공자련려인공화
ᅩ. 혜선서 련봉 동 39만구
운 룡

JOURNEY THREE

XIV

August 3, 1997

After making sure no one was following me, I jammed my foot down on the gas pedal and accelerated past the speed limit toward my parents' house in La Crescenta. The warm summer breeze rushed through the window and around my head. I'd been given less than a week's notice to pack after my father had flown back from Seoul on the twenty-seventh of July. He was there for only two short days to deliver twenty thousand dollars to the guide and meet with the SBS director. When he returned home, he looked worn and worried. The number of people had increased yet again to nine. Hak Churl had a one-year-old son. His wife had to come now with their child, and there was no time to waste. Every day counted. The North Koreans had increased the security along the Yalu River, and high-speed boats aggressively patrolled the maritime border, due to the May 20 defection of the North Korean fishing boat.

This forced us to set a new escape plan in motion. Instead of my family sailing by Chinese naval boat from Dalian, they would have to travel by land through China, but unfortunately, help from China was still not an option. After Hwang Jang Yop's diplomatic stand off staged at the South Korean consulate in Beijing, it was highly unlikely that China would risk upsetting North Korea—their longtime political ally—again.

North Korea had initially accused the South of kidnapping Hwang Jang Yop and threatened to retaliate. Hwang Jang Yop was the highest member of the Central Committee of the Workers' Party ever to defect. He was the chief architect of North Korea's ruling ideology of *juche* (self-reliance) and a former secretary of the Central Committee. In an effort to cool off North

Korea's anger, China asked the Philippines to allow Hwang Jang Yop to stop over for a month.

Hwang Jang Yop arrived in Seoul on July 11 via the Philippines on a chartered Air Philippines Boeing 737. At a press conference, he said that the North Korean regime had turned a blind eye to the suffering of its people and seemed to believe its only option was to use its armed forces, which had an arsenal of nuclear and chemical weapons. If that was the case, the failed inter-Korea Red Cross talks for food aid were probably a sham, and that would explain why the North Korean delegates had unreasonably walked out on the talks.

I couldn't help think how unbearable conditions must have been for the peasants if someone like Hwang Jang Yop, an elite member of the Central Committee who lived a privileged life, fled from North Korea. We had to find a way to get Yong Woon Uncle's family out of North Korea, out of China.

My father and I researched all the areas that bordered China. There weren't that many safe and convenient options. Macao and Vietnam were possible choices. Of the two, Vietnam seemed the better one. In 1999, Macao, a Portuguese colony, would return to Chinese rule, like Hong Kong. Vietnam had reestablished diplomatic relations with Western nations, even the United States, since the collapse of the USSR in 1991 and had developed prosperous economic ties with South Korea. Companies such as Daewoo Motors already had a joint-venture assembly plant there. It was financially smarter for Vietnam to maintain friendly relations with Seoul rather than Pyongyang, which had nothing to offer them.

When I got to the house, my father was counting out a thick wad of hundred-dollar bills. Thirty thousand dollars, to be exact. Seeing all that money reminded me that this was a business transaction and not simply a communion between people out to accomplish a humanitarian mission.

My father separated the bills into three even piles of ten thousand. Anyone carrying above that amount in cash had to declare it at customs. Surprisingly, a stack of one hundred hundred-dollar bills wasn't as bulky and impressive as I thought it would be. My father was able to hide his portion inside a thin money belt tucked inside his loose jeans. I stuffed mine in a powder blue tampon box and sealed it back up. As with toilet paper, I had learned it was wise to be armed with my own supply in China even though I'd stopped menstruating due to all the stress.

The third and last bundle was given to Halmoni. She carefully wrapped the bills in a flowery blue-and-white scarf and secured it underneath her blouse. It was a pretty cream chiffon blouse with petal sleeves that blossomed out just below her elbows, which added a nice softening touch. She looked beautiful and vibrant, but I was anxious about Halmoni going on such a long journey again at her age. Just a walk around the block was an epic adventure, but if she didn't reunite with her son in China, there was a great chance that she might not get to see him for another year. Once in the custody of South Korean authorities, all defectors were detained for questioning, then whisked off to a reeducation facility, where they'd learn to adjust to South Korean life. Halmoni didn't want to risk the delay. She had waited long enough.

I was going to China at the request of the SBS director, who wanted me, the author of Halmoni's book, in his documentary. Documentary or not, I was going. Even the guide's orders to stay home couldn't keep me from fulfilling my promise to Halmoni.

The area around the Korean Air counter was mobbed by disorderly passengers hurrying to check in for the flight. My father managed to sweet-talk the female ticket clerk into giving us priority boarding and priority seating. Our seats were in the first row, three paces away from the lavatory and right behind the blue curtain that separated business class from the rest of us economy travelers.

Reclining the seat back, I attempted to find a comfortable position. I felt like a bonsai tree, confined, cramped, and distorted. I wriggled and shifted and groaned, exhausted. It was impossible.

Halmoni couldn't sit still, either. Her stomach began to act up. I scrounged in the bottom of her purse for Tums. My fingers groped through all the other bottles and packages of medicine my mother had so wisely packed. Finding the correct bottle, I read the directions: chew. Easy enough. With one flick of the wrist, I knocked two perfectly round pastel-colored tablets into Halmoni's palm. When the pills didn't settle her stomach, I coaxed her into eating some white rice mixed with warm seaweed soup that the flight attendant scavenged from business class. Most of it spilled down the front of Halmoni's chiffon blouse. I dabbed out the stain using a wet napkin, then covered her with a fleece airplane blanket. Short of hijacking a first-class seat, it was all I could do for her.

The eleven-hour flight to South Korea was pure torment in those narrow, uncomfortable seats, and yet our journey wasn't over. At Seoul's Kimpo

International Airport we had a three-hour layover before we could board our flight to Shenyang, China. We found an upstairs lounge area where there were large-screen Samsung televisions and Formica tables with cushioned benches. Halmoni immediately curled up on one of the cushioned benches and passed out. I fell asleep alongside her but was awakened by a faint beeping sound. A small lens was aimed at my sagging face. The last thing I wanted after a grueling international flight was to be so closely and critically scrutinized by a video camera and have it record my disheveled, smudged image. Suppressing a yawn, I slowly propped myself up. I adjusted my shirt and hair and wiped the sleep from my eyes so I could get a better look at the person operating the camera. He was a young South Korean man, about twenty-six or twenty-seven. His hair was shaved closely around the sides and pushed up and spiked on top with gel. The skin on his face was slightly scarred from an old burn, and he wore thick black-framed glasses that looked like props.

I was tempted to reach over and flip off the camera, but I reminded myself that this was the price we had agreed to pay for SBS's assistance and government connections. From that moment on, I had to deal with the reality that there would be no more privacy. The video camera, hidden in a regular-size leather date book, recorded our every move. The entire plane ride it rested on the meal tray, across the narrow aisle, pointed directly at us. It stayed on us all the way to the jetway in Shenyang, where a male attendant with stooped shoulders and a doughy nose waited with a wheelchair. Halmoni insisted she could walk the distance, but I was more insistent. The attendant energetically wheeled an unhappy Halmoni through side doors and private elevators, cutting in front of every line.

Once we entered the immigration area the young man with the camera lingered slightly behind our group. He was nervous. I could read it on his face. During a lull in the plane ride, I had struck up a conversation with him, and he'd told me a little about himself. His surname was Kim and he was a freelance cameraman. The burns on his face were from back in the days when he was a college student demonstrating for democracy and a flaming Molotov cocktail exploded on his back. This was his second assignment in China in two months. The first assignment had been to videotape North Korea's ruined landscape along the Yalu border. As he was making his way back to Yanji to catch his flight, the Chinese police arrested him. They confiscated all his equipment and tapes and detained him for two weeks before expelling him from the country, which explained the disguised appearance that matched his false documents.

We lost sight of the cameraman on the other side of the customs barrier, but we kept moving toward the exit with a flood of people. Outside the heat was scalding, and the humidity robbed the air of oxygen. I couldn't get enough of the syrup-thick air into my lungs.

"Where is he?" Halmoni drawled warily, her blinking eyes searching.

"You'll see him soon," I told her, yawning. I yawned so widely that my jaws cracked.

"I thought maybe he'd be here. I just have to see him this time."

Another yawn. Another crack. "You will," I affirmed, looking around to see if anyone was watching us too closely.

The cameraman caught up to us at the taxi stand, wild-eyed and sweaty. He was absolutely no help. He didn't speak a word of Mandarin. It was up to my father to negotiate a cab fare while I held on to Halmoni. He fumbled to communicate with a group of men squatting on their thighs and leaning against their cabs. They all wore their trousers rolled up to the knees and muscle tank tops drawn up over their dark nipples. They were eating their lunch from tin vessels, and none of them seemed too interested in earning our business. One driver, sucking fish bones between his teeth, hand-signaled numbers to us. He wanted 150 yuan (about twenty dollars). He was over-charging us because we were foreigners, but we scrambled into his un-air-conditioned cab anyway. My father slipped the driver the name of our hotel through the steel grille. It was written in three Chinese characters on the back of a business card. The driver took the card but paid no attention to the hotel name, instead turning the card over and admiring the golden embossed English calligraphy. Once his curiosity was satisfied, he belched and ground the clutch at the same time.

The car quivered, then jolted forward into the honking Shenyang traffic. The streets were jammed with taxis, motorbikes, trucks, and buses that coughed noxious black fumes into the already smoggy air. Our driver was unwilling to halt at signals and blasted his way through traffic lights, racing past one matchboxlike building after another.

Shenyang was not a beauty spot. It was a grim city of concrete buildings, abandoned state-owned factories, and rusty smokestacks, but it had the best railway lines in China and a well-developed highway network. At the beginning of the seventeenth century, Shenyang was the capital of the Manchurian empire—the center of ginseng trade. At the turn of the nineteenth century, the Russians occupied it and industrialized it into a Russian railroad town, but during the twentieth century the city changed hands frequently. The Japanese took it over after they were the victors in the Russo-Japanese War of 1904–5. When the Chinese Communist Party came into power in 1948, Mao Zedong's new China added to the industry, making Shenyang a key city in the industrial drive of the 1950s and 1960s. With the new switch to market reforms, Shenyang lost its edge to busy coastal cities such as Dalian.

Today, Shenyang was the capital of Liaoning Province and had a population of over six million. It was a place of ceaseless noise, overcrowding, and high unemployment. The wide, characterless streets were full of people standing around doing nothing. Several generations of family members lingered outside on the sidewalks, fanning themselves, napping, enjoying as free entertainment anything out of the normal, mundane flow of life. Because of the poverty and cramped living space, the streets had become living rooms, kitchens, and bathrooms. A woman cooked on the footpath. A man relieved himself against a urine-stained wall. Not far from him, an old barber hung a mirror on the wall and set up a shaving stool, waiting for customers. Groups of men squatted around a food stand slurping noodles for longevity (the lengthy noodles are said to represent long life). Two women were hanging laundry on a line stretched from the bars of a window to a telephone pole. As we sped by, the hot breeze from our car puffed out the shirts and trousers, making them look like strange kites.

Our driver suddenly swerved wildly just in time to steer clear of the endless line of rickety bicycles that hurtled out of a side alley into the intersection. The bicyclists didn't even look sideways to see if cars were coming straight at them. Obviously they were under the belief that what they couldn't see wouldn't run them over.

Our driver enjoyed himself as he dodged bicycles and swung the car around sharp corners. He beamed with pride as the car bounced sickeningly against the curb, then slammed to a stop with such force that I was almost unseated. As I scrambled back and up I saw a very tall and sleek building in front of us. The Gloria Plaza Hotel was different from any other building I had seen here, and much more pleasant. It was a gleaming high-rise constructed of white tile and tinted glass with three prominent flagpoles standing erect out front. The red Chinese flag wilted in the airless heat between two motionless white flags. My father had chosen this hotel for the staff's higher standard of English and because it stood opposite the North Railway Station.

Two bulky doormen, standing obtrusively at the entranceway, scrutinized everyone who entered the hotel. Their massive guts bulged against the seams of their tank-green uniforms. Smiling broadly, I made an attempt to win over the bigger, more threatening man. His official facial expression didn't change. Giving up, I walked past him and spun through the revolving glass door into the cool oasis of privilege. The hotel was equipped with a grand piano bar, business center, satellite TV channels, men-only sauna, and European-style café that served flavored lattes and shots of Italian espresso. It also came equipped with surveillance cameras. I spotted four of them wedged in the corners of the ceiling and another one near the elevators as a bellhop escorted us to our rooms upstairs. Who knew how many more were hidden that I couldn't see.

Once Halmoni and I were inside our double room and I tucked her into bed, I found myself scanning everything. My hands silently swept the furniture and vents the way the guide had taught me. Satisfied we weren't being bugged, I relaxed and walked over to the window. From our room, we had a smoggy panoramic view of the busy train station across the street. The station was also a modern design, not traditionalist or bland communist. It actually reminded me of a slice of cake—an eleven-layer vanilla cake with fudge filling in between each layer. Burrowed into the center was a huge black-faced clock. Just as the clock chimed three I caught my father leaving the hotel. He was going out to call the guide from a pay phone, to tell him we had arrived. He was supposed to say, "Can you tell the bearded man that the *halmoni* from Seoul moved to a new address?" By the address given, the guide would know which hotel we checked into and our room numbers.

I tried waiting up for my father, but at around eight my eyes felt grainy and my craving for sleep overwhelmed me. I staggered to bed, gratefully sinking into the mattress. With a sigh of contentment I pulled the crisp sheet over me. In seconds I was gone. At some point between eleven and midnight, the phone rang and I came out of a heavy sleep. The left eye flickered open while the other stayed closed. I couldn't convince the right lid to part. I had to pry it open manually, but I still couldn't see. I groped for the receiver. It wasn't there. Someone had rearranged the furniture in my bedroom. These weren't my soft Egyptian cotton sheets. I didn't know where I was. Then my eyes adjusted to the darkness and I saw in the twin bed next to me the covers rising and falling over a lumpy mound. Reality returned to me, one small piece after another. I picked up the receiver in the nick of time, before the caller hung up.

"Where is your father?" The guide's voice rushed into my ear.

"Sleeping," I muttered, not completely awake.

"He isn't in his room. He shouldn't be out this late."

"He went out to call you."

"That was hours ago." The guide went on to mention something about a delay. I tried hard to stay attentive, but I kept drifting away. "Put Halmoni on," he said.

"Can't it wait till the morning?"

"No, I have something important to tell her." The sudden drop in the guide's pitch startled me so much, I became alert.

Crouching by Halmoni's bed, I shook her as gently as I knew how. She didn't wake. She slept soundly, curled up on her side in the form of an S, her inside hand cradled between her head and the pillow. "Halmoni . . . you have to wake up." I shook a little harder, and her wrinkled eyelids lifted open slowly. She was aware, but she remained lying on her side. When I handed her the phone, she took it and laid it on top of her ear.

"Hello?" Halmoni's voice cracked from exhaustion. "Who is this? . . . Lee Yong Woon? Is it really you, Yong Woon-ah?" The name, her son's name, came out in the form of an exhalation. There was a long pause, then she continued. "What good is it if only you are safe? Don't do anything foolish. . . . Of course you have suffered. We have all suffered, but it's not necessary to say all those words to me. I already know your feelings. Keep your mind straight and stop drinking. You can't leave her behind. Is she not the mother of your children? . . . There is nothing you can do about that now. Don't speak of it again. Say nothing more. Return quickly. No matter what happens from here forward, I've asked God to watch over you. He's kept you alive for almost fifty years, and I've asked Him to protect you for fifty more. Go, go, safely. There is still a chance for us to meet after this life," she said in a cool voice that amazed me. Then her whole demeanor changed and she sat up. "You've done a good job. You've done a good job. Yes . . . yes, that I know. Return my son quickly. . . . What? . . . I heard you. She is very clever. . . . Are those your thoughts or hers? . . . I heard you clearly."

Halmoni handed me back the phone. I tried to make sense of it all, but not having heard the other end of the conversation, my mind could not do much with it.

"The day after tomorrow I'm coming to Shenyang to speak to you all," the guide said softly.

"Are you coming alone?" I asked.

"I'll fill you in when I get there. Until then all of you must be very careful. Your father mustn't go out alone so late except when related to this project. Understand?"

"He probably had to take care of something," I replied, wondering why I sounded so apologetic.

"Just stay in the hotel," said the guide, and then the phone clicked off.

I scooted closer to Halmoni, studying her tired eyes veiled with despair. An irritated look crossed her face. "That person doesn't speak straight. He wastes time. He asked me who Yong Woon was. Does he think I don't even know my own son's name? Retard. Why did he have us fly out in the middle of the night when they haven't even crossed yet? All on his own he's decided to go ahead with everything, knowing Ae Ran's mother doesn't want to come. What is he going to do? Kidnap her? He couldn't even rescue his father and older brother, and they're his flesh and blood. But I thanked him for the good job he's done. I did it so he'd leave my son alone. He can't be trusted. He's sitting around drinking. They've both been drinking tonight. I could tell by the way they dragged their words." She stuck out her pink tongue like a drunk and slurred her words, mimicking them. "Yong Woon was going on about how much he missed his mother. I told him to keep his mind straight, to save his sentiments and tears for later. My goodness, we're doing all this and he's sitting around drinking. He complained to me that he lived all these years without fun because of Ae Ran's mother. It's probably because she wouldn't tolerate him sitting around the house all day getting drunk." Halmoni rose slowly to use the rest room. I followed her to turn on the light.

"It's because life's hard over there," I defended him, but deep down I worried Yong Woon Uncle might become a liability once he got to Seoul. Sometimes freedom was harder to use than to win. If he wasn't able to cope with it, he might drink more. His drunkenness would torment Halmoni.

"Then what's that other person's excuse?" She flushed the toilet and shuffled back to bed. She took off her glasses and dislodged her dentures with her tongue, severing the strands of saliva, and dropped them into a glass of water. They sank to the bottom and sent up little bubbles. "I want to leave tomorrow. Call your daddy and tell him," Halmoni sighed, and settled into her pillow.

"In the morning," I stalled, wondering where my father could be. What was he doing out so late?

"I'm going to tell him we must leave."

"Tomorrow." I turned off the lights in hopes that the darkness would lull Halmoni to sleep. I listened carefully for her soft snoring, but I didn't hear it. For a long time we lay awake. I wasn't sure who fell asleep first.

XV

The sound of running water in the bathtub woke me even before the sun rose. Unable to fall asleep again, I eventually crawled out from under the sheet and headed for the bathroom. Halmoni pressed past me, wearing only a tank undershirt and the baggy bloomers with secret pockets she had sewn herself.

I put my shoulder to the door frame and watched as she retied the money wrapped in her blue-and-white flowered scarf underneath her breasts. I stood there a little longer as she stepped into a roomy pleated dress that ended halfway down her shins. When she was done dressing, she smiled at me. I was relieved to see that she was no longer showing signs of despair. Retreating into the bathroom, I took my time brushing each tooth thoroughly, wondering about my father. Where had he gone? What had he done? Had he been with someone? Suddenly I became furious at the guide for planting such nasty thoughts inside my head. It was cruel to suspect my father of anything.

When my father summoned us to his room, I hurried Halmoni down the thickly carpeted corridor. The moment we walked in, the video camera was aimed at us again. I became instantly flustered.

"Mother, listen very carefully," my father requested.

Halmoni gave him all her attention. She sat regally in the armchair pushed up against the window with her knees propped up close to her chest. The bottoms of her bloomers, tucked inside the thick tangerine-toned stockings, showed.

"Mother, before we arrived in Shenyang, your son crossed over for the second time with Ae Ran to meet with the guide. They told the guide that the whole family was ready to go, even the ill son, Hak Churl. The only person they were waiting on was the youngest son, Mun Churl, because he wanted to attend his college graduation. Because of him and your son's inability to control his wife and children, everything was delayed."

"How do you know all this?" I questioned my father.

"The guide told me. *Ii-sh,* he said something else. During the time the family was awaiting Mun Churl's return, Ae Ran's mother did something totally foolish that may have jeopardized this entire mission. She sold their house. The amount received was less than sixty dollars. She should have just left everything as it was. When she tried to give her older sister the bags of rice and clothes we sent them, the older sister became suspicious. The entire country's starving, yet they have rice and new clothes, and Ae Ran's mother was just giving it all away. The older sister became hysterical when the plans were exposed. She threatened to report them to her son, who's a member of the Secret Service."

My father said more, but I couldn't concentrate on what else he was relaying because my ears caught the sound of a half knock and a passkey in the lock. Before I could react, the door swung open and the maid was already in. We all jumped up and shut our mouths. It wasn't wise to presume Chinese maids and bellhops couldn't speak Korean or English and didn't have sharp eyes. I sent her away promptly, propping a chair against the door.

My father continued in a more cautious voice. "The guide told your son that the mission was off, to go back. Before he sent them across the river he showed them Hae Ri's book. Seeing his picture on the book, your son became so terrified he was willing to throw away his wife and children and stay in China."

My eyebrows soared and I sort of sagged down in my chair, winded. It felt like I had jumped out a second-story window onto a hard patch of concrete.

"When Ae Ran saw her letter printed in the back of the book, she started to shake badly. She didn't want to go back, either, but the guide secretly told her if she went back and calmed down the situation with her mother's older sister, pretend life was back to normal, he'd keep going. No one knows except Ae Ran or else the plans will unravel again."

"Let's go home. It's in God's hands now," Halmoni said, sounding resigned.

"If nothing happens in three days, we'll give up this mission."

"I want to leave now."

"Three days."

"Leave now. There's nothing more we can do."

"It'll at least take that many days to get flights out of here. The planes are all booked because of the many Korean and Japanese tourists coming here this time of year to visit the Changbai Mountains."

"Don't you see this is God's will?"

"Don't say that," I said harshly. "Why are you giving up so easily?"

"Even defeat is God's decision." Halmoni took my arm and held it. I could feel her fingers tense, as though by squeezing my bones she might instill the Holy Spirit in me, but I was fed up with her brand of Christianity, which demanded that she be long-suffering and unquestioning. I was fed up with God and His silence. How many time had I pleaded with Him to let Halmoni see her son, to save him from that wretched place? How many years had Halmoni prayed? I refused to pray and believe in God when He had turned His back on an old woman who had only served Him faithfully. He had let her suffer again and again. He had let me suffer. As people were judged and measured by their actions and compassion, I judged and measured God, too. In my heart I found Him guilty of committing the greatest sin—causing pain. So much unnecessary pain.

"Why did that person have to show them the book? Let them be," Halmoni moaned.

"Mother, he had to show them."

"Why did he?"

"So they'd see what danger they're in." My father tried to get through to her, in frustration scratching his arms until they were red.

Halmoni wasn't listening to what he said. She kept echoing her question. "Why did he have to show them?"

"The situation was already dangerous before they saw the book. We can't change what's happened. If we could change one thing, the book should have never been written."

My father's words sank deep inside my stomach. With all the other feelings of guilt and regret twisting around down there, I could hardly speak. I forced myself to finally admit what I had done. I had to. Dropping to my knees in front of Halmoni, I let my confession pour forth in a pool of tears as I groped at her hands. "This is all my fault. I was stupid. I should have known. Now they're all in danger because of me, because of something I wrote. It's all my fault. I'm sorry. I'm so sorry, Halmoni."

"Don't cry. You don't need to cry. You did nothing wrong." She squeezed my hands back. This time I felt her anguish.

"What's done is done. The book's already been written, so we have to keep going, or else." My father was about to say something else, but Halmoni reeled around and lashed at him.

"Why are you scaring this child?"

"Halmoni, please," I begged, "we have to help them. We have to. We just can't give up and go home, not after everything we've seen. I can't—I can't—"

For a long moment Halmoni was silent. Her expression was simultaneously glazed and pious, like that of a saint about to be tortured. Then at last she uttered in a contemptuous tone, "What can I do? Even if I told that person to stop, he has his own mind. He will do it anyway. I don't trust him. He's a drunk."

"Mother," my father huffed, removing his polo shirt and pushing his pant legs up over his knees. Wearing only his white tank top and the improvised shorts, he scratched furiously. "The guide is under tremendous stress. Don't condemn a man for trying to relieve his burdens at night with a drink or two. Don't view him like a criminal."

"I never said that. Don't put words into my mouth," she snapped, enraged.

I took a stabilizing breath. "Halmoni, we need the guide. You need to change your thinking. From here on, instead of praying all the time, you need to take action. We need to rely on each other. This is not over."

Halmoni leaned to one side of the chair, hooking a foot around the chair leg. "What isn't meant to be isn't meant to be. Let us leave them alone, in peace."

I snorted. "What peace? There is no peace over there."

"Why are you upset at me?" She tried to smooth out the wrinkles in her dress.

I forcefully grabbed her hands again. "Because you're being selfish. Stop thinking about your fears. We're all scared."

"Your hands are too cold. I know you. Whenever you're burdened, your hands become cold. You're worrying yourself sick." Halmoni tried to warm my hands with hers. "I don't like anyone scaring you like this. Feel her hands," she said to my father.

"Halmoni, promise me you won't give up and leave," I pleaded.

"How can I leave alone? I just follow you. If you say go, I go. If you say stay, I stay. I am an old woman. What does it matter what I say? I'm just like that black shoe on the floor—baggage you bring along. I still don't trust that person. He's trying to keep us here for some other reason."

"My goodness, Mother." My father put out his hands in a gesture of helpless dismay, palms up and empty, and then dropped them into his lap. "Still you think badly of him."

Halmoni's eyes narrowed to sharp points. "We were led to believe my son was already here! That's why we came so quickly, like thieves in the middle of the night. But he's not here. He's still in North Korea."

"How was the guide supposed to predict that Ae Ran's mother would sell her house and tell her older sister? Your son's family withheld information from the guide. They should have told us the older sister's family is connected to the Secret Service. We're not mind readers."

"But when a person makes a promise, he must fulfill it even though there is a knife pointed at his throat. Open your eyes. He's setting us up. He fills our minds with fear so we won't use the phone to tell people where we are."

"You're not thinking positively. All you can do is complain!" my father exploded, pulling off his glasses. "Mother, you said—"

"Stop telling me what I said! That person is up to something and you're too blind to see!"

"Why are you yelling at me?"

"Okay, stop. That's enough." I used my body to block their view of each other.

Halmoni hefted herself up to her feet. "I will only listen to Hae Ri, not to you," she said, cocking her head to the side, away from my father.

"Fine, then you two handle everything. I'll go home," he fired back.

"Go if you want."

"I will."

"You'd leave your daughter here? What kind of father are you?"

"Stop it!" I screamed, so close to hysteria that everyone froze, rock still. No one spoke. No one moved. When I turned to Halmoni and gestured toward the door, I became suddenly aware of the camera peeking at us. I had forgotten it was in the room. It was on us the whole time we were arguing. Embarrassed, I pushed past it and jerked open the door. Halmoni didn't understand. Grabbing her under the arm, I physically removed her from the room. I had to keep her away from my father till they both cooled down, till my own nerves settled down. I had seen a new side of them. They weren't behaving like the people I knew, and it frightened me.

Halmoni acted as if no harsh words had flown between her and my father. In fact, the next morning she denied even having fought with him. I think it was

all the stress and exhaustion of the journey that was wearing on her mind—
wearing on all our minds, and making us behave strangely. I bounced between
agitation and anticipation, knowing the guide was on his way. I couldn't sit
still. I showered twice, then paced the room, shaking my arms and legs as if I
were doing some tribal mating dance.

Finally, about a quarter to seven, the guide checked into a room on the
fourteenth floor. It was near ten before he came knocking at our door. It was
an almost inaudible knock. I pressed my ear against the wood and asked who
it was. Recognizing the guide's voice, I unlocked the top bolt and let him in.
He seemed leaner, more towering, and more imposing, even though he
appeared to have been up for the last forty-eight hours. As he traveled from
the door to Halmoni's bed and bowed to her and my father, I shamelessly
ogled him. Stubble darkened his golden tanned face, and the white T-shirt he
had on just deepened the tan. I gave myself a mental shake and forced my eyes
away from him. It was dangerous to be attracted to him.

There was another man with the guide, hauling a duffel bag. He was a
squat, thick-set man with an unusually large head and bushy brows. The Coke-
bottle glasses he wore made his bulbous eyes look more magnified. He seemed
slightly younger than the guide but had a cocky, I'm-in-charge-here air of
haughtiness about him. I could sense the friction between the two of them.

"Hello, Halmoni, I'm Kim Chon Hong, the chief director on this project
for SBS." The large-headed man bowed courteously, then motioned to a
straight-back chair. "Halmoni, why don't you sit over here at the table next
to me?"

"I can hear you from here just fine. You talk from over there." She stared
at him blandly from where she sat on the bed.

The director dragged the straight-back chair over to Halmoni and settled
into it himself. He sat with his legs spread and his elbows sticking out so much
that he looked like a sumo wrestler readying for a bout. When the camera
was set up on a tripod and the tape was rolling, he turned his attention back
onto Halmoni. "Halmoni, I hope you're in good health." His on-air voice was
too big for him, as if maybe he'd taken voice lessons and felt it necessary to
use what he'd learned. "Halmoni, ever since my coverage team and I arrived
in China, we've been waiting on the younger son, Mun Churl. He wants to
match everything around his graduation. Graduating isn't important. We had
told Ae Ran's mother to send a message to Mun Churl that his father was ill,
so he'd come home promptly, but we discovered that Ae Ran's mother never
sent the message. She was having second thoughts. Only Ae Ran, with her

baby strapped to her back, and your son, Lee Yong Woon-ssi, came to the safe house. Ae Ran came to get away from her husband. He treats her terribly. He beats her and throws things at her that leave visible bruises all over her arms." The director paused to let us imagine the horrors that had happened to Ae Ran, then brought out several fragile bundles of letters. His blunt, stubby fingers opened them with exaggerated care, then read two letters written to my aunt from Ae Ran and my uncle while they waited in Changbai for the rest of the family to escape.

Mother,

Why didn't you come to the river? Is Mun Churl there yet? Mother, if this mission gets out in the open, we are dead people even if we remain alive. We can't keep this a secret forever. We are involved too deeply now, and there is only one road to go on. If our family is to survive, you must cross the river no matter what. Our guides are planning to leave tomorrow if you don't cross today. I cannot go by myself. I will not go. We have the guarantee of safety. We have Uncle and Grandmother here, and they will be traveling with us, so you can rest easy. Grandmother means to bring us all to South Chosŏn, not just Father and me.

The die is cast and we cannot change its fall. The fact that Father has already crossed over two times is unforgivable. Receiving rice and clothes will not be forgiven, either. We shouldn't have taken it then. We shouldn't have met with Uncle and Hae Ri in the first place.

Rice must be served in time or else it turns to cake. Delays weaken our situation in the worst way. Mother, if I am to be treated like an animal there, I would rather take my poison here and die here. Death is a better way.

Mother, please let us know your intentions quickly. If you decide to come, I'll leave the baby here and fetch you. Mother, tell the neighbors that you are going to Kangseo to collect a debt. Tell them that you are going with Hak Churl and that Mi Ran is staying with Father at the other house because of his high blood pressure. Then tell Mi Ran's friends that she and you are going to Kangseo. And inform the people at Mi Ran's work that she will be taking a vacation or some time off.

Mother, if you decide to stay, I won't come your way at all. I have no home and no place to go. There is no point in going on.

When the rain starts, it will be all over. I am not threatening you, I am telling you the truth.

Ae Ran

Dear,

What happened yesterday? I have already been put out in the public along with Ae Ran, Hak Churl, Mun Churl, and Mi Ran, so you cannot scatter about. We need to act effectively. Tonight you have to do everything Ae Ran tells you, with or without Mun Churl.

You must bring the People's Certificates, diplomas, and pictures. There is nothing else we need. Time is extremely short.

I had a hard time reading the expression on Halmoni's face. It was a weird mixture of despair and humor.

"Ae Ran has gone back, but Lee Yong Woon-ssi stayed behind, hoping Ae Ran could convince everyone to cross. Every day at one Ae Ran came out to the river with the baby and signaled that Mun Churl would return tomorrow, tomorrow, always tomorrow. Ae Ran kept stalling us because she was afraid we'd leave. She should have just been honest with us. Finally, on the sixth, at one in the morning, Mun Churl arrived at Hyesan. The next day, at one, Mun Churl, Hak Churl, and Ae Ran showed up at the river and signaled that they were at last ready to move that very night. They were told to come to the river at six in the evening to receive instructions. At six, the guide's aide swam over to give Ae Ran directions, but instead she handed him these two letters. One she wrote to the guide; the other is to her father."

I could see the pages were still damp. The director unfolded the paper, taking his time, and then began to read:

1997, August 6

Respected sir,

How busy you must have been because of us. I don't know how to express my gratitude. My heart is heavy bringing you such disappointing news. Mother agreed to escape but changed her mind when her older sister arrived from Haedae on the third. Discovering the news, Aunt screamed at the top of her lungs and created chaos. She threatened to report us, but we managed to stop her. She plans to stay here for a month to keep her eyes on us. Leaving now will most likely result in failure, and we will not even make it to the river before Independence Day.

I am sorry. I am really sorry we took such a long time, causing delays and loss. We are not concerned whether we live or die, but under such circumstances we must abandon the original plan—something we never imagined. I worry that someone in your party will go crazy because of the trouble we have caused you. And I am most sorry for having fallen short of Grandmother's expectations. Please explain to those waiting for us.

If you, sir, are willing to help us again, then I have confidence that we will do well the next time, since we are experienced now. Failure is the mother of success. Sir, thinking of Grandmother, please help us until the end. Watch over us until the end.

Ae Ran

To FATHER,

Are you in good health?

Our plan is totally destroyed. We cannot think of leaving at such a time. We should not have let Aunt come, and now the situation is out of control. We must consider the troubles we will be inviting afterward, the horrendous investigations. Since Aunt's arrival, our home has become a grieving house, a funeral parlor. And since we sold the house, we will have nowhere to live. We made a big mistake in believing in Aunt just because she is a relative. Mother is a naive fool. There is no compromising in matters of life and death, no matter who is involved.

If the guide can offer just one more opportunity, it would be good. Thinking of Grandmother and Uncle, please ask the guide for his understanding and to help us to the very end. I don't know what's ahead for us now. The future is bleak and I can't breathe.

Perhaps our escape wasn't our destiny. With your return, we shall decide our fate. The other day, I spent our life savings and bought rat poison and we are all carrying it in our pockets. Depending on what the situation is, we are prepared to take our own lives. Dying comes only once.

Ae Ran

The director peeled open the last bundle of letters. "These two are from Lee Yong Woon-ssi. This one he wrote to his wife's older sister, but we thought it was best not to send it."

MADAM,

It is not that my ideology is bad, nor am I ready to betray the motherland. I only want to abide by my mother's lifetime wish. Granting her happiness cannot be considered a crime.

You probably already heard from Ae Ran, but I shall reiterate the situation. I, my wife, my children, and my grandchildren can no longer live there. This son's picture from North Korea was sent across the Pacific with the first letter written by the granddaughter. My name, my wife's name, my children's names, workplace, and so on . . . all these things are out in the open all over the world; hence, it is only a question of time whether today or tomorrow we are captured.

Madam, please understand the spirit of this and behave in a just manner. Time is tight and urgent, so please allow your sister, nieces, and nephews to make their move this evening. Not one member of our family must fall out. As a guard, I will not cross over the river again. I swear it on my life. I am prepared to die in front of my mother rather than go back.

Lee Yong Woon

"Since he wrote this letter, your son was persuaded to go back. We believed that if he didn't return, his wife's older sister would have carried out her threat and turned them in," the director concluded.

Halmoni sighed in silence. It was a deep, long, sorrowful sigh. The director let the silence hang a moment while he rolled all the letters into a tube. When he was done, he placed the tube primly in his lap like a diploma, then stepped rapidly into the gap and began again. This time he brought out four cases of digital videotapes from a secret compartment in his duffel bag and organized them on the bed. Selecting a carefully labeled tape, he inserted it into a Sony Handycam and pressed play. Halmoni and I leaned forward to get a better view.

"That's Ae Ran," the director pointed out.

A middle-aged-looking woman wearing a pioneer-style bonnet was squatting at the river's edge, pretending to wash her feet. A baby was secured to her back with a dark blanket wrapped around her chest. I tried to make out the violent shades of purple and blue on her arms, but the two-inch flip-out screen was too small. Then the camera quickly zoomed out to catch a young, slender man swimming over to Ae Ran. When he stood up in the thigh-high water in his forest-green underwear, I recognized him immediately. He was the younger Chosŏn brother, whom Jambbong, Jambbong's wife, and I had accidentally bumped into that frightful evening in Changbai. As he attempted to talk to Ae Ran, a border guard shouted at them, brandishing his rifle.

"You see the gun, Halmoni? Ae Ran has guts. She's acting very laid-back. Later we bought that border guard ice cream and beer. See there, Ae Ran is passing the guide's aide the letters."

"Who took these pictures?" Halmoni's tone carried a sharp edge of suspicion.

"I brought two other cameramen with me. They're still in Changbai. Halmoni, when this is all over you'll have to buy us all lots of tasty food."

"Who's that young girl?" Halmoni wasn't paying attention to his teasing.

Across the screen flashed a close-up image of a small girl, nine or ten years old. Her face was a patchwork of brown and black skin, and her hair was matted and filled with burrs. Ugly scabs and red sores covered her arms and legs. She was a throwaway child. The situation was so bad in North Korea that parents threw away their own children, even abandoning babies. There were thousands of children roaming the train stations at Hyesan and other cities along the river.

"This throwaway girl hadn't eaten for many days, so we clothed her, fed her, and kept her overnight, but she came back again with a pack of kids younger than her begging for food. It's been confirmed that they eat people over there," the director said gravely as he fast-forwarded the tape and found what we'd been waiting for.

Halmoni crept closer and narrowed her eyes. She turned her head first one way and then the other. "That's him! He looks better than I imagined." She at once livened up.

To me, the old man on the screen didn't look okay at all. His gaunt, silver-bearded face was deeply lined, and there was something wrong with him—his facial features didn't work in synchrony. His mouth moved independently of his small, dark eyes.

"When you see this old man, do you feel like he's your son?" asked the director.

"Of course. Am I a cold woman?" Halmoni was annoyed.

"I'm amazed that after all these years you can still recognize him."

"Where would his looks have gone?"

"He remembered practically every detail since you two were separated. He told me he last saw you just before Christmas 1950. He went as far as Haeju."

"That's right. That's where he was captured, in Haeju. The day after his father fled, Yong Woon went off with two of his friends from church. I packed him a small sack of clothes and what food we could spare. When the boys arrived at the Haeju-Sinmak crossroads, an old farmer standing on a rock told everyone to go to Haeju because Sinmak was unsafe. I know because I saw the old farmer. I remember him so clearly. He had on a wide-brimmed straw hat and an A-frame basket on his back. He said if we went to Haeju, there were boats to take us down south to Inchon. If we went to Sinmak, the Reds would capture us. I was so tired, I couldn't think straight. The children and I had been walking in the snow for so many weeks, with barely any food or sleep, planes shooting at us day and night. Duk Hwa saw Yong Woon's friend. He had gotten separated from the other two just before we arrived. Yong Woon had been standing right where we were just moments before. I said, 'Children, we must hurry and catch up with your older brother in Haeju.' But just the mention of Haeju sent my second son, Kun Il, into a feverish rage. He kept screaming, 'Sinmak, Sinmak, I want to go to Sinmak.' I told him he was speaking nonsense. He was only a child. What did he know? He wouldn't listen. He kept screaming 'Sinmak, Sinmak' until he passed out. I didn't know what was causing him so much pain. I tried massaging his arms and legs, but it was no use. He wouldn't wake up. Yong Woon's friend offered to carry Kun Il on his back, but I'd given up. I was so exhausted I just wanted to turn around and go back home. I sent the friend away, asking him to tell Yong Woon to return home when it was safe. So alone, the children and I dragged Kun Il on a broken door to Sinmak. When we got there the village was completely empty except for a few wild dogs. We had our choice of abandoned houses. I picked the cleanest one and cooked us a feast from the rice and *kimchi* I scavenged. Each child got a full bowl of steaming rice, even the baby. Because our bellies weren't used to food, our mouths couldn't swallow it. I had to threaten the children with punishment to eat, and finally they did. Knowing the children had food inside them, I was able to sleep peacefully that night, though I thought the Reds were coming for us. But they never came. I found out months later that the Reds raided Haeju instead. While Yong Woon waited in Haeju, hoping I had changed my mind and we would soon join him, an explosion of gongs and drums woke everyone from their sleep, and they were forced onto a truck. They took my Yong Woon." Halmoni's voice broke on his name.

"No, it didn't happen that way. He walked back to Pyongyang on his own feet," said the director.

Halmoni objected to the correction of her memory. "No, he was caught in Haeju by the Reds. The old farmer was a Red spy."

The director delved into his pocket again and extracted a worn notepad with his own messy handwriting. "These are some notes I took during my interview with Lee Yong Woon-ssi. After he walked back to Pyongyang, he and his friends organized the YMCA and an anticommunist youth league. That was 1951. A year later, in 1952, he was arrested for his activities and received a seventeen-year jail sentence. Since he looked so young, he lied about his age and was sentenced to a youth detention center. He was only imprisoned for a few years due to good behavior, then released. Once released, he spent the next two years wandering around Pyongyang like a homeless gypsy until they drafted him into the army. After he served his time, he got married in 1963 and worked at a factory that made coal mine machinery in Pyongyang. He became the Chosŏn Athletic Association's director of operations. In September 1974, when he had to reregister his family status report, the police discovered his parents' past. The fact that you were rich landowners and Christians classified your son into the lowest group. He was labeled hostile and purged to a labor camp far away in the mountains of Yanggang Province, known as the land of death, where political prisoners are kept. Five years later, in 1979, after his release, he and his entire family were banished from Pyongyang and relocated to Hyesan, where there's no plumbing, no hospitals, no transportation, no food, nothing. Yong Woon-ssi and his wife fought a lot because he had hidden his criminal record from her. He told me she still blames him because the police wouldn't even let her say good-bye to her mother. She begged them to let her leave their younger son with her mother because she knew they wouldn't be able to feed all their children where they were going." The director paused and looked out the window to make a dramatic point. "Your son has had a hard life. He's been able to withstand many difficulties, but now—being older, and also hearing from his mother and having this project fall apart—he drinks quite a lot."

"That's enough. I was led to believe my son would already be here." Halmoni's voice didn't break again, but she sounded as if she was in shock.

"Yes, why wasn't this better coordinated?" my father questioned the guide.

I could see the muscles in the guide's cheeks tighten and release.

"Lee Teacher, that was my doing," the director confessed. "I have two purposes. First, the safety of your family. Second, to make a sixty-minute documentary. It's more effective and dramatic if you three await their arrival. The effect is lost if they have to wait for you. Trust me, the scene will look cold.

We want the viewers to feel with their hearts as they're watching. That will help your cause. So, please, bear a little inconvenience and be patient. All sides are frustrated. Also, I know Lee Yong Woon-ssi has two younger brothers. Lives are on the line here. Why are you, the son-in-law, and the granddaughter here and not them? It's very strange," he said, trespassing into the minefield of my family's affairs.

"Their situation is very complicated," my father replied, shifting in his chair. Then he promptly switched the focus and asked, "How much longer will this take to complete?"

The guide, rubbing his stubbly chin, stepped forward, taking over at this point. Before speaking, he made sure he wasn't being taped. "It could be three or four more days. But with a project such as this, no one can ever control the unexpected happenings," he said in a low, subdued voice.

I felt distracted. My mind wasn't on the mission anymore. It was on the guide's hands. I couldn't get over the way they were so strong and so delicate at the same time. The satiny golden skin was stretched over superbly proportioned bones. How had I missed this during our days together in Dalian? I wondered what those hands felt like, what his touch would feel like on my skin.

"It'd help if one of you came with us to Changbai. It'll give your relatives courage and speed things up," I heard the guide say. Just at that moment I glanced up and caught his glittering eyes for a split second; then he turned away carefully, trying not to be so obvious again. He continued, "Halmoni should be the one to go, but the journey is much too rough for her, so Lee Teacher, can you go?"

The guide's choice threw me. I was certain he had me in mind, but he had changed his selection at the last second. "I'll go," I offered in a clear, big voice. Everyone swiveled their heads around and glared at me as if I'd done something wrong; instantly I felt ashamed. I retained my poise, standing very straight with my hands to my side. "I'm younger, the ride won't bother me," I explained.

"It's too dangerous," my father objected promptly.

That was not what I wanted to hear. I didn't need him to be paternal, protective. All I wanted was for him to back me up. "I've already been there twice," I reminded him and everyone else in the room.

"Just stay here. You're a girl," he said.

Girl. I balked, crossing my legs the way men do, an ankle resting on a knee. "What does that have to do with anything?"

"Listen to me. You'll only get in the way. Let the men handle it."

I was dumbfounded, hurt, livid. My father had never spoken to me like that before—my father, who had drummed into me ever since I was little that I was as good, as fast, as smart as any boy, that I could achieve whatever I wanted to do. I was about to holler a personalized proclamation of emancipation, but I restrained myself. I had my father's honor to protect. Raging daughter equaled father losing face. Here, everyone was bound by this honor code in some damn way or another—women and daughters were especially bound. It was so unfair. I raged at that egomaniac named Confucius, an illegitimate child himself, who had codified hundreds of years ago the proper gender roles and behaviors between men and women. He gave the men all the power, privileges, and benefits.

The director and cameraman used this strained opportunity to politely excuse themselves. The guide lingered behind for just a moment to speak to my father. "At all costs we have to protect the identity of the people helping in this project. You must make certain SBS does not mention any names in their documentary or report anything until this project is complete."

"Absolutely." My father gave his assurance, bowing.

After everyone and my father had left, Halmoni sat Indian-style on the bed observing me. She sensed my uneasiness. As usual, her instincts were right on. My feet were twitching to run after the guide. "What's the matter with you?" Halmoni asked, cocking a brow at me.

"Nothing," I said, making an effort to manufacture a smile. It felt false from the inside but must have looked believable to her, because she stopped questioning me and began to peel an apple with a knife. When the phone rang I was glad to answer it and break the silence. It was the guide. The director wished to view the footage I'd shot on my own video camera sometime in the morning. "Oh, the director wants to see what I've shot with my camera? He wants to see it now? No problem. I'll bring it up right away," I improvised in a loud enough voice so Halmoni could hear that some professional business was being discussed.

"Not now, it's almost midnight. Bring it in the morning," the guide repeated.

"Okay, I'll be there in a moment." I hung up, my part of the conversation finished. Randomly I collected a few video cartridges and shoved them into my pockets.

"Take your father. You're an unmarried woman and they're old men," Halmoni said sternly.

"I'm just going upstairs. I'll be right back," I answered nonchalantly as I rushed out of there. Inside the mirrored elevator, I touched up my lips and checked my hair as I was lifted to the guide's floor.

Before I knocked on the door I stood still for a moment with my eyes closed and one hand on my stomach to calm the roller-coaster feeling inside. I was filled with a crazy confusion and was surprised that I was feeling a little bit afraid. I asked myself what I was really doing there. Had I come out of necessity or curiosity or gratitude or defiance? If I'd had any sense at all, I should have gone back downstairs. But I didn't have any sense. I knocked.

The cameraman let me in and shut the door behind me. My knees went rubbery as I trespassed into the smoky den of men and absorbed their collective stares. I held my breath as I looked over at the guide, sitting cross-legged across the small breakfast table, which had been moved between the twin beds as a makeshift bar. An open bottle of Johnnie Walker whisky and beer cans were placed at the three corners. The director was leaning back in the other bed, his arms crossed behind his head, one leg spiked forward, the other raised and bent at the knee.

"Why are you here?" the guide asked with his familiar deliberate arrogance.

I answered back, equally deliberate and equally arrogant, but my mouth was parched. "If you're going to take anyone to Changbai with you, it should be me."

I held my breath again, not sure how the guide was going to react. His mouth took on a fond quick smile, and he lifted his whisky glass to me in a toast. "In some ways you're very predictable."

I drew a sharp breath. "You know I'm right. I'm younger and quicker and it's my book."

"If you come, it'd be good for my documentary. We can start out by having both grandmother and granddaughter entering together, and later the granddaughter can lead the story. But it's up to your father," said the director, refilling their glasses with whisky, then offering me a soda from the tiny refrigerator.

"I'd like some of that." I pointed to the bottle of whisky. I didn't have a craving for it, didn't like it. It was to prove a point.

The director took off his Coke-bottle glasses slowly and looked curiously at me. Without the glasses, his eyes seemed more froglike. "Would your father mind if you drank?"

I returned his curious stare with a hard glare. I let him and the others know in clear, slow English that I had earned my own bread and keep for over ten years. For over a decade I had fended for myself and had not only remained alive but done well.

I helped myself. I ceremoniously poured a full glass of whisky and carried it back to an available chair. *"Cheers!"* I toasted, and drained it. Instantly, my eyes watered, and I couldn't help but make a face. It felt like I'd swallowed rubbing alcohol. I managed to refrain from coughing.

The men kept their stares fixed on me while they continued to suck on cigarettes. They mumbled a few unmentionables about a shaman woman the director knew who could drink any man under the table when she went into a trance state as General MacArthur.

"You mean MacArthur is still in Korea. He just can't get enough, can he?" said the cameraman, and they all laughed.

I gave an unamused chuckle, but I missed the rest of the exchange. I was impatient for the director and cameraman to be gone. As if reading my mind, the guide had a brief, low, cryptic conversation with the director. The director returned his eyes to me, then threw back his shot with a beer chaser. Quenched, he promptly left the room, followed by his associate.

Suddenly the guide and I were left alone. I was nervous and thrilled and disgusted and amazed. It was an intoxicating combination. I began to imagine all the wild things we could do together. It was impossible to keep from grinning, briefly. I decided to pour myself another drink, just to do something. I got up and walked over to the refrigerator, rejecting the whisky. Inside the refrigerator were cans of Coca-Cola and Sprite, lychee-flavored carbonated drinks, and miniature bottles of Chinese wine. Dynasty and Great Wall were the two choices. I twisted open a bottle of Great Wall. I chose it for the name. It was so sugary it made my lips curl.

"Hae Ri, you're more useful here. Halmoni's very fragile right now, and there's tension between her and your father. You know how to soothe her." The guide looked at me warmly and smiled.

I let out a long sigh. I couldn't argue my point when he looked at me like that.

"Things are already complicated as it is. I have nine other lives to worry about."

"Don't think of it as nine. It's really seven adults plus two kids," I said kiddingly.

"Your thinking is so off, but if it wasn't, it wouldn't be you." He chuckled to himself.

I laughed, too, enjoying the sugary wine now. "I was surprised you agreed to let SBS follow us around."

"The director's a son of a bitch, but I've seen his work before. He's good. We can use him," the guide said, pushing up his sleeves a few inches. He opened a new pack of 88 cigarettes. While he selected a stick, my eyes went to the red scars on his forearms.

"Did you see a doctor about those?" I asked, pointing, almost touching.

The guide looked down at the bite marks. He traced his fingers along the raised skin. "The doctor suggested I should have the scarring surgically removed."

"Will you?"

"I decided against it."

"Why?"

"Because . . . they're a remembrance of you," he said in a thick voice that made the roller coaster in my stomach fly off its track. I wanted him. That was the truth. I knew he sensed my desire, because he was looking at me with a mixture of astonishment and mischief. I could barely stand it as he slipped quietly from where he sat on the bed and walked toward me. My cheeks burned. My heart pounded hard.

He was standing tall before me.

I sat very still. I wanted him to make a move.

The phone cut in. It rang a long trill, and the guide turned away. He didn't pick it up right away. He was trying to decide if he should answer it or not. After a few more rings, he got it. "What?" he said gruffly, and at once changed his tone. "Yes, yes, a moment please." He handed me the receiver.

I silently cursed the phone as I took it.

"What are you still doing there? It's two in the morning. Halmoni's worried sick," my father barked into my burning ear.

I peered down at my chunky wristwatch. It had been two hours since I entered his room.

"Go to your room right now," my father ordered.

I wasn't sleepy. I wanted to stay up a little longer and enjoy the fact that I was drunk, hopefully, wonderfully drunk. But my conscience got to me even through the haze. So, on liquidy legs, I sauntered over to the door, my movements stretched in time by the alcohol. When I groped for the doorknob, two hands pinned me to the wall. Before I could react or even utter a syllable, the guide's powerful body smashed against mine, and he roughly kissed me on the mouth. It was a hot and scratchy kiss, and he tasted like cigarettes and whisky.

As he deepened the kiss, I could feel myself being carried away in a flood of clumsy, desperate passion. All at once the feeling of aloneness I had pushed away returned, and I was reminded of Steven.

What was I doing?

My body went rigid. I suddenly felt Steven's presence so strongly, it was as if it were his lips, his hands, his body touching me. He was too close. The guide was too close. With all my might I pushed them both away.

The guide sharply caught my wrist, taking hold of me, and he slowly tightened his fingers and bent his head to kiss me again. I wrenched away from him and scrambled backward out the door.

I made my way along the corridor, staggering badly from the intensity of the contact and the liquor. When I entered my darkened room I nearly tripped over Halmoni's stockinged feet. She was sitting at the foot of her bed, waiting for me in the dark. "Do you know what time it is?" she shrieked, flicking on the light. "You've been drinking." Her words pounced on me.

"Shh, it's okay." I tried desperately not to slur my words, but even to my own ears I sounded drunk. I was drunk, but in a bad way now, having not eaten anything since lunch. I had to clasp the wall to steady myself in the swaying room. It didn't help, and I became nauseous. I ran to the bathroom and slumped over the toilet, hugging it. When nothing else heaved up but air, I crawled to the tub on my feeble hands and knees. Leaning over the side, I turned on the tap. The water cooled my blood and I was able to pull myself up by gripping the sink tightly.

Exhausted, I swam by Halmoni to bed. When I shut my eyes the room tumbled and whirled again. I dug my nails deep into the mattress, trying to hold on. My ears nearly exploded when there was a loud pounding on the door.

My father came bursting in.

"She's drunk!" Halmoni told him.

My father's lower lip hung low as he stared me down in total shocked disgust. "You drank?" he roared, pointing an accusatory finger at me as though I had committed some horrible crime.

How dare he judge me?

Outraged, I rocketed into a sitting position. I was about to shout back at him, my mouth opening to form the words, but then I was forced to lean against the headboard because the sudden movement made me almost retch again.

"You're going home," my father said angrily with a wave of his hand.

Just when I thought it couldn't get any more humiliating, I saw the guide's blurry face appear from behind my father. He was standing not five feet away. I strained to level my shoulders and hold my head in the center, desperate to maintain an air of dignity against impossible odds. My shoulders wouldn't stay level.

I wanted him and the others to disappear, but they began to multiply and spin around me.

XVI

Under half-closed lids, my eyes swiveled weakly. I was at the mercy of a tremendous headache, the worst headache I could ever remember having. Even the feel of the air-conditioning on my skin hurt. When I tried to cover myself with the tangled sheet, Halmoni drew it away, leaving me exposed. She wanted me up. She was already bathed and dressed. I struggled up to one elbow, head hanging limply, then very slowly eased my feet out of bed. It took me some time to find the floor. I called on every last bit of strength I had to put on my clothes and drag myself out of the room. I had to show everyone I could handle my alcohol.

Halmoni and I joined my father at a quiet corner table in the restaurant. The guide, director, and cameraman were absent, probably still in bed sleeping off the alcohol. When the food arrived, I struggled for a minute. Halmoni fixed me a plate of toast and phlegmy eggs anyway. She leered at me as she sank her dentures into a slice of buttered toast. I shuddered at the noise of her top teeth scraping against the bottoms as she ate.

Biting down on my lower lip, I turned away from Halmoni. I was in no condition or mood to force unwanted food into my dry mouth and chew just to placate her. What I needed was a strong antidote for a dragon-size hangover. I settled for jasmine-scented herb tea. The sweet-bitter taste took away the acrid taste still in my mouth.

"I don't trust people who drink so much," Halmoni declared scornfully.

"Then you must not trust a lot of good people," my father said back.

"Don't you care that that person got your daughter drunk? Because of him she started drinking."

"That wasn't the guide's fault. Hae Ri should have known better."

They both turned their attention like a searchlight on me. If it hadn't hurt so much to wrinkle my forehead, I would have scowled back at them.

"He's not even married," added Halmoni.

"So what?" my father said evenly.

My throat locked and my mouth gaped open. It struck me how ridiculous it was that it was okay for the guide at his age to be single but I was judged harshly. A surge of despairing resentment tore through me. I knew that showed.

"What we should be discussing is the fact that there is no affection in your son's marriage. Hak Churl's marriage is also in trouble. Since he's been in the hospital, his wife hasn't visited him once, not even on his birthday. She and their son are living with her parents. That's why we didn't know about them. Ii-sh. I don't understand what's going on in their family. All three marriages have fallen apart. We might have to reevaluate our original plan to bring everyone out," my father finished, then turned to me. "What do you think?"

I touched my mouth, wanted to laugh. He was asking me my opinion. I was allowed to decide the fate of nine other lives but not allowed to have a drink without my daddy's permission. Staring at a spot on the table, I tried to push aside the resentment and concentrate. It took me a while to get my head working and carefully sift through what little information I knew about the nine people. As I arranged my thoughts, an image of a woman encased in a smoggy yellowish red aura emerged. I couldn't get a clear look at her lean face, but I did see dark fingerprints on her cheeks, and realized it was blood. I tried to blink the grisly vision away, but it persisted. I blinked two or three more times to make sure that what I was seeing wasn't really there. That only set off the violent thumping in my head again. "She shouldn't come, then." My mouth was moving before I knew what I was saying.

"What?" my father asked.

"Leave Hak Churl's wife, but it's up to Hak Churl what he wants to do about his son." I brought the words out very, very carefully, as if each were capable of slicing my tongue.

The image of the bloody-faced woman faded, then disappeared altogether.

"What about your aunt?" he asked.

What about her? I thought. "She has to come. Her children won't leave without their mother," I said with conviction, thinking of my mother.

Finished with breakfast, we headed back to our room and called the guide, who was still asleep, as I had thought. My father asked him to come and speak with us. I wanted to duck into the bathroom. I had made a fool out of myself on top of everything else.

After some twenty nerve-racking minutes, the guide showed up. He walked in slowly, as though he had all the time and confidence in the world. He looked like hell. His face was bloated, and underneath his tan was a sick pallor.

The guide sat in the chair farthest away from Halmoni. He could see from her narrowed eyes and tight mouth that she meant him harm. He didn't glance in my direction once as I stood rigidly poised next to the lamp, my head held a bit higher. I was determined not to look as though I had anything to be ashamed of.

"We're willing to reconsider who should come," my father began, and the guide listened quietly. He appeared to be thinking everything over seriously. I tried to read him, tried to figure the flow of his thoughts, but his eyes gave nothing away. When my father was through speaking, the guide scratched his head, then nodded thoughtfully.

"My goal is to bring everyone out, but at this time I can't predict the number. If Ae Ran's mother does decide to stay behind, she could stall her older sister, giving her children time to get away. Then again, if she stays, there's a chance that Mun Churl won't come, either. He's extremely close to his mother. As for Hak Churl's wife, Ae Ran will let her know the plans—"

"Oh no, you mustn't tell her. She might turn them in." Halmoni's eyes widened.

"Ae Ran will let Hak Churl's wife know at the last minute, just before they cross. But like I said, it's my goal to bring them all."

The guide rose to his feet, patting his chest as if looking for a pass. He very deliberately glanced around the room, swiveling his head just so that he could see me without getting caught. All at once he gave me a quick wink. I almost fell against the lamp.

As I watched him go, a fresh wave of loneliness washed over me, and I felt that desperate craving again. I thought I must be completely derranged to still have these feelings. He was an unpredictable, unknown, arrogant, dangerous, and suffering man. I told myself to forget about him. I was a level-headed person, despite a lot of recent evidence to the contrary.

The following Sunday morning, after the guide and the director had left for the airport, Halmoni came unglued because my father and I wouldn't take her to church. It wasn't safe. We tried to reason with her. The guide had warned us about the Chosŏn churches in China. They were heavily censored by North Korean spies because it was the most obvious place to monitor those who were a threat to the communist system. Christianity went against their beliefs. In their society there was room for only one god, and it was their Great Leader, Kim Il Sung.

"That person has got both your minds so twisted, you can't even see what he's trying to do. He's pumping us with fear so that we'll be terrified of everyone and obey only him. It's his plan to keep us in the dark and isolated while he organizes with the Reds to kidnap us to North Korea. Why do you think that other man with the camera follows us everywhere, recording everything we do?"

"That's ridiculous," my father scoffed. The farther out Halmoni's imagination soared, the more agitated he became. He didn't know how to handle her fears, and their arguments kept escalating.

"We need someone to watch our backs without those men knowing," she urged.

"You don't know what you're saying."

"Stop being a fool!" Halmoni shot back, glowering at him. "This is all a setup. The Reds could be coming for us tonight. It doesn't matter if they get me. I've already lived my life. We need to protect Hae Ri. Act quickly."

"There's no talking to her!" my father erupted, and then, turning on his heel, he stepped crisply out the door.

For the rest of the day, I kept them apart again. I was very aware of how terrified Halmoni was. It was plainly visible in her eyes. Reaching out to her, I placed both my hands on her tense wrist, saying with the pressure of my fingertips, Everything is going to be all right. You have to trust me.

She didn't respond. She looked around for several seconds, then groaned. "*Omona*, I fear we will never leave this place. Hae Ri, look at what's happening here and act accordingly." She took my elbow, a physical plea. "We need to contact a reverend. He is the only person we can trust here, not those people." Her hand suddenly became a vise, and her nails dug into my arm. I pulled, but she snatched me back. "You need a bodyguard!" she half growled, half shrieked.

Seeing that Halmoni was about to lose it again, I finally told her what she wanted to hear to calm her escalating panic. Halmoni heaved a long sigh of relief as I dialed my father's room to fill him in on the deception.

"Dad, Halmoni wants us to find a Chosŏn church and ask the reverend to assign us a bodyguard during the time we're here. We need to pretend we'll do it." I spoke only in English.

"What?" he snapped, still holding on to his anger.

"It's just pretend. To make it appear like we are, we need to leave the hotel later today for a few hours."

"We can't reveal this mission to a reverend. Is she crazy?"

"Dad, do you know what the word *pretend* means?"

He didn't respond immediately.

It dawned on me suddenly that he wasn't fluent in English. All my life I had taken it for granted that he understood everything I said. I felt both surprised and yet not surprised; it explained a lot. I took a long, deep breath to try to keep my voice even, but it was getting harder to act normal because of the underlying hostility I felt toward him. I bit down hard and resumed speaking in a slower, remedial manner. "Listen carefully, Dad. *Pretend* means 'not real, fake, make-believe.' Halmoni wants us to go get help. But we're not really going to do it. Understand? It'll make her feel better. So, when you see her later, just play along. Okay?"

What I was suggesting finally got through to him. "No, that's not right. The guide and the director have helped us out so much. Instead of accusing them of being spies, we should be doing all that we can to assist them. That's why I've decided to join them and go to Changbai as requested of me. I leave tomorrow." He sneaked the news in at the very end.

Oddly, I took it well. I wasn't upset. In fact, I wanted him to go, to liberate myself from him. "Okay, then, let me handle this my way, since I'll be the one left behind with her. All right?"

"If you want to lie, go ahead, but I won't."

"Fine." I hung up, smiling.

Halmoni was watching me. "Was he mad?"

Dropping my eyes, I answered in bright monosyllables. I knew I couldn't tell her the truth about my father leaving us and joining the guide and the others in Changbai. It would only upset her more. I would make up whatever needed to be made up to help her keep what remained of her sanity. She had been losing it little by little ever since we arrived in Shenyang.

"Halmoni," I said, grabbing her attention away from the phone, "if you'd like to go back to Seoul tomorrow, we'll take you to the airport, but Father and I will have to stay here. There's only one seat on the plane. It's a very busy time." I left the decision up to her, knowing what her answer would be.

"Oh no, I have to stay with you. I can't let you out of my sight." Halmoni's voice was passionate, almost normal.

I kissed her cheek softly. "We shouldn't give up the seat. Should we let Father go first, and you and I can wait until we can fly out together? It'll be easier to get two seats than three," I said innocently. To my ears it sounded believable.

"What about that person with the camera?"

My mind sped. The cameraman was being sent back to Seoul with the video footage shot at the river. It was dangerous to hold on to the tapes. I couldn't tell Halmoni that or she'd catch my lie. "He has another job in Beijing. He's already left."

Thinking he was gone, Halmoni sighed inwardly, and she was finally able to rest. But the next evening, as the sun vanished and the darkness settled, the room swelled with the emotional pitch of Halmoni's panicky voice.

"The Reds have captured your daddy! Why else didn't he come by last night or this morning to say good-bye? He hasn't even called us once today. It's not like him. Your daddy's a very responsible man. He should have called us by now. Think. Can't you see they're closing in on us? Think of your mother. Think of her!" Halmoni shrilled, as if she were venting decades of fury.

In my most soothing voice, I reminded her of the videotape she had seen of her son as proof that the guide was on our side.

"He could have easily crossed over to North Korea and taped your big uncle there, making us think it was done in China. The Reds are paying that person to do this. That's why he hasn't asked for any payment for himself. It's because he doesn't need it. You know what he'll earn if he turns us in? He won't receive a lot for me. I'm too old. He'll get a lot for you, because you're pretty and young."

"I thought you said I was old." I tried to make her laugh, but she wasn't hearing me.

"The Reds like kidnapping important people. They took Kim Dae Jung. They dragged him into the ocean and then pulled him onto a boat, but a KCIA helicopter thought something was suspicious, so they followed the boat. Finally, the Reds dumped him near his home. They also took a famous actress. They tricked her into thinking she was going to star in a movie in Hong Kong. Once in Hong Kong, the Reds gagged her and carted her off. Later they kidnapped her husband, who was a senior movie director, because Kim Il Sung's son wanted to make movies. Hae Ri, you're better than that actress. All she can do is act. You can write. Every minute we stay here, the Reds get closer. We need to sneak out. You need to act quickly!" Her expression grew taut.

"China isn't like North Korea. People can't just come into our hotel and take us. We're Americans."

"Stop being an idiot! Do you think you'll have time to show them your American passport when they're gagging your mouth with tape and covering your head with a sack? America has no power over North Korea. The only person that can help us right now, right here, is a reverend," Halmoni kept insisting. She was so blinded by her faith, she thought if a person was ordained, he was instantly washed of all evil.

"Just because a person's a reverend doesn't mean we can trust him. The reverend could be a Red spy."

"Wicked girl." Halmoni shrank back, and her savage eyes warned me not to speak again. "I want to leave this wretched place. You don't know how brutal the Reds can be." She made her voice quiet, but so lashing that I blanched. I knew that Halmoni said the things she said and thought the things she thought because she had seen North Korea from the inside. She was the only one. The rest of us only saw it from a distance. The reason she had survived this long and achieved the things she had, things that were beyond the reach of normal men and women, was her sharp instincts. But this time her instincts were wrong.

"That's why we're doing all this, Halmoni. To save your son's family from the Reds."

"Leave them there. That's their life, their fate, but you don't belong there. You'll die. I can't just think about my son anymore. I have to worry about you and your mother as well. She'll die if she loses you. I know."

The phone rang. Saved. A wave of thankfulness so intense rushed through me, it weakened my knees. "That's probably Father calling," I said joyfully, picking it up. On the other end of the line I heard breathing, then only the dial tone remained. This happened four more times. The phone would jingle, and then the crank caller would abruptly hang up.

"See! They're coming!" Halmoni shrieked. "I refuse to stay here a moment longer." She started looking around for her shoes.

"Halmoni, stay here." I grabbed her arm, but she yanked it away.

"Call for protection!" A tremor passed over her pained face. She was literally shaking and began to pant, her chest heaving rapidly. Halmoni was having a hard time breathing. "If you're not smart enough to save yourself," she wheezed, "I'm going to find someone who will. I'm going to call Choi Soon Man in Yanji." She hunted around for her shoes. Finding them, she squatted down to put them on. When she tried to raise herself from the floor, her veined hands clawed the air as if reaching for some invisible hold.

I moved away from her, hiding my hands behind my back, but she managed to heft herself up, staggering for an instant. She stared bewildered around the room for a moment, suddenly unsure where she was. Then she remembered her purpose and took a step toward the door. I jumped in front of her and blocked her path in the narrow hallway, holding the wall on one side and the bathroom doorknob on the other. She tried to dodge past me. I had to think of something fast. If she talked to anyone, they'd certainly call the police.

"Okay, Halmoni, I'll find a reverend. But it's too dark now. Tomorrow, I'll go to the Chosŏn district and find a church. I'll ask the reverend to help us."

"You will?" She slanted her eyes at me.

"Yes, I'll go tomorrow." I nodded, stalling for time.

Halmoni heaved a sigh of relief. "Good . . . good . . . speak only to the reverend. If he can't watch after us, ask him to assign someone while we're stuck here in China. Someone with a car in case we need to get away quickly."

"Yes, I'll do that," I assured her.

The next morning, as Halmoni watched television, I secretly unplugged the phone on the nightstand and turned down the ringer in the bathroom before going on my pretend errand. When I closed the door behind me a trollish maid was dusting just on the other side of it. Her eyes combed me with interest as though she'd caught me coming out of someone else's room. I nodded blandly as I passed her by and moved on.

I ventured only as far as the lobby café and slid into an out-of-the-way corner table. Acting like a tourist plotting her day, I spread out a guide to the city taken from the hotel desk. I tried to study the colorful map, reading in *pinyin* the names of buildings and streets, but all my thoughts returned to Halmoni. I couldn't believe how unmanageable she had become, how unmanageable everything had become. I feared Halmoni more than the Reds. I wondered how I was going to get through the next several days with her. My brain clicked like an adding machine, trying to figure out the number of days. I knew how long it would take my father to fly to Yanji—three, maybe four hours. Then the drive from Yanji to Changbai—fifteen hours if road conditions were bad. It'd be dark by the time they got there, so they'd have to wait till the morning—five, maybe eight hours. Make contact at the river to arrange for the crossing—two to twenty-four hours. Once everyone was across, they'd have to calm down, change clothes, eat something—one to three hours. Drive or take the train back to Shenyang—fifteen to twenty-five hours. The total maximum hours were sixty-nine. That was three full days and seven hours away.

You can do it. I cheered myself on to boost my morale.

I lingered downstairs for about two hours. I was afraid if I stayed away any longer, Halmoni might wander around the hotel and expose our plans. Just as I reentered the room, the bathroom phone shrilled thinly. It made me jump, but Halmoni didn't hear it. She was napping. On the third ring, I shut myself inside, closing the door soundlessly, making sure it was locked.

"Who's this?" I whispered threateningly.

"It's me," the guide responded in English.

My heart twisted. "Are they out?"

"Not yet."

"When?"

"Your aunt's older sister hasn't left their house yet, so we're all still in Yanji. It'll be at least four or five more days."

"What!" A shudder rushed through me. I had set my heart on three days and seven hours. That was it. That was all I could handle. Suddenly I wanted my real life back, the life I'd lived before. I was starved for my books, my friends, my apartment, my Starbucks coffee. I asked myself why I had volunteered. Why hadn't my mother come? It was her brother. Why hadn't my sister come? She was older by two years. Why hadn't my brother? It would have been much easier for him, being male. No one would have hassled him because he was twenty-eight and unmarried. Halmoni's two other sons should have come!

Because, Hae Ri, it was your book. I could hear the guide's voice inside my head. I heard my father tell me it never should have been written, and the words were like bullets exploding. I leaned my back against the door, one hand cradling my neck. My fragile crust of restraint was about to crack. It took all my willpower not to wilt to the floor, but I could feel myself losing the fight. "No way. That's too long. I can't keep Halmoni here that long."

"You have to."

"I can't."

"You have no choice. If you must, take Halmoni sightseeing. Get her to exercise. Make her laugh," he said firmly.

"What are you doing in there?" I heard Halmoni's hoarse voice through the door.

I rushed off the phone. At least four or five more days. I started to run the numbers in my head again. There were twenty-four hours in a single day. Sixty minutes in an hour. One thousand four hundred and forty minutes in a day. Sixty seconds in a minute. How many seconds in a day? I couldn't add up that many numbers.

I told myself that no matter how hard it was for me, it was much harder for Halmoni. If it took every last ounce of courage I possessed, I had to stay strong and composed for her until the very end.

XVII

When the sunlight flashed through the window, the first thing I did was think of ways to pass the day. Whatever the guide's motive, I decided to follow his advice and take Halmoni sightseeing. The fresh air and exercise might raise her spirits, but more important, it would distract her mind.

Halmoni gave me an intense, pleading look. When she spoke, it was in a little-girl voice: "I don't want to go out."

A survival instinct kept me focused on not accepting no for an answer. It took forty-five minutes of cajoling and sweet-talking, and in the end she gave in, barely.

I took Halmoni's elbow and propelled her through the hotel doors. The heat was just starting to intensify. It was going to be another hot, roasting day. On the ground, our two long, thin shadows stretched out ahead of us. They were more eager than Halmoni. She dragged back, vocalizing her fear, but I locked my arm around her waist and urged her into a taxi.

The taxi dropped us off at a busy intersection in the city's center next to Zhongshan Square. Unlike Sun Yat-sen Square in Dalian, this one had a giant Mao Zedong statue. The statue was by far the most distinctive landmark that I'd seen in the city. The monolithic Mao, wrapped in an overcoat, stood straight and aloft with his hand raised, surrounded by ecstatic PLA soldiers, peasants, students, and miners thrusting up the Little Red Book of Mao's selected quotations and stomping on a traditional Chinese lion. To me, the balding Mao didn't look like a god or Superman—he looked like a regular man directing the congested traffic with his raised arm, and everyone in the merry band below him was reaching for a Coca-Cola ad.

We followed Mao's extended arm southward toward an outdoor market. Halmoni wanted to tour the rows of sweets and fruits and dough sticks sizzling in blackened woks filled with hot oil. She stopped at a workhorse bicycle cart piled high with fruit. It was parked in front of a butcher's stall with whole pigs and skinned dogs hanging by their necks on hooks, the length of their bodies split open to show off the layers of meat. The noise of fat, iridescent flies buzzing around was overwhelming. As I waved them frantically away from my head, Halmoni went to work poking and probing fuzzy golden pink peaches. She ignored pleas from the vendor with only three front teeth to stop her inspection. Only when she had made her choices did she stop. She pointed them out to the vendor, saying some words in Mandarin. I was impressed. The language was coming back to her from the distant past, and she was able to haggle brilliantly. For less than one dollar we greedily carried away ten large juicy peaches, four pounds of lychees, and a bag of sugar cakes made from glutinous rice.

Halmoni seemed completely herself now, her mind clear and her fear tamed, but she wasn't able to travel the same distance as she had a few days earlier. Her pace had slowed down considerably. She was sweating, and her bangs were plastered to her forehead by the time we reached the end of the row of fruits. I kept pressing her to move forward into an alleyway with one-room shops that doubled as homes. I wanted to tire Halmoni out completely so that she wouldn't have the energy to work herself into a frenzy again.

Seeing an open hair salon, I hooked her by the elbow and steered her inside. I sat Halmoni down at the only workstation. In front of her was a wall-to-wall, ceiling-high mirror with faded plastic ivy serving as a border. The mirror was cracked and taped in three places, fracturing Halmoni's face. Next to the workstation, there was a small private room with a massage table. Tacked above it on the ceiling was a huge black-and-white Calvin Klein poster ad with a beautiful naked woman leaning into the muscular chest of a beautiful man wearing only tight jeans.

Two women worked in the salon. The younger of the two was a tall, dark woman with a loose, jowly face and no makeup. The other woman was older, prettier, and made up. She reminded me of a Chinese Dolly Parton, with cascading curly hair, a rhinestone-studded denim miniskirt outfit, pink cowboy boots, even false eyelashes, but she was flat-chested. It seemed like it was Dolly's job to stand in the doorway to lure the clientele off the street with her sassiness and musical laugh.

In sign language, I pointed at Halmoni's hair, then at Dolly's hair. A perm would eat up at least a few hours. Understanding, the women nodded and rolled Halmoni to the pink sink. I stepped back to let them do their work, but when I saw that they were about to comb black dye into Halmoni's silver hair, I immediately jumped in and stopped them. The silver strands were Halmoni's crowning glory. She had earned each one, and no one was going to color them.

Disappointed, the two women moved on to preparing the pink perming solution. It came in a glass bottle with a rusty cap and peeling label that had a hand-sketched profile of an Asian man with a big Afro. And the Crayola-colored rollers that were brought out were relics. They were the same ones my mother used back in the seventies to give me bad home perm jobs. I was beginning to have serious doubts about letting Dolly and her girlfriend tamper with Halmoni's beauty, but there was nothing else for us to do, so I let them continue, quietly hoping for the best. Halmoni, on the other hand, made no effort to hide her displeasure. She complained that the rollers weren't rolled tight enough, that they needed to be secured with bobby pins, to squirt more fixer on the sides. I'd never seen her act this way. She had never cared about her appearance before.

When everything was set and blow-dried, Halmoni had a tight Afro, just like on the label, and she reeked strongly of fixer. I smiled, pointing at my grinning mouth, then tipped the women generously, not for a job well done but for their lively company. I dreaded leaving them and their open salon and returning to our upholstered cage, where the minutes and air pressed down on me. But we had to get back. I was becoming paranoid. A crowd of people swirled around the salon, gaping in from the street to see the foreigner get her hair permed. They gawked and pointed at us long after we had left the salon and passed them by.

Halmoni was exhausted by the time we made it to our hotel. Her pale face drooped with fatigue. I could see that her eyes were about to close on her in spite of herself, and I helped her to bed. I drew the heavy wine-colored drapes across the window and sat in the armchair listening to the quiet. Everything was quiet. Too quiet. I couldn't hear even the sound of Halmoni's breathing. To my astonishment, she didn't make a peep or move at all. A few times I had to tiptoe up close to her and wait for her chest to move up and down slightly. When I was certain she was still with me, I returned to my post and kept vigil. I tried not to fall victim to gloomy thoughts and made myself think positively to rev my spirits, because I was the guardian of Halmoni's life.

Around four in the afternoon she awoke on her own, and I turned on the television. Television had the power to distract Halmoni for stretches of time.

She would crack up at the over-the-top slapstick humor on the Korean channel. It was amazing she could still laugh after everything she had been through, but the diversion lost its power as the sun went down. I couldn't prevent the orange-and-gold stripes across the sky from fading any more than I could prevent Halmoni's terror from resurfacing. Frantically, I wove more stories as the night absorbed us and the last bit of sunlight was squeezed from the sky. I made up elaborate tales about undercover FBI and KCIA agents and reverends disguised as street sweepers and hotel maids watching after us. Sometimes I'd maneuver a story so outrageously far to stay ahead of the disaster, I couldn't keep them all straight in my head and Halmoni would catch me. I'd have to scramble to recover with another tale, which only made matters worse. She'd become hysterical and her face would shrink in horror.

"Something terrible has happened to your daddy. We haven't heard from him since he left us here. That's not like him. He's very dependable. You're a bad daughter. You aren't even concerned. You should be calling the police. When did you turn so stupid? Why are we just sitting here? Are you retarded? I'm not going to listen to your lies anymore. You can stay here if you want, but I'm leaving this awful place. Give me back my passport and plane ticket." She thrust out her shaking hand.

I looked at her with shock. The sting of desertion was sharp. Halmoni was willing to leave me now. I tried to tell myself not to take it personally, that she didn't mean it, that she was panicking. Besides, it was best not to argue with her—you never knew who was listening.

I looked around the room for something, anything, to offer her. I gave her a cold soda. Halmoni's rejection rushed out so fast, a string of spittle dangled out of her mouth. "I don't need a drink! Give me my passport and ticket! Give them to me!" She grabbed my wrist with such unsettling strength, I winced.

I didn't know what to do. It felt as though I was holding my own grandmother prisoner. I really felt like Brutus, and it was tearing me apart. What should I do? I tried to figure something out while Halmoni continued to throw words at me. "I can't believe you're such a retarded girl. And so is your daddy. He just flew off all on his own and left us here unprotected. He only thinks about himself. I warned your mother about marrying him. I should have kept a closer eye on her, but Duk Hwa always had a mind of her own. She did what she wanted. While I was treating people, trying to make a living for us, she was meeting him behind my back. He used to hang around outside our church and her university in his army uniform like a lovesick fool just to see her. When I found out about him, I said no. His mother was a Buddhist. I didn't go to jail, leave our home in Pyongyang, and risk our lives so she could marry a Buddhist. But your mother was determined. All on her own she decided to bring him to the house. Young people back then didn't do such things. She has guts, that one. The moment I stepped into the house and saw him, I knew he would be trouble. He is too handsome, like your grandfather. It's a burden marrying a man who's too handsome."

"But you loved Grandfather. You had a wonderful marriage." I wanted to keep her busy talking about him. She told the whole story to me again.

Halmoni's marriage to my grandfather had been arranged late by a match-maker. She was twenty-two and he was nineteen. Her father, having grown up in a small family with only an older sister, enjoyed the company of his chil-dren, especially his three daughters. He admired their strength and curiosity and spoiled them even though girls belonged to someone else's family after they married. Halmoni had been trained and disciplined and prepared for her future wifely duties, and she never expected to find love. It wasn't something a woman hoped for. To her surprise, her baby-faced husband turned out to be gentle and open-minded, and he encouraged her to use her sharp mind. When he moved his family to China, he didn't confine her to the house. He supported her desire to go into the sesame oil business, then to become an opium madam and a popular restaurateur. Halmoni made so much money that her husband, who had blossomed into a handsome man, was able to live the life of the gentry. As a man of the upper class, he spent most of his time at expensive teahouses in the company of beautiful *kisaengs*, professional female entertainers. Filled with jealous rage, Halmoni stormed after him one day inside a teahouse and chased him home.

"If you love a man too much, it only brings endless agony and lonely nights. A smart woman marries a man who loves her a little more."

"No, it should be equal."

"Is anything ever truly equal? In a marriage, love fades in and out. That's life. So there has to be more than love. It's not enough. I know you loved Steven, but he wasn't right for you," she said, knowing though I had kept the breakup a secret. "That's why you struggled about marrying him. Isn't that so?"

I couldn't answer her.

"I know you've gone through a lot recently, but you still brought me to China. Deep inside, I can feel you. When you hurt, I hurt. You don't know how much I've cried. You still think about him, don't you?" There were tears in the folds of skin around her lashless eyes.

"I'm okay. Really." I forced myself to smile.

Halmoni's eyes held mine, willing the truth out of me. I, on the other hand, wanted to keep that liquid time with Steven far behind me, years behind me. I managed to look away before my eyes betrayed me.

"I pray that you will forget him quickly and that your heart will heal quickly. I pray all the time that you'll meet someone outstanding in the world. Someone who won't make you cry. I'm grateful to God. He protected you from making a mistake and ruining your life, because you're too valuable to him. That's why if I must choose between your life and my son's, I'd save yours. I'd save yours over Ae Ran's and Mi Ran's. I'd save yours over all of theirs and mine. You don't have to do this. Save yourself."

"Don't say that." My hands shot up to my ears, because my heart wouldn't accept such a thing.

"I don't know any of them, but you I know. That's their fate." Her eyes begged my understanding.

"No one deserves that. And fate isn't set in stone. We can change it."

"Who do you think you are? God?" she hissed. "I have wanted to see my son for so long. I still dream about him all the time, but I will not trade your life for his. The Reds can take me, kill me. I've lived my life. They won't leave you alone. They'll break your mind and rape your body until you're under their control."

Halmoni's dark premonition made my stomach turn and contract. I refused to listen anymore; she was starting to get to me. I tried to manufacture fantasies to distract myself. Usually I was very good at this. All I had to do was stare at a blank space on the wall and I'd escape into a fantasy to preserve my mind. As Halmoni raged on and on, I lost my ability to concentrate and couldn't block out her shouts. "You think if they catch you they'll just kill you quickly? No! They'll drag you all over town by your nostrils like a cow, then shoot you or set you on fire or both. That guide doesn't know this. None of you do. I've lived there and have been in their jail before. It's a very frightening, dark place. All you young people know is secondhand rumors picked up from Chosŏn people!"

"Please, Halmoni, don't do this," I murmured, staring down at the watch strapped to my arm. The hands seemed like they were splinters in time.

"Because you drank with that man, you think he's your friend. He's too old for you, and he's got a grown child." She paused to study the effect of this news.

I tried to relax my facial muscles, control any visible signs of surprise, and keep my voice matter-of-fact. "Now you're making things up."

"Hasn't he told you?" she snickered, leaning far forward toward me. "I heard the director and cameraman talking about his son. That man's using you. I've seen the way he talks down to you like you're his whore or something. I don't like it. When he speaks to you he should be more proper, distant. Ah, this is so frustrating. I thought you were smarter than this. When did you become so stupid? A woman has to use her head if she's to survive. . . ."

Halmoni went on and on. I scarcely knew what she was saying anymore. She was unreachable, untouchable. The woman who was always a pillar of strength and assurance to me was about to snap, and I was fumbling around trying to adjust.

"Stupid girl!" she flared at me one last time before succumbing to fatigue again. She had worn herself out finally, and sank into bed. As she slept, it seemed as if the weight of her skin was pulling her right into the white pillowcase. But her sleep was troubled and feverish. I found myself straining with her. I wasn't certain anymore that I was doing the right thing.

Halmoni would no longer leave the room. When I pressed her, almost in desperation, she refused, even for food. We had to order all our meals in, and soon half of the room was littered with a collection of plates coagulated with grease because Halmoni wouldn't allow housekeeping to come in and clear the food. She was storing my uneaten portions. I just couldn't eat. My growing paranoia about the Reds had taken all the pleasure out of it. Every time the food cart was rolled in, I looked at it like someone who expected to be poisoned. I raked through the rice, removed suspect slivers of meat, rejected any or all odd formations of vegetables.

Now there was nothing else to look forward to, nowhere to go. It was draining doing absolutely nothing, just idly watching television all day and taking a lot of nervous naps. I tried to convince myself to do sit-ups or write to release the anxiety, but I wasn't motivated. Over time there was no distinction between today, yesterday, and tomorrow. The days were all so long, so much longer than I ever imagined, and I became disoriented. I no longer knew the number of days since our arrival in China, the number of days since the guide left, since my father left. It was somewhere between a week and a lifetime. I tried to recount the days, get them straight in my head, but had to stop counting, because it really didn't matter. All that mattered was that another day was almost over and I let myself drift off to sleep. When I woke up from a nightmare, the same one I had after coming back from Dalian, Halmoni was looming over me, leering at me threateningly. Unprepared, I shrieked and shot sideways away from her like a rubber band.

"I'm watching you," she whispered darkly. Her small gray eyes grew round and large, filling up the whole room from one end to the next. A demented light was behind them.

I turned over on my stomach and sank my face deeper into the pillow, unable to take the weight of her eyes. I would have given anything for this all to be over at the touch of a button. My nerves were completely shot.

"I would rather see you dead than the Reds capture you. They'll strap you to a bed, then shove a spout down your throat and pump you with water until it comes out of your nose. They'll rip off all your clothes and whip you with a leather strap and twist your fingers with pine tree sticks. The pain's so horrible, you'll beg them to kill you. They won't. They'll beat and rape you so badly, your whole body will swell and the skin will peel back. They won't stop until they've broken your mind and you're completely under their spell. You will never find yourself again. You will become one of them. Why won't you listen to me? You don't know how sneaky and brutal they can be. I'm telling you the truth. They kidnapped Kim Dae Jung. They dragged him into the sea and pulled him onto a boat." Halmoni was repeating herself, having forgotten she had already used the threat of doom and torture to frighten me.

"I'm not Kim Dae Jung," I whined. Kim Dae Jung was a fiery, outspoken opposition politician. He was South Korea's Nelson Mandela, who ceaselessly struggled for the promotion of democracy and human rights. In 1971, he'd nearly toppled President Park Chung Hee's military rule when he ran against him in the national election. Kim Dae Jung was a man of courage and belief, a spellbinding orator, a leader. I was just Helie Lee.

"They're coming to get you tonight. They're just waiting for us to fall asleep." Halmoni's voice rumbled with manic terror now, and her eyes darted back and forth uncontrollably, up and down from each corner of the ceiling to the walls to the floor to the door.

Fear for both of us swept through my body, and thoughts in two languages spun around endlessly inside my head. What's taking the guide and my father so long? Why haven't they called? Something must have gone wrong. Everyone could be dead, for all I knew. I felt like I wasn't going to be able to hold it together much longer.

"Give me my ticket and passport! Give them to me!" Halmoni's panic made her as strong as Hercules, and she yanked me out of bed. I was standing up now.

"Halmoni, please stop it already. We're safe here." I barely managed to get the lie out.

"I said give them to me!" She slapped me hard across the face. My head snapped sideways, knocking me off balance, but I didn't make a sound as the blow cracked my cheek. I just stared at her in the shock of the moment, holding my cheek as she blindly spat more venom and crass, insufferable insults at me, spraying my face with her hot, stale spittle that smelled faintly of garlic. In my frenzied mind, I tried to think through what few options I had, but I was so distracted by shock and exhaustion that I wasn't able to concentrate.

In desperation, I reattached the bone-colored phone on the nightstand. In front of Halmoni's blazing eyes I quickly dialed my parents' number. The moment I did so, I had a feeling that the call was being listened to, and I remembered the guide's warning to me. But there was nothing else I could do. My mother was the only one who could get through Halmoni's madness. She'd know how to look beyond the problem.

A recorded message in Mandarin came over the line. I tried again, but my hands shook so badly that my fingers kept slipping. On the third try I managed to push the correct combination of digits and reached the international long distance operator, who put the call through for me. I heard the line ringing thousands of miles away. I twisted the cord around my fingers as the ringing tone went on and on and on.

"Hae-ro," my mother yawned. When I heard her warm honey voice, scratchy with sleep, it caused a lump to form in my throat. As I spoke I could hear the echo of my own frailty. I told her about Halmoni accusing the guide of being a Red spy. I told her about being cooped up. I told her about the actress and Kim Dae Jung. I told her about the rotting food. When I was done telling her everything, I heard her exhale thousands of miles away, then take a deep breath. "I'll take care of Halmoni." My mother's reassuring words fed me courage by wire.

I handed over the receiver to Halmoni. There was a hostile silence, then she took it. "What?" she said angrily into the mouthpiece. "I see he's twisted your mind, too. . . . I can tell by his heavy-lidded eyes and how they leer at everything suspiciously. And that director has big bulging eyes that pop out. . . . No, I don't believe we'll make it home. What? . . . They know our room number. They're coming to get us tonight, and she's doing nothing about it. What? . . . All right, all right," she grumbled, her tongue darting spitefully as she dropped the receiver back into my hand.

"Hae Ri, she's worse off than I thought. You need to bring Halmoni home as soon as possible. If her mind goes, we'll never get her back. I'll call the travel agent as soon as it's morning here. In the meantime, call the front desk and change rooms. That'll ease her mind a little. Make sure she tries to get some sleep. She's too fragile. She has to conserve her energy for the flight back."

"Okay, change rooms and take her home," I repeated dully, then said it again more confidently than I was feeling.

The clerk at the registration counter was very suspicious and wanted to know how much longer we intended to stay at the hotel and if everything was fine. The maids probably reported that we never left the room and that the room stank of rotting food. I told the receptionist we'd be leaving as soon as Halmoni was feeling better. When she summoned a bellhop to transfer our bags, I declined the assistance because I couldn't risk Halmoni's terror flaring up again. I couldn't handle another horrific episode. So, I carried everything myself while Halmoni puttered behind me to our new room on the third floor. When we got inside, I made sure the door was securely shut and the bolt slid into place. While Halmoni watched, I systematically combed every inch of the room. I opened every single cabinet and drawer. I dropped to the floor and looked underneath the beds. I looked inside the vents, the phones, the clock. I ran my hands under the table, the desk, and the ledge. When I was completely finished, there was no bug. Still, I couldn't swallow back the fear and panic that gripped my throat. I was actually starting to believe the Reds were coming to get us.

XVIII

Sickness racked my body. All the stress and tension and misery had finally gotten to me. I could feel the illness seep through my system. I tossed and turned in sweat-covered nightmares, waking up several times during the night. My throat was painfully dry, but I didn't dare get out of bed, afraid to wake Halmoni. I forced myself to go back to sleep, and in the morning when I awoke again Halmoni was missing.

I struggled to get to my feet, bracing myself against the nightstand, calling out for Halmoni. My voice sounded harsh, gruff, as if someone had mutilated my vocal cords.

The Reds!

I looked around desperately for signs of a struggle or forced entry. There weren't any, but I couldn't be sure. I was on the verge of hysteria.

Somehow I managed to stagger to the elevator, half falling to the side. The lobby, the people, the furniture looked so weird. The fever was making me see everything through drunken eyes, and I collided into a janitor pushing a mop across the marble floor. She stared at me with a blank expression. I thought, She could be one of them. The pail and mop could just be a cover. She could be a trained North Korean kidnapper. She could have Halmoni tied up and gagged in the janitor's closet somewhere in the basement, waiting to be hauled across the border and shot. Then I saw her. Halmoni was sitting at the concierge's desk, unharmed.

"Halmoni, what are you doing?" I gripped the desk. My legs were weakening.

"Making a Coca-Cola." Halmoni meant collect call. "This nice lady is helping me." She pointed to the concierge, who was holding Halmoni's tattered phone book.

"You must be the granddaughter," the concierge said in her musical accented Korean, then asked, "Did your father get off okay?"

I turned and cocked my head. "You know my father?"

"Yes, I helped him with his flight to Yanji. He told me you're a writer. I enjoyed talking with him very much. He's very nice and funny." She smiled shyly.

Her sense of familiarity disturbed me. I studied her more closely. Her smile and politeness weren't accompanied by a disconcerting indifference, as they were in the other employees. She was close to my age and slender, with small gentle eyes and a face that was very pale, almost white, except for the flush in her cheeks. She only came up to my shoulder. The name on the plastic tag pinned to her chest said Miss Cho. Suddenly I didn't like her. I didn't want Halmoni around her.

"Sorry, Halmoni, this number isn't working." Miss Cho handed Halmoni back the phone book.

"That's odd. I Coca-Cola that number before." Halmoni scratched her ear, bewildered. I had altered Choi Soon Man's and other numbers in her phone book by changing some of the digits while she was napping days ago. "I'll be back," Halmoni told the concierge, sounding like the Korean Terminator. Arnold Schwarzenegger couldn't have topped her delivery.

Once we were sealed off in our room again, I only had enough energy to crawl into bed. The instant I did so, all my strength left me. Pull yourself together, I said to myself, angry. I hated being so weak. I told myself that for centuries women used to have their babies one day and get back to the rice paddy, cotton fields, or battlefield the very next day, whereas I couldn't deal with a microscopic flu bug.

Halmoni glowered at me with quiet suspicion for a while, then touched the back of her cool hand on my feverish face. Shaking her head, she shuffled over to the sink and brought back a glass of water. She sat on the edge of my bed and held the glass to my chapped lips. The liquid went down my dry throat like rocks. I choked. Most of it came back up and soaked into my shirt.

"You need a treatment," Halmoni diagnosed.

I didn't protest. It wasn't because I wanted to be pinched and hit and scraped, but I knew ch'iryo was another way to occupy Halmoni's mind. For both our mental sakes, I told myself I could endure more physical pain.

Halmoni bowed her head over me and called on God's mercy to guide her hands as she performed His healing. She began by pinching the flesh around my neck between her index and middle finger. At first, her touch felt sooth-ing. As she became more zealous and energized, it began to sting. My entire body flinched in anticipation. It tensed up every time she grabbed a chunk of soft flesh and pinched it hard, making a popping sound. Soon rows of dark purple bruises and burgundy hickey marks circled my neck and blossomed down my chest, all over my breasts. If nothing else, the pain confirmed that I was still alive.

After three intense hours, Halmoni decided we both had had enough for one day. Her hands were as red as if they had been held over a fire. But she was the calmest I had seen her. "Rest for now. You'll feel better soon." She ran her fingers over my forehead and cheek. She made me feel cared for and loved, which was what I desperately needed after the physical and emotional beating. Suddenly I wanted to grab her and hug her, but my body was depleted. It felt like I had just run a marathon. All I could manage to move was my eyes. I let my gaze drift away through the wide crack in the wine-colored curtains, those awful curtains with the crazy confetti design. I stared up at the glowing moon and the scattering of twinkling stars against the inky black sky. Back in L.A., I used to look up at the massive sky and dream about exotic places and things happening in far-off countries. Now that I was halfway across the world gazing at the same sky, the same moon, it reminded me of home, and I was stabbed by a pang of homesickness. I wanted to climb on top of the window ledge and curl up against the glass, to get closer to the moonbeams.

Closing my eyes, I began to fantasize again, leaving this room and this place. I fantasized about the simple, pleasant things I took for granted but loved to do. I even missed all those hated things like washing dishes, doing laundry, vacuuming. Sometime during all this reminiscing, the bathroom phone drew me away and out and back to my bleak reality. It was still dark outside. I wasn't sure if it was the same night or another. It could have been another because the view through the window looked different. Less stars.

Slowly, very slowly, I limped across the room on stiff legs. I felt every bruise.

"Where are you going?" Halmoni asked sharply.

"Shower," I said.

"So late?"

"I'm sweaty."

"Aren't you feeling well?"

"Yes, better, but sticky," I said, hoping that the caller wouldn't hang up.

"I'll help you."

"No, I'm feeling much much better. I can do it myself." I shut the bathroom door behind me before she could protest. I stuffed a towel underneath the door and cranked the nozzles, then gently lowered myself down on the toilet seat. The water blasted out from the showerhead and in a matter of seconds the tiny space was clouded with steam. Around the tenth ring or so I pulled the receiver off its hook and pressed it to my ear.

"Get Halmoni ready," my father whispered, then the call ended.

My heart lifted with hope and anticipation. I visualized everyone speeding toward us. They'd be here in maybe fifteen hours, I calculated. That wasn't bad. Holding on to this thought was the only thing that kept me from scratching up the walls. In fifteen hours I would have relief from all the waiting and hysteria.

The bathroom phone rang again near four in the morning. Halmoni snapped awake the moment I pulled myself to the edge of the bed by my heels. I was convinced more than ever that she heard and saw everything, even when asleep. She possessed a sixth sense, a sensitive antenna, that beamed her a chart of my movements.

Avoiding her darting eyes, I went inside the bathroom and soundproofed the tile room again by stuffing another towel under the door and cranking up the shower. "Hello," I said in a hurried manner, cupping my hand over my mouth to mute the sound.

"Hae Ri." My father screeched out my name breathlessly into my ear. Instantly I sensed trouble. "Only four pieces of baggage made it across."

I almost dropped the receiver. I wanted to stop the flow of information, wanted to block it, but the magnitude of his words had already cut into me, and every inch of me was shaking so hard that the toilet seat rattled beneath me.

"The director wants to bring them anyway to Halmoni."

"No way. This isn't his decision," I whispered even more softly as I kept my eyes glued to the doorknob. I couldn't believe what was happening. I gritted my teeth. Suddenly it all seemed like an impossibility. I was thinking Halmoni had been right—we should have left things alone. This was insane. Only four made it out. Five left behind. I wanted to rip the toilet out of the floor and hurl it against the mirror. Calm down, I ordered myself. I had to get hold of my emotions. Taking a deep breath, I dominated my insane panic so I could speak again. "Send them back."

"I tried, but they threatened to kill themselves."

Then I heard the guide get on the phone. "Ask Halmoni what she wants to do."

"You can't speak to her. This can't happen," I snapped at him.

"If we can't convince them to go back soon, we have to move the baggage. It's too dangerous to keep them here."

"Send them back. Less than half is not okay."

"Ae Ran thinks—"

"Ae Ran's there beside you? Let me speak to her."

"Why?"

"Put her on," I barked. I had no time for his question. As I waited for her to get on the line, I struggled to picture in my mind the whole chaotic turn of events from every angle. It was as though a firecracker had gone off inside my head.

At once I recognized Ae Ran's thick North Korean accent. "Yeh?"

I continued in a more determined voice. "Ae Ran Older Sister, you all have to come together."

"I know. My father and I tried. I even wrote them a letter begging them to cross, but they won't listen."

"Try, try again. Write another letter—a hundred, if that's what it'll take. Write the best letter you've ever written in your entire life. Beg them to come," I said. Brilliant, Helie! Is that the best you can come up with? My brain cast about wildly, sending my fragmented thoughts spinning in hopes that I could come up with a better suggestion. I cursed myself as I kept coming up empty. Then I hit upon an idea, and I asked to speak to the guide.

"You want me?" he said.

"I've thought of something. Send across my book. Let the others see what Ae Ran and Big Uncle already know."

"It's too big. The border guards will intercept it."

"Then rip off the cover and last chapter and send that."

There was a hesitation, then the guide said in a pleased voice, "Very clever. Okay. I think that'll work. We'll be there as soon as we can, but around a quarter to midnight, eleven-forty-five tonight, I want you to go downstairs and meet Jambbong's wife in the lobby. Tell her we're running late, but have her wait there for me." He clicked off.

I sat on the closed toilet lid, shaking, calming down, shaking again. My father and I had totally lost control over the mission. In truth, we'd never had control. The guide and now the director had all the momentum. I wondered how far the director would go to get his documentary. I wondered why the guide was so determined to make this happen even at such a high cost to everyone. Yet it had to turn out all right, because I didn't know how I'd go on living a normal life if it didn't.

There was a loud bang on the door. I froze. "What are you doing in there?" Halmoni demanded to know, banging on the door some more.

"I'll be right out. I'm almost done," I called back airily, stripping off my clothes and shoving my head under the shower for a second. Then I threw one white bath towel around me and one over my head like a turban. When I opened the door, Halmoni stood right on the other side, leaning against the frame, narrow-eyed. My hands began to shake again. I crossed my arms over my chest and tucked them under my armpits to still them.

"What were you doing in there all this time?"

How can we possibly do this to her? I thought in anguish. It isn't fair. "Showering," I said.

"Again?"

"I couldn't sleep and there's nothing else to do." I crawled back into bed, still wearing the towels.

Halmoni reached over and checked my forehead. "You look pale. You need another treatment." She lifted up the hem of her dress and got out the metal Chinese soup spoon she always carried around inside the secret pocket sewn into her bloomers.

I let her go to work on me, glad to be doing something. Halmoni scraped both of my inner arms with the edge of the cold spoon, lubricating with water so as not to tear the skin. It kept her busy for as long as her energy lasted. When she had no energy left in her, I encouraged her to nap. Then she started up again on the back of my thighs. I worried I'd run out of body parts before my father and the others reached us.

Perhaps it was Halmoni's *ch'iryo,* perhaps it was the slim hope that my idea had given me, but I began to feel a lot better. I was able to eat some congee and get dressed. As I tunneled my legs into a pair of black slacks and pulled on a baby doll T-shirt, I found I was talking to myself again, rambling on. It was because I was trying to keep things straight in my head, to keep the weight of my thoughts evenly distributed so I wouldn't forget what I had to do.

Around ten in the evening I began fidgeting. I kept glancing down at my watch, tapping the face lightly. I knew it'd be a battle to get past the door alone. I couldn't even go to the bathroom without Halmoni questioning me. I made up a lame excuse. "We're out of coffee. I'm going to get some downstairs in the café."

"Have them bring it up."

"It'll be cheaper if I get it myself," I said, knowing Halmoni constantly worried about the cost of the mission. Suddenly the craving for a freshly brewed cup overcame me, and I began salivating. There was something familiar about warm coffee. I think that was why I drank it so often.

"I'm going with you."

"It's too tiring for you."

Halmoni was close behind me. "I'm not tired."

"I'll be right back."

"I won't bother you." She went and stood by the door.

"Halmoni, please let me do something by myself."

"Why do you need to do things alone?" She took my arm.

Exasperated, I gave up. Clearly she was not going to let me out of her sight. At that moment, I decided I couldn't postpone the inevitable. I sat Halmoni down in a chair and confided in her that the family had escaped, withholding the number of people. I only gave her the version of the truth I thought she could handle. I told her about the two phone calls I received in the bathroom from my father. He was with them. He hadn't gone to Seoul. I told her that her son was coming. When I was all done talking, I leaned back against the desk in order to show her I had said the whole truth and nothing but. Halmoni didn't react. I had the feeling, as she continued to watch me, that she had listened less to my words than to the things I hadn't said.

"How do I know you're not lying to me?"

"They're coming. I swear it. Hope to die if I'm lying." I placed my hand over my heart.

"Are they all coming?"

"That's what we wanted," I answered. Another half-truth. She'd find out the rest soon enough, I thought wearily.

"I won't believe it till I see my son's face with my own eyes," she replied coolly, but I knew she wanted to believe so badly. I read it in her expression. "My goodness, you and everyone else have lied to me so much, even now I can't help wondering."

"Big Uncle is coming. That's the truth."

"It's wonderful that you can believe so effortlessly. I was so terrified that I asked God to watch after the guide if he is truly helping us, but if he's our enemy to let his ears and nose fall off. They must come. They must all come." She laced her fingers on top of her lap and smiled for the first time in days. As Halmoni kept talking, she seemed to bounce back to life. I recognized the look immediately, because it was the face I was so used to.

Before leaving the room, I plugged the nightstand phone back in the jack, put a long-sleeved charcoal gray jacket on over the T-shirt, and tied a black-and-white leopard-print scarf around my neck. I was completely overdressed for the hot summer night, but I had to conceal the bruises and hickey marks that had deepened in color.

"Be careful," Halmoni warned, but her eyes sparkled.

I nodded heavily, then backed out the door as though I were backing out of a cage. When I got inside the elevator the power and lights suddenly shut off and the whole thing jerked and then stopped. Blackness. The hairs on the back of my neck rose. My pulse sped. I tried not to think about the Reds. Tightening up my courage, I stepped forward and with both hands quickly explored the panel. I felt around for the buttons. Finding them, I stabbed every one. I wasn't convinced it would work, but it was the only possible route of escape. Fortunately, when I hit one of the lower buttons the elevator lurched again, then the doors gave way slightly and a faint shaft of light spilled in from the corridor. But the opening was only about five or six inches wide, and my hips were wider than the gap. I tried to wrench the doors apart a few more inches, but they wouldn't budge. Emptying my lungs and thinking only thin thoughts, I twisted, wriggled, and squeezed through, scraping the sides of my hips and ears raw. Freed, I hurried down the dim corridor back to Halmoni, alone in the pitch-black room.

"Halmoni?" I called out.

"Who's there?" The terror in Halmoni's voice had returned.

"Where are you?"

"Go away!"

I felt my way along the floor from memory and reached the window. I drew open the curtains to let the moonbeams and artificial lights that splashed off the other buildings stream into the room. There in the farthest corner, I found Halmoni curled up on the floor, in a tight ball like a small animal.

"Here, take my hands," I said, bending down.

Halmoni threw up her arms in a defensive position to protect herself.

"It's me, Hae Ri," I purred softly.

She blinked. "Hae Ri, is that you?"

"Yes, Halmoni. It's me."

Her gray eyes grew wide. "Oh, thank God. I thought they got you."

"Halmoni, things like this happen all the time in China," I told her, putting all the confidence I could muster into my voice. I had no idea if what I claimed was true or not.

Halmoni refused to move from her corner, so I slid down next to her and slipped my arm around her shoulder, relieved when she allowed it. Her body was like a block of ice. I tried to jiggle her shoulders in an attempt to loosen her up. It didn't help. She only began to rock back and forth.

For thirty minutes or more I sat there rocking with her before the lights flickered back on as suddenly as they had gone out. Even with the lights restored, Halmoni couldn't release her fear. Her face was paler than ever, and it remained contorted. I agonized over what to do. I couldn't leave her in this state. I couldn't stay, either. It was a quarter after midnight. The guide had said eleven-forty-five, being very specific about the point in time.

"Halmoni, I have to go back downstairs. You understand? I'll be right back. Do you think you can lock the door when I leave?" I strained to get myself and her onto our feet. Halmoni clung to my hand as I dragged her over to the door. "Turn the lock and put on the chain when I'm gone. I'll be back soon. Everything's going to be fine." I gave her hand a slight squeeze, then pried loose one small finger after finger until she disengaged.

The door clicked shut behind me. I waited until I heard the bolt grate into the slot, then turned away. Unable to brave the elevator again, I took the stairs. Still stiff and unsteady on my feet, I went down the steps carefully. As I reached the second floor, a second blackout occurred, and I lost my footing, but I managed to grab on to the iron railing. I held on to it all the way down to the ground floor, then I slipped through the emergency exit door. The lobby was lit with dozens of candles. My eyes flew around the room, looking for a house phone. Seeing one, I immediately called Halmoni. With relief I detected no madness in her voice, and her breathing sounded regular. I continued on across the lobby, carefully skirting the clusters of people.

Jambbong's wife was sitting in the café at a table that had a view of the street and the entry. She wore faded blue jeans, a blue-and-white checked button-down shirt, and my black jacket with the zip-away hood and monster pockets I had given her to pass on to my relatives. I didn't mind. All that I had on me I would have gladly given to her right then. That's how happy I was to see someone familiar. When I caught her eyes, she looked up at me with a sense of urgency, then immediately rearranged her facial expression to appear nonchalant. She signaled me to take a seat. I casually walked over to her table and settled into a chair across from her. Up close I could see she had puffy bags underneath her eyes, and her vivaciousness was gone. I reached over the table and touched her hand. In a low voice, I thanked her for the pains she'd taken on behalf of my family.

"You don't have to thank me," she whispered, laying her other hand on top of mine and patting it in a gesture that was so kind, it nearly made me cry.

"It's so good to see you. How did you get here?"

"I arrived early this morning by train to secure a place for your relatives to stay."

"Were you in Changbai with the guide and my father?"

"No, but I did meet your father when we picked him up at the airport in Yanji. He's very nice. He has a great personality," she praised.

I chose not to acknowledge her last comment. It bothered me in the same way Miss Cho's familiarity had. If I thought about it too much, all I would see was my mother's face, and everything I believed in and had faith in would be shattered if their marriage weren't rooted in stability and loyalty and love. I forced myself not to think about it. I passed on the guide's message, then fixed my eyes on the entrance. Just outside the revolving glass doors, the same two bulky guards monitored the taxis pulling into the curved carport, dropping off late-returning hotel guests. Several more taxis came up to the carport but passed by without stopping when they saw that there were no passengers to pick up.

Compulsively, I checked my watch against the slightly slower clock on the face of the train station. The fifteen-hour estimate had been optimistic. Around one in the morning Halmoni came out of the elevator. Her rubber soles squeaked noisily on the marble floor. I pulled out a chair for her and introduced the two women. Halmoni gazed keenly at Jambbong's wife.

"Do you know my son?" Halmoni asked.

"No, not directly."

"So you must know the guide, then?"

"Yes, my husband and I are working with him on this project."

The muscles in Halmoni's face tightened, loosened, then tightened again. I could see her mind churning, her guard rising. All at once a glow of red tail-lights backing into the curved carport distracted her, and she wandered over to the window, propping herself against the glass.

Let it be them. Don't make us wait another minute.

The red taillights drove off like all the other cars. Halmoni watched them as they moved farther away. But my eyes weren't on the taillights. They were focused on the security guards studying us through the window. I saw their stare dart to the side, just behind us. In the window's reflection, a slight, bespectacled man was spying on us over a newspaper from the lobby.

I left the table and went over to where Halmoni stood. "It's getting late. Let's wait upstairs."

She moved away, protesting.

"Just do as I say. All this is for you." I caught her roughly by the wrist and elbow. I could feel her body tense in resistance, but I refused to let go.

"What will you do?" Halmoni questioned Jambbong's wife.

"I'll wait here a little longer," she responded politely.

"Why don't you go home and get some sleep," Halmoni said, but it was more of a statement than a suggestion.

"Thank you, but I'll wait a little longer." Jambbong's wife bowed.

I returned the bow.

Back in the room, Halmoni was quiet for a long time because, like me, she was afraid to say anything. In the heavy silence, we lay in her bed together, on top of the covers, fully dressed. I folded my arms around Halmoni and held her tightly. Tonight was supposed to have been the night. I had promised.

All night, that night, I wouldn't let myself relax and succumb to sleep. I forced my eyelids to stay open no matter how heavy they became, because deep down I felt that if I slept, something terrible would happen to all of us.

XIX

August 17, 1997

At six-thirty in the morning, the phone propelled Halmoni out of her sleep. It was my father calling us from inside the hotel. The rush of relief almost caused me to pass out. Five minutes later we were out the door and hurrying to his room, forgetting to brush our teeth, forgetting to wash our faces.

My father had just bathed. He was wearing a blue shirt, the shade of blue that the sea becomes at midday. Seeing him, smelling him clean and soapy with just a hint of musk, the nightmare softened, and I almost felt giddy. Then the morning light played against his face and the spell broke. He looked awful to me, worn and depressed and shaken. He seemed to have shrunk. Even his face seemed smaller. On his forehead there was a red gash half an inch long. I edged in front of him to get a better look because I couldn't believe he had changed so much since I had last seen him seven days ago.

My father filled us in on his journey. After he left us, he'd flown directly to Yanji, where Jambbong and his wife met him at the airport. They drove him to the safe house where the guide and the director had been staying. As the car pulled up to the seven-story building, my father immediately recognized the building—because we had stayed there. Choi Soon Man's daughter and son-in-law lived on the fifth floor. Jambbong's wife had unknowingly rented an apartment unit one floor above our former hosts. They had to sneak my father up the stairs, past the fifth floor. Once inside the safe house, he couldn't leave. He was trapped in the apartment while I was cooped up with Halmoni in our upholstered cage, thinking he and the guide were making their way to Changbai.

They couldn't make a move until Aunt's older sister left Hyesan. Only once a day, at one in the afternoon, did Ae Ran come out to the river. Each time she made an X with her arms, signaling that all was not clear, that her mother's older sister refused to leave.

Finally, after three days of waiting around, the guide and my father decided they should head for Changbai anyway. Jambbong drove everyone to the border town and dropped them off at the Chosŏn brothers' home. The one-room brick and plywood home was located a few streets back from the Yalu River. It had a shed tucked away in the dirt backyard where they all stayed out of sight, waiting for Ae Ran's signal that came just once a day.

On August 15, the day commemorating Korea's independence from Japanese occupation, my father went out to the river to meet Ae Ran. To disguise his appearance, he changed into a tattered green shirt, cutoff shorts, and slippers, and removed his Western-looking glasses. He carried a washrag and soap and walked with a little boy to the edge of the river. Squatting beside the water and washing himself, my father waited for Ae Ran to appear. On that day, Ae Ran came to the river with her baby and drew a circle in the air, indicating that all was clear, her mother's older sister had at last left. In return, my father held up three fingers and yelled, "Tomorrow," instructing her that they should cross the river at three the next morning.

All the guides, my father, the SBS team, even the North Korean border guards stood by on alert. Two days before, the younger Chosŏn brother had paid off the guards and their superior officer. After a lengthy negotiation, the price for the safe crossing of nine people went down from ten thousand yuan to four thousand ($465).

At the designated time, only Yong Woon Uncle, Hak Churl, and Ae Ran with her baby strapped to her back showed up at the river. Mun Churl had run away again. He had decided not to defect to South Korea. Recently admitted into the party, he had been promised a job after graduation, and that was what he intended to do—graduate. Even when he was fainting with hunger, he was determined to graduate. He'd go out to the woods behind his college and pick grass to boil into a watery green broth to stave off the hunger pains so he could study. That was all Mun Churl was focused on. To him, the government's promised job was life itself.

Because of Mun Churl, his mother stayed behind as well. She refused to leave without her younger son, knowing he'd be killed if they all defected. Mi Ran was all ready to escape with the others. As she was putting on her shoes to leave, her mother dragged her back inside the house. Hearing her mother's sobbing plea, Mi Ran couldn't abandon her and watched from the doorway as her father, older brother, and older sister with the baby left without them.

Hak Churl didn't even reveal the escape plan to his wife. He simply told her that they were crossing the river to meet Halmoni, then they'd return. Initially, she agreed to join them. Three nights before the crossing, their son, Chun, became ill and had to be admitted to the hospital. His health did improve, but then Hak Churl's wife changed her mind, concerned about her parents. She encouraged Hak Churl to go and said she'd come out to the riverbank the next day with a red umbrella, which would be her greeting to Halmoni. She had no idea as she said good-bye to her husband that he wasn't coming back.

When the four showed up at the riverbank, the border guards caught Hak Churl by the arm and hit him hard across the face. The guards yelled at them to get off the riverbank. Terrified, Hak Churl was about to swallow the chalky gray cube of rat poison they all carried with them in case they were captured.

Ae Ran stopped Hak Churl from taking the poison and pleaded with the guards to let them cross to meet Halmoni. The guards became confused. Their orders were to let nine people cross the river at three in the morning. Realizing Ae Ran's group were the people they were waiting for, the guards allowed them to jump into the water, where the younger Chosŏn brother met them.

With the younger Chosŏn brother leading the way, they waded clumsily through the murky water, clinging to each other. The water level had gone back down to waist height, making the crossing less treacherous but no less terrifying. With each step they took toward China's muddy border, they expected to hear gunshots and feel bullets piercing their backs. But there were no shots, no bullets. A mere $465 had bought them their lives. They made it to the China side.

From the riverbank, the younger Chosŏn brother led them quickly up and over a stone fence and through the confusing maze of narrow, unlit alleyways. When they reached the dimly lit brick house and saw my father waiting to greet them, they collapsed to the floor around his feet in tears.

Seeing only four of them, my father went into shock. Once the realization seeped in that five were left behind, he became so upset that he was nearly sick. He told them to go back. They refused. They threatened to run away. They swore they'd kill themselves.

Unable to change their minds, the guide and my father had no choice but to move them out of Changbai. The longer they stayed at the Chosŏn brothers' house, the more dangerous it became for everyone involved. Quickly the four refugees were fed and clothed, and they washed their faces. That was all they had time for. By six, as the early morning mist was lifting and the sky became tinged with gold, they were ready to leave.

Originally the guide had prepared three cars, parked at different locations in town. But with only half of the group out, the third car was discarded. The guide, the director, a cameraman, the younger Chosŏn brother, and Hak Churl rode in the front car, since everyone except Hak Churl had identification documents. Their driver was a Chinese man who worked regularly as a truck driver. He knew all the back roads around the western base of Changbai Shan to Shenyang.

Jambbong drove Yong Woon Uncle, Ae Ran, her baby, my father, and a second cameraman in his red taxi. The two cars communicated by walkie-talkie from about a mile's distance. There were no words spoken at all. One click from the first car warned the second car to halt. Two clicks urged Ae Ran's group to abandon the taxi and hide in the dense forest.

The two cars went through one practice run before approaching the first security checkpoint, an hour outside Changbai. The guide had cautioned everyone to be extremely alert and ready for anything. The Chinese police had tightened security along the border and at all the checkpoints due to the countless number of North Korean refugees hiding out in the mountains and forest. Some desperate refugees had broken into homes and stolen food. As a result, the Chinese people were eager to report them, and the police were eager to track them down and repatriate them to North Korea, where they would face retribution. On December 26, 1996, *Dong-A Ilbo,* a South Korean newspaper, reported that over four hundred North Korean refugees had been arrested by Chinese authorities and forcibly repatriated, though it was a clear violation of international law.

Even if the refugees avoided capture, their chances of survival were slim. They were up against extreme weather conditions and terrain, tigers, black bears, leopards, and other wild animals hunting for food in the inhospitable forest.

When the two cars reached the first checkpoint, Hak Churl, Ae Ran and the baby, and Yong Woon Uncle exited the cars to bypass the checkpoint. The younger Chosŏn brother led the refugees by foot through the wilderness as the front car and then the second car paid the toll and passed safely through. The younger Chosŏn brother and Ae Ran's group caught up with the two cars on the other side of the roadblock.

At the second checkpoint, halfway to Shenyang, soldiers holding machine guns across their chests blocked the road. Immediately the guide clicked the walkie-talkie twice, warning the second car of the danger. Hearing the two clicks, Jambbong stepped on the brakes so suddenly, the people in his car jerked forward and my father's forehead struck the dashboard. Quickly, the refugees, the younger Chosŏn brother, and the SBS cameraman fled into the forest.

When they were safely out of sight, Jambbong rounded the bend and drove slowly toward the roadblock, stopping several feet from the candy-striped guardrail. An unsmiling young soldier questioned Jambbong while another soldier stood by my father's open window, gazing down at him. Their IDs were requested. My father handed the unsmiling soldier his passport. Seeing my father's navy blue U.S. passport, they aimed their machine guns at him and Jambbong. The soldiers demanded to know what they were doing at the border. My father insisted he was sightseeing. Suspecting he was an American spy, the soldiers thoroughly scanned his passport and visa, then searched the taxi. They checked under the hood and inside the trunk and felt underneath the seats. Finding nothing, they allowed my father to go.

Jambbong inched the taxi forward. Within a few minutes they were clear and barreling up the empty dirt road. They drove about three or four miles and pulled into a small service station that resembled a wooden outhouse. The first car was parked out front with its hood propped up, pretending to have engine problems. Jambbong turned off the engine and did the same. The two cars waited there in the hot sun for three hours until Ae Ran's group came stumbling out of the forest.

The younger Chosŏn brother had taken them deep into the forest, toward a hill that rose sharply to a village of small huts. He was supposed to stay clear of villages and fields and people, but he took a shortcut through the village because of Ae Ran. The sweltering heat and unfamiliar motion of the car had made her almost helpless with nausea. Many times along their perilous journey they had to stop so she could vomit. She became so dehydrated and weak, my father was terribly concerned that she wasn't going to survive the long, jolting ride. She sat limp with her head lolling back and forth, unable to nurse or comfort her baby, but the baby never cried out. Through all the bumps and jolts and suffocating heat, he just lay quietly in his mother's nearly lifeless arms.

At four in the morning, twenty-five hours after Ae Ran's group defected from North Korea, the two cars, cloaked in mud, bounced into Shenyang.

Promptly Ae Ran's group was taken to the safe house that Jambbong's wife had secured and prepared with food and bedding for nine people.

—————

Finishing his story, my father removed his gold-rimmed glasses and dragged his palms down over his face as if he were wiping water from it, then he placed the thumb and forefinger of his other hand to the bridge of his nose, as if adjusting its position.

A shadow passed across my father's strained face. His frown deepened. "Ae Ran begged us to try again to get the others out, but I think there's no convincing the mother and Mun Churl. They're true Red patriots. No one on the mother's side of the family fled to the South during the war, and she's been a party member since eighteen."

He hawked up mucus the way the Chinese did and spat into a napkin. Then, as though it was too much for him, he sat back in his chair and sighed. "Of all the children, Mun Churl could have convinced his mother to escape, but he couldn't see beyond his diploma and ran back to school. If it wasn't for Mun Churl, everyone could be across by now. As angry as I am with him, I know he doesn't know any better. Since birth he's been fed their propaganda. At twenty-five a young man's the most passionate and idealistic."

My father's words percolated through my brain. I tried to step back from who I was and look at it from Mun Churl's standpoint. He probably knew nothing about the world outside and what it could offer him. All he knew was what the party's propaganda pumped into him. The party controlled the newspapers and broadcasting stations. The Korean Central Television Station in Pyongyang offered only three channels. Other cities only received one channel. North Korea had just two AM radio networks and one FM network. Radio dials were fixed to receive only designated frequencies, preventing the reception of foreign broadcasts that might reveal the truth to its citizens.

"Was the book sent over?" My voice was ominously quiet.

"What?" My father glanced at me.

"The book. Did you send it?"

"Ae Ran's letter, along with your book cover and the ending chapter, was folded into a tiny square and carried over the water to Mi Ran. Even after seeing their names exposed in the book, they said they couldn't go against the party."

"Fear cripples people and prevents them from making good decisions. The

Reds control them with fear. Their brains are washed," Halmoni said, wiping her eyes with the hem of her dress.

"When Ae Ran's mother realizes half of her family is truly gone and there's no future for her there, she'll come."

"What if she doesn't?" I asked shakily.

My father touched the gash on his forehead with the back of his hand, thinking deeply. For a moment he seemed to forget we were waiting for his response. He brought his palms together as though he were praying, resting them against his lips. Finally he looked up at me and said softly, "We can do no more for them." He opened his mouth to speak again, and I heard in my mind what he meant to say—they're dead—but no words came out, not even in a whisper. Instead, he nodded.

My heart thumped against my sternum. Hope joined deadly fear and converted the adrenaline that pumped through my veins into pure energy. I flew around the room gathering up baby products and dumping them into a backpack. My older sister, Julie, had carefully prepared a care package for Ae Ran's baby. She'd bought bottles, disposable diapers, diaper rash ointment, moist wipes, a plastic thermos, orthodontically correct pacifiers, infant clothes, booties, and powdered formula. The formula was loaded with vitamins and nutrients that Ae Ran's body probably lacked. Julie had opted for the soy milk mixture in case the baby was lactose intolerant—something I would have never thought of, but Julie did. She was smart and sensible like that.

With two quick jerks, I zipped everything up and draped it over my shoulder. As I was about to step through the door, my eye landed on the camera bag. I'd almost forgotten it. I went back in and grabbed it.

We were moving.

For once I didn't have to slow down for Halmoni. The bags hanging off my shoulders, pulling at my bruised neck muscles, felt like anchors, and the lack of exercise had left my legs weak and stiff. We shuffled along at about the same pace, bumping up against each other as we made our way downstairs, across the lobby. The closer we got to being outside, the better I was feeling. When I saw the revolving glass doors, I threw all my weight against one of the heavy panels and spun out into the fresh air. Immediately, I became disoriented in the bright sunlight—the sun, after we had been in the dark room for thirteen days, had the effect of back lighting with a hard spot. I used my hand to shield my eyes, then slowly the dots disappeared and I could see again. I removed my hand, leaned back, and opened my face and body toward the sky. The hot sun and fresh air cleared my head, and gradually I felt myself grow stronger, gathering strength for the reunion ahead. We found a cab and I settled myself as calmly as I could next to Halmoni, who was holding up well, all things considered. She seemed almost at ease except for the hard gleam in her watchful eyes.

Five minutes later the cab came to an abrupt stop in front of a spectacular-looking palace with glazed green-and-yellow tile rooftops and golden dragon guardians, scaly and clawed, perched at their corners to protect the grounds. Shenyang Imperial Palace was located in the center of the old city on the east side of town. It was one of the two imperial palaces that hadn't been destroyed in China during the Cultural Revolution. Begun in 1625 and completed in 1636, the palace had been home to the founder of the Qing Dynasty, and stood as evidence of the period when Shenyang was the capital of Manchuria. Now this miniature version of the Forbidden City in Beijing functioned as a popular tourist attraction. A rusted English sign wired above the ticket counter said Wisitor in faded red letters. For thirty-five yuan, visitors could tour the ancient grounds where Emperor Nuerhachi and his son once sat on their jeweled thrones.

I wondered why the guide had picked such a conspicuous location. The sidewalks weren't wide enough to accommodate all the people hanging around, so they spilled out onto the streets and swirled around our cab as we climbed out.

"Hae Ri." I heard my name being called and glanced around. Two seconds later I saw Jambbong's wife pushing through the hectic, bustling swarm. With a wave of her small hand she urged us into a waiting cab. I slid in between Halmoni and my father in the back.

Jambbong's wife directed the driver in Mandarin. He nodded sluggishly and ground the gears. The cab puttered and bounced around for several blocks, then headed back in the same direction we came. I could see the Gloria Plaza Hotel in front of us grow bigger and then smaller again, until it was gone. I was sweating by the time the cab turned off the main road and rolled up onto a sidewalk in a residential area. The dreary cluster of dormitory-style concrete-block buildings was actually a company compound that housed employees and their families. Once again, I had to question the guide's logic. How safe could this compound be, with everyone both working with and living with each other?

Jambbong's wife motioned us to stay back, unmoving, as she walked around the corner, hands jammed in the front pockets of her cutoff jean shorts. We were left all alone, out in the open, in the heat. The sun on my back grew increasingly hotter with every minute. Somewhere nearby a frustrated cat or child yowled. I carefully glanced around. Goose bumps prickled all over my arms. I became very aware of neighbors idly watching us from their open doorways: a woman sitting on a stool and knitting with a bright yellow ball of wool, a line of hard-faced people sweating at the bus stop, kids buying ice cream from a two-wheel pushcart. It felt like they all knew what we were doing.

At the exact moment Jambbong's wife reappeared from around the corner, a slender man with a boy-smooth sunburned face approached us. I recognized him immediately. It was the younger Chosŏn brother, who had swum across the river in his green briefs and received Ae Ran's letter. Seen up close in the bright sunlight, his eyes were translucent, almost golden, instead of being dark brown like everyone else's.

The younger Chosŏn brother took Halmoni's arm, then turned and instructed the rest of us not to follow until they reached the end of the block, which was about sixty paces ahead. I instinctively grabbed on to Halmoni. I didn't feel easy about trusting anyone else with her. It was the old familiar fear that I couldn't lose her. I forced my hands to let go. As they moved farther and farther away, I kept my eyes trained on Halmoni's hair. I never lost sight of her. Her shiny silver locks were like a tracking beacon, and everything else blurred out of focus.

When they hit their mark, the three of us began trailing after them with our heads slightly lowered. At the end of the block, we cut across a gravel yard and into a grim maze of buildings wedged close together. Communist urban planning seemed to have been designed to cram the largest amount of people into every available square foot and to send people's sense of direction into a nerve-jangling tailspin.

My eyes remained on Halmoni as the younger Chosŏn brother led her into one of the seven-story boxy buildings set in the back. Reaching the entryway, I saw the two of them standing at the foot of the stairs, staring up at the steep, metal-tipped concrete steps. The safe house was on the top floor. The younger Chosŏn brother, who was smaller than me, offered Halmoni a lift on his narrow back. She mulishly refused and forged on, climbing the steps sideways. I could imagine her overtaxed heart pumping against the strain, her legs shrieking for rest. Halmoni got only as far as the third floor before her muscles gave out. Huffing, she tottered against the railing, leaning on it to take some of the weight off her feet. Finally she surrendered and we pushed her onto the young man's bent back. To my surprise, his five-foot-three narrow frame was incredibly strong. He was able to haul Halmoni up the remaining four flights of stairs.

At last we made it onto the top landing. All of us were breathing hard. I was bent over at the waist, hands braced on my knees, head drooping. I forced myself to inhale and exhale through my nostrils. Once I was able to breathe somewhat normally again, I peered over at Halmoni from my bent-over position to see how she was doing. Strands of hair were matted to her forehead with sweat, and the petal sleeves on her cream chiffon blouse had wilted. When she saw me surveying her appearance, she became conscious of how disheveled she looked, and smoothed out her blouse and raked back her bangs with her trembling fingers.

"You okay, Halmoni?" I asked.

"Fine. Let's go." She sucked in her breath. It was a rough, ragged-sounding inhalation.

On her go-ahead, the younger Chosŏn brother pressed his ear to the heavy steel door and discreetly rapped a signal. Half a second later the door clunked and screeched partway open, as if the people on the other side had been listening for us. When I slipped inside behind Halmoni, the first thing I saw were video cameras, the red recording dots glowing. I made no attempt to be polite. I pushed them aside to give Halmoni breathing space to collect herself. The cameramen stepped back just enough so I could crouch down and help Halmoni take off her shoes. It was an odd thing to make time for, but the custom was so deeply ingrained in us. As I unbuckled my strappy shoes, I flicked a sidelong glance around the room. The sparsely furnished living room was a combination kitchen, television room, piano room, and bathroom. The bathroom, which occupied almost half of the living area, was encased within clear glass walls. It was as if the proud owners were displaying their gleaming white sit-down toilet and tub. I told myself to hold it in.

The director urgently gestured toward a closed door on our left. Looking around a second time, I wondered where the guide was. The director motioned to the door again. I knew the family was just a few feet away behind a thin wall. After all those years of wondering, of fantasizing, about Yong

Woon Uncle, about Ae Ran, about this moment, they were at last here. I was finally here.

This was the moment.

My heart was hammering away like crazy as I neared the door. My excitement suddenly transmuted to a sense of alarm. Who were these people, really? What if Halmoni couldn't identify the man as her son? What if they were imposters planted by the Reds? If they were genuine, was I to feel instant love toward them? Would it show on my face if I felt nothing?

Halmoni was the first to go inside the room. I held the door open for her, then followed. I almost choked from the sour stench of nervous sweat that reeked from the three depraved-looking strangers standing in front of us, with forced painful smiles on their shiny faces. They gave me the shivers. They were so emaciated that they looked as though they had just escaped from a concentration camp. Hak Churl's face was stained black and covered with red welts, and his scrawny frame was lost in the fresh pair of navy blue shorts and T-shirt he had on. The light cotton material just hung off his shoulder bones as if they were a hanger. The woman with the frazzled pageboy haircut, wearing black slacks and a white collared blouse, was Ae Ran. She was only six months older than me, but her skin was weather-beaten and discolored and puffy. When I looked into her hard, sad, young-old face I saw her wasted beauty, and it spoke volumes on the harshness of North Korean life.

Standing between Ae Ran and Hak Churl was a real live ghost from the past. He looked both haunting and haunted. His skull seemed to press through his brown parchmentlike skin, rendering his cheekbones more prominent and his cheeks hollower. Deep grooves ran across his forehead and were like parentheses around his straggly gray goatee. His brushed-back hair was also gray on top, but his thick untamed eyebrows were jet black, shading his small crescent eyes. The irises were almost as black as the pupils. They seemed cold, empty, bottomless.

Shocked into a state of animation by our arrival, they rushed at Halmoni, dramatically embracing her, talking and crying.

"Mother, Mother, oh, Mother," Yong Woon Uncle whimpered again and again.

"Halmoni, Halmoni, Halmoni," Hak Churl and Ae Ran sobbed in agonizing unison.

They clung to Halmoni for dear life. As they continued to call out her name the tune became slower and stranger, and it sounded like they were howling. There was no sound to Halmoni's sorrowful crying, but tears coursed down her sagging face, following the pattern of creases around her sunken eyes and turned-down mouth. Her chin quivered.

My chest grew tight as I watched the heart-wrenching scene just inside the doorway. I had to glance away when I felt my own tears gathering in my throat. It took me a few minutes to recover and breathe normally. Just as I looked back, the three of them simultaneously came at me and flung their arms around me, holding me so tightly, trembling. "Hae Ri, Hae Ri," the trio howled. They smothered their hot, sweaty faces into my neck and back. My weary legs couldn't support them any longer, and we all crumbled to the floor. We sat there holding each other, our arms and legs entwined. I felt nauseous. I had to untangle myself. I pulled away.

Halmoni began a prayer. She spoke so softly, her words floated above us, and I couldn't quite distinguish them. The others, seeing Halmoni pray, solemnly bowed their heads and shut their eyes. I kept mine wide open and let them rove around, from Halmoni's clasped hands to Yong Woon Uncle's bare feet. His feet looked grotesque and disfigured, his toenails thick, yellow, and cracking. Moving on, my eyes traveled up his khaki cargo pants and past his clean white T-shirt and his thin neck, finally settling on his face. A fly crept around his cheek and mouth, as if he were already a corpse. Too much had happened for him to notice. I searched his face for any traces, any family resemblance. I couldn't see any similarities to Halmoni or my mother or myself.

"Amen." Halmoni ended her prayer. She stuffed a stiff napkin under her oversized glasses to dab her eyes.

"Mother, your lifelong wish has been fulfilled," Yong Woon Uncle muttered, kneeling before her on one knee.

"The rest of the children and Ae Ran's mother must come," Halmoni said gravely, her words hanging in the stale air. Then, remembering, she peered at the kneeling old man closely and asked, "What was the name of the church we attended in Pyongyang?"

"Sangbok Church," he answered promptly.

"That's right," she said with a hesitant smile. "Your younger sister, Duk Hwa, told me to ask you that."

It was my turn to test him. I pulled out the tiny, yellowed snapshot that my mother had entrusted to me. "Do you know this person?" I questioned him.

Yong Woon Uncle drew the photo right up to his left eye, squeezing the other one shut. He examined it for less than a second, then laughed real big.

"You think I wouldn't recognize my own father's face? My father was a very distinguished and handsome man," he said proudly.

This gnarled old man was Lee Yong Woon.

I was convinced of it—not so much by what he said or what he knew, but by the feeling I had. And that truth brought with it a deep sadness that spread through my body. When I looked at him I felt both sympathy and disgust. A family was a high price to pay for freedom.

"How perfect it would have been if you all had come together. The rest must come. They have to come," Halmoni said again.

A baby's hearty, high-pitched wail startled me. I glanced over to the wooden frame bed. A very large baby was lying on his stomach on the bamboo mat spread there. He was diapered in a coarse cloth sealed with blue plastic that looked as if it had been cut from a cheap picnic tablecloth. The cloth and plastic were secured with a rope. I was shocked by the baby's size. He was substantially larger than I expected a North Korean baby to be. He appeared perfectly healthy and fine, except for the back of his head, which was severely flattened.

"He's your great-grandson," Yong Woon Uncle announced over the wails.

The baby was named Ko Churl Hyuk, but they called him Bul Churl. It was the most unwanted pet name imaginable, I thought. It literally meant "no come," because he was born during the worst famine in North Korea's history.

Hearing his grandfather talk about him, baby Bul Churl hiccuped and whined, but his arms didn't thrash about like a normal baby's. He just lay helpless on his round belly, drool seeping out of his heart-shaped mouth. He hiccuped and whined some more before Ae Ran finally hoisted him up by his arms as though he were a doll and attempted to burp him. When that didn't work, she unbuttoned her white collared blouse and, in front of everyone, drew out her hard, dark nipple and guided it into Bul Churl's mouth. Gagging, the baby pushed her breast away.

"May I?" I held out my arms, asking if I could hold the baby. Ae Ran gladly handed him over.

Baby Bul Churl, for all his size, didn't weigh a ton, but he did stink of urine and baby sweat. His dark halo of feathery hair was beaded with moisture. When I wiped his head he looked up at me with sad, haunted eyes. I felt their heavy weight. Already he had lost too much, suffered too much.

"Did you get married?" Yong Woon Uncle asked.

"Choi Soon Man told us you were engaged," Ae Ran relayed.

"Yes, there was someone, but she didn't want to marry him." My father stepped forward and spoke up, coming to his daughter's rescue so she wouldn't seem pathetic on videotape.

I tried to pretend I didn't care. But it made me crazy that the marriage question was always marched around. Every cell in my body longed for a baby of my own, ached for one, even while I resented the way my worth was measured by it. Just thinking about it made me burn. Desperate to be free, I peeled off my jacket and the leopard scarf that seemed to be getting tighter and tighter around my neck like a tourniquet, cutting off the oxygen supply to my head.

Suddenly they were all looking at me horrified, looking at my inner arms and neck. I had forgotten about the bruises and hickeys inflicted by Halmoni. Ae Ran especially appeared frightened.

"It's okay. Halmoni did it to me," I assured them.

Their facial expressions still didn't soften.

"Really, I'm fine. They don't hurt." I tried to explain the treatment but was distracted by Baby Bul Churl's cries again. Reaching into the backpack I pulled out the bottle of formula I had prepared in the hotel room, and offered it to him. He wasn't used to the stiff rubber nipple and rejected it with his loosely curled fists. I tried again. This time I squeezed a few drops of warm soy milk into his mouth, letting him get used to the taste. He didn't like that either and spat it out.

Bul Churl was crying now, a full-throated frustrated cry, milk gurgling out of his mouth. Not knowing how to soothe him, I let Hak Churl take him from me. Hak Churl was very careful with the baby, cradling his weak neck and head. He rocked him gently and offered his finger for the child to gum. Comforted, the baby's cries began to weaken, and he snuggled against his uncle's concave chest.

I wanted to ask what hidden reason had compelled Hak Churl to abandon his wife and child, knowing they would suffer severe punishment, if not death. I was sick at heart, knowing I had cast them away as well.

"Why didn't you bring Chun and your wife?" I asked, overcome by the desire—no, the need—to know everything.

Hak Churl lowered his face. He didn't respond.

I wouldn't let him off the hook. "Don't you love your wife and son?"

Hearing my second question, the others in the room laughed uneasily, unnerved by my frankness. I didn't care. For my own sanity I needed an explanation. Love was humanity's only salvation, not a bag of rice or money or their Great Leader. I needed to know.

"Yes." Hak Churl lowered his face again, as if it weighed as much as lead. "I was afraid to tell Chun's mother the whole truth. When we first got married, I couldn't tell her about Halmoni living in America. That's not something you proudly tell another person, even your wife. For her and our son, I wasn't going to come, but Father said it was Halmoni's wish."

I couldn't accept his reason. Because Halmoni wished it? What kind of answer was that?

"Leaving a sick child . . . I don't know how to feel right now," Hak Churl said, seeming to collapse in upon himself.

Leaving a child, period, I thought in anger.

Ae Ran continued for her brother. "Before we ever received that first letter from Kun Sam Uncle in America and learned Halmoni was still alive, Father would often wander off by himself. I would ask him where he was going, and he'd say he was trying to verify seven people's deaths. How was he going to do that? I thought. In 1989, a government organization dealing with Chosŏns abroad called Father to their office. The officer in charge asked Father if he had relatives abroad. He said no. Later the officer questioned him again, and that was when he told Father he had surviving relatives living in a different country. He wouldn't reveal where. After hearing that news, our family waited, but no more information was given to us. While I was in Pyongyang in 1990, I went to the office and begged them to help us, saying you were the only family we had left. Then in 1990, we were given your letter and encouraged to correspond with you. Each time with your letters you sent us a check for a hundred American dollars; our government kept ninety of it and gave us ten. That amount helped us to survive these last six years because food rations were completely halted. You don't know how frustrating it was not being able to write what we really wanted to say to you and just waiting and waiting all those years for you to visit us. Finally I couldn't bear it any longer. I was so desperate, and on top of that I was pregnant. When I met Choi Soon Man, he agreed to help us if we gave him a thousand won and got him to America. He only became nice to us after he spoke to you on the phone. After that Choi Soon Man credited us a few things to sell on the black market."

"I did try to visit you many times," Halmoni murmured glumly.

"For six years we believed you were coming, so we all waited and waited," said Ae Ran.

"Our government even fixed our house in preparation for your visit," Yong Woon Uncle informed us. Their government didn't want foreign visitors to see all the disrepair and decay.

My father explained to them what had happened. "When North Korea started allowing tourists inside the country, we were hoping to make the trip in 1993, but then the doors shut again. I managed to find a Korean travel agency in America that was allowed to organize groups into North Korea. At the last minute, I found out that we were required to sign documents pledging our loyalty to the Communist Party. When I refused, we were cut from the group and lost our deposit."

"When you didn't come, I went to Pyongyang several more times to find out what happened. They kept saying you were coming, but in reality I know now that it hadn't worked out," Ae Ran sighed.

"Mother, how did you get out of North Chosŏn during the war? I didn't think you did. I thought you turned back at the Daedong River," Yong Woon Uncle said, placing his hand over Halmoni's and rubbing it tenderly. She slipped hers away to wipe a stray tear.

"No, your younger brothers and I crawled over the part of the bridge that was blown apart by the bombs. Duk Hae was tied to my back. Duk Hwa was the only one to cross the river by boat."

"You crawled on the bridge, Mother?" There was awe in his shaky voice.

That year the Daedong River wasn't frozen over, like all the other winters past. Fishing boats and junks were ferrying people across to the other side. So many people were fighting each other to get on the already crowded boats, because the river stood between them and the South. Even women were shoving and cursing like men. My mother, Duk Hwa, who was only eleven years old at the time, was the only one able to get on a boat and hold on. So the boys and Halmoni had to climb up the footpath to the mangled bridge. The two ends were still standing, but the middle was only twisted steel rods. Still, people fought to get on it, pulling and shoving each other aside to cut ahead.

"What happened to Father's older sister and her family? Did they get out with you?"

"They all died except your uncle. But I never found out what became of him."

"They all died?"

"No one in that family lived long. But they lived longer than your father."

"Ah, Father, he died too soon," Yong Woon Uncle groaned sorrowfully.

His eyes scanned from left to right, then back again, as if he was mentally flying through the annals of his childhood.

The director interrupted at this point and asked Yong Woon Uncle, Ae Ran, and Hak Churl to squeeze in around Halmoni. They moved only after receiving a confirming nod from the guide, who suddenly appeared. He deliberately stood in the back of the room, away from the cameras.

Yong Woon Uncle sat in the steel folding chair next to Halmoni, shoulder to shoulder with her. His eyes were wide open, exposing the red capillaries marking his yellowed eyeballs. He looked scared to death in front of the cameras. They all did—no wonder, coming from where they had.

"Lee Yong Woon-ssi," the director called out in his deep broadcaster's voice.

Hearing his name, Yong Woon Uncle straightened and sat stiffly upright on the edge of his chair. He pressed his lips so tightly together that his mouth looked like a long-healed scar.

"How does it feel to see your white-haired mother and you yourself a grandfather?"

"He's not that old. At least he's not all shriveled up." Halmoni squinted crookedly at him.

The director nodded, not letting her annoyance affect him. "Lee Yong Woon-ssi, when you first learned of your mother's survival, how was your heart then? It must have been quivering."

"I was speechless," he mumbled in a small voice, glancing toward the guide again.

"Speak louder, please," the director requested strongly.

"I was speechless!" Yong Woon Uncle's voice rattled.

"Why were you speechless?"

"I—I thought they had all perished. When I received the information that she was still living, I wanted to go home and tell everyone, but I couldn't right away. I was afraid." He grabbed Halmoni's hand, feeling the skin and massaging it. Halmoni's fingers didn't grip back. She sat stiffly in the chair, looking more distant than I'd ever seen her.

"Halmoni, if your son had died instead of being lost, would your heart have been better?" The director asked the difficult question in hopes of prying an emotional response out of her.

"If he had died in my care and I had buried him, my heart wouldn't have ached so much. When I discovered he was alive, I worried if he was well. Was he eating? It would have been better if two of them were left behind, so they could have had each other. He was all alone. It always tormented my heart." She freed her hand and gripped her blouse with her fists as though to squeeze the pain out of herself. Worse than the pain, though, must have been the helplessness she felt.

"Yong Woon-ssi, what would you like to do for your mother when you reach South Korea? Do you have any thoughts? She doesn't have much time left," the director asked.

"Me?" Yong Woon Uncle blinked.

"Yes, what would you like to do for her?"

Yong Woon Uncle turned and faced Halmoni straight on. "Mother, since I'm the eldest son, I have to take care of my duties. Mother, I wish for you to live with us so I can take care of you." He clutched her hand again in both of his.

Halmoni let her hand drop for the third time, physically retreating. She didn't look at him directly. "That's not necessary. Everywhere I go people want me to live with them," she said strangely.

There was instant silence in the room, choking silence.

"Mother, at least let me treat you to a warm bowl of rice." Yong Woon Uncle reached over and clasped her stiff arm, holding it down like a balloon that was threatening to get away.

The director relentlessly pressed on. "Lee Yong Woon-ssi, what else would you like to do when you get to South Korea?"

Yong Woon Uncle paused to reflect. "More than anything else, do something good for the church." Inspired, he began singing a hymn he had memorized from his childhood.

> *Without Jesus there is no hope*
> *Jesus, You are my life and my friend.*
> *Without Your presence, I could not exist, not even live for a moment*
> *May I awake each morning with You in my heart*
> *May I sleep each night with You in my thoughts*
> *When I labor in the fields, may You be my overseer*
> *When I am alone at home, may I feel Your overwhelming love*
> *Even if a fish can live outside of the water*
> *Our spirit apart from You cannot survive.*

Yong Woon Uncle suddenly stopped singing, seeing Ae Ran's eyes shoot warning sparks at him.

"My father is a bad person. He could never be a true communist because he hid the hymns in his heart all those years. He should have been purged. He should have been killed by the firing squad." Ae Ran laughed nervously, brushing back a wayward wisp of hair.

Her response blew my mind.

"I didn't say Kim Il Sung is bad," Yong Woon Uncle said almost in desperation, trying to explain himself.

"Believing in Jesus Christ means that you respect the United States. Father should have been singing worshipful hymns to our Great Leader instead." Ae Ran suddenly brightened her expression and began to sing a song.

> At dawn in the morning
> I am thinking about our Great Leader
> In the evening looking at the moon
> I am thinking about our Comrade Leader.

Ae Ran sang with such sincerity and affection that I began to understand a little better why they did what they did. North Korea's system and ideology were so powerful, they could turn one family member against another. You couldn't even trust your own spouse or children for fear they'd betray you if you said anything against the party. To them, this was normal.

"Ae Ran, have your opinions changed at all since being in China?" asked the director.

Ae Ran swallowed. She straightened her back. She was trying so hard to look brave, but then she dropped her eyes and nodded guiltily. "All my life I have been told that our country is the best, that our socialist system is the best. Our stories and songs reflect that thought. They said we North Chosŏns are better off than any other people. The country gave us housing and rice—" She stopped abruptly, closing her eyes as though she couldn't bear the pain. When she opened them again, the tears poured down her cheeks. For a long time she said nothing, then all at once she said in a strangled voice, "Life in North Chosŏn is disastrous."

She looked shattered. Her father and Hak Churl nodded sympathetically. They knew exactly what she was talking about. No one would elaborate or say anything negative about Kim Il Sung, their Great Leader. They didn't have to. Their sagging, tormented eyes said what their mouths could not say yet.

The director filled in the silence. "Lee Teacher, please come here." He offered my father a collapsible chair up front. "What's going through your mind right now?"

My father sat back. His eyes were fixed down at his hands, trying to focus on something that wasn't there. "I feel guilty. Seeing only four here today, I'm filled with guilt that I've committed a great crime. We've separated three families. When things began to get complicated and Mother begged us to leave them alone, I just couldn't walk away, because I knew that my daughter's book might already be in the wrong hands. I place no blame on her, though. I blame myself, because while Hae Ri was writing her book and traveling around on tour speaking out against North Korea, I should have counseled her more seriously. It's dangerous to get North Korea upset." He sighed.

"When I saw Hae Ri's book in Changbai, I knew that if the police discovered Lee Yong Woon was our father, it would have been the end of our family, because if you do something wrong against the party, everyone dies or is crippled or disappears. Therefore, we had to go. We have to live," said Ae Ran, but it sounded as though she had lost hope.

"Have to live." Halmoni laughed, a strange, hoarse laugh.

"We have to live. And Halmoni being our grandmother, would she tell us to come if it was bad for us? Would our uncle come and do all this for us if it was bad? I also have a child. For his benefit I crossed."

"Okay, everyone," the guide cut in. "Lee Teacher, my man will escort you three to the street and see that you get into a taxi safely."

"So soon?" I swung around and cast him a wild-eyed glance in disbelief. The suddenness of the end of our reunion caused me to panic. It hadn't even been an hour yet. I had been sure we were at least going to spend one night together.

Ae Ran, Yong Woon Uncle, and Hak Churl all had the same crestfallen expressions. I could tell they yearned for more time as well, but they slowly rose to their feet. They seemed to be under the guide's spell. I'd noticed it earlier. They sat when he instructed them to sit. They spoke when he told them to speak. They straightened their backs when he told them to sit up straight. It seemed like they had traded in one dictator for another, and I didn't like it.

After everyone scrambled to take pictures and say good-bye, I slipped off the double-banded rings I had worn for a long time and placed them in Ae Ran's callused palms. "Give one of the rings to Mi Ran for me when you see her," I said, my voice barely above a whisper. My tongue stumbled over what else I should say, but I found myself lost for words even after all my rehearsed daydreams about what I would say to her on this day.

Ae Ran looked down at the two rings joined together by a thin gold clasp. Her eyes misted with tears again as she wrapped her slender fingers around them tightly. I wanted so badly to comfort her, to feel closer to her. But I couldn't. I could hardly look at her. I couldn't shake the gnawing, agonizing thought that we had saved only four lives. As much as I wanted to pass moral judgment on Ae Ran, Hak Churl, and Yong Woon Uncle for leaving the others behind, I reminded myself that they had been indoctrinated under North Korea's dictatorship system—a horrible system that destroyed humanity from the core.

XX

August 20, 1997

During the remainder of our stay in China, we didn't see Yong Woon Uncle and the others again. They were busy getting their hair cut, brushing their teeth, and scrubbing their faces. The guide had them brush and scrub hard four or five times a day with toothpaste and soap, luxuries that weren't available to them in North Korea. Hak Churl especially needed it. Black coal dust and sweat and sun exposure had stained his skin deeply. Even though Hak Churl had graduated from college with an engineering degree, the party had assigned him to hard labor in a coal mine because of his father's bad record. Ae Ran suffered the same discrimination. She had applied to the prestigious Kim Il Sung University in Pyongyang but was assigned to a trade school, which was the lowest type of educational institution in their society. Later Ae Ran had figured out a way to trade her assignment and managed to attend Shinuiju Light Industry College. After graduation, she worked in a beer factory and got married.

Having seen what had befallen his older brother and sister, I couldn't understand why Mun Churl believed so strongly that the party would favor and protect him. I was still holding on to the hope that once he returned to Hyesan and discovered that half of his family had defected, he'd realize there was no future for him in North Korea.

We received word from the older Chosŏn brother that Mi Ran had come out to the river and signaled that Mun Churl would arrive home on the twenty-third. Mi Ran had phoned him at school. Ordinary citizens didn't have private telephone lines. Phones were mainly available at government offices, factories, cooperatives, and workplaces. Fortunately, Mi Ran worked as a switchboard operator. Her job allowed her to sneak in personal calls, and she was able to contact Mun Churl immediately. She had told her brother that their father had suffered a severe heart attack so Mun Churl would return quickly.

The guide was preparing to leave for Changbai on the twenty-first to offer Mun Churl and the others one final chance. He had come to our hotel room the day before to pick up the still shots I had taken at the reunion. He planned on sending the photos across to Mi Ran with another letter from Ae Ran telling them about their journey after crossing the Yalu River. Ae Ran wrote about the grandmother she met for the first time, how the streets of China were developed beyond imagination, and the delicious food.

I was desperate to accompany the guide to Changbai, not for the adventure or because I desired to see the border again but because I had lost confidence in him. He was great with logistics but painfully awkward with people. Since the beginning, he hadn't known how to deal with my relatives to inspire trust and courage. Yong Woon Uncle responded to him because North Koreans were trained to follow orders and my uncle so desperately wanted to see his mother. It would take a lot more finesse to convince Mun Churl and the others to defect. It would require soothing words and gentle prodding. I believed I had a better chance of getting through to them. The guide's awkwardness could cost us five lives.

My eyes stayed on the guide as he strode toward the window, then stood by it, his strong yet delicate hands resting flat on the window's ledge. The light from the morning sun, fully up in the sky, sensually threaded itself around him and made a slit of bright color along the left side of the double bed. Remembering what Halmoni had said, I checked to see if he would roll the thumb and index finger on his right hand around the fourth finger on his left, where a wedding band was usually worn. He didn't do it.

The guide looked briefly at the sun, then drew the drapes closed, snuffing out the light. The room became instantly depressing. Turning back around, he looked me straight in the eye without speaking. I knew he read my mind, but I waited. It was to my advantage to deal with the guide face-to-face, in private, or my request would be shot down in the presence of my father and Halmoni.

"Can you make us some coffee?" The guide wanted to remind me of my woman's place.

I felt my face flame, but I smiled pleasantly and walked over to the alcove bar. I plugged in the hotpot. While I waited for the water to boil, I saw the guide lean over to my father and whisper. My father unbuckled his leather belt and reached inside his pants. He handed over his portion of the money, all ten thousand dollars, to the guide. Halmoni and I were told to do the same. I hesitated a moment before bringing out the blue tampon box. I didn't understand why we were handing over the full amount when the navy ship had been canceled.

"Are they still going by boat?" I asked.

"No. That route's not an option any longer," the guide replied.

"Then why do you need so much money?"

"Yes, how will you be spending it?" asked Halmoni.

"Now that the group is split, everything is going to cost double. I have to bribe the border guards again and pay my aides. This time everyone might want a lot more. I have to be prepared for anything."

"But the whole amount?" I asked again.

"What about my coffee?" the guide reminded me. A faint smile quirked his mouth.

I was itching to say something biting, but I controlled my temper. I turned away from him and walked back to the hotpot. The water was boiling. I prepared three cups with creamer and sugar. On a lacquered tray, I brought the cups over and served Halmoni and my father first, then the guide last. I watched with great satisfaction as he took one sip and his lips slid into an ugly curl. His coffee I had made extra sweet with six pink packets of Sweet'n Low.

The guide took a second sip, then collected the money. He pursed his lips, let them go with a smack, and then he left. He barely drank his coffee.

My opportunity to speak to the guide away from my father and Halmoni appeared when Jambbong's wife called at six to ask if I would shop with her for supplies and clothes for Ae Ran's group. I was overjoyed, and surprisingly Halmoni released the reins a little, affording me some freedom. I raced out of the hotel and jumped into a cab before she had a change of heart.

It was exhilarating to be able to go out on my own and meet a friend. It had been a long while since I'd been able to think about unimportant things such as shopping. I checked my wallet. There was enough cash for something to eat and a few gifts. Just thinking about it made me happy.

Eager to stretch my arms and legs, I had the cab driver turn a corner and let me out early. I knew I shouldn't have been out in the middle of the street all by myself, but it felt liberating to walk the remaining block to the Chosŏn Hotel. I was in no hurry to get there. The temperature was much more pleasant than the day before. A cool, choppy breeze carrying the savory smell of sesame oil and garlic fluttered the bright yellow scarf tied around my neck and played with my ponytail.

I burst through the hotel's revolving glass doors. As soon as I entered the lobby, I saw Jambbong's wife. She was all dressed up in a double-breasted pinstriped navy suit with a long skirt slit high on the side and ankle socks over nylons. Her hair was neatly pinned back with sparkling rhinestone barrettes.

Straight ahead, behind her, I spotted the guide sitting in the empty coffee shop. On the table there were two full cups of coffee on saucers, no steam, and the ashtray was littered with smashed butts, which told me he had been there for a while. The guide flicked his smoking cigarette at me, issuing another imperial order for me to come. Suddenly I was seething with anger. I didn't want to speak to him anymore. I wasn't going to ask him for anything. I wasn't going to fall on my knees and beg. Before I could execute a U-turn, Jambbong's wife slipped her arm into mine and held me in a tight, friendly grip.

"Talk to him nicely," she said.

"He doesn't deserve it. He's—he's mean," I said very sassily, one hand on my hip.

Jambbong's wife found me amusing.

"Well, he is. All he does is yell orders at me. I'm sick of him."

"All Chosŏn men are like that."

"Your husband's nothing like that."

Her eyes widened playfully. "My husband's terrible. He won't even wash a sock. He pushes me around all the time. Men are all the same, I tell you. Hae Ri, the guide is truly a good man. He's just difficult to deal with sometimes, but he adores you so much, I know. I've never seen him act like this over a woman before."

Lucky me.

"Won't you talk to him? For me?" Jambbong's wife said it with such warmth and deep caring, I couldn't deny her request. I let her drag me to his table, tossing a glance over my shoulder to see if my father or Halmoni had tailed me. I stopped just in front of the guide's table, slanting a look at him with unconcealed distaste. I decided that he was definitely not a handsome man. He had sharp, angular cheekbones and thin, flat lips that fused into a straight implacable line. The skin along his mulish jawline was pitted, and another scar marked his obstinate chin. When I thought about the kiss, I wanted to cringe.

"Sit." He flicked his cigarette at the chrome-legged chair directly across the table from him.

I whacked down my purse on the table, splashing the coffee, then gingerly arranged myself on the chair diagonal from him. I treated him to a view of my stony profile.

"Now, you two stop acting silly. Let's enjoy this time." Jambbong's wife tried to soften the tension.

"Why is Hae Ri so pretty?" the guide said without the slightest bit of embarrassment.

The compliment, so unexpected, made me blush.

Pleased, Jambbong's wife gave me a big smile.

I rolled my eyes to the ceiling and responded with a simple "You're crazy."

Jambbong's wife patted my hand and laughed. "That's good, you're talking to each other." With a little twinkle in her eye, she excused herself and exited the café to go shopping on her own. It was suddenly clear that this meeting was a setup. I wasn't going shopping.

The guide moved around the cigarette butts in the ashtray with the burning tip, then smashed the one he was holding. I didn't know what he was thinking. Every time I thought I had him all figured out, I realized how little I understood him.

"Are you upset with me?" He curved his shoulders forward.

"If I go with you to Changbai, I may not be anymore," I said in a nicer voice, placing my hand on his bare arm for emphasis. He looked at my hand, then covered it with his own, rubbing the back of it and toying with the silver ring on my thumb.

"I've fallen for your charms before."

"So I can go?"

"No," he muttered, as if he was trying to convince himself.

I yanked my hand away and crossed my arms firmly over my chest, giving him a killing look. "If you had listened to me in the first place and dealt with Ae Ran instead of her daddy, we'd all be in Seoul by now. You know it's true. She would have organized her family more quickly and effectively. Because you relied on her father, he created delays and chaos. While he was drowning his sorrows in alcohol, his wife sold the house and called her older sister, and

Mun Churl ran back to school. Now everything's all messed up," I spat in English.

"Yes, that may be true, but my answer's still no."

"That's so unfair," I shot back.

"Death isn't fair."

"Let me speak to Mi Ran and my aunt. I know I can convince them to come over."

"Look, be a good girl and drink your coffee. I ordered it black, just the way you like it." He pushed the cup in front of me.

"I don't want it. You drink it!" My voice began rising, and I let my temper go this time. I was over him and his chauvinistic, superior attitude.

"Hae Ri, don't be like that. Why are you getting so emotional? Be reasonable. Your presence will only complicate things."

"Your ego can't bear the thought that a woman may just be smarter, stronger, and do your job better than you. You can't stand it. But it's true. I can see right through you. Deep down you're weak. You're scared!" I jabbed my index finger at his face, an inch away from his nose.

The guide's black eyes blazed. He was seething with outrage. His face and neck were turning reddish purple, and for the first time I was reminded that he used to be a gangster. A second after that realization, almost on cue, a gust of wind slammed into the window behind me with such force that it sounded like thunder.

"Remove your finger," he said in a low, menacing tone. His own fingers flexed and unflexed, and the muscles in his bare arms tensed and bulged as if he ached to send me crashing to the floor. A smidgen of fear rose in my chest. If he did smack me, there'd be nothing I could do about it in this part of the world, where men made the laws and traditions to exclusively fit their needs and greed.

Defeated, I lowered my finger.

"Damn it," the guide swore under his breath, running a hand through his hair, then rummaged for something inside his jacket pocket, seeking a distraction. He took out an unopened pack of 88. He tapped the top end against his white palm, ripped open the plastic seal, and carefully selected a cigarette. Blue smoke poured from his nostrils and circled around his head. The nicotine eased his nerves, and he regained control of himself.

"If your father says you can go, I'll take you." His voice was sounding easy again.

"Let me say this one more time: I don't need to get my father's permission. I work and pay my own bills. I drink when I want to drink. I'm my own person. Get that through your head." My voice was low, fast, and bitter, so that he could hear and know that I had swallowed my share of universal hardship.

"I'm a Korean man, and so is your father. This is how we function."

I didn't answer.

"Hae Ri, we have two choices. That's all. Do you know what they are?"

I was uninterested in his little game to test whether I'd been listening or if I was intelligent enough to grasp the vast knowledge that he was about to bestow on me.

"Hae Ri." He said my name more tenderly to draw my burning eyes to his. As much as I hated to admit it, those hooded dark eyes of his had a powerful hold on me. When they stared at me at such close range I could feel the vibration from deep within. The feeling made me mad all over again. What was the matter with me? I wouldn't allow myself to be moved by his strength. I wasn't going to acknowledge it.

"We shouldn't marry; we should just have a child. Or we can decide not to see each other after this project is complete."

If it hadn't been so preposterous, I would have been completely floored. Now, he wanted me to have his baby without the commitment or liability of marriage. What made him think I didn't want to get married? What made him think that I'd want him as a lover? Suddenly his ridiculous proposal provoked a fit of belligerent laughter, high and shaky, the way you laugh when you've been too close to the edge.

The guide sat up straighter. "What's so funny?" he groused.

"I have higher ambitions for myself than to be your baby-making mistress."

"Why would you say that? You wouldn't be my mistress."

"Really? What about your wife and kid?" I knitted my fingers together loosely and rested them beneath my chin.

"Who told you I had a wife?"

"Doesn't matter, does it?" I blew a breath, rising to my feet. I turned my back on him to leave, but then stopped. Spinning back around again, I leaned way over the table, brushed my lips against his ear, and whispered in a sexy alto voice, "I still think you're rude."

I struck home. I could tell by the clenching of his jaw.

I walked away, purposely emphasizing the sounds of my heels.

Outside, the humid air was heavy with the fecund smell of saturated earth. It was pouring rain now. Slabs of aluminum-colored clouds blocked out what was left of the sun and darkened the street to a slippery snake, scaly with car headlights. I joined the half dozen people waiting for a cab under the shelter of the hotel entrance.

I was let off in front of Gloria Plaza, yards away from the revolving door. Tipping the cabdriver generously, I got out and sprinted through the driving rain into the hotel. I skated across the slippery floor in the direction of the elevators and went up to my father's floor. At his door, I knocked firmly three times and went charging in, bringing with me the smell of damp denim and the ozone odor of the storm.

My father's eyes were bloodshot. He had been crying or drinking, I didn't ask which. I didn't want to know. When he saw my dripping appearance, his mouth grew wide and he rushed into the bathroom to retrieve a towel. I mopped the end of my wet ponytail and sponged my clothes off quickly, then got to the purpose of my visit.

My father protested at once.

"Explain to me why I can't go."

"This is not the fun. This is not the cartoon," he said in English.

"I am going," I said with a firm voice.

"Why you want be rebel?" He narrowed his reddened eyes, looking at me as if without recognition.

"Now I'm a rebel. I wasn't a rebel when you sent me to Dalian."

Frustrated with me, he switched back to Korean. "Things have changed."

"Yeah, things certainly have, and you can't even see what's happening."

"Listen to me. This last trip to Changbai, I saw how really scary it is there. Even I don't want to go back again."

"Well, I'm not scared."

"We could have all gotten caught."

"It didn't happen, did it?"

"It's not safe, especially for women. This is very serious. They kidnap women."

"Men get kidnapped, too."

"Hae Ri, I have a headache. The three of us are leaving for Seoul tomorrow."

"You can't make me." I tried to sound commanding, but I knew it was a whine, a soft, plaintive, pathetic whine.

"You'll obey me or we give up this mission. That's final."

What my father said stole my breath, and words of protest died without making it past my lips. This was not my father. This place had changed him, and I hated what he had become, hated what he represented. He now demanded that I shut up, behave, and be unquestioning. His betrayal wounded me in the most extreme way.

Draping the damp towel over the desk chair, I laboriously walked out of the room. My spirit retreated even further into an almost weird state of detachment. I felt emotionally anesthetized, yet hyperaware, as I wandered back outside into the storm. I walked to the far side of the hotel and found a private spot to sit. A soft moody light burned from sconces by the emergency door. I sat there listening to the liquid sound of the night and looked out at the eerie scenery. The streaming summer storm around me unleashed rain in driving sheets and obscured the buildings, rendering them flat and erased. Thunder boomed in the distance, faint but powerful. Moments later came another boom of thunder, and the sky cracked with fissures of fire.

The lightning brought more rain, falling hard and thick, thicker than I'd ever seen rain, streaking down my hair, streaking down my face, streaking down my neck, washing away my features.

XXI

August 21, 1997

Jambbong had driven the guide back to Changbai to convince the five remaining family members to cross the river. Jambbong's wife stayed behind to escort Ae Ran's group farther southwest to Beijing. They couldn't remain in the safe house in Shenyang much longer. The owner had made an unexpected visit the day before and became very suspicious when she saw Ae Ran's fearful group. In Beijing, the guide had another safe house lined up. Ae Ran and the others could hide there until the rest of the family joined them. Once reunited, all nine members would ride the new Beijing-Hanoi passenger train to the South Korean embassy in Vietnam.

The train ride from Shenyang to Beijing would take them nine hours. Jambbong's wife booked two first-class soft sleeper compartments for the long-distance journey. The compartments contained four soft bunk beds, clean bedding, lace curtains, porcelain teacups, and a washroom with a Western-style toilet. Ae Ran and her baby stayed in one compartment with the SBS cameraman, who acted as her husband. Jambbong's wife stayed with Hak Churl and Yong Woon Uncle in the other compartment.

As they rode the train toward Beijing, my father, Halmoni, and I flew out of China without even having had a chance to say good-bye to them. The guide felt it was too risky. To be frank, I was relieved. It was wiser to avoid the guide, wiser to act as though nothing had happened.

In Seoul, I stayed in the terminal to await my flight to Los Angeles, and my father and Halmoni headed for customs. He was escorting Halmoni to Elder Kim's *ch'iryo* clinic. It was better for her physical and emotional health to remain in Asia till the mission was complete instead of flying back and forth.

I, on the other hand, couldn't stomach the thought of staying there for even one more day. I found out later that while I was safely boarding my plane, an agent of the KCIA intercepted my father and Halmoni at the bottom of the escalator. He ushered them through the airport, bypassing immigration and customs, to a private door that led right out onto the street. A black sedan was waiting to pick them up just outside the door. Once inside the car, the agent interrogated my father as to the purpose of our trip. The agent naturally assumed that my father, as the male head of our family, was the mastermind behind the mission, and therefore I was spared the interrogation. Under pressure, my father revealed our entire ordeal in Shenyang, ending with a plea for the agency's permission to bring the refugees to South Korea. The agent wouldn't commit to anything. All he said was that he'd see what he could do.

Those vague words triggered alarm bells rather than providing any reassurance. The KCIA was capable of anything. I had learned from my father that the communists had indeed kidnapped the South Korean actress Halmoni had been talking about, but it was the KCIA that abducted Kim Dae Jung. After he nearly toppled the dictatorship of President Park Chung Hee in 1971, Kim Dae Jung was marked as a troublemaker. In 1973, the KCIA and the secret police kidnapped Kim Dae Jung while he was touring through Japan to gather support for the restoration of democracy in his country. The agents burst into his Tokyo hotel, blindfolded him, gagged him with a chunk of wood, put him aboard a small boat, and sailed him out to sea. He would have been murdered if it weren't for the worldwide uproar that demanded his safe return. He was released near his home in South Korea.

Outside Los Angeles International Airport, I planted my feet on the solid pavement and sucked in deep lungfuls of car fumes as if I were smelling the sweetness of vanilla. It was one of those very perfect days that L.A. was famous for, not too hot and not smoggy. The sky was a pretty pastel blue and full of cotton-ball clouds. I spread my arms and embraced the whole city. I was home, and there was no other place in the world like it. I wanted to do something typically American like eat a juicy hamburger dripping with ketchup and topped with pickles.

My roommate, Tiffani, picked me up on the curb in her boyfriend's leaf-green Honda Accord. A faint smell of cologne permeated the car, and the stereo was cranked all the way up. In my two-and-a-half-week absence, Tiffani had totally changed her appearance. Her quarter-inch twists had been replaced by shoulder-length extensions, braided and gathered on the crown of her head. The braids accentuated her dark chocolate complexion and cat eyes. She looked younger, girlish.

"How's Harmony?" she asked as she hugged me, her smile wide.

"Fine," I replied lightly, slumping comfortably into the seat, one knee propped up. "She's staying in Seoul a little longer. But my father'll be back in a few days."

"How are you doin'?"

Burnt. Shitty. "Good. It's good to be home." I put on my sunglasses and adjusted them against the spangled sunlight ricocheting off the geometric buildings that lined the long stretch of Century Boulevard. I couldn't share with Tiffani all my strange and troubled thoughts. Nobody was supposed to know about my North Korean family's defection. My friends believed my trips to Asia were a continuation of my book tour, and my neighbors were so used to me going out of town to visit my boyfriend in Hong Kong that no one ever pried.

"So, what's goin' on? What did I miss?"

Tiffani's cheery banter distracted me all the way up La Cienega Boulevard, past Beverly Hills, into West Hollywood. We reached our tree-lined block so fast, I couldn't believe it. In front of our apartment complex, Tiffani swerved over to the curb and dropped me off, engine still humming. I felt like running inside, but the energy just wasn't there. The adrenaline that had kept me going through most of China began to dissipate. I was so tired I could barely lift an arm to wave good-bye to Tiffani as she put the car in gear and peeled off to meet up with her boyfriend.

When I hobbled into the apartment again, halting at my bedroom doorway, I felt anxious again, not calm. It was hot, and the dust got caught in my throat. I threw open the window and sat down on the ledge. The fresh scent of summer mixed with the smell of sun and flowers. The buds had all turned into huge blossoms of red while I was away. There was a book I hadn't finished still lying on the floor where I had tossed it last April. It was *A Moveable Feast*, by Ernest Hemingway. I picked it up and dusted the cover off a little, then placed it on the nightstand, next to the answering machine. The red light was flashing. I hit play, switching on the incoming messages. I heard Julie's voice. "Hey, I heard you were some kind of rabble-rouser. Call me when you get back." *Beep.*

My jaw clenched. Hearing my sister say that touched a nerve. I wasn't a rabble-rouser or a troublemaker or a fanatic.

Suddenly I wanted to concentrate on my life, alter it. An impulse drove me forward even though I was exhausted. I tore down the romantic mosquito netting above the bed along with the cream silk curtains and my pictures, rolled up the woven bamboo mat, and pushed all the furniture into the center of the room. The next thing I did was drag out the stepladder and get out the tape, newspaper, rollers, and unopened paint cans I had bought the year before. I'd wanted to liven up the apartment, but Steven had disapproved of the color.

Now I put the newspaper down on the wooden floor and mixed the paint with a twelve-inch ruler. I'd never done this kind of work before, but I didn't feel the need to read any directions or ask advice from anyone. I just did it.

Dunking the fuzzy pink roller directly into the can sideways, I painted my room a deep Mediterranean blue. Paint dripped on top of my head and onto my face, into my mouth, so that I could taste it on my tongue. I didn't stop. I didn't mind the ache in my back and shoulders. Hard physical labor felt great. It kept me from thinking too much. I could see the progress. Painting produced immediate results. In one short single day, I had improved my life.

But in the days that followed, everything spun out of control again. I received crank calls, sometimes five to seven calls in one hour, at all hours of the day and night. No one ever left a message, but someone was there. I could hear breathing. Several times I dialed *69 to identify the number, but evidently the caller was not traceable. In desperation, I stopped answering the phone and let the machine screen the calls. When the caller started leaving messages, I was mildly surprised to find that it was the guide.

"Hae Ri, this is me." *Beep.*

"Hae Ri, I need to talk to you, please." *Beep.*

"Why haven't you called me?" *Beep.*

"You need to call me. I shouldn't have to be the one constantly calling you when you should be the one calling me." *Beep.*

"I need to talk to you. Why aren't you listening?" *Beep.*

I tried to avoid his calls as long as I could, hoping he'd forget me and move on, but his hostile messages kept choking my machine. Finally, after forty-some hours, I knew I couldn't put him off any longer—it was too dangerous, his messages were becoming more belligerent. The next time the phone rang, I picked up the receiver. There was a lot of static and background traffic noise.

"Hae Ri? Is that you?"

"Yes," I answered, my voice flat.

"Why do you treat me so badly?" he snarled. Before I could answer, he cut me short. "I've done everything for you. You're really a wicked woman turning a man's head, making him dream of you. Who are you? Who are you to me? Do you know who I am?" he hissed.

I gave no response. I didn't lash back. The desire to do so wasn't in me anymore. I was tired of being belittled and beaten down and disappointed. I had decided that from here on I would shut up, sit down, and act ladylike. I'd let them, the men, handle everything.

"Nothing," he said. "I'm no one."

I wasn't moved by his humility. All I wanted to do was get off the phone. "I have to go," I said. As I pulled the receiver away from my ear, I heard his piercing scream: *"Hae Ri, I love you."*

I hung up the receiver, ending the call. I pressed and pinched and pulled the skin at the bridge of my nose, trying desperately to extract those three words, fighting back the flood of emotions they provoked.

Don't think about that.

I went over to the kitchen, opened the corner cabinet, and looked inside for a moment. It was too early in the morning for a drink, but the wine with the sour-apple-green label talked to me, and I was thirsty. I hefted the bottle off the shelf and clumsily poured myself a glass. As I gulped the wine, I retraced in my mind all the things I had done and said to get me into this crazy, dangerous predicament with very little room to maneuver. I should have been less emotional, less flirtatious, more amiable. Now this man, who had control over the mission, wasn't thinking about the nine lives that depended on him, but locked on his distorted love for me.

The phone rang again. Startled, I backed away from it so fast that I crashed against the refrigerator and crushed the glass of wine in my hand. I tottered, almost fell, but caught the edge of the sink to keep my balance. For some reason, the machine wasn't picking up. I should have left the receiver off the hook. I closed my eyes tightly, as if that could block out the sound, but after a dozen long shrills I reluctantly answered it before it woke up the entire neighborhood.

"I need to see you," the guide slurred. His liquidy voice immediately put me on guard. He was drunk.

"Why are you doing this?"

"Why? Don't you know?"

I waited. I realized that my hand was cut and dripping with blood.

"Ever since I first saw you at the Shilla Hotel, I haven't been able to get your face out of my mind." He stopped, then let out a surprising chuckle. "Can I tell you something funny?"

"Sure." I shook my head, dreading what he might reveal.

The guide's voice sobered. "For many years, I didn't think about sex. When I was younger I had to be drunk to be with a woman. The moment I was finished I felt her body turn cold while I was still inside her. I hated that feeling and I hated them for it, so I'd walk for miles to shake off the anger. When I got older I realized it wasn't them, but me. I think it'll be different with the woman I love." In his trailing words, I heard the fear that he'd told me too much and the obvious pain.

His confession was unbearable. My emotions struggled between disgust and sadness, and I began to feel ill. First, a faint dizziness hit me, then an intense nausea rolled over me as the wine unleashed a terrible memory inside my head. I knew the feeling of being with someone who didn't, couldn't, love you. After it was all over, I lay bare on the damp mattress feeling cold and empty, as if I had just vomited. Nothing left of me . . .

Suddenly I understood so much about the guide, why he was the way he was. He had had sex, but he'd never made love to a woman. He had never experienced the magic, the feeling of being home.

"I need to see you. I'll fly out there," said the guide.

"No. Don't come here. What about Mi Ran and the others?"

"That's all you care about, isn't it? You don't really care about me. All of you are using me." His voice was contemptuous.

Each time I attempted to answer him he overrode me, battered me, accused me of all sorts of other terrible things, as if he were cross-examining a criminal in a court of justice. I felt myself withering. I thought of options. In the end, I realized that there weren't options. I had no choice but to obey his request, or else he might abandon the mission. Without the guide we were lost. He had all the contacts, the safe houses, the guides, the experience, and our fifty thousand dollars.

"Okay, I'll fly out to China," I returned, exhausted.

"No, meet me in Seoul on the twenty-seventh. Until then I'll drink," the guide swore, and ended our conversation.

I was on my own. As I planned my travel arrangements, my whole being focused on what needed to be done. I had to smooth things over with the guide, return his attention to the mission, then fly back home. All of this without my family finding out.

On August 25, four days after I arrived home, at nine P.M., I secured the apartment and went down the back stairs carrying my overnight bag. My car was parked in the garage, just beneath my living room window. A bare fluorescent bulb in the ceiling socket gave just enough bluish light. The garage was deserted.

I had to maneuver past a badly parked red convertible Miata to get to the driver's door. When I slipped the key in and tried to open it, I discovered the lock was busted. My car had been broken into. They hadn't stolen anything inside as far as I could tell, and no other car in the garage appeared to have been tampered with.

Slowly, I backed out of the dim garage and ran upstairs. I fumbled for the right key on the chain. Finding it, I hurried inside the apartment, locked the door behind me, and went to the phone. When I was holding the receiver in my hand I didn't know who to call. The sheriff? The police? The FBI? AAA? What would I tell them without sounding paranoid or crazy? It was impossible to determine who broke into my car. It could have been an agent of the KCIA or the Reds or simply a petty criminal who'd wanted to steal my stereo but didn't have time to pull it out.

I decided to call for a taxi to take me safely to the airport. Just as I was about to leave for the airport, I received a collect call from Jambbong in Changbai. The guide and the director had been captured at the river while waiting to make contact with Mi Ran. Jambbong didn't know whether it was the Chinese or North Korean police who arrested them.

The shocking news hit me full force, and my heart gave a sickening leap as I looked wildly around for an invisible enemy. I ran around the apartment double-checking all the windows, drawing the curtains together, and propping chairs against the front and back doors. The place was at once secured, but no room could be made secure enough to protect me from the brutality of my own thoughts.

My imagination dredged up horrible scenes of armed Red soldiers overpowering the guide and the director. Their nostrils were pierced as though they were steers, and they were dragged across the crashing river. The Reds carted them through a remote path that led to a dark valley surrounded by steep mountains, totally cut off from the rest of the world. At the base of the valley was a massive concentration camp with guard dogs and ten-foot-tall watchtowers holding guards with loaded machine guns. In front of thousands of ragged prisoners, all so skinny and weak, their captors condemned the guide and the director without a trial to a public execution as spies working for the capitalist American devils.

The gruesome picture intensified, and I saw Mi Ran, Aunt, Mun Churl, Hak Churl's wife, and her son bound together. Gasoline was being poured over their heads. Before they were torched, each person was shot in both knees, both arms, and the side of the neck. Right before death came to them, they were set afire.

Stop it, I told myself fiercely, but it was impossible to stop thinking like this. Halmoni's paranoia had really gotten to me. I kept imagining the execution. I kept seeing the hot flames rising. I was shaky for days as I waited at my apartment. I had postponed my trip to Seoul, waiting, not knowing, worrying about the guide, the director, and my uncle's family.

It was only after my father returned to Los Angeles on August 29, my thirty-third birthday, did I recover. He had come back without Halmoni but brought with him the news that the two men had been released. When the Chinese police had spotted them creeping around the riverbank with camera equipment, they were arrested, and the director's cameras and footage were confiscated. For twenty-four hours the men were roughed up and interrogated, then they were released and put on a plane out of China.

Before the guide's capture he had messengered to my father and Halmoni in Seoul three letters from Mi Ran.

DEAR RESPECTED UNCLE,

What a tremendous hardship you have gone through making the long, long journey to the motherland. It is not that we don't appreciate all you and Comrade Guide have done for us, but if our entire family disappears, the motherland authorities will look to you for answers. Also, we will be committing a very serious crime, be considered traitors, the consequences of which reach beyond death.

Mun Churl Older Brother and I are in the prime of our youth, and we know our time, place, and fate, but we worry about Chun and his mother. After Hak Churl Older Brother left, Mother and I tried to get Chun's mother to cross the river on the twenty-second by telling her that Halmoni desperately wished to see her great-grandson, but she refused to go. She thinks Older Brother will return in several days. She continues to check the river until three or four every afternoon. Young Chun still ails from a sinus infection and he cries constantly for his father. The situation is not something we can discuss so we sit in angst.

Father and Older Sister's whereabouts haven't attracted any attention yet; however, Hak Churl Older Brother's disappearance is a problem since he *was in the midst of a medical treatment. So please talk to him, Uncle, and send him back.*

I was ready at dawn on the sixteenth to go, but my feet would not leave the ground because leaving Mother behind all alone was unthinkable. The wall of tears blocked my steps. I couldn't let go of Mother's hands.

Why does separation happen? How it splits my heart.

An hour later at seven, I went out to the river and searched for the younger Chosŏn brother, but he didn't appear. I waited until nine, then returned home. I kept returning to the river and finally met with his older brother, who told me that Father and the others had made it across safely.

Uncle, I truly believe us staying behind has made it safer for the others. The army commander has come by, a relative from Kil-joo visited, and Choi Soon Man Uncle stopped by. He shows up once a day to ask where everyone has gone. I said that Ae Ran Older Sister was away to earn some money.

With all these people appearing unannounced, how fortunate that I at least remained behind. It would have appeared suspicious if only Mother was left.

I talked to Mun Churl Older Brother on the telephone. His graduation ceremony was finished on the twenty-first. He was planning to depart school on the twenty-third. But yesterday, the train jumped the tracks due to an accident involving a military vehicle, so he'll arrive on the twenty-fifth.

My heart is racing and my pen is running all over the place.

Uncle, please don't worry too much about us, but I request that you care for our father and Ae Ran Older Sister, and send back Hak Churl Older Brother. We need him here for our own sake.

When reunification finally happens, I promise I will be there to share the joy.

From
Mi Ran

DEAR RESPECTED GRANDMOTHER,

You've traveled a long way to the motherland, thousands and ten thousands of miles, to care for us, but instead we've made your heart heavier and we are in agony because of it. We want so much to be next to you, run to you, but there'll be a huge rumbling even before we reach you.

You probably have heard from Father that I could not leave Mother, old and weak. Her eyes aren't very good these days. When she's under great stress they become bloodshot, blinding her totally. I'm terribly sorry that we weren't able to bring you joy. I have many things to tell you, but most of all I wish you a long life till the day of reunification.

Grandmother, no matter where I go I will never forget your love for us. Even in my dreams, I envision Grandmother, Uncle, Aunt, and Hae Ri.

From Mi Ran
in the motherland

AE RAN OLDER SISTER, THE ONE I LONG TO SEE,

Day after day we worry to death about you and Father. I have a huge headache due to Chun's mother. Aunt's son is a problem, too. He comes almost daily. He arrived on the morning you left and asked if you went to Hwa-po. I told him you did.

On the seventeenth at seven in the morning, I went out and talked to a border guard. He didn't want to reveal anything, but I managed to drag out of him the fact that you had money to collect in China and thus crossed the river. I breathed easily then.

After reading this letter, send back Hak Churl Older Brother. It would have been all right if he just left without saying a word, but he told people about his trip. He also left in the midst of his medical treatment and the business manager keeps inquiring about his whereabouts. I don't know what else to do.

Remember you must not do anything to deface the motherland even after you get out. Make sure for our sake or we will all be dead.

Older Sister, if you get near Grandmother, give her our regards.

Mi Ran

For all our planning and suffering, we had achieved only more pain, more tears, more wondering. In my mind, I pleaded, threatened, and begged Mi Ran and the others to act quickly and cross the river. Otherwise I couldn't bear to think about their fate.

Journey Four

XXII

September 30, 1997

The farther Ae Ran's group moved away from the Yalu River, the more certain I felt that Mi Ran's group was being hurled headlong toward death. After the guide's release from jail, I waited for instructions to fly to Seoul, but he didn't contact me. A week later, he called my father from Vietnam. The guide had sneaked back into China on August 29 by international ferry. The ferry departed from Inchon, South Korea, during the night and arrived the next morning in Dalian. From Dalian, the guide rode the train to Beijing. He wanted the first group out of China and off his hands. The strain of the mission had become too much for him.

The guide dressed Ae Ran's group in new clothes and had their hair cut short and styled. Ae Ran and Yong Woon Uncle were given fake gold-rimmed glasses and Hak Churl a gold watch and tennis shoes—signs of civilization. Their looks were vastly improved by the neater dress and the lighter complexion that resulted from scrubbing their skin four to five times a day. They were even given lessons on how to walk and act with confidence. Backs straight, heads up, they safely boarded the train with the guide and the SBS team. Jambbong, his wife, and the younger Chosŏn brother headed back to their homes before their extended absence was questioned.

It was a two-day journey to Vietnam on the new Beijing-Hanoi passenger train. The train had begun operating the year before, in February 1996. It crossed China diagonally, going southwest through a great variety of terrain and provinces. On the second day of the journey, the train reached Guangxi Province. Guangxi bordered Vietnam on the northeast corner, which was the most mountainous part of the country with sheer rock escarpments and deep valleys.

At the popular Friendship Pass border checkpoint, the group exited the train and waited in the background as the guide negotiated with Vietnamese soldiers posted near the checkpoint. He paid them off in U.S. dollars to deliver Ae Ran's group over the border. While the group made its way on foot, the guide and the SBS team entered Vietnam legally, using the road entry into Lang Son Province. Once reunited on the other side of the border, everyone squeezed into a hired taxi. They traveled south through the Hoang Lien Mountains, through remote areas that were home to many ethnic-minority hill tribes living in small wooden houses built on stilts. At Lang Son, a town about nine miles south of the border, they got onto Highway One, which was a potholed, narrow dirt road. They drove on this road over a hundred miles to Hanoi, where the South Korean embassy was located.

The capital city of Hanoi was about eight hundred square miles in size, and the city center consisted of four districts. The South Korean embassy was west of the center, in the Ba Dinh District, where most of the foreign embassies were housed in classical architectural masterpieces that had remained intact since the end of the French colonial era. The South Korean embassy was housed in the mammoth Daewoo Hotel, currently Hanoi's largest and most expensive joint venture.

At the door to freedom, Ae Ran's group suddenly lost confidence. Since leaving North Korea, they had experienced mood swings, from delight in their new surroundings to deep remorse for the family they had left behind. They weren't sure what to do anymore. Once they set foot inside the embassy and requested political asylum, there was no turning back. Their fate would be sealed.

The guide gave Ae Ran's group one night to think everything over clearly and carefully. That night, in their hotel rooms, Ae Ran was haunted by memories and slept fitfully. Clinging to her baby, she worried about how her nearly blind mother and her younger siblings were going to survive. Yet at the same time Ae Ran realized that her son had his whole life in front of him. She would never marry again. She would devote her life to taking care of her child, her father, and her younger brother, nothing else. That would be her salvation.

Blinking back the tears, Ae Ran, Hak Churl, and Yong Woon Uncle decided to go forward.

The morning after they arrived in Vietnam, the group headed up Kim Ma

Street to the South Korean embassy in the Daewoo building. They were instructed to ride the elevator up to the fourth floor, then rush inside the embassy and declare themselves North Korean refugees requesting political asylum. The problem was, they had never seen or heard of an elevator before, so they didn't know what to look for once they entered the lobby. So the guide had to shepherd them the last few feet of their journey to the elevator. When the doors opened, he shoved them in, pressed the button for the fourth floor, then dashed off.

After ten minutes passed, the guide decided to check on the group. When the elevator doors reopened, Ae Ran, Hak Churl, and Yong Woon Uncle were still standing inside, scarlet-faced and shaking with fear. They had somehow jumped off on the wrong floor. When they didn't see the embassy, they ran back inside the elevator and rode it up and down until they came face-to-face with the guide.

As my father relayed the guide's story, I could picture the scene in my mind—something out of the Three Stooges. It would have struck me as funny if the situation hadn't been so deadly serious for them and for those left behind.

Just when we had given up on Mi Ran and the others, they finally crossed the Yalu River on September 6, twenty days after Ae Ran's group escaped from North Korea.

Suddenly everything didn't seem so bleak. Since the guide's capture, I had retreated into my apartment and rarely ventured out. I spent long hours writing in my journal. It had been a while since I had done so. The words and emotions and descriptions didn't come slowly. They rushed out, filling page after page. When I took a moment to look at all the words, tracing them with my fingers, I was suddenly seized with panic that I had strayed too close to the edge. I forced myself to keep writing, because it had always been my salvation. It enabled me to divert real breakdowns by transferring troubled, sometimes incoherent thoughts onto paper. The instant I started to write I could feel all the negative thoughts that had built in my head and gut meet at my shoulder and travel down the length of my right arm to my thumb and fingers, through the ballpoint pen, and onto the paper.

I had been writing at my desk when my father called to tell me the fantastic news. "The others made it out! Can you believe it?" he said, overjoyed. I felt almost weightless, as if something had dropped, some hard thing had loosened. My entire body literally tingled as I took in deep breaths of cool air. It filled me. All at once my pent-up emotions erupted and I let out the hugest cheer.

They'd done it!

On September 5, Mi Ran had signaled the younger Chosŏn brother. She pleaded with him to ask my father to help them escape. Once Mun Churl returned to Hyesan City and learned that his father and older siblings were gone and that his mother had sold the house, their dire situation at last sank in. Still, he thought they should stay in North Korea, but as the days passed it became increasingly difficult to cover up the disappearance of four people. It was only a matter of days before the police discovered the truth and arrested them.

They were quickly running out of time. But my father and I were back in the States, and the guide was in Vietnam. It would be days before anyone could reach them. The Chosŏn brothers decided they would rescue our family on their own, without having to be enticed with more money. They, like everyone else, had become emotionally involved with the people who had entrusted their lives to us.

Together, the two brothers eagerly planned the midnight escape. They pooled their savings and paid another four thousand yuan to the North Korean border guards for the safe passage of five people, though we had already paid for their passage. At midnight, Mi Ran, Aunt, Mun Churl, and Hak Churl's wife with her one-year-old son, Chun, showed up at the river-bank, prepared to cross. The Chosŏn brothers waited for the family in the cold water. Right as Mi Ran's group was about to jump into the water, the border guards were suddenly switched. The Chosŏn brothers signaled them to abort their plans. As they were being chased off the riverbank by the new guards, the younger Chosŏn brother managed to signal to Mi Ran an alternative meeting place and time. Fearing for their lives, the group fled to Ae Ran's abandoned house and stayed hidden until nine-thirty in the morning. The younger Chosŏn brother had said to meet at eleven in Wiyun-dong, a neighborhood in Hyesan, which was about an hour and a half away on foot. When they arrived at the location, the Chosŏn brothers weren't there to meet them. The hours passed but the brothers still didn't show. Finally, at seven in the evening, eight hours late, the brothers appeared on the other side of the river and gave them the signal to cross. Though the river was narrower in this area, it was more treacherous. The water was deeper. It swirled up to chest level. Clinging to each other, they trudged through the water, following the brothers' instructions on where and where not to step.

Once safely across, they were rushed to the Chosŏn brothers' house, where they were fed and clothed. They stayed there until transportation could be arranged to sneak them out of Changbai to Shenyang, where they were to meet up with the guide. At four in the morning, nine hours later, two cars were secured. The older Chosŏn brother drove Mun Churl in the front car. The younger Chosŏn brother took Mi Ran, my aunt, Hak Churl's wife, and her son in the second car. The route to Shenyang was different from the one Ae Ran's group had traveled. The alternative route was a longer and tedious drive, but they would avoid checkpoints and soldiers with machine guns.

During the long, grueling drive to Shenyang, the front and rear cars remained only forty feet apart, as Mi Ran and my aunt suffered severe carsickness. In the event that the refugees had to suddenly flee from the cars, Mun Churl could run back and assist the women.

Some thirty hours later, they reached Shenyang, exhausted and dazed. A few days after their arrival, the guide and the director joined them at the safe house. Upon meeting Mi Ran's group, the guide sent the Chosŏn brothers back to Changbai and called in Jambbong and his wife for the next leg of the journey to Beijing.

Immediately, the guide had everyone brush their teeth and wash their faces ten times over the course of two days, and he bought them new clothes to make them appear like South Korean tourists. He then loaded everyone onto the train on September 11. In Beijing, they were taken directly to another safe house and kept there instead of being transported to the South Korean embassy in Vietnam. The guide feared if the second group traveled the same route into Vietnam before the others were granted political asylum, the embassy might reject both groups, suspecting that an outside person or persons had illegally masterminded the escape. If that happened they would be repatriated to North Korea and our guides uncovered. It had to appear as though our family defected on their own initiative and wits.

Mi Ran's group had to stay hidden in China until Ae Ran's group cleared the interrogation process, which would verify that my relatives were actually refugees in need of protection. Through SBS's government contacts, we discovered that the South Korean embassy had requested that the United Nations High Commissioner for Refugees (UNHCR) handle the case in order to avoid additional conflict with North Korea as well as with the Chinese and the Vietnamese governments. Until then, Yong Woon Uncle, Hak Churl, and Ae Ran and her baby were being kept in separate rooms in the Daewoo Hotel.

If only Mi Ran's group had escaped a day or two earlier, we could have stopped Ae Ran's group from entering the embassy, and all nine members could have gone together. Now all we could do was wait. But as the investigation time stretched into days, the days into weeks, and the weeks into an entire month, Mi Ran's group started to grow suspicious of the guide and the SBS team. They convinced themselves that the guide and SBS team were North Korean agents leading them to a death trap. Even little Chun would hide from the cameras or burst into tears. The director tried to calm their mounting fears by showing footage of the first group's reunion with Halmoni. Even after seeing the images, there was no calm for Mi Ran's group. Trapped in a state of waiting, their nascent hopes plunged to agonizing grief as they thought about the family that had abandoned them and the family they had left behind. Their consciences tortured them.

Mun Churl dealt with his pain by drinking. When drunk, he fought bitterly with his mother and Mi Ran. He was angry with them and everyone else for taking him out of the only home he'd ever known. He'd been content where he was. He believed that the party and their Father Leader had guided and supported him all his life, and that he had betrayed them. His betrayal affected him deeply.

Emotions swirled out of control.

The guide became very concerned that Mun Churl and the others might try to run away or do something more desperate. He urged my father to fly to China to defuse the dangerous tension. For once, I was glad he didn't choose me. I wasn't prepared to deal with the guide just yet. I didn't want to distract him.

My father wasn't gone for long. He flew to Beijing and was back four days later, exhausted. He looked as if he had traveled to hell and back, but his brief trip quieted the hysteria. He managed to assure the family that the guide and the SBS team weren't North Korean agents. However, he wasn't able to ease Hak Churl's wife's pain. She hadn't eaten or slept or said anything, just cried, since she discovered the real plans for defection. Before they left, Mi Ran had lied to her and said that Halmoni was throwing Yong Woon Uncle his belated sixtieth-birthday celebration in China and wanted her great-grandson to attend. Koreans considered the sixtieth birthday, the *hwangap,* a momentous event. The body had passed through the five twelve-year zodiacal cycles that constitute the proper life span of the human being. Mi Ran had promised Hak Churl's wife that they would return promptly after meeting Halmoni. Hak Churl's wife's father had been against the crossing, but her mother gave her blessing, not knowing she would never see her daughter again.

All at once something dawned on me. The nightmare I'd had after I came back from Dalian—the mysterious woman sobbing and pleading to go back as Ae Ran and Mi Ran argued and I screamed amid the searchlights and stomping boots—it was her. Hak Churl's wife.

Seeing her anguish, my father had offered to take her back. If that was what she truly wanted for herself and her son, he'd personally escort her safely to North Korea. If I'd been in her place, I don't know what I would have done. Would I choose my parents or my child?

As Hak Churl's wife agonized over the two impossible options, her years of political indoctrination slowly began to loosen. Her tears gave way to the shattering realization that she had been lied to by her government. As Ae Ran had said, all their lives it had been drilled into them that their socialist system was the best in the world. The moment Hak Churl's wife crossed into China, she saw with her own eyes that it wasn't true. People in China didn't live a gray, captive existence like North Koreans. Even Changbai was a paradise compared to where they had come from. She had never seen so much food, so many colors and vehicles and people talking freely in the streets. For the first time, Hak Churl's wife could actually envision a future for her son, Chun, who turned two in China.

To celebrate Chun's hopeful future, my father threw him a Western birthday party when he was in Beijing. He went out and bought a Tweety Bird cake and candles that lit up like Fourth of July sparklers. While my father sang "Happy Birthday" to Chun, the others clapped along, absorbing their first New World custom.

In the Korean custom, a child's earliest birthday, the *tol,* was a very significant event. In the days before modern medical care was available, few children survived their first year of life, so the *tol* was as celebrated as the sixtieth birthday. The toddler, dressed in colorful traditional clothes, was seated before a table laden with symbolic objects that would foretell his or her profession—pen, book, money, food, thread, arrow, and dagger. If the child chose the pen or book, it pointed to a career as a scholar. Money or food predicted great wealth. The thread indicated long life. The arrow or dagger represented a great warrior or soldier.

After Chun blew out his birthday candle, his mother somberly decided to stay. Now, whatever Chun chose to be—scholar, doctor, warrior, artist—no barrier would be unassailable and no aim too high.

As a safety precaution, the director recorded each person stating on three separate occasions that they did not wish to return to North Korea, in the event that they changed their minds once they reached the South and accused us of international kidnapping.

Unfortunately, the tape couldn't resolve our own conscience. While Mi Ran's group was held up in Beijing, we had learned some very disturbing news, which we kept from Hak Churl's wife. Choi Soon Man had contacted my parents on his return from Hyesan. He reported that the North Korean Secret Service had torn apart Ae Ran's and her parents' houses, searching for clues. When they discovered the only possessions missing were family photos and documents, the police knew the occupants had escaped. Ae Ran's husband and Hak Churl's wife's parents were arrested directly after the raid. Choi Soon Man said that the police knew the family hadn't reached America or South Korea yet because it wasn't in the news. They suspected the family was having trouble getting out of China.

At the end of the phone conversation, Choi Soon Man strongly hinted that we sponsor his family's visas to America and pay for their airfares. We took it as a threat. Choi Soon Man let it be known that he had possession of the Chosŏn brothers' names and phone number, which he had obtained when Mi Ran, confused, disoriented, and mistrustful, had secretly called him from the Chosŏn brothers' home after they crossed into China, thinking he might be able to help. As a result, the Chosŏn brothers had to flee Changbai and go into hiding.

Mi Ran's one action had endangered the lives of the very people who helped them escape. If I had learned one thing over the course of these several months, it was that one action, though carefully thought out, could result in a deadly domino effect.

There was no going back for any of them at this point. It was too late.

XXIII

October 13, 1997

My roller bag was ready to go. It only took me a second to leave the apartment, because I was always packed and prepared to take off on a minute's notice. It was a habit I had formed—even a travel outfit hung against the closet door. All I had to do was jump into it and I was ready to go to China once again.

This trip was at the guide's request. Without the assistance of his aides, he needed my father's help to relocate Mi Ran's group to a new safe house. The place they were currently staying belonged to a female South Korean student who was attending Beijing University. The student had become fearful—Mi Ran's group had been staying with her for over a month, and their prolonged presence had aroused the suspicion of neighbors. The group needed to be moved quickly.

Halmoni asked my father to take her to Beijing with him. Her health had deteriorated even more, and she felt that she couldn't wait for the second group to reach her in Seoul. However, she didn't want me to accompany them. She hadn't forgotten about my one night of drunkenness, and neither had I. I hadn't forgotten about the kiss, the fight, or the manic phone calls. I dreaded facing the guide. However, I was even more concerned about Halmoni's mental frailty. In Shenyang, my father hadn't known how to handle her fears, and the tension had become explosive between them. I had to go to be the buffer. Also, I felt obliged to keep a close eye on my father. Each time he traveled back to Asia he changed a little more. He was buying into the whole notion that men were superior and could do whatever suited them and that women should be obedient, loyal, and silent. It wasn't because he was macho deep down. It was the environment in that part of the world. Everyone there was raised under a strict notion of filial piety. It was one of the first concepts my father had learned as a child, but America and a strong, independent wife had transformed his beliefs and behavior.

Before we left, my mother pulled me aside and asked me to be more understanding toward my father. She had sensed my hostility toward him. "This is a strain on all of us, especially your daddy. There aren't that many sons-in-law who would do such difficult and dangerous work. He's doing a great thing for Halmoni," she reminded me.

I felt ashamed that I needed reminding and tried so hard to understand what my father was going through. In Asia, it was as if he came alive the way a brilliant actor came alive on the screen. He wasn't discriminated against for being an Asian man or for not speaking English properly. But each time I went back to Asia, I changed, too. My sense of inadequacy and bitterness advanced because I was fighting for equality and respect, and always trying to over-compensate for having been born a woman. This confusion threw me off balance and made it difficult for me to talk to my father. Yet, for the sake of the mission, I ignored the awkwardness and just moved on.

At the crack of dawn, my father and I landed in Seoul and headed for our connecting flight. Arriving, I saw Kim Chon Hong, the director. He was accompanying us to Beijing. His face was disguised under a sparse beard. The dark growth around his mouth shaded the fleshy shape of his chin and jaw. He was dressed casually in a navy blue and yellow nylon windbreaker with the collar turned up.

Halmoni was parked next to him in a wheelchair, wearing a loud, tacky red blazer that sparkled. She looked older, but not because of the wheelchair. There was a faraway, unfocused look in her gray eyes that made her look more like ninety-five rather than eighty-five. It was as though our task had compressed the passage of time, taking ten precious years off her life.

I stooped over the wheelchair to give her a hug. Halmoni's cheek was hot to the touch, and the smell of urine rose from her clothes. She had lost control of her bladder and wasn't aware of it.

"I treated four people yesterday. I think it was too much for me," said Halmoni hoarsely, then released a succession of nasty, heaving coughs that turned her face red and left flecks of saliva at the corners of her lips. She fumbled in her purse for a tissue. When she didn't find it, she rummaged in her pocket and pulled out a used rag. She hawked noisily to clear her throat, then spat a wad of yellowish green phlegm into the tissue and examined it. Under any other circumstances, I would have at that very moment whisked her back home and into a hospital.

"You shouldn't have worked so hard." I placed my hand gently on her back, afraid that a stronger pat would set her off again.

"I wanted to earn some money to give to your parents. I know this is costing them a lot," Halmoni sighed.

I couldn't fault her. At this point we were all desperately trying to pitch in. Flying back and forth from China plus hotel expenses just for ourselves had taken a hefty toll on our credit cards. We were badly in need of a cash injection, but nothing seemed to be free or easy at that stage.

The hot and stuffy plane spent more time on the ground than in the air, which disoriented Halmoni. She thought we had landed in Beijing before we'd even taken off. When the plane finally took off, we were in the air just over two hours—a breeze compared to the grueling overnight flight from Los Angeles that had robbed me of an entire day.

Just after the plane touched down in Beijing's Capital Airport, passengers crammed into the aisle and dragged down their large carry-on bags. Swept up by the frenzy, Halmoni slipped into the aisle while I was reaching underneath the seat to retrieve our belongings. When I looked up, I saw bodies jostling her from several directions. I flipped off my seatbelt and called out to her, but she was already four rows ahead. Clutching my camera bag and Halmoni's purse to my chest, I jumped into the aisle and plowed a path to her. I positioned myself a few inches away to prevent the stampede from squashing her. Panicked, Halmoni reached out and held on to my arm to steady herself. Her grip was weak.

I was greatly relieved when my father and the director came up from the rear to help Halmoni down the steps to the tarmac. The weather hadn't turned cold yet. It still felt like summer, but it wasn't hot and humid. The air was dry and the sky unusually clear and blue, which made it easy to believe that all was right with the world.

On the tarmac, a wheelchair and an escort with jug-handle ears and crooked teeth were waiting for Halmoni. I was surprised to see her sit in the wheelchair willingly. Evidently she was more exhausted now than stubborn.

Because of our escort, we didn't have to wait in any lines, and cut to the head of immigration in front of crowds of foreigners ushered by tour guides waving bicycle flags. Welcome to Beijing was stenciled in bold black letters overhead. Apart from the red People's Republic of China medallion, punctuated with five golden stars, everything else was dull and had an air of neglect. The walls and floors were scuffed up. On the ceiling, rusty water stains, left there by years of seeping rain, wiggled into the shapes of winged gargoyles.

A lethargic immigration officer in the standard tank-green uniform checked our arrival cards, U.S. passports, and the health declaration papers that we had to sign. In the segregated line next to us marked Residents, a tall, dark-skinned man with wiry black hair was being harassed. His documents were thoroughly checked and passed around among three frigid immigration officers. The dark man humbly dealt with the harassment, obviously having had to deal with discrimination before. He looked Uighur, one of the minorities in the northwestern region near the Silk Road. They spoke a Turkic language and for centuries used Arabic script. The Uighur were Muslim and their faces were a combination of Indo-Iranian and Mongol.

The immigration officers were still scrutinizing his travel documents as we left the area. It had taken us less than twenty minutes to pass through all the checkpoints and to retrieve our luggage at the carousel. However, the director wasn't anywhere to be found. He had become separated from us somewhere between the busy terminal and immigration. I anxiously looked around for him in the chaos of all the coming and going, because he had taken my camera bag with him.

After much contemplation, I had decided to bring along my camera. Though it was dangerous, we needed backup in case the director's footage was confiscated again. Also, I was beginning to feel insecure about our relationship with SBS. We had a verbal agreement with them, but nothing down on paper. In the end they could betray us. Having worked in the entertainment business, I had seen it happen many times. My greatest fear was that SBS would go back on their word and broadcast our story before everyone made it safely to South Korea. No one had anticipated it would take this long. And in the event that the South Korean government rejected the refugees, the family would have to hide out in China indefinitely. The footage could never be shown then. Would SBS just willingly destroy the footage after all the time and money they invested?

At my urging, my father had contacted his old schoolmate, the executive at SBS, and requested a written contract. The friend assured my father the contract could be written up formally at a later time. When my father pressed for one to be drawn up promptly with specific conditions, it reflected badly on him, because Koreans believed a contract was not as important as the interpersonal relationship between good friends. My father didn't ask again, afraid to offend his friend. We needed to remain on good terms with SBS.

I finally spotted the director as he was placing my bag and his onto the customs inspection table. The inspector loudly jabbered something in Mandarin at him, and the director feigned confusion. He kept pushing his large glasses up on the bridge of his nose. In seconds, three more customs officers arrived at the scene. They were all speaking at once as they took their time sifting through the director's belongings. They seemed more interested in the bottles of duty-free Johnnie Walker whisky and cartons of Marlboro Lights than the expensive camera equipment. Clearly, these Chinese inspectors had learned a mutant form of socialism whereby a little work goes a long way.

During the commotion I casually walked up to the table and retrieved my camera bag. My father and Halmoni trailed me as I headed straight for the glass windows and exit doors. Once outside, I turned in a circle, studying the area to see if anyone was watching us too closely. For the most part, it seemed the only people targeting us were roving taxi drivers. They attempted every verbal stratagem to lure us into their overpriced taxis. We shooed them away, waiting for the director.

Twenty more minutes passed before he was at last waved forward. He caught up with us outside, his forehead glossy with perspiration. He sparred with the taxi drivers in what sounded like fluent Mandarin. He got the price he asked for from a driver with a two-inch-tall rust-red lacquered Buddha stuck to the dashboard—probably put there to counteract China's traffic hazards.

It was a long drive from the airport to the city center. We drove about an hour on the smooth eight-lane highway, busy with Japanese-made automobiles. Identical high-rises lined the route. Somewhere near the city center, our cab whipped to the right, maneuvering around speeding cars to the exit. The local streets were congested with traffic and construction sites. Smartly dressed people and students in the latest baggy fashion and colored hair crowded the streets, walking, riding bicycles, jammed into buses, cars, and shops. It was easy to believe that one-fifth of the world's population, more than one billion people, lived in China. Seeing all the people, I saw the wisdom in the government's law of one child per family. China's greatest threat to the world wasn't its nuclear arsenal, it was overpopulation.

Beijing was incredibly different from all the other cities I'd visited in China. Everything was gigantic, almost inhuman in scale, with hard straight lines. Chang'an Avenue, the capital's main thoroughfare, was a very straight and mammoth lane heaving with tourists hurrying to see the two most famous sites in Beijing. Tiananmen Square "Gate of Heavenly Peace" was the center of the People's Republic of China and the world's largest public square. The concrete square, dotted with statues, was the size of nine football fields put together and bordered by monumental buildings. It was here, on October 1, 1949, that Chairman Mao Zedong hoisted the red flag to proclaim the foundation of the People's Republic. Tragically, its international notoriety had come from the televised bloody military crackdown on protesters peacefully demonstrating against the slowness of reforms, lack of freedom, and widespread corruption in June 1989.

Opposite Tiananmen Square, in dramatic contrast to the socialist present, was the Imperial Palace, better known by its unofficial title, the Forbidden City, because during the Ming and Qing dynasties, ordinary Chinese were forbidden from even approaching the thick crimson wall of the palace.

Affixed on the wall above the moated entry was a larger-than-life portrait of Mao Zedong. It was flanked by slogans in giant white characters that proclaimed, Long Live the People's Republic of China and Long Live the Great Union Between the Peoples of the World. All the other portraits and statues of Mao Zedong towering over the masses had been removed from the capital and replaced with neon signs advertising French cognac, Japanese electronics, and American fast food. That was why this one giant portrait, hanging all alone, had such an impact on me. Mao Zedong's spirit dominated the space and air. Something about his baggy-lidded eyes staring straight out suggested that somewhere beneath this once-deified, all-powerful man was a deep sadness—as though he had wanted to achieve so much more but fell short of his grand goal.

We had our driver drop us off in front of the Imperial Palace to change cabs, as a safety precaution. I suddenly felt quite insignificantly tiny, walking across this huge frozen ocean of concrete, amid the overwhelming throng. Tripping over tourists, we flagged down a crawling cab that was keeping pace with pedestrians. Our new driver used his horn to encourage slow vehicles and bicycles to get out of his way. When no one listened, he took a near-fatal risk and made an illegal U-turn in the middle of the street, narrowly missing a bus.

We left the inner ring of the city and drove along a network of smaller streets that crisscrossed the long, straight boulevards and avenues, past parks, the Beijing Zoo, and endless twisting gray stone alleyways to get to our hotel on Haidian Lu.

A group of Asian investment banker types carrying laptop computers and chattering into cell phones congregated in the sparkling lobby, blocking the way to the registration desk. I hung back with Halmoni in the lobby while my father and the director filled out the necessary forms.

I wondered where the guide was. Was he in the hotel? An echo of fear and anticipation rippled through me as I recalled his confession on the phone. I wasn't sure what to expect of the coming encounter or how to handle him.

When the men were all done checking us in, I put my arm around Halmoni's waist and we slowly made our way upstairs. Halmoni walked with a pronounced shuffle, and she felt so light I could have carried her. At the far end of the corridor, two men standing near a giant potted plant glanced in our direction, then turned discreetly away. I gently hurried Halmoni along.

Once inside our room, I prepared a warm bath for Halmoni so I could send out her soiled clothes to be laundered. She struggled to get out of her dress. It was painful for her, as it required her to lift her arms. I had to help her wiggle free and lower her into the filling tub. Seeing her naked, her obvious physical decline and frailty left me speechless. The muscles of her legs and buttocks were atrophied, and her flesh hung like drapery. There was a long surgical slash half an inch wide from her belly button to her pubic bone where two golf-ball-sized gallstones had been extracted back in 1988. To the right of the scar, it looked as though a grapefruit had gotten lodged underneath the skin. The surgeon had done a sloppy job sewing her up because he really didn't expect her to live, but sheer willpower and the longing to see her son had kept her alive. Ever since the tragic reunion in Shenyang, though, her will and strength had withered away. I worried that she might not last to see everyone make it to freedom and that she would die with her guilts and regrets.

Over the sound of the water running, I could hear Halmoni's coughing in the other room as I folded back the bedspread on her bed and plumped up the pillows. Each hawking, tearing cough went straight through me. When she finished her bath, she slowly toddled out of the bathroom wearing the fresh-smelling pajamas my mother had sent along. Now Halmoni looked better, with her skin pink from the warm water, but her eyes were still dull. The fear that I had seen in them had now given way to overwhelming fatigue.

Halmoni's hands shook as I tucked her into bed. Leaving the spread folded around her feet, I drew the blanket and top sheet over her, tucking it between her shoulder and the wall.

"When will I get to see them?" she asked weakly.

"Tomorrow," I said, because there was no way she could have seen anyone in her present condition. Then I added quickly, "Tonight we both need to rest." I included myself, knowing that if I didn't, she'd insist she was fine, although she had sat in the wheelchair willingly.

Halmoni wanted to say something else but was unable. Almost instantly she fell asleep. I switched off the harsh ceiling light and flicked on the soft floor lamp, then pulled a wooden chair beside her bed. I sat next to Halmoni, watching over her. From time to time she opened her eyes, but when she drifted into a dream, I finally allowed myself to doze off, slumped in the chair. I hadn't been asleep for very long when I heard a knock at the door. My eyes popped open and I bolted upright in my seat. I glanced down at my wristwatch. It was almost nine in the evening.

The knock sounded again, more demanding this time.

Halmoni inched up in bed and attempted to get up, but I motioned to her to remain where she was. In the semidarkness, I ambled to the door, over the half-unpacked suitcases and parcels on the floor.

"Who is it?" I called out to whoever was making the racket. These days I thought twice about throwing open the door without checking to see who was on the other side.

"It's me, Kim Chon Hong."

Cautiously, I unbolted the door and drew it open with the chain still attached. Through the crack I saw the director's magnified eyes smiling at me through his glasses.

I stepped back to let him in. A hard white light suddenly lit the room. A short, stocky young man trailed in the rear. As they both turned the corner and saw Halmoni sitting up in bed, the young man suddenly pounced on top of her, knocking her back against the headboard. The length of his body smothered her. I was paralyzed, totally unprepared, as I stared at them, my eyeballs almost popping out. Everything seemed to be in slow motion, as if this were a weird, blurry dream. I saw myself reach out and heave him off her and throw him against the wall, hard.

"Is this man drunk?" Halmoni asked me groggily.

"Halmoni," the young man wailed. "It's me, Mun Churl. It's me, Mun Churl."

Halmoni's glazed eyes instantly came alive. Her splayed fingers reached out to touch him, her whole body trembling. "Mun Churl?" It was a whisper. "*Omona, omona,* is it you, Mun Churl? Finally, finally, you're all out," she said in a breathless rush, and drew him to her breasts, clinging, clinging. Mun Churl's arms wrapped tightly around her waist and his head was buried in her lap. For endless moments they remained clutched together, holding tightly to each other. There were huge tears coursing down Halmoni's cheeks. She cried more now than when she had seen her own son. It was as if Mun Churl was the child she had been searching so long for.

Mun Churl wiped the back of his hand across his eyes and rose slowly to greet me. He was about my height, maybe an inch shorter, shoulders built squarely—not too thin, because he'd been in China for a while. I could see that his teeth were crooked and stained yellow, his mottled complexion coarse and prematurely aged with deep lines like the others, but his skin wasn't nearly as blackened as that of his older brother, Hak Churl, who had been forced to labor in a coal mine.

Mun Churl stood awkwardly with his shoulders hunched forward, hands in his front pockets and head bent. The way he was standing and the clothes he was wearing—a tan linen vest, a green-and-red striped shirt, baggy tan slacks, and soft leather shoes that could have probably fit my size 6½ feet— made him look like a middle-aged Chinese man. I wondered if he had picked out the outfit himself or if it was a reflection of the guide's or the director's sense of fashion.

"Hello," said Mun Churl quietly.

In one spontaneous, swift movement I smacked him on the arm. "I've been waiting to do that," I said half jokingly.

Mun Churl didn't step back. He just hung his head lower. "I deserve it. You should hit me again, harder," he muttered in a low, husky voice.

Hearing the remorse in his voice and seeing the bleakness in his eyes, I lost all desire to shove my fist square into the center of his gut for all the delays he had caused. He had been through so much, more than I'd ever know. I dragged him to me so I could hold him. His body was stiff, his eyes sunken. While he wasn't exactly hugging me back, he wasn't fighting my hold. He was trying his best not to collapse inward.

"No, I've changed my mind. I'm just glad you're safe." I smiled, trying to be comfortable and upbeat for him as I looked at his face in detail, searching more closely for any family resemblance. I thought he could have inherited his eyes from my grandfather. The crescent-shaped eyebrows, spaced unusually far apart, and the wide forehead might have been Halmoni's.

Self-conscious, Mun Churl reached up and ran his palm over his crudely cut hair. Little clouds of dandruff spilled onto his shoulders. "They made me cut my hair," he said.

"It looks good," I complimented, then asked if he had graduated.

Mun Churl nodded without meeting my eyes.

"Did you bring your diploma?" I asked, curious. The one thing that Ae Ran had brought with her was a bag of diapers for her baby. I was amazed that among all the things that Yong Woon Uncle could have brought, he chose to carry a stash of tobacco to roll cigarettes.

"It's not a diploma. It's a license," Mun Churl answered slowly. "I brought it, but then had to tear it up along with the other documents and family photos, because we became scared that if we got caught, they'd know who we were."

"What made you finally leave North Korea?" Halmoni spoke up weakly.

"When Mi Ran sent for me saying that Father had a heart attack, I returned home quickly. He wasn't there." Mun Churl fell into silence and stared down into his upturned palms, apprehension in every line of his face. Something inside him made him continue and spill out his heart. "I cried so hard. I asked Mother what we should do. She said it's our destiny to go. I thought our chances would be better just to stay and endure the consequences. I didn't know if it was worse outside or not. Never in my life did I think I should go to the other side of the dividing line. I couldn't even imagine it."

The paucity of information in North Korea and its people's ignorance of another world outside was hard for me to grasp. Living in the West, especially in America, whether I wanted it or not, liked it or not, I was constantly bombarded with news.

"Did your mother come, too?" Halmoni asked, though she had already been told everyone made it out. She wanted confirmation from Mun Churl.

"Yes." He sank down at the foot of Halmoni's bed, his hands holding tight to the edge of the mattress.

Halmoni released a great crackling sigh and rubbed her chest to ease the pain. She began to cry again. "What a relief. The thought of one person left behind tore at my heart. . . ." The rest of her soft, clipped words were drowned out by dry, hacking coughs mixed with heavy sobs. She hawked the phlegm into a tissue.

"For Mother, who bore me, I came. You don't know how much I've hurt her growing up. She tried to rear me to be a honest person, to be conscious of every rule, every code of conduct. Mother always worried I would waver and go the bad way of living because I do what I want and live as I want. So she lived for me every step of the way. Her love is great. But the person who made her suffer when she was younger is still making her suffer in old age." He abruptly cut himself off again, unable to continue.

I waited, knowing he wasn't finished. I knew he needed to tell it at his own pace.

When Mun Churl was ready he spoke again. "I understand now why Father drank so much. Life is hard, and when it turns out different from what your mind was set upon, you drink. All those years he thought he was an orphan . . . he could never speak of it, even to his family."

Halmoni was roused by what he had said. "From here on, you should all live a clean life. You shouldn't drink."

"Alcohol is like medicine. It makes you forget your emotions. I drink when I feel bad. I'm only human. When I heard that Older Brother left Sister-in-Law and their young son behind, that Father left, my heart felt cold. Whenever I think about them, I drink. I drink when I think about—" Mun Churl looked at the floor, his whole body shuddering with longing.

"Your father was sharp as a knife and very brave when he was a young man. When he was only sixteen, he made a sign protesting against Kim Il Sung and marched around school. He wouldn't back down even after the Reds beat him up till he bled. That's your real father. That's why God's protected him till now. When the Reds told him to renounce God, he refused to the very end." Halmoni wiped her eyes with the hem of her pajama top.

Mun Churl glanced up in disbelief. He knew so little about his father's history. He fell silent for a long moment and closed his eyes, his hands folded on his lap. He almost seemed to be meditating.

"What's going through your mind, Mun Churl?" I wanted him to cleanse himself of his suffering.

"I think about much. I think of my friends and—" He cut himself off again, his voice wavering.

Reading his face, a horrible thought flashed across my mind. "Did you have a girlfriend?" I asked.

He slowly nodded once. "We were engaged in April and planned to marry after my graduation."

Hearing he had a fiancée, that there was another person involved, was like an electric shock. It took a moment before I found my voice again. "Does she know where you are?"

Mun Churl ignored my question. Then in a stronger voice, scratchy with bitterness and hurt, he said, "I don't want to think about my past anymore. All I want to concentrate on is the future and how I am to pursue it."

Responding to the simmering fury in the undertone of his voice, I probed gently. "You say that, but you hold on to your anger."

"Yes, but now it's . . . I guess when I see Father I'll have to sit down with him and tell him all that's in my heart."

"And what would you say to him?"

Mun Churl's face crumpled, and tears spilled onto his cheeks. He quickly looked away—I guessed that if he met my eyes at that moment, he might not have been able to express the rest of what he longed to say. "That I'm a child that was thrown away, but I've walked back on my own feet. Then Father will feel something. He will feel some new emotions." He retreated to the safety of silence again and drew his shoulders forward, as if he were truly an old man.

I backed off. Mun Churl's pain was palpable. I had been overly optimistic about our chances for success. If I had known the countless perils and hardships all of them would be exposed to, my decision to go forward with the plan would not have been so easily made. It would have been preceded by far more soul-searching than had been the case five months earlier.

XXIV

October 16, 1997

Halmoni woke up coughing. The fit got stronger until she was forced to give in to a series of wrenching coughs that turned her face purplish red and racked her body, partially doubling her over. Slowly the coughing stopped, and she subsided like a rag doll and fell asleep again. She looked so defenseless, lying there flat on her back, her cheeks and jowls drawn down by gravity.

I decided not to wake her for breakfast. At the moment, what she needed more than anything else was rest in a cozy bed. So I went downstairs alone to meet my father. I was relieved to see that at least he was well rested. Leaving him at the table, I toured the lavish international buffet. I returned promptly to the table with a bowl of warm rice congee and a saucer of *kimchi* to take back to Halmoni, black coffee for me. The coffee didn't taste good. It wasn't the quality of the beans or the way it had been brewed. Coffee had lost its power over me because I no longer wanted to be comforted. I just wanted to get through this, to get it over with.

When my father heard about our late-night visitors, he became visibly upset that the director had acted irresponsibly. On the contrary, it wasn't irresponsibility. I was sure he had thought it all out carefully. By bringing Mun Churl to our room in the middle of the night, unannounced, the director knew he'd catch Halmoni off guard and startle her into tears. He didn't want her emotionally prepared. He wanted unedited sobs, and he was determined to catch it on videotape because the reunion with Yong Woon Uncle had been unsatisfactory for his dramatic documentary. Again I wondered where the guide was and why he had allowed Mun Churl to wander around the hotel with the director. I couldn't figure it out. I thought there might be something going on between the director and the guide; my instincts warned. They might have some kind of secret agreement that we didn't know about.

Suddenly I felt the energy shift in the room. I swiveled my head all the way behind me and saw Mun Churl and the guide coming toward us. Their faces were flushed and their hair was ruffled, as if they had had an intense night of drinking. The guide looked especially disheveled, with a touch of madness in his eyes. He took a seat opposite from me. He sat very still, very calm and watchful. For a brief moment our eyes met. There was an intensity in his hooded gaze. My heart began to pound. I had insanely mixed emotions about him. I'd known our first encounter would be awkward, even hostile, but I'd been hoping that I would feel nothing. I told myself it wasn't him that I desired; it was what his body might make me feel that was the thrill, and that thrill compounded with loneliness and danger was what had made me kiss him before.

I averted my eyes to avoid meeting his again and devoted my attention to a long-legged waitress saucily walking over to our table with a pot of steaming coffee. Her sleek uniform was fitted tightly, like the traditional Chinese cheong-sam, buttoned down one side, and slit very high on her thigh. For the briefest second, her predatory eyes, outlined in dark pencil and heavy mascara, glanced at the guide. He didn't notice.

I drained my cup and asked the waitress to refill it. She filled the guide's cup without him even asking. When Mun Churl picked up his cup to examine it, she filled his, too. Mun Churl looked at his coffee, at a loss as to what to do. He sneaked a look at me to observe how I took my coffee, and saw the guide add creamer and sugar to his. Mun Churl decided to copy what the guide did. He splashed in milk and four packets of sugar, then looked worried that he might have used too much.

I thought about engaging Mun Churl in a conversation but decided against it because of his strong North Korean accent, which might reveal him. Instead, I noted what he brought back from the buffet table: scrambled eggs, bacon, sausage, fried noodles, two slices of watermelon, and two cherry tomatoes. He ate thoughtfully, as if each morsel was a separate delicacy and he needed to consider each bite. I thought about advising Mun Churl to move his chair closer to the table—he was sitting unnaturally far away from it—but decided against that as well. I didn't want to make him any more self-conscious. The guide was constantly telling Mun Churl what to do—I heard him whisper to sit up straight, use the fork properly, wipe your mouth, and sample the pineapple. It was almost too much. When he was done telling

Mun Churl what to do, the guide revealed his plans to my father. He intended to relocate Mi Ran's group to Harbin, the capital of Heilungkiang Province, China's northernmost province, which was a five-hour journey by train.

I was opposed to the move. Harbin seemed potentially more dangerous. It was closer to North Korea's border than Beijing, and Harbin wasn't as well traveled by foreigners. Locals weren't accustomed to seeing many outsiders. Only in Beijing did a foreign face elicit barely a second glance, because it was home to many embassies and international businesses. Here, you could find KFC and A&W Root Beer restaurants. I held back because I knew I'd be silenced, and I wasn't going to risk it anymore. I wouldn't give them the power to withhold or to grant. I simply stopped myself from voicing my opinion.

The guide's eyes were watching me as I swirled the coffee around in my cup. I could feel him thinking about me, and it made my face burn hot. I heard my father say something, but I couldn't hear the words over the roaring in my ears. Evidently the guide hadn't been paying attention, either. There was a pause. "Excuse me?" the guide said dryly and coarsely. The vibration of his voice sent a whispered warning through my nerve endings.

"In the countryside, won't they be more visible?" My father articulated my concern.

"That's a natural assumption, but it's not the case. Here in Beijing, if they get caught, we'll all be in serious trouble. In the countryside, the police easily overlook things."

"I know someone who lives here. He may be able to help us find a better place for them to stay in the city."

Who? I thought, looking across the table at my father. I had no idea he knew anyone in Beijing.

"I can't trust anyone I don't know," said the guide.

His face didn't give away any emotion. Only someone who had been watching him carefully, as I had these past months, would notice the way he ran his hand through his hair. He was agitated by the interference. He wanted my father to do as he was told.

"Why don't we meet with my friend, then decide?" suggested my father.

"Who is this friend of yours?"

"A missionary."

"I can't trust your missionary."

The muscles of my father's right cheek contracted and his mouth went stiff. He was angry. "I know him. He can be trusted," my father said through clenched teeth.

"Lee Teacher, do you want me to help or do you want to handle this project all by yourself?" The guide's voice was thinner than ever, like the sound of wind passing over dead leaves.

"Safety must be our first concern. I said my friend is completely trustworthy," my father threw back at him, his face held tightly in icy fury. I'd never seen my father that firm and confrontational with anyone other than his children.

The guide wiped his mouth delicately in an effort to get a firm grip on his patience. When he had done so, he pushed his plate away and placed his hands flat on the table. "Then, Lee Teacher, you deal with it," he said. He got up and walked away. Mun Churl stopped chewing and promptly raced off after him.

The guide's words echoed in my mind as I watched to see if he would come back. He didn't even give a backward glance. I knew he wanted to see what our reaction would be to his sudden departure. He wanted to show us that he was in complete control of himself and was accustomed to being in control of the situation around him. Then again, he could turn on us, and if he did, he had the means and the knowledge to put an end to the mission.

I exchanged a long look with my father. He was pale and silent, perspiration glowing on his face. He strove to repress his anger and fear. Sitting with his arms folded across his chest, he remained still. When he had quelled his emotions somewhat, he narrowed his eyes, trying to analyze and assess what had just happened. My father grappled with the puzzle, trying to get the pieces to fit.

"Something else is going on with him. Did he seem distracted, nervous, to you?" he asked, the muscles in his cheek working.

I hesitated, feeling guilty. "I didn't notice."

My father removed his glasses and rubbed his red-rimmed eyes. There were two red indentations on the bridge of his nose from the weight of the glasses, and his face looked careworn but determined. It was then that my father became a man of action. He decided that we could not sit around any longer and let everyone else call the shots for us. We should remove Mi Ran's group from their present location and hide them in a new safe house before the guide could try anything. "It's our family, and it's time to take this project into our own hands. If we don't, we'll have only ourselves to blame in the end," he said.

The serious look in my father's expressive eyes told me that he meant it, and I could see him move into another gear, the way he did when someone he cared about was hurt. Suddenly he moved more quickly, totally self-assured.

Promptly he left the hotel and contacted his friend from an outside pay phone. At noon that same day, a wizened man with thinning hair arrived at our hotel room impeccably dressed in a well-tailored gray suit and a nicely matching silver tie. My father politely addressed the man as Sa-jang-nim (company president). He was actually an undercover Christian missionary posing as a foreign businessman. I was intrigued by this secret agent of God, who was hoping to plant new Jesus seeds in China's red soil. If his activities were discovered, he, his wife, and their children, as resident aliens, would be subjected to abusive interrogation and deported. Underground churches were illegal and regarded as cults. The risk, however, was much greater for nationals. They were only allowed to attend legal, government-sanctioned churches. If they were caught worshiping at an underground church, they would be imprisoned and beat up. Sometimes the punishment could be death. Even faced with such persecution, membership at Sa-jang-nim's church continued to grow steadily.

Halmoni's wrinkled eyelids lifted like crushed-velvet curtains as she slowly heaved herself up from the bed. She smiled warmly and gestured to a vacant chair. Sa-jang-nim bowed reverently as he took the seat.

My father slid Sa-jang-nim a thick white sealed envelope of money, then another, thinner one. "This is a small token of our appreciation."

"That's not necessary." Sa-jang-nim wouldn't accept the second envelope of money. It was passed back and forth about five times.

"You must take it for your difficult work here," my father insisted.

"Thank you. Thank you very much. I will take it for that reason, then." Sa-jang-nim bowed his head again and paused to say a silent prayer over the envelopes. When he was done, he raised his head and asked, "What brings you to Beijing?"

"It's a continuation of our April trip, regarding our North Korean family. They've all made it out."

Sa-jang-nim clasped his small, manicured hands. "Wonderful. Wonderful."

"Half of them are safe, but the other half are still stuck in China."

"There are many North Korean refugees like them hiding here and in Russia. Their numbers go into the hundreds and thousands. It's a tragedy. The South and North are the same people, but our government won't grant them entrance. Shame on our country and other countries for abandoning these helpless refugees. Your family's extremely fortunate because they have you. How long do you think it'll be before you can get them out?"

"We're not sure. In the meantime, they need a secure place to hide."

"We should send them to a church." Halmoni's voice sounded halfway between a gasp and a grunt.

"Not a good idea, Halmoni," Sa-jang-nim quickly cautioned. "It's dangerous. The two sanctioned churches here are filled with spies, and the police like to crack down on the underground ones. I do know of a place for them to stay, though. An apartment just became vacant today in the same complex my family lives in. The transportation is a bit inconvenient, but that won't matter to them. It's very safe. The former tenants were also South Korean missionaries, so the neighbors won't be curious if another Korean family occupies the unit. My wife and I can keep a close eye on them and take care of their needs."

"Are you sure you want to take on this burden? There's no pressure." My father let his words hang for a moment to give Sa-jang-nim an opportunity to change his mind.

"I don't see it as a burden. This is the reason why we came to China."

The place and situation sounded more than ideal. My father and I decided to inspect the space right away; unfortunately, we had to leave Halmoni behind. Her cough wasn't getting any better and she had the chills, but she refused to go to the hospital. She was afraid the doctors would keep her there and she wouldn't get to see the family. All I could do to make her more comfortable was to offer her two Tylenol. Obediently she swallowed the pills, barely lifting her eyelids, then she slid back into bed.

The apartment was located in a large cluster of high-rise apartments that looked so much alike, the developers had to mark everything with large red numbers to distinguish the concrete-block structures so people wouldn't get lost. As we wandered along, trying to be discreet, a young Caucasian man with blond hair leisurely rode by on a purple bicycle with vegetables piled in his metal basket. Seeing that no one seemed to notice him even though he was obviously more foreign-looking than we were, I was able to relax a little as we went deeper inside the expansive property. The deeper we went, the more construction there was. Cranes skewered the flat line of rooftops. At least half a dozen skeletal buildings were being demolished, and three dozen new concrete ones were being built at a furious pace.

The available unit we had come to inspect was farther back, to the left. It was in the oldest building we saw—standing not quite straight—and it was the only block painted canary yellow. After all that concrete and red, yellow had never looked so good. Someone on the third floor had made an attempt to encourage a garden on the balcony.

Sa-jang-nim let us into the drafty, poorly lit studio. The grimy light made the room feel like it was under water. I padded in and looked around. It was almost empty. There was a small gas stove and a twelve-inch sink in the closet-size kitchen, and the bathroom had a stained Western toilet and tub. That was all. With the starkness and cold cement floor, it made me think of jail, but to Mi Ran's group it didn't matter. It didn't matter if it lacked fancy molding or lots of closet space or character or reliable plumbing, or even if it resembled a jail cell. It was decent and available, and it would keep them safe. In the end, that was all that mattered.

My father and I agreed to rent the apartment with Sa-jang-nim's help. The landlord required three months' advance payment as a security deposit. We gave Sa-jang-nim 775 dollars for three months' rent plus extra cash for utilities and living supplies—a total of 1,000 dollars.

Having been betrayed by Choi Soon Man, I was suspicious of anyone and everyone offering us their services. There were always strings and conditions. Personal motives would always be attached. Sa-jang-nim was different, though. We could depend on him, but not because he was a religious man and spoke in a soft, caressing voice that inspired confidence. No, he needed us as much as we needed him: My father confided in me that my parents' church in Los Angeles financed his entire mission and provided for his family. Monthly the church wired him 800 dollars. That was an exorbitant amount, considering that the average Chinese earned about one-eighth that amount.

By the time we got back to our hotel, the guide still hadn't left us a single message at the front desk, and he wasn't answering his cell phone. We hadn't seen or heard from him since breakfast. We had no idea when or if he would show up, or what his intentions were.

"Get ready. As soon as the apartment becomes available, we have to move quickly," my father told me as I left him at the lounge bar to check on Halmoni's condition. Four o'clock was a little early for drinks, I thought, and then pushed the comment out of my mind. My father had been working so hard that he'd earned the right to any diversion, I tried to tell myself.

When I opened the door to my room, my eyes collided with the guide's.

He was framed in the doorway bearing a meal tray with an empty soup bowl. Seeing him standing there, my heart tripped crazily. I wanted to strangle him on the spot for worrying us, and yet throw my arms around him for coming back.

"I brought warm wonton soup for Halmoni to soothe her cough." He flashed a thin smile, then slowly stepped to the side to let me in.

Halmoni vaguely noticed me come in. She was curled on her side with her knobby knees drawn up and a wad of crumpled tissue in her slack fist. She worked hard for each breath, and her dentures made funny clicking sounds.

The guide looked undecided about whether to leave or stay. I remained very distant, trying to recover my composure. I walked to the far end of the room and pretended to search for something on the desk, leaning way over to hide my face behind a curtain of hair to avoid his stares.

The guide coughed deliberately from three feet behind me. Startled, I nearly knocked over the lamp on the desk. I wondered how he'd gotten so close without me realizing it. He was practically breathing down the back of my neck. He was so close I could smell the mixture of sweat, soap, and sandalwood. I could feel myself weakening. I waited until my legs felt strong enough to support me, and then, bracing myself against the edge of the desk, I turned back around and faced him.

"I was, ah, about to, ah . . . ," he said, paused, took a deep breath, then began again before he lost his will. The words tumbled from him. "Have dinner with me tonight?"

It took a minute for the invitation to penetrate, and I was aware that my mouth had fallen open. I looked up at him blankly, trying to concentrate, seeking the right method for dealing with the dinner invitation and him. I decided this was the perfect opportunity to press my advantage, because he wanted something from me. "My father and I met with his friend," I told him, to see what his reaction would be.

The guide gazed at me, one eyebrow lifted quizzically. I knew better than to mistake the sparkle in his eyes for amusement. I proceeded gently. "He's a missionary from my parents' church in L.A."

"I already told your father that I can't trust his missionary," he said flatly.

"I see," I said, forcing myself to keep my voice at a smooth, polite level.

"Will you have dinner with me tonight?" he pressed.

"If I do, will you meet with him?"

"Probably not."

"Then what would be the point?"

"I won't have to eat alone."

"I don't mind eating alone. I eat alone all the time."

The guide thought for a while about what I'd said, meditatively studying the tray he held in his hands and the empty soup bowl on top of the tray. When his eyes came back to mine, I didn't like the cool intensity I saw in his gaze. I had the impression he had made a major decision.

"I eat alone a lot, too. Too often," he said, his voice soft, then he walked to the door and let himself out, closing the door quietly behind him.

I bolted the door and groaned, wondering if I should have treated him more kindly. I had heard the wariness in his voice. Maybe I should have gone to dinner to seduce him into cooperating. But it was too late. I began to fear that I had done more harm. Had I made the guide lose face again? My thoughts ran riot as I tried to consider carefully all the ins and outs and implications and ramifications, and as I did so I became more and more frantic. Just then my father phoned. The guide had agreed to inspect the apartment.

That night, while I cared for Halmoni, my father showed the guide the apartment. The new safe house met with his approval.

XXV

etting Halmoni bathed and dressed the next day took some effort. She was growing weaker. It was difficult for her to stand up and balance. She had to hang on to me with one hand the entire time, but I finally managed to get her ready. I had picked out something nice for her to wear for when she met her daughter-in-law and grandchildren for the first time. It was a simple black-and-white long-sleeved collared dress that gathered at the waistline, giving her body some curvy form. Over her shoulders I draped a pink cardigan, and I wrapped a long red scarf around her throat. The colors didn't match, but somehow the look worked on her. Lastly, I sprayed her with floral perfume in the event that she had another accident with her bladder.

"You ready?" I asked, grabbing my camera bag.

Halmoni nodded even though the moving and changing had sapped most of her strength.

At a quarter after three in the afternoon, we all headed out to the old safe house. Mi Ran's group hadn't been moved yet to the new location. My father and the guide went ahead in the first taxi. Halmoni, the director, and I piled into a second cab.

Seated, the director turned to her. "So, Halmoni, when you see the others, are you going to cry again like you did the other night?" he teased.

"Whether I cry or not is my choice." Her voice ended in a small cough.

"Why did you cry when you saw Mun Churl and not when you met your son?"

"Do you think I have to cry outwardly? I cried inside. I was very upset and sad, knowing my son had left his family behind. It was not my wish to sacrifice lives to see my son. This time I'm going to communicate with him. My son and I have a lot to say to each other."

"He isn't going to be there, Halmoni. He's in Vietnam with Ae Ran and Hak Churl," I reminded her.

Halmoni absorbed the information, then patted my arm. "I'm getting everything I ever wanted. I know I'm being spoiled by you and your father these days. I thank you for writing your book while I'm still alive. I have to repay you before I die. Isn't that right?" She brightened up. I was surprised by the energy that filled her voice.

We drove only a few minutes and made three changes of direction before I saw a recognizable landmark—the white granite gates of Beijing University. The exterior resembled that of many East Coast colleges in the United States, with beautiful autumn-colored ivy draping over a stately brick wall enclosing the campus.

The director instructed the driver to drop us off near a very busy intersection, crowded with haggling vendors and their carts and a row of barbers with their shaving stools and straight razors. The tires screeched up against the curb, nearly hitting a street cleaner who was working vigorously to sweep up the tumbling debris with a broom whose bristles were bent.

While I helped Halmoni get out of the cab, the director slammed the passenger door and dashed across the street without a word of direction. I couldn't chase after him. It took Halmoni a long time to climb out of the backseat and straighten up. I scanned the street, searching for my father or the guide, needing assistance with Halmoni.

We were on our own.

I slowly walked Halmoni around the many obstacles on the sidewalk to the chalked-off crosswalk at the intersection. There wasn't a street signal to halt the accelerating cars and trucks that charged at us. No one seemed to care about pedestrian right-of-way, much less traffic lanes. Crossing the street in Beijing was like crossing a street in downtown New York City, except worse, as in addition to the vehicular traffic there were millions of daredevil cyclists that didn't give way, either. I had to act like a crossing guard, holding out my free hand while gently guiding Halmoni across the wide street. Several times when she felt my grip tighten she picked up her pace, causing her to wheeze.

Once across, I spotted the director down the street, leaning against the wall of a building, smoking leisurely. When he was sure I'd seen him, he ducked away into an alley. I led Halmoni toward the alley. We moved aside to let a man dressed in a stained white smock pass. His stride was funny, with a sailor's roll. He purposely brushed up very close to me. When he did that, a shiver went through me.

I steered Halmoni into the mouth of the alley. Suddenly we were sandwiched amid the shadows of tall, squalid tenement buildings. Every sound echoed, and my stomach tightened. All my senses screamed caution. I pretended to keep my eyes on the broken walkway, but the whole time they were scanning side to side for any possible danger. From the corner of my eye, I thought I saw furtive movement behind the folds of draperies on the other side of glass windows.

We followed the walkway to the end, and when we turned the corner I caught the director's hunched profile going down another passageway, around another corner, and entering an apartment building. I was thoroughly lost in the maze. I tried to quicken Halmoni's pace so we wouldn't lose the director, but she was moving with an odd sort of calm—a calm born of exhaustion.

Inside the building, the entire corridor was a black, dark tunnel. It smelled awful, like a sewer. At the very far end of the tunnel was a rectangle of faint bluish gray light.

"I can't see very well," Halmoni murmured in a small voice.

I clutched both her hands firmly so she could feel our contact. Carefully I began to walk backward, feeling with my feet and guiding her with my voice. The deeper we went in that dark tunnel, the more the flesh crawled on the back of my neck. The crawling feeling didn't subside, and I was convinced that a spider was on the nape of my neck. I put a hand back there to check.

"*Ayee!*" Halmoni exhaled explosively, a sound that carried ten feet.

"I'm here. I'm here." I gripped her hand again. I kept talking to soothe her fear and mine. I could hear her labored breathing and her uneven footsteps as she moved along. "I won't let you go. You're doing great," I praised as I pulled her closer to the light.

At last we made it, and stepped into the pale blue-gray light. I looked around to get my bearings. The interior of the corridor was filthy with trash, and the plaster was cracked and mildewed. There were steel doors on either side, making it look like a long, gloomy cell. My straining eyes spotted the director gesturing to us from an apartment several doors ahead.

I let Halmoni rest for a few minutes to steady herself, knowing that what was next would be hard for her.

"Let's not keep them waiting," Halmoni said, her voice barely audible. She took the deepest breath she could, gathered her last bit of strength, and slid her feet forward. I counted off the number of steps it took for her to reach the door. Thirteen. Depending on how you looked at it, thirteen wasn't such a horrible number. Americans consider it bad luck, but I viewed it as lucky.

The door opened, and we cautiously stepped in. The director and a tall, fair-skinned woman in a long black bib dress were the only ones to receive us. She could only have been the student from Seoul whom the safe house belonged to. Everyone else, including my father, was missing. I waited for the director to say something, but he just stood there, taping us. It was as if he wanted us to figure everything out for ourselves. I felt the muscles in my stomach tighten even more.

Pushing him out of the way, I took inventory of the place with my eyes, not moving my head. Nothing out of the ordinary. It was a small, cramped room with rough blue carpeting and wall-to-ceiling bookshelves sagging and bulging with Chinese textbooks. The only real luxuries were a television set, a boom box, and an air conditioner. There was no furniture, really, except for a low wooden table, which the television was placed on, and a waist-high refrigerator pushed into the corner of the living room because the kitchen was too narrow to accommodate it.

Recalling the last reunion, the director had had the family hide in a separate room for dramatic effect. I counted two closed doors, one on either side of the narrow kitchen. Helping Halmoni slip off her shoes and kicking off mine, I followed my intuition and led her to the door on the left. As soon as I curled my fingers around the knob and twisted it, it was flung wide open and Aunt and Mi Ran engulfed us in desperate hugs.

Halmoni cried out with the suddenness of lightning. "You poor things," she moaned. "I'm so thankful that I can see my children. I'm so thankful. God is great. Every day I will live for you, God, every day, great God that you are." Her voice broke into loud heaving sobs, finally releasing all those years of *han,* suppressed anger and sorrow and regret.

I thought I should cry or something. I had every reason to cry, but I felt curiously empty of emotion. No tears could be summoned. I imagined pretending to cry for my family's sake, also for the cameras. It was no use.

"Hae Ri." Aunt sighed my name close to my face. Her iron-gray hair was newly dyed black and permed, and the white gauze eye patch was gone from her left eye, revealing a clouded cornea. The other eye was still dark and clear, but it didn't have any real sparkle to it—dulled with hardship, it had lost its vitality, like everything else about her. The skin around her eyes and mouth was as wrinkled as walnuts.

Mi Ran was just the opposite of her mother. She was red-cheeked and smiling, and she radiated life. Her efflorescent spirit was accentuated by the brilliant tangerine-pink lipstick she had on. When she tilted her head up, the light highlighted the heavy foundation that she had smeared on unevenly.

Mi Ran hugged me firmly. She was strong for her five-foot-two frame. Her body was sturdy and thick—she had gained weight since arriving in China five weeks before. Her weight concerned me; perhaps we'd gone too far in trying to make the family look healthier. No one was going to believe that she was a North Korean refugee. It was imperative that she and the others look and act the part of poor, gaunt refugees needing political asylum. They had to win sympathy.

When Mi Ran finally released me and stepped aside, I saw my father and Mun Churl standing in the back. Then I caught a glimpse of another person just behind them. Instantly I knew who she was, though I'd never seen her picture. It was the mysterious sobbing woman from my nightmare.

Hak Churl's wife was called Chun Jung Soon. Chun Jung Soon—the name filled my mind inescapably like a drumbeat. She had a hard, sharp face, sort of storklike, with a high-bridged nose and small icy black eyes. Her lips and cheeks were hard and red, and her hair was cut severely short above her ears. Underneath the tight-fitting silvery turtleneck she wore, it was easy to notice that she had enormously large breasts for her slim figure.

Jung Soon stayed at the periphery with downcast eyes, clutching her two-year-old son, Chun, to her chest for protection. Chun's deep frown matched his mother's, making him look far more grown-up than he was.

I wondered, not for the first time, if it wouldn't have been a better idea to tell Jung Soon about her parents' arrest, and as always, the answer was the same. What good would it do? Even if she spewed Kim Il Sung quotations and claimed that we had kidnapped her, it wouldn't restore her life back in North Korea nor save her teaching position as a high school mathematics instructor. She would be branded the wife of a defector, and her son would be left with no future in a country that demanded absolute devotion to its deceased leader and now his son, Kim Jong Il.

Abruptly Jung Soon's eyes snapped up. I was momentarily put off balance by the suddenness of our contact, and I smiled awkwardly. There was a startling dignity about her.

"Hi," I said, determined and cheerful, then immediately regretted greeting her. I thought she was going to say something back, something venomous, maybe, because in her icy dark eyes I could read agony and anger. In that moment, I realized she knew the news about her parents and that there was nothing I could say to comfort her. Her pain was immeasurable, and I didn't know how to talk to her. My inadequate apology pounded through my head. I was so sorry, more sorry than I had ever been in my life.

Jung Soon remained self-contained and crossed out of the room with her son. The others followed into the main room, except for Mi Ran. She slipped her arm into mine, wrenching my attention away. Mi Ran cuddled up to me. Her warmth and softness and the sweet smell of her shampoo comforted me.

"I can't believe this is all happening," Mi Ran hummed, her accent thick. As she talked, her eyelids fluttered under her upslanting brows. I recognized the dancing lance of her intelligence and her inner playfulness. I liked her just for that. It made me want to find out everything about her.

Spellbound, I listened to Mi Ran as she filled me in on the last five months without any prodding.

The first time the guide's aide, the younger Chosŏn brother, came knocking at their door, only Mi Ran was at home with her parents. When they heard him call out for Lee Yong Woon, they became frightened, thinking it was the police coming to arrest him. Yong Woon Uncle stayed hidden inside the house. When he didn't appear, the younger Chosŏn brother called out for Mi Ran next. Hearing her name, she felt compelled to emerge and talk to the late-night caller. The younger Chosŏn brother flashed her the photo I had given to the guide at the Shilla Hotel. He asked Mi Ran if she recognized the married couple in the picture. When she denied knowing such a couple, he went away. Mi Ran hadn't lied. In fact, she told the truth. I had mistaken the woman sitting on the lawn next to Yong Woon Uncle as my aunt. It was actually Choi Soon Man's wife. I should have examined the photo more closely. The confusion cost us precious time.

The next day, the younger Chosŏn brother returned to the house. He asked Mi Ran again if she recognized the man in the photo. Seeing the neighbors spying on the mysterious visitor, Mi Ran confessed that the man was her father, then quickly lied and said that he had gone away for a while, so that the younger Chosŏn brother would leave before the neighbors reported them. Three days later, he showed up with Halmoni's birthday picture and a note that gave a meeting place and time. The note warned if they lost this opportunity, it would be a misfortune and they'd regret it. Wondering what the misfortune could be, Yong Woon Uncle was terrified into complying.

On June 4, the younger Chosŏn brother floated Yong Woon Uncle across the Yalu River in an inner tube to meet with the guide. During the crossing, the river water was rushing so fast and forcefully that they were nearly swept away. Had it not been for the young man's bravery and swimming ability, Yong Woon Uncle would have drowned. The younger Chosŏn brother had risked his life and suffered deep cuts on his legs to save Yong Woon Uncle. Two other men trying to escape to China that same evening weren't as lucky. Dog-paddling across the river, they were pulled down by the deadly current and were gone—as if they had never been there at all.

Badly shaken by the crossing, Yong Woon Uncle stayed at the younger Chosŏn brother's house for several days to gain some strength and courage. When it was time for him to return to North Korea, he was instructed to discuss the plans for defection with his family. Hearing the plans, the family didn't think it was possible for all nine of them to leave, so they considered just sending Ae Ran and her baby. They'd tell their neighbors that she had died while wandering around looking for a way to survive. But when Hak Churl and Yong Woon Uncle left as well, it became impossible to cover up their disappearance. Mi Ran and the others finally faced the fact that if they stayed, they'd be executed, or crippled and taken to some horrible place to die.

Mi Ran was quiet for a long time, her painted lips slightly parted. Then she said in a subdued voice, "We've sinned against our aunt and Chun's mother, and because of that all our hearts ache." A tear rolled down her cheek. I didn't know how to respond, and Mi Ran, seeing this clearly, realized it was better to change the subject. She shrugged, as if shaking the sorrowful thought from her mind. "This place is so wonderful. Every day we eat three times a day, different delicious foods, and there are never less than five side dishes at each meal. Being here, we're living without being envious of others. I'm so thankful," she sighed happily, smiling at me.

I stared at this young woman, who had spoken so freely and easily. I marveled at her innocence and startling self-confidence. Being born into such an oppressive and conformist system hadn't robbed her of her ability to laugh or express her feelings. There was nothing guarded about her.

My thoughts were interrupted by the sound of Aunt summoning us to dinner. Mi Ran promptly stood up and grabbed my hands. I allowed her to lead me to the living room, where a low portable table was covered with delicious food. The entire day had been spent shopping and cooking for us. It felt like *Chusok*, Thanksgiving, because of the special rice cakes that had been prepared. They were made out of glutinous rice and shaped like half moons, the inside packed with sugar-sweetened red bean paste.

I took my place at the table. I sat down on the floor in between Aunt and

Halmoni. Mi Ran didn't sit right down. She went to the other closed door, just right of the kitchen. She rapped on it and called out in her sweet voice, "Comrade Guide." When she jarred open the door and peeked in, I saw the guide sitting on the bed, his legs loosely crossed and puffing on a cigarette. He caught me staring at him.

"Mi Ran, won't you come inside and close the door," he requested, and she did as he asked, shutting the door. In spite of myself, a twinge of jealousy gripped me. I couldn't help feeling mildly jealous of Mi Ran. I felt that was in the worst of all possible taste and unjust, but I had a feeling that the guide knew, and that was why he did it.

Smothering my ridiculous hurt feelings, I bowed my head and laced my fingers together on my lap as Halmoni said grace. Even though I was sitting beside her, her voice was so soft that I couldn't hear a word she uttered. Neither could anyone else, but we all sat absolutely still and quiet out of respect for Halmoni. I thought about saying "Amen" when she was done but decided against it.

Everyone started digging in, bulldozing mounds of food into their wide-open jaws as though it'd be taken away in a minute if they didn't eat it all. I sat back watching, because after a few spoonfuls of the gooey, tasteless rice, corn, and red lima bean gruel and a sample of the rock-hard rice cakes, bland kimchi, and dry bulgoki (marinated spicy beef), I couldn't eat any of it. Neither could my father. He was picking the food from his teeth with a toothpick, signifying he was done.

"Hae Ri, don't you like the food?" Aunt asked, concerned, her mouth full and chewing away.

"It's good." I took another bite into a hard rice cake to prove it to her. When she wasn't looking in my direction, I buried it under the gruel to make it appear like I had finished it.

From the corner of my eye I made note of Mi Ran reemerging from the bedroom. She wedged herself between her mother and me and grabbed a bowl of gruel. I wondered what she and the guide had spoken about. Mi Ran didn't say.

After a while, we found ourselves slipping into the familiarity of a family dinner despite everything we all had been through. We discussed the merits of living in China as opposed to North Korea. Even Jung Soon and Mun Churl had lost their sullen look. During their exhausting, dangerous, but fascinating trip from Changbai to Shenyang and then to Beijing, the real face of China was revealed to them slowly, mile by mile. They saw the daily hardship of farmers, the grinding poverty in the cities, the bureaucratic inefficiency at the train station, and yet it was all far better than where they had come from.

Mi Ran wanted to know about our lives in America. My father had a captive audience for his stories of how America's democratic system worked. They were stunned when they learned that citizens were allowed to elect our president every four years and could impeach our leader for bad behavior, and that we had the right to choose where to live, how to work, how to worship. They followed every word of my father's encyclopedic knowledge and commentaries. They were riveted by the new possibilities and endless horizons his words revealed. Their eyes grew wide with wonder when I told them about apartment prices in Los Angeles, the fact that I had my own car, and that my roommate was black.

"Haven't you ever seen a black person before?" I asked.

They shook their heads.

"But you must have seen people with different-colored skin and hair, right?"

"We heard that there are some," Mun Churl responded. "Wait. I did see one just briefly at a hotel in Pyongyang in 1988 while I was in the service. The foreigner had yellow hair and red nails. I remember thinking to myself, 'Ah, that's a foreigner.'"

It took me several moments and a great leap of imagination to picture the absolute homogeneity of the society that they had lived in. At the source of North Korea's isolation from the outside world was the ideology known as *juche*. It was designed to inspire national pride and identity and consciousness centered on Kim Il Sung and the party. *Juche* meant rejecting dependence on foreign nations and declaring that they were a self-sufficient economy with a self-reliant defense—a reaction to Korea's past political and economical subjugation by foreign powers in the twentieth century. The ideology had been so effective that my relatives had virtually no concept of another world across the border, and that ignorance had made them fearful and suspicious. The suspicion was so profound on both sides, North and South, that the tension increased and so did the military buildup. It was all very dangerous and very sad.

"Mun Churl, what's the first thing you want to do when you get to South Korea?" my father asked.

Mun Churl's eyes flicked down to his hands. "When I go there, I have to learn the art of driving," he said, wishful.

"Then you shall," Halmoni said, coughing and hawking into a wadded tissue.

"Anything and everything is possible now for you. If you want to go to school again, you shall. In South Korea, you can study whatever subject you wish. With an education, you can become a big person," my father encouraged him. Then he turned to Mi Ran. "And you'll be able to find a nice husband who'll treat you well and show you around."

Mi Ran giggled, and her whole face lit up. Behind her smiling dark brown eyes, she dreamed of getting married and living happily ever after. She was, in a strange way, so pure. They all were, actually. There was something old-fashioned about them, a degree of gentility and sincerity that had evaporated from the rest of us.

While everyone was talking, I got out the tape recorder and video camera. I pressed the red recording button on the Walkman and camera. When the others noticed the recording equipment, their lips automatically shut. Not until they could see that all my equipment was safely out of sight did they relax a little. When no one was looking, I reattached the tape recorder to the teeny microphone clipped to my bag and positioned the video lens through the hole in the front pocket, then settled onto the floor again next to Halmoni, out of the shot.

"One, click. One, click," Chun yelled in happy excitement as he snapped everyone's picture with an imaginary camera.

Chun was a squat child with small slitted eyes and a runny nose. He had on a bright yellow sweatshirt with the English words crab, cat, and snail written on it in a tilting, happy font. He displayed no signs of stunted growth due to malnutrition. The only thing about him that resembled the pictures of North Korean children lying listless in their bare cribs was the way his wide head was flattened in the back, similar to Ae Ran's baby. Other than that, he acted hyper, like a normal toddler just discovering the amazing strength of his legs and voice. His high-pitched screeches and excitement echoed across the room. He was having a great time dancing, falling down, picking himself up, and dancing again. He performed for us his own original dance steps with both index fingers jabbing the air, walking and squatting like a sumo wrestler.

"Where'd you learn that?" I applauded.

"Tee-bee." He grinned happily.

"What a fine boy," Halmoni praised.

"You've grown." My father hoisted Chun up into the air for a quick greeting, then set the boy down on his lap. Chun snuggled up to my father and grabbed his large ears. I could see that he liked my father very much. In fact, they all did. The women buzzed around him as if he were a returning hero. They offered him beer and coffee and laughed at his jokes. Even Chun laughed with delight. When my father sipped his coffee, Chun copied and helped himself to a cup. His mother didn't stop him. She let him drink it. To them, it was food.

Finished with his drink, Chun went off to investigate the phone. He lifted the receiver to his ear and pretended to make a phone call.

"Daddy," he said in his cute baby voice, then made another call. "Grandpa."

Suddenly the conversation at dinner stopped flowing. On the surface everyone was laughing and saying, "What a smart boy," "What a lucky boy," but there were undercurrents. I could see the constraint everywhere, between everyone. Chun felt the tension as well and wedged himself between his mother's knees, but he was too young to understand. It was good that he was too young, because how do you tell a child that his father had left him behind to die?

Jung Soon held her child fiercely against her.

"What about you, Chun's Mother? What would you like to do when you get to South Korea?" I asked, making my voice soft, trying to break through her protective barrier.

Jung Soon flicked a quick glance at me and then looked away again. Her eyes narrowed, barring me access. Everyone waited, watching her as she thought.

"Every time I eat well, live well, I become afraid for my parents. I'm trying to concentrate only on how we will live in the future. I would like to learn more about other societies. We were told our socialist system was the best in the world. The fact that we lived a lie, that they tricked us, is most regretful," she said tightly, her voice a mere thread of sound.

I could tell she was troubled by her own frankness and disloyalty, as were the others. I bet it was the first time these four had questioned their party's ideology openly. Before, they had simply accepted what they were told—that their country was a utopia, a paradise on earth. I think much of North Korea's boastfulness and isolationism were an attempt to compensate for its inferiority in technology and commerce in comparison to the rest of the world.

It was going to take some time for them to adjust to the dialogue and to understand what freedom really meant. It was going to take some time for them to trust us—they had spent their entire lives thinking that we were the enemy, when in fact we were the same people, united by our race, our language, our *hangul* script, our ancient history, our future.

~

My heart sank when it was time for us to leave. My father and the guide wanted to relocate Mi Ran's group to the new safe house that very night. We had spent almost three hours with them, two hours longer than with Ae Ran's group. Still, it wasn't enough time. Time had passed too quickly.

Again Mi Ran reached out and clutched my arm. I could feel her fear strongly, and I hated the thought of leaving her there. "It won't be long before we see each other again," I told her, trying to sound convincing, but I knew I wouldn't see her for a while. We were leaving Beijing the next day to take Halmoni to Elder Kim's *ch'iryo* clinic for a treatment. We were planning to leave her in Seoul so she'd be there to greet the family the moment they arrived in South Korea, but my father and I would continue on to Los Angeles. I had no idea when this second group or the guide would reach South Korea. At least they'd have food, warm clothes, and a secure place to stay for the time being.

Aunt tried to rearrange the creases in her face into a smile, but it didn't come out well because of the worries tucked into each fold, weighing everything down. I glanced over at Jung Soon. Even her face pleaded with us to stay. She looked so small and so scared and utterly alone. I didn't budge.

When no one moved, my father said, "This isn't the end, only a great new beginning. Until then, Sister-in-Law and you children, live comfortably and eat well, and especially be extra kind to Chun's mother."

Jung Soon didn't reply. She just remained slumped on the floor and inclined her head faintly to indicate she'd heard him. Tears streamed down her face. The brown irises of Chun's eyes filled with wonder at what all this was about, but when he looked up and saw his mother's tears, he started crying himself.

My heart broke for her as I remembered her parents. I took a step forward to caress her arm, to console her by touching, affection. She remained immobile, inconsolable. I had an overpowering urge to gather them both in my arms with all my love and strength. I wanted to promise them that everything would be all right, but I no longer believed it myself. So how could I make them believe?

My father continued in a kindly voice, "Though your heart is heavy, you must do what you said. You must look ahead toward a bright future for your son. I promise you that where you are going is a much better place."

I was the first to walk out. I hated good-byes. The door clanged behind me. As I waited in the dim, foul-smelling corridor, I saw a rat with a long kinked tail move around my feet. It was disoriented and scurried about trying to find its way out.

The student brought Halmoni out on her arm. My father was with them. He was going back to the hotel to pick up the large care package of jackets, long underwear, medicine, and dried food for Mi Ran's group.

The student led the way down the darkened corridor. We followed her. Her black dress made her almost invisible. We retraced our steps through the black tunnel and all the way back to the street. Bright headlights from an approaching car washed over us as it rounded the bend. Once the car was safely past and we were alone, the student turned to us and said, "I don't mind your relatives staying with me. Really, it's no problem. They can stay as long as they need. They're good people."

My father and I looked at her, bewildered, then realized the guide had deceived us. It wasn't her idea to move Mi Ran and the others, but his. I tried to imagine why he had done it. Mentally I flipped through a variety of possibilities, and the more I thought about it, it seemed possible that he had done it in order to manufacture a means of seeing me again.

XXVI

November 23, 1997

Thanksgiving weekend. We had a lot to be thankful for, yet I was feeling ungrateful. The worst part was the waiting. It was maddening just sitting in my apartment. It had been seven months since everything began, and for all we knew, it might be another seven months. The guide told us to be patient when we were already exercising supernatural patience. He said that we would hear some good news in about another week. It was always one more week, one more week. I was certain the guide didn't know what was going on. He was speculating. He hadn't expected our North Korean family to split into two groups and the mission to last this long. Now both groups were stuck in political limbo due to the South Korean presidential election coming up on December 18 and the economic crisis in Asia. Currencies had dropped all around the region, and South Korea faced its worst economic crisis since the founding of the Republic of Korea. The country was on the brink of bankruptcy and had to go to the International Monetary Fund (IMF) for a bailout loan. The future of South Korea was uncertain, and everyone was nervous. The KCIA still wasn't willing to commit to helping us until they knew the results of the election and what the future would be.

Regardless of who won the presidency, one way or another we needed to get Mi Ran's group out of China. Once again, my father and I realized it was up to us to find a way. We could not sit around any longer and let everyone else call the shots for us. It was our family, and we had to take matters into our own hands. If we didn't, as my father had said, in the end we would have only ourselves to blame.

However, the KCIA did hint that Mongolia might be an alternative escape route for Mi Ran's group. Nobody, neither myself, my father, nor the guide, had considered the Mongolian People's Republic as an option. The socialist republic was a remote and vast region between Russia and China, looming over China in a great arc. It was the land of Siberian blizzards and the scorching hot temperatures of the Gobi Desert, home of nomads and the legendary Genghis Khan, who led armies of herders riding horses the size of large ponies and butchered millions in the thirteenth and early fourteenth centuries.

The first emperor of the Qing Dynasty built the Great Wall to keep out Genghis Khan's armies from China, but the wall—the only man-made structure that can be seen from space—couldn't hold them back. They conquered China and founded an empire that stretched from Vietnam to Hungary.

During this period, while my father diligently communicated with the KCIA, the guide, and SBS, Mark Oh, from the FBI, contacted me again. He had slipped his business card underneath my door. I decided to see what he wanted and invited him to my apartment, since he already knew where I lived. He agreed and promptly drove over. His tall, tan, and remarkably handsome Hawaiian looks were more suited for a modeling career than secret intelligence work that required him to blend into the scenery. His straight white teeth, slightly arched nose, smoky dark brown eyes flecked with gold, and smiling mouth gave him the sort of all-American look that people tended to trust on sight. I had to admit there was something very attractive about Mark Oh, something beyond his nice features. The word that came to mind as I smiled up at him was *charisma*. When he held out his hand I took it.

"How've you been?" he asked. His handshake was solid. "How's the writing coming along? You writing anything new?"

His questions were too simple and direct, not layered and manipulative. It put me more on guard. "Not recently. Just been spending a lot of time with my grandmother."

"Great. How did everything go with your book about your grandmother? No trouble?" he asked, still smiling. He was referring to a package I'd received in the mail the year before, which I had told him about. An anonymous sender had given me a rare book titled *Song of Ariran—A Korean Communist in the Chinese Revolution,* by Nym Wales and Kim San. Arirang was actually an ancient folk song that had become symbolic of Korea's tragic history of suffering. Near Seoul there was a hill named Arirang, and on top of that hill was a giant pine tree. During the Yi Dynasty, thousands of prisoners—bandits, dissident scholars, farmers, anyone who spoke against oppression and injustice—were hung from the gnarled branches of the pine tree, their bodies suspended over the side of the cliff. The story of the Song of Ariran was one of several versions. This version was said to have been written by a young man during his imprisonment, and as he trudged slowly up the Hill of Arirang he sang this sad yet beautiful song in farewell. The song had become a symbol of climbing obstacles only to find death at the end. Yet death did not mean defeat. Out of many deaths, victory may be born.

The black-bound book had come with no signature and no inscription. I honestly didn't know what to make of it. I hadn't really thought much about it until I began to receive anonymous calls in the middle of the night. The husky male voice wanted to know everything about me, wanted to know my views on life, attempted to become friendly with me.

There was nothing the FBI had been able to do except advise me to change my phone number or move. My situation back then wasn't a threat to national security, but now the FBI considered me a possible troublemaker. Mark Oh used his charm to draw out information concerning my travels and activities abroad. I think he was trying to deduce if I subscribed to communism and held a membership in the party. He offered me my own cell phone, all expenses paid—"for your protection," he said softly. "Remember, Helie, if anyone ever gives you trouble or you just need someone to talk to, you can call me."

"How do I know you're not the bad guy?" I teased.

"I don't wear a big black hat, do I?" He grinned.

I laughed politely, accepting the phone. When Mark Oh was gone I tucked it away inside a shoebox in my closet. I thought of all the other people I knew who might be able to help us. I sifted through all the contacts I had made in the past, even if it was for a brief moment. A person did come to mind, someone I'd been introduced to by one of Steven's high-powered friends during a social event. This man had connections with the South Korean leadership, Kim Il Sung, *and* the U.S. State Department. He was fully appreciated by all the governments concerned. Without his efforts, suspicion and paranoia might have escalated to war over the years. By acting as the medium for unconventional dialogue between the two Koreas and the United States, he was able to ease tensions.

I went down the street to a pay phone because I no longer trusted the phone in my apartment. I called information in Washington, D.C. After several wrong leads, I finally reached the right person. With his generous assistance, I was able to secure an appointment with Ambassador Richard Schifter at the European Bureau of the U.S. State Department. I should have thought of this earlier. Why not bring the refugees to America? After all, I was an American citizen, and they were my relatives. I was eager to meet with the ambassador. It might be a comparatively simple task for him to advise President Clinton to order a small, well-trained military force to sneak into China and rescue Mi Ran's group. At the least, I hoped that after hearing about my family's harrowing escape, the ambassador would be moved enough to champion our cause and convince the State Department to grant political asylum.

I flew out to Washington on the red eye the first week of December. It was vital I get there before the Christmas holidays, when the government would shut down. It was my first trip to America's capital. Being there, climbing up the stone steps to Ambassador Schifter's stately building, I was reminded of Jefferson and Adams and Jimmy Stewart's movie *Mr. Smith Goes to Washington*. I felt giddy with excitement, like a schoolgirl about to come face-to-face with the president, until I walked through a metal detector and had my purse thoroughly searched for contraband. I was given a name tag to attach to my jacket before being admitted further into the building. I was told I had to wear the name tag the entire time I was on the premises.

A private secretary appeared to escort me to the ambassador's office suite. "Hello, Miss Lee. The ambassador will see you now."

I had to admit that I was a little nervous when I was shown into the office, which was cluttered with a massive wooden desk, a large brown leather sofa, several uncomfortable chairs, and glass-fronted cabinets. But the ambassador put me at ease as he stood to greet me. He was about six foot three, a distinguished elderly gentleman with thinning white hair and a warm smile. From his rubicund cheeks, I guessed he regularly enjoyed a good bottle of wine and was very comfortable in his political-appointee job.

He offered me something to drink, then reminded me that the first responsibility of being an American citizen was to vote for those who represented my interest. I listened politely to each well-delivered, hollow word, knowing that he was basically advising me to write to my congressman and senator.

I felt disappointed and frustrated. My family didn't have that kind of time. I had presumed too much. It had been naive of me to think the ambassador could bring my family to the United States. The devastating reality was that the United States wasn't in the business of accepting North Korean refugees. According to the *Newsweek* story "The CIA Lands a Big Fish" in the September 8, 1997, issue, the United States had accepted only two cases since the Korean

War. North Korea's ambassador to Egypt, Jang Sung Gil, had defected from his Cairo post into U.S. CIA agents' open arms the past August. Around the same time, his older brother, also a diplomat, who ran a shady trading outfit that reportedly funneled foreign exchange into Kim Jong Il's personal treasury, also vanished with his family into the custody of the CIA. There was speculation that the CIA may have courted the brothers because Cairo was the nerve center of Pyongyang's Middle East secret weapons trade. Jang may have had details of two missile factories North Korea had built in Syria and Iran.

What about the regular people who didn't possess a gold mine of top-secret information to barter for their lives? Who would help them? Who would help us?

We had to help ourselves. We would have to force doors open. Fortunately, we had the tools to do it. Of all the decisions we had made, of all the precautions we had taken, the one thing we did right was to make all those videotapes. Back in Los Angeles, my father and I decided that as soon as the guide and Mi Ran's group reached Mongolia, we would use the video footage of the escape from North Korea to issue a plea to the world to pry the government's doors open.

December 10, 1997

Eight days before the South Korean presidential election, we received an unexpected message from the KCIA via SBS. All it said was that it was a good time to move Mi Ran's group but to avoid the South Korean embassy in Mongolia. They didn't want the Mongolian government upset.

Why now? It seemed possible that the KCIA knew about my trip to Washington and our plans to go public with our story. Whatever the reason or motivation, we intended to go forward.

My father and I immediately surfed the Internet. We assiduously researched the roads and railway lines from Beijing to Mongolia's capital, Ulaan Baatar. We discovered that what looked like a simple but long journey on the map would be both a personal and physical challenge even on the best public bus or the fastest train. The Trans-Mongolian Railway leaves Beijing on Wednesday mornings and arrives in Ulaan Baatar the next morning, but there are many delays. At the China-Mongolia border, Mongolian officials take passports for inspection and stamping, which can take as long as six hours, and because the train crosses the border during the middle of the night, the officials have the mental advantage, since passengers are groggy with sleep.

I wasn't certain Mi Ran's group could survive being confined on a crowded train or bus for some thirty hours across several hundred miles of frightening desert. Also, if they went by train or bus, there was a greater danger of being discovered along the route by Chinese police, Mongolian border officials, or North Korean agents, now that it was known that the family had escaped. The guide and my father agreed that a plane ride was more direct and would be less risky. They'd be in Mongolia in two hours.

Led by the guide and Jambbong and his wife, Mi Ran's group entered Beijing's Capital Airport on December 10 with falsified South Korean documents. Several days before their departure, the guide had taken their photographs and given the pictures to Jambbong's wife, who then had the documents made up on the Chinese black market. Everyone was jumpy and apprehensive. The guide was very concerned about Chun's talking and exposing them. Repeatedly he warned the little boy not to utter a word, not even to his mother. The guide also took precautions with Mi Ran and my aunt's motion sickness. He gave them each a motion sickness patch to stick behind their ears to prevent nausea and vomiting.

Once inside the busy airport, two new guides from Mongolia approached the group. At that point, Jambbong and his wife slipped away. The two Mongolian men, posing as my aunt's eldest sons, escorted Mi Ran's group the rest of the way to their departure gate. The guide boarded alone, apart from the group.

At ten before nine in the morning, everyone was seated in their seats on Air China. The two Mongolian guides silently demonstrated how the seatbelts fastened and unfastened, so Mi Ran and the others wouldn't attract attention to themselves when it was time to deplane. At nine twenty-five the plane began running forward and went into the air. Mi Ran and the others weren't frightened, even though this was their first trip on a plane. They were more worried that someone would discover their counterfeit documents or that Chun would expose them. Once the plane had reached cruising altitude and they were floating effortlessly above the clouds, the refugees finally began to think that they might actually make it to South Korea.

Mi Ran's group arrived in Ulaan Baatar during the time of year when sudden snowstorms were frequent and it was extremely cold. The temperature had dropped down to minus ten degrees. My relatives wondered if they had fallen from the sky and landed in another world. They saw people wearing fur hats and long one-piece gowns and living in large white felt tents called *gers.*

The two Mongolian guides led the group to a hotel in the city and booked three rooms. Mun Churl shared a room with Hak Churl's wife, Jung Soon, and her son, acting as a married couple; Mi Ran roomed with her mother; and the guide stayed in a room with the two Mongolian guides. As everyone waited for further instructions from my father, who was working on getting the KCIA to grant permission for my relatives to enter South Korea, Jung Soon became concerned that her son was ill. Chun was unusually still and quiet. When she asked him what the matter was, he wouldn't answer her at first. It turned out that he was merely following the guide's orders not to speak. Even at such a young age, Chun had been well trained to obey authority.

Two days later, on December 12, the KCIA finally came through. They instructed my father to put Mi Ran's group on the next Korean Airlines flight bound for Seoul. Immediately, everyone was loaded into cars and driven back to the airport to catch the noon flight. At the departure gate, with four KCIA agents waiting at the entrance to the jetway, the guide said his good-byes to Mi Ran and the others. Mi Ran, realizing that this was the end of their journey with him and that he was leaving them, began to cry.

"These people will look after you now. You can trust them completely. Do exactly as they say," he said, trying to comfort her and the others. Then without ceremony he handed them over to the agents and vanished into the swarming crowd.

At noon, the plane took off, and it arrived in South Korea four hours later. Upon landing in Seoul, the agents quickly ushered my relatives into an awaiting shuttle and transported the group to a heavily secured building somewhere in the city. When the shuttle pulled up to the security gate and the gate slid open and closed automatically, trapping them inside, Mi Ran had an awful feeling that they'd been brought to a prison camp. She began to feel very afraid when they were locked away in separate rooms, photographed, and questioned intensively. The refugees were drilled about their lives in North Korea and what persecution they had suffered due to their family background and political and spiritual beliefs.

After the grueling interrogation process was completed, everyone was sent upstairs to different sleeping quarters. For three days they were kept apart from each other. Mi Ran became a nervous wreck wondering what was happening. She didn't think she could stand it another day. She begged her captors to let her see her family. She begged them for information concerning her father, Hak Churl, Ae Ran, and the baby. The KCIA wouldn't divulge any information concerning their whereabouts or well-being. They wouldn't even confirm if the group was in South Korea. Mi Ran became so frightened and exhausted she collapsed in tears, hope lost.

It wasn't until December 15, Mi Ran's twenty-sixth birthday, that the two groups were finally brought together. Before that meeting, Ae Ran, Yong Woon Uncle, and Hak Churl had had no clue that the others had escaped from North Korea. They too had been kept in the dark and isolated since secretly being flown into Seoul on October 20 at the South Korean government's expense.

The KCIA agents escorted everyone into a large conference room. When an agent came for Mi Ran, she walked down the long corridor in a state of bewilderment and turmoil, wondering what was taking place.

"Where are we going?" Mi Ran asked, uneasy.

"We thought you might like to attend a birthday party," the agent said as he opened the door to the conference room, where her parents, older siblings, sister-in-law, and nephews were gathered around a birthday cake.

For a moment no one spoke. Everyone was nervous, scared, and unsure. They stared at each other for a brief moment, and then all at once they rushed into each other's arms.

December 25, 1997

Celebrating Christmas was the last thing on my mind. My parents begged me to go with them to church and give thanks before we flew out to South Korea the next evening. The KCIA wanted us in Seoul to address the press now that the election was over. Kim Dae Jung—Korea's Nelson Mandela—won the presidency by a narrow margin because the ruling party candidates split the majority vote. At the age of seventy-two, this was Kim Dae Jung's fourth bid for the office, and after having survived a kidnapping, an arrest, a death sentence, an exile, and a house arrest, his time had finally come to lead his country. His victory was a victory for democracy.

But I didn't have it in me to celebrate or accompany my parents to church. I spent a quiet Christmas alone with a pile of cards wishing me happy holidays and a wonderful New Year. No one shared my Christmas dinner, which consisted of take-out Indian food from Tandoori House.

When the food arrived, I arranged the white containers of yellow rice and curry chicken on the end of the empty table. The stereo played Diane Reeves's *Bridges* CD. I thought food and music could console me. They didn't. Now that everything was almost over, I felt an awful sense of despair instead of the great release that I had imagined the long-awaited news would bring. The rescue operation had provided a refuge from my own life. By keeping my focus on something immense beyond myself, I was able to function. By concentrating so intensely on nine other lives, it allowed me to push Steven into the background. As long as I kept running, I could pretend most of the time that everything was all right.

I couldn't pretend anymore, couldn't run away from reality.

All of a sudden I realized the CD was over and that I could hear the watch on my wrist thickly ticking. I felt more alone now than I'd thought a person ever could be. I cranked up the music to block out my thoughts, yet the more I struggled to push Steven out of my mind, the more he became alive. I began to see his face, to hallucinate his hands cupping the back of my neck, rubbing my belly in slow circles. The weight of his hands felt so real that I was confused, almost drunk without having had a single drink.

I told myself there was no reason to see him, no good in returning to rejection, but not having any contact with him for so long awakened something desperate inside me and I felt like I would die if I didn't at least hear his voice.

Finally around midnight I couldn't stand it anymore. I called Steven's home number before I drowned in anxiety. Ringing. My heart raced. The housekeeper answered. She informed me that Steven was in Seoul.

"Do you have the number?" I asked, breathless and dizzy.

"No, but he's expecting you, Miss Cho." The shock of hearing another woman's name made me drop the receiver in the cradle. Why was it so easy for men to move on? It had been only seven months. Had he forgotten my face, my scent, my touch? Did he care that I still dreamed about him, that I was a mess? These questions took hold of me for hours and hours, and the urge to reach Steven grew until it made me insane. Suddenly I didn't want to be strong and brave and stand alone anymore. I wanted him back. It was that simple.

Frantically, I rummaged through past long-distance phone bills and tracked down the number to the Shilla Hotel. Somehow I knew he'd be there. It was three in the morning in Seoul. Refusing to think that another woman might be occupying my space beside him, I dialed the number. The hotel operator put me through to his room. My heart was hammering, as if I had run up a dozen flights of stairs.

"Hello?" I heard his sultry, hoarse voice come through the earpiece.

"Hi, it's me," I uttered softly, trying desperately to stop the rush of emotions from breaking up my voice.

"Hey, Helie. How've you been?" He spoke comfortably, familiarly, sounding genuinely pleased.

Tears ran down my cheeks. It was as though time hadn't passed, as though it would be possible to pick up from where things had crashed and burned.

"Is something wrong?" he asked softly.

My lips moved silently for a long moment before forming sounds again. "No . . . yes, I mean, I just . . . wanted to hear your voice." I took a calming breath, then started again. "I miss you."

"What?" he muttered, but I knew he'd heard me.

I repeated the lonesome words. "I miss you."

"Yeah, me too," he finally admitted.

Some of the tightness in my chest released. "Everywhere I go, I'm always looking around, hoping we'll run into each other," I confessed, half laughing, half crying. Every time I was on a plane or in Asia my eyes watched for him, because I carried a belief tucked in a secret crevice of my heart that somehow fate would one day bring us together again.

Steven didn't answer me.

"Say something, please." I couldn't bear his silence.

"I'm just listening."

I tried not to whine about the past or my regrets. Instead, I let the hurried, desperate words spill out. I let him know how intensely I needed him, dreamed of him, still loved him. I was long past the point at which my dignity could be salvaged. I went on to tell him I'd try harder to make him happy, to be everything to him a woman could be. I'd be caring, faithful, his friend, his companion, the mother of his children. There was so much to say, it felt as though I'd never be able to say it all. I rubbed my forehead, scouring my senses for the precise words. If only Steven would say "I love you," I would go to him right then and there. We could live happily ever after. We could be Cinderella and Prince Charming, whatever we wanted to be.

I stopped, unable to continue. I heard my own words and I realized how unconvincing they sounded. "I'm sorry I was wrong. I shouldn't have just left," I said miserably.

"No, you did nothing wrong. Don't apologize. It was me. I failed you. I—"

Steven faltered. I could feel his guard going up from across the distance. "Hey, Helie, I have an important breakfast meeting in a few hours. Can I call you later?"

I felt the words go through me like a knife. It hurt to breathe. I thought I might pass out. "Sure," I managed to say, feeling my senses desperately reaching out to him.

All morning I waited in bed, curled up like a ball around the phone. I was wearing Steven's white dress shirt, the one I had taken before leaving his apartment in Hong Kong. I brought it out of the closet and put it on, aching for him. It still smelled of him. The aroma of his tobacco, his cologne, his hair oil, and his body all blended into a marvelous smell. I raised the soft fabric to my face and inhaled deeply, waiting. My anxiety magnified with each passing minute. Periodically I lifted the receiver to my ear, checking and rechecking to see if there was a dial tone.

Steven never called back. In my gut I knew it was really over. A bubble of anger and hurt and indignation swelled up until I was overcome by a kind of maniacal rage I had never experienced before. Punching the pillows with my fists, kicking the furniture, and tearing clothes from the closet, I swore at him, using every cuss word I could think of, and I could think of plenty. I only remembered the rare, sweet memories, and buried the fact that Steven had chosen power and wealth over love. And I blamed myself for everything: I didn't know how to fulfill his needs, I couldn't cook, I dressed too promiscuously, I talked too much, I was too proud, too stubborn, too career-focused. The truth was that while we were together, I had been slowly going crazy with unhappiness, all the while trying to please him. I would never fit into that mold, never turn into some banker's little housewife.

When I had finished trashing my bedroom, I sat down with a pair of scissors and shredded the letters Steven had written, full of empty promises. Then I shredded his dress shirt. As the last piece of shirt fell to the ground, I felt myself sinking lower and lower. I wasn't crying for the world outside or anyone else anymore, but for myself, because I, who had always known where I was going, was ultimately lost. What lay in store for me? It was depressing to think that at the halfway point in my life, I was single, childless and lost. This was not where I had expected to be at thirty-three.

"Now what, God?" I cried, surrendering.

Slowly from somewhere deep inside a message came to me. It said that if I could withstand this, I might be able to see the thing that I was supposed to see.

선동인수각련려인공화
소. 례선서 련불 동 39만구
운 룡

FINAL JOURNEY

XXVII

My spirit felt clean. I'd been so close to the edge of a cliff for so long, afraid to fall off, that it was a relief to finally plunge into the pit of rage, kicking, thrashing, and ripping things apart. Then something rare and wonderful happened. I fell into a dreamless sleep. I slept like a lumberjack until morning. The clock said ten-twenty, and I felt revitalized. I was ready to go again. As my parents and I buckled ourselves into our plane seats, I felt ready to face whatever lay ahead of me.

As the plane took off, I stared out the window at the airport, the palm trees, the highway that led to the Pacific Ocean. The day was cloudy, and soon I could see nothing. Then the plane rose above the clouds and the sky was a beautiful dark, hard, clear blue.

My mother was animated with excitement. She had packed large suitcases filled with gourmet coffee, chocolates, and cosmetic products to give to old friends and relatives she hadn't seen for almost thirty years. I assured her South Korea had everything, just cheaper now that the Korean won had plummeted from 890 to 1,560 per U.S. dollar and was still dropping.

"I can't believe I'm going back home." My mother's voice rose with nervous laughter. This was the first time I had heard her refer to Korea as home. That quiet word, *home,* carried with it a desperate homesickness. I wasn't aware of just how much she missed Korea, how much she had suffered during the last forty-seven years, until my father had brought her a souvenir of the Yalu River in an Evian bottle. During the war, when the North Korean army was forced back to the Yalu River, many South Korean soldiers bottled the river water and presented it to their president, Syngman Rhee. It was the purest and cleanest water in all of Korea then. The water in the Evian bottle was murky, and because of my mother's practical nature I thought she would have thrown it away. She didn't. Instead, she washed her hands and face in it.

"Family is the most important thing in life," my mother said to me, looking straight into my eyes. Her eyes were dancing, and a sudden vast smile went across her face. "Now I want you to enjoy your life. I want you to be happy. You're a special lady. You can achieve whatever you want, but I don't want you to miss out on a family of your own. Find someone who'll appreciate and support your dreams. Then you'll have bigger wings."

"What if he doesn't exist?" I asked.

A small grin hovered on my mother's lips as if she knew something. "He does. When you meet him you'll know, because he's descended from heaven just for you. Halmoni and I have prayed so much for you. God has a whole file cabinet full of prayers, so don't worry."

Actually, I wasn't worried anymore. I realized that finding a husband was not a priority for me, not now that Steven was out of my system. I knew better than ever before that everything in my curious life had happened for a reason. And if it took forty-seven years to find that spectacular someone just for me, I was willing to hold on. I was not going to settle. I would never settle again. He would come to me correctly. No games, no cultural constraints, no empty promises.

I promised myself that.

Coming through the automatic glass doors at Kimpo International Airport, pushing a squeaky cart loaded with goods from America, I easily spotted Halmoni's silver permed hair. She was being wheelchaired up a ramp by Elder Kim, through the wave of sleepy people who had come to the airport at the crack of dawn. Halmoni had on the same clothes I last saw her in and a tight cream-colored padded jacket that fell just below her waist. When our eyes locked, she favored me with a wonderful smile, her face cracking into warm creases. I was glad to see that she looked a little better, brighter, healthier. There were times I hadn't thought she was going to make it, but she did. We all did.

I smiled back and threaded my way toward her. A joyful swell of relatives' undulating voices buffeted us; a tangle of arms lifted high, then embraced us. My mother became blind with excitement in the glare of recognition, the victory of return. Her energy was contagious. Cousins she hadn't seen since they were all young adults reminisced with her. Their conversation was continuously punctured by laughter. They talked gleefully about old neighborhoods, old hangouts, old people that no longer existed.

As we pushed through the revolving doors toward Elder Kim's van, we were hit by a blast of arctic wind, although it wasn't snowing yet. I'd forgotten how cold Seoul could get in December. I struggled with both hands to hold my leather jacket closed against the fierce wind trying to tear it off me. Inside the van, it was just as cold as it was outside, like stepping into a refrigerator. Our combined warm breaths immediately fogged the windows. My mother wiped a spot clear in the glass and peered out as the van followed the zigzag course out of the airport onto the highway. She pressed her face closer to the glass to stare at all the chrome and glass and glitter. I couldn't help but notice that the modern city of Seoul was a bit of a letdown for her. She had envisioned the city the way it was when she left in 1968. Even though at that time Seoul was just starting to rebuild itself after being completely gutted by the war, and my mother's family had been scraping by as refugees, it was a nostalgic time.

"Seoul looks just like L.A. except everyone's Asian. It's so strange." My mother raised her eyebrows, then asked how the country was doing. The hot topic on everyone's mind, besides the upcoming reunion, was the crashing economy and the International Monetary Fund bailout. There were signs all over the city advertising IMF Sales and IMF Lunch Specials. What was surprising, though, as well as impressive, was the attitude of my relatives. They weren't bemoaning their situation, but saying it was a blessing in disguise for the country. To them, IMF stood for "I M Fine" and "I M Fighting."

Elder Kim said that the country needed a serious wake-up call because the people had been so wasteful of energy resources. People lived like it was winter in the summer and summer in the winter, cranking up the heat when it was cold and blasting the air-conditioning when it was hot. South Koreans, like the rest of us, were caught up in the quest for material gain and success. Through purchases of goods and services, they hoped to find happiness and security.

"It's all fine. It's all fine. Now we'll have to pull together as a country. Only then can we truly work toward reunification. Only then will we know true happiness and security," declared Elder Kim.

My mind wandered as we drove. I found myself reflecting on the trials these people had endured. Then I remembered the fact that *hangul* script remained intact and that the Korean identity still existed after almost four thousand years of invasion, subjugation, and colonization by all its neighbors—the Japanese, the Chinese, the Mongols, the Manchus, and the Russians. All traces of those defeats and the Korean War were gone, and

Seoul looked as modern as Los Angeles. South Korea had huge industrial empires such as Daewoo, Hyundai, Gold Star, and Samsung—created by self-made men, by poor men, by farmers, soldiers, and engineers—and this proved that they, the people, were capable of overcoming the Asian economic crisis. The Korean spirit was indomitable, unwilling to be subsumed. And now, with a new democratic president leading the nation, it seemed possible that once the country was back onto the path of prosperity, I'd live to see peaceful reunification, perhaps even within my parents' lifetime.

Our hotel, the Koreana, was located on T'aep'yong-no, or Great Peace Street. T'aep'yong-no was a very long and wide street that stretched out to the much-hallowed Kwanghwan-mun, Gate of Transformation by Light, in the old city. The concrete gate was a classic double-roofed wooden structure with three arched passageways. It was an impressive landmark. In the olden days, the center arch was reserved for the king's use only, and the side arches were used by all others.

In front of Kwanghwan-mun was Admiral Yi Sun Sin's bronze statue, propped up on a tall pedestal. Admiral Yi was Korea's greatest hero. He had annihilated the Japanese in the 1590s during Japan's invasions of Korea by building the world's first ironclad battleships, called *kobuksun*, or turtle ships. The ships were covered with iron plating and sharp iron spikes. The bow was a dragon's head that puffed out sulfuric fumes from its mouth to create a smokescreen. Each time the Japanese fired their cannons, the story goes, the cannonballs bounced harmlessly off the turtle ships and splashed into the sea.

A uniformed doorman promptly opened the door for us, and we dashed inside. We rode the escalator upstairs to the lobby, decorated with large Christmas wreaths and poinsettias. The piped-in music was merry and light. I was pleasantly surprised to discover that the lobby was nice and toasty. From what Elder Kim had said on the drive over, I had expected the hotel to be unheated and noncelebratory.

A bellboy led us to our adjoining rooms on the eighth floor. The rooms were small and modest but had all the niceties—a television set, clean linen, and bottled water. My father had chosen the Koreana because of its close proximity to Toksu-gung, or the Palace of Virtuous Longevity, where we were told the big reunion with all nine members of our North Korean family would take place. It seemed a bizarre location to hold a serious government press conference. The press conference was the KCIA's idea, in exchange for political asylum. They wanted us to put on a good show to boost South Korea's image to the world in the face of economic disaster and the unsuccessful attempt to provide North Korea with famine aid. It was the least we could do. If they had asked us to perform human doggy tricks, we would have done them willingly.

Halmoni and I shared one room; my parents shared the other. Halmoni wasn't impressed with the new velvet outfit my mother had sewn especially for her. She just wanted the next day to hurry up and arrive. She hadn't seen or spoken to Yong Woon Uncle or the others since they arrived in Seoul. It was very hard on her to know that they were so close and yet she couldn't see them.

I wasn't in such a hurry. I wanted to savor this final trip and enjoy myself for once—take in some sights, go see a movie, eat, sing karaoke even though I couldn't carry a tune, whatever my mood favored. Unfortunately, I had to stay within the hotel, as a KCIA agent was to brief us on the scheduled press conference.

While I waited in the room with Halmoni, a question popped into my mind. I'd wanted to ask her this for a long time, and it took me a moment to work up my courage.

"If Big Uncle had been a daughter, would you have searched so long for her?"

Halmoni raised her eyebrows high and laughed silently, almost a grimace. "Life has taught me to think differently. For me, a daughter is dear."

"So if Mom had been trapped in North Korea—"

"I would have gone there myself and searched for her." Halmoni's breathy words rushed out. "If you don't have a daughter, it's all for nothing. One good daughter is equal to a hundred sons."

This was the affirmation that I had been yearning to hear, and it moved me deeply.

The KCIA agent didn't show up till eight the next morning. We all rose as he entered my parents' room, introducing himself as Special Agent Kim. He was smartly dressed in a dark blue double-breasted suit and a short tan trench coat. His wide face had a high, smooth forehead and minimal lips. He sat back on the desk chair very comfortably and crossed his legs, giving us a glimpse of the hairless skin where his trousers failed to meet his socks. This agent was more relaxed and amiable than the other agent my father and I had met at Denny's in Los Angeles. That actually made me more cautious about him.

My parents, Halmoni, and I arranged ourselves around Special Agent Kim to hear what he had to say. Speaking in a calm, intimate manner, he confirmed that the reunion was taking place on the grounds of Toksu-gung in front of the international media. Following the reunion, we'd be ushered inside a building for the press conference. We were to keep our answers simple and avoid mentioning the names of people and third-party countries involved for the sake of international peace. He looked pointedly at me when he said this and then proceeded to explain what would happen to Yong Woon Uncle's family following the press conference.

All nine members would be whisked away, out of the city. Under the tutelage of KCIA agents and generous financial support from the government, the family would spend the next three to six months being "reeducated" so that they could adjust to freedom and South Korean life. The assistance program for defectors used to last longer, but owing to the country's economic crisis, the time period had been reduced. The KCIA wanted to get the defectors adjusted as quickly as possible. They would learn to deal with strangers and con artists, shop in department stores larger than the town they came from, and learn to read the variety of foreign words South Korea used, such as *shampoo, supermarket, aspirin,* and *computer.* When they made the transition from communism into the twenty-first century, the family would be given free housing and jobs to support themselves.

"What if they need more time to adjust?" I asked.

"That may be the case, especially with the younger son, Mun Churl. He's having problems. He definitely needs careful education to reverse the effects of brainwashing." The KCIA wanted to make certain that Mun Churl wouldn't be a security risk.

"The elder son's wife, Chun Jung Soon, may have some difficulties as well," my father noted.

"Yes. She was near tears when I spoke to her. She honestly feels she doesn't have the right to be here because of her parents. As I see it, wouldn't it have been better if she was left behind?" said the agent.

An intense discomfort filled the room.

"I'm sure they're all having many different thoughts, even regrets, right now. We all have to understand that," said my mother calmly.

Special Agent Kim wrinkled his forehead. "Let's hope the process of adaptation and integration goes well."

Halmoni spoke up. "It will. For the sake of the children, it will."

Once the short meeting was over, Special Agent Kim launched himself from his chair, walked to the door, and left. When he was gone, I noticed a sudden change in my mother's face. She had on a worried frown. I could see that she was thinking over all that Special Agent Kim had said. With seriousness she leaned toward me and made an appeal. She didn't want me to write about the last seven months. Reflexively I looked up at the ceiling for guidance. There wasn't an easy answer. Unlike the SBS's documentary, cleared by the KCIA to air on the first of the new year, the stuff I had written in my journal was personal. My most intimate feelings and moments were exposed. I wasn't sure if I could share them with the whole world, even if I wanted to. I honestly hadn't thought about another book. But now, faced with the question, I also knew I couldn't commit to not writing about what had been an undeniably life-transforming experience—and one that spoke so directly to the dire situation in North Korea. I knew it would be easier to just move on with my life, because once I committed to a book, really committed to doing it, I'd have to relive the experience all over again. That prospect unnerved me. Also, I was ashamed of some of my behavior over the past months. I was afraid of losing face myself.

"How can she not write about it? She has to tell," my father said unexpectedly from where he stood next to the window.

I was curious to hear what else my father had to say.

"Even if we all have to look over our shoulders for the rest of our lives, it's a small sacrifice. This story needs to be told, or all our efforts are just self-serving. Hae Ri must let people know what horrible hardships we endured and what desperate people will go through for the chance at freedom. And"— he paused, raising his hands in a steeple against his mouth— "it'll make her a great lady."

I looked directly at my father. In the sunlight, I could see all the details of his face. Lines were appearing on his forehead and around his eyes. He had lost his rich tan, and there was a large, unsightly cold sore on his lower lip. For the first time in his life he was beginning to look his age, sixty-two, and no doubt the continual and considerable stress of the last few months had played a part in that. My father and I were silent, yet we were talking more than we had in a long time. In his burning eyes was mirrored all the love and pride and protectiveness he felt for me. He hadn't betrayed me or let me down. He had done all this for me as well. At his age, my father should have been enjoying his retired life. He was two years past his sixtieth birthday. He had successfully completed the proper life span of a human being, and he had earned the right to spend the rest of his years in ease as a respected elder. As his child, it was my duty to make his retired life as comfortable as possible, and yet he had spent his time in Asia by my side to keep me out of harm's way.

"You keep writing," he encouraged.

XXVIII

December 30, 1997

My parents' room was a chaos of clothing. My father had gone downstairs to read his newspaper in peace while Halmoni and I reclined on the king-size bed watching my mother get ready. She was making up her face in front of the dressing table mirror in her flesh-colored slip. With expertise, she applied glistening cream all over her face and neck, and blended in foundation that was a shade too light for her natural olive complexion. She then skillfully drew on black eyeliner and filled in between the black hairs of her eyebrows, extending the ends. It gave her a slightly dramatic expression. Her mouth she painted the usual rosy pink. Using a small brush, she drew in her own borders rather than settle for the ones she was born with.

"Three more hours," Halmoni announced, marking off the time ritually. She was already dressed in her black velvet outfit and had been ready to go since six. For the occasion, she had let me fuss over her hair. I'd combed, teased, and sprayed the permed curls into place like a sculptor molding a piece of clay until she cried out.

For myself, I didn't need a lot of preparation time. It took me only twenty minutes that morning to shower, make up my face, sweep up my hair into a high ponytail, and pull on an outfit. Out of necessity, I had trained myself to minimize everything from makeup to clothes to money, and I'd discovered that I could actually get by on very little.

When my mother was done filling in her lips, she pressed them together twice and inspected her work in the mirror from various angles. Satisfied, she pulled a simple knitted suit over her head. Her combed and sprayed hair became disheveled, standing up as if a gust of wind had blown through the room. Using my fingers, I brushed her hair back into place. I wanted her to look her best because today was as much her day as it was Halmoni's. She was the one who had held down the fort at home and managed the day-to-day business to pay for the mission.

My mother's hands trembled with nervous excitement as she clipped on pearl earrings. When the gems were in place, she put a hand to her fluttering heart and whispered, *"Omona."* It was all she could say.

"You look stylish," I complimented, appearing in the mirror behind her.

"You look stylish, too," she returned, and we both laughed the same girlish laugh. Then my mother slowly swiveled around and faced me. Her eyes held me motionless. "Hae Ri-ssi," she said softly. It was the first time she had inserted the honorific ending to my name, humbling herself. "I've been doing a lot of thinking since yesterday. Your daddy's right. We have to think bigger than ourselves."

"Yes." Halmoni nodded in sage agreement. "The spirit spoke to me through my dream again last night."

"That's wonderful, Mother. What did it say?" my mother asked, suddenly excited. Halmoni's dreams were always right. When the communists had imprisoned her for not turning in her husband and eldest son, she wasn't allowed to speak to the other prisoners or even pray. Those caught praying were beaten or taken to the woods and shot. Out of sheer hopelessness, Halmoni crawled into the privacy of the wretched toilet stall in the middle of the night and prayed for her release. She had to get back home. Her younger children and one-month-old baby needed their mother. There was no food, and bombs were blowing up the city. But Halmoni had no party connections or money to bargain for her life. All she had was her faith, and she prayed every night, sometimes falling asleep in the cramped, soiled stall.

One night, after Halmoni had fallen asleep in the stall, she heard an angelic voice calling out her name in a dream. "Baek Hong Yong, come with me," the voice said. The voice belonged to a woman cloaked in all white. "Come, this way," she called again, and Halmoni followed her to a dark concrete tunnel. "Trust me," the woman said. And Halmoni did. She followed the woman into the pitch-black tunnel. The voice calling to her was her only guide, but she wasn't afraid.

As Halmoni walked deeper into the tunnel, she saw a light at the very end. When she reached the light, she found herself in a lovely valley with snow-capped mountain ridges, emerald-green hills, and a pristine lake nestled at the base. "Go in," the woman urged, gesturing for Halmoni to go into the lake. Unable to swim, Halmoni became afraid. "It is safe," the woman assured her, floating to the center of the lake. Halmoni's fear was soothed by the woman's honey-sweet voice, and she submerged herself in the water all the way up to her neck. The refreshing coolness seeped into her, cleansing her. "You are free," said the woman.

The next day, the twenty-ninth of her imprisonment, the guard called out Halmoni's name and she was freed.

My mother and I listened anxiously as Halmoni revealed her latest dream.

"The spirit spoke to me last night," Halmoni repeated, and cleared her throat. "I was at my father's house, and my mother told me we should cook plenty of beef for our guests. So many people had come and gathered on our lawn to see Hae Ri, Dae Kun, and all my other grandchildren swimming in the blessed lake like Olympians. Everyone was watching you, wondering how you children could swim like that. Then I thought to myself, ah, they must have learned it in America."

"What's so great about swimming?" I questioned.

"You were showing us a new way to swim. Because you were trained in America, you have a different way of doing things, looking at things, than a Korean. Our people have for a long time tried to reunite our country but failed. It'll take someone like you, with your Korean face and American know-how, to make it happen for the rest of us."

"That's why you must write this story, or else all this will be merely self-serving." My mother touched my face gently with her warm, strong hand. Her touch was like a blessing.

Everyone was immensely relieved when the waiting was over. We all got our coats. My mother draped her previously unworn mink coat over Halmoni's shoulders. The sight of the expensive fur caused me to grunt my disapproval. It was too extravagant with the IMF crisis going on. I protested the mink, but my mother insisted. She wanted her mother to look triumphant.

"This is a great day. Halmoni should look her best when she sees my big brother," my mother decreed, her eyes alight and proud.

All of a sudden the realization hit Halmoni. "I'll see Yong Woon soon."

I could see the thought expand in her mind and figured she was remembering the long-lost innocence of those bittersweet days before the war but also thinking about the present and dreaming of good times yet to come.

At the exact appointed time, one-thirty, Special Agent Kim came for us in an unmarked white shuttle. We were efficiently herded into the vehicle and locked in. Two ramrod-straight men were already seated inside. They were both dressed in ordinary dark suits and had serious faces. They did not speak to us. Common sense told me that they were also special agents. I resisted an impulse to ask them what had motivated them to join the KCIA, and took a seat in the back between my mother and Halmoni. My father sat in the front passenger seat, looking over the headrest to make sure we were all in.

I could feel my blood move more quickly and my arms prickle all over with gooseflesh as the vehicle surged through the frenetic traffic on T'aep'yong-no. We wove quickly between cars and passed several of the city's major hotels before reaching our destination.

Toksu-gung was located across T'aep'yong-no from City Hall. The palace seemed dwarfed by the shadows of the nearby skyscrapers. The vehicle passed through the high, tile-capped wall that surrounded the grounds, and I noticed that the thick stone wall damped the sounds of the congested city traffic and the shrill din of horns. I shifted forward to get a better look at the palace that had been sitting on this very spot with stoic majesty since the mid-1400s. It was here that the five hundred years of Yi Dynasty rule (1392–1910) drew to a painful and tragic end as Japanese domination finally resulted in annexation. In August 1910, Songjung, the twenty-seventh king, issued a proclamation yielding his throne and his country to the Japanese.

Toksu-gung is now a park open to the public. It's popular for its lovely gardens of peonies and roses, water lilies and chrysanthemums. I spotted young couples dressed up in fancy black tuxes and white wedding gowns dotting the lawns. They posed in melodramatic embraces, blissfully oblivious to the cold, as studio photographers snapped their pre-wedding photos in the chilly December air.

After some time went by, there was a bang against the driver's window. I flinched. Special Agent Kim was pounding on it with his gloved fist. The driver reversed out of the parking spot. Gravel sprayed up, clattering against the wheel wells. He moved the van farther up the path to get us as close to the lawn as possible, then shifted into park, letting the engine idle. In front of us there was an imposing neoclassic stone building designed by an English architect. It was the first large Western hall in the country. At the end of World War II, the hall was used for the failed meetings of the U.S.-Soviet Joint Commission on Korean Trusteeship. To our left was one of the traditional palace buildings, with window panels ornamented with interlacing woodwork designs, exposed on the outside side and papered on the reverse side.

The door of the minivan made a loud screeching noise as it slid open. I was the first to step out, and I helped Halmoni ease out of the car. She lumbered down, one leg at a time, clutching my shoulder. Her velvet pants rode up her thin calves, revealing her thick tangerine stockings. As I bent down to adjust Halmoni's pants, I saw my father go up to my mother and gallantly take her hand on his arm. Straightening herself, my mother brushed a stray hair back into place with the automatic gesture of a girl, shy and nervous. She leaned her entire weight into my father, who stood solidly beside her with his feet firmly planted on the ground. They go so well together, I thought, and at that moment I saw him look at her with such love.

"It's time," said Special Agent Kim, glancing down at his watch.

That was our cue. I was jittery with excited energy as I locked arms with Halmoni. My mother clasped Halmoni's other arm while still clinging to my father. Together, the four of us moved along, linked in such a way that we were holding one another up. I carefully lifted my feet over the soft carpet of dried grass laced with small crusts of ice. It felt as if the air around us had thickened to the consistency of honey as we made our way along the side of the palace building, which was connected by an enclosed walkway to another almost identical building.

"I can't believe this is really happening." My mother's jaw trembled with the emotions she could no longer keep in. A few breaths snagged on sobs.

Halmoni, on the other hand, was totally relaxed. Her face had the serene look of the very old. It seemed as though she didn't even notice the almost absurd surroundings—palaces, wedding gowns, and media. A flock of reporters in brightly colored windbreakers aimed their telephoto cameras at us and shouted at us to look their way, but we listened only to Special Agent Kim and the other agents, who formed a circle around us. They urged us toward the open lawn area in front of the two connecting buildings. As we rounded the corner, I saw all nine members of our North Korean family lined up on the grassy platform. They didn't approach, but looked at us anxiously.

I couldn't get over their transformation. I was struck by how handsome they looked. Their hair was stylishly trimmed and slicked down with glistening gel, and they were well dressed in dark suits. Yong Woon Uncle, Aunt, and Ae Ran were even fitted with prescription glasses. However, it was Hak Churl who made the most startling transformation. He looked like a totally different person. His face was dramatically younger and lighter. The deep wrinkles had noticeably vanished, and his complexion was now a polished olive. He was very attractive.

Standing beside Hak Churl was his wife, Jung Soon, smiling shyly, and their son was in his arms. Mun Churl stood very straight, solid, next to them, smiling hesitantly. Seeing them was fantastic and painful all at the same time. Beneath the disguise of fine department store clothes and new haircuts and smiles, the events and circumstances still existed. The betrayals and old loyalties, philosophies, and distrust weren't forgotten. Everyone had been profoundly scarred.

As if suddenly awakened and shaken alive, everyone burst into wails. I was caught up in the shuffle and sway, the friction of movement. The edges of our bodies blurred into one massive, undulating shape, and our tears mingled. Low, moaning cries and high-pitched laughter flew from our mouths in plumes of steam.

My mother's cries were the loudest. Her shoulders rose and fell as she gasped for breath in the midst of her sobs. Yong Woon Uncle threw his arms around her, embracing her tightly, almost strangling her. The touch of him made her wail even louder. Her mouth stretched wide open across her shiny crinkled face. The sound they made together had a rich inner harmony, with Yong Woon Uncle's rapid, chirpy speech overlaying my mother's deep, slow voice. I willed my mother to release the war demons and ghosts. They couldn't haunt her any longer.

Then Yong Woon Uncle staggered over to Halmoni on unsure feet. When she saw him, she tearfully reached across, and he flew into her arms. She cradled him tenderly to her breasts like an infant, as if trying to undo all the harm that had come to him. He burrowed his face into her and sobbed with the anguish of a lifetime.

Free at last. At last.

I smiled and closed my eyes over warm tears. A stillness settled over me. I couldn't remember the last time I had experienced such peace. I let myself float suspended in a state of quiet timelessness, letting out the deepest breath ever. The feeling that washed over me right at that moment was so divine, so exquisite, it felt baptismal.

When I opened my eyes, Ae Ran stood directly before me. I looked at her with a sharp intake of breath. A kaleidoscope of emotions pounded through me as I considered exactly how I felt toward her, Yong Woon Uncle, and Hak Churl. Anger, compassion, love? I decided I felt all of the above, plus admiration. It took a lot of courage to defect, casting themselves away from everything they had known, trusting us. If it hadn't been for Ae Ran's tenaciousness, we never would have found them.

I pulled her to me and bound my arms around her. Ae Ran's arms went around me immediately, and we held each other close. She squeezed me hard around the neck with the crook of her arm, my face pressing into her clean, creased collar. Her baby, hitched on her hip, was smashed between us, but he didn't protest the smothering.

I felt Ae Ran's heavy tears and hot breath against my cheek as she cried into me. I felt her years of anguish making everything inside me quake again. I held on to her even tighter, our bodies fused together, until the energy between us conquered the trembling and we began laughing out loud uproariously. Suddenly I saw her as she was, bright and attractive. I wanted to hug her again and again, but she broke away and joined her family.

All nine of them formed a semicircle in front of Halmoni. All together, they brought the backs of their palms to their foreheads, knelt down slowly on the grass, and lowered their heads to the ground, bowing deeply in the most respectful way.

As Halmoni stood before them, she held herself with a simple and powerful dignity. She was absolutely beautiful with her hands folded in front of her, her head slightly lowered, and her eyes squeezed shut. I could see her lips move in prayer. In this amazing scene, Halmoni's life was a testimony to Korea's tragic history, desperate longing for unity, and destiny.

Should I ever doubt that God is great, please let me remember this day.

XXIX

December 31, 1997

On the eve of the new year, my thoughts floated from the reunion to the guide. I had looked around for him at Toksu-gung, but he wasn't present. I couldn't believe he'd miss the moment he had worked so hard for. He deserved to be there. I felt a need to see him, to resolve our unfinished business, before I resumed my life in America. I couldn't just wipe him out of my consciousness and pretend that he didn't exist. I wasn't going to do that anymore. I wanted to start the new year clean. When I finally tracked the guide down and asked him to meet me, I was concerned he would refuse my invitation, but he agreed. I let the guide choose the time and place—four o'clock at the Windsor Café in the Lotte Hotel.

The café was an exceptionally luxurious formal room with rich oil paintings, yet it also looked like an intimate English pub. From each table glowed pools of inviting light made by small candles. The place was pretty empty. A small group of businessmen and a couple were scattered at the highly polished wooden bar. I spotted the guide seated in a paneled alcove in the rear. He was leaning back in the deep leather booth, his legs stretched and crossed at the ankles. His clothing was a surprise. He had on pressed black trousers, a black knit turtleneck, and a blazer that was an indistinct smooth color—taupe, maybe. Very trendy and not at all the kind of thing I expected him to wear.

I began to thread my way among the furniture, high heels clicking against the marble, approaching him. Although I usually abstained from wearing anything too glamorous, wealthy-looking, or sexy, today I had permitted myself to dress up in a red chiffon dress. The dress wasn't suitable for the streets of Seoul or the winter weather, but it was just right for me. I had bought it at an

337

expensive boutique after littering the floor of my hotel room with the contents of my luggage and finding fault with every outfit I owned. It made me feel pretty and self-confident, even more aware of my femininity.

Slowly the guide stood. His dark hair shone, and I realized again that his features exerted some kind of fascination over me. He had his own beauty, a kind of rugged, solid quality—not too smooth and not too perfect.

The guide reached over to help me take off my jacket. He measured my décolletage with his eyes so swiftly that I almost missed it.

"Thanks." I acknowledged his chivalry with a smile as I slid into the cushioned booth. The guide had taken the liberty of ordering me red wine. I glanced at the glass. I didn't have a craving for it anymore. In front of the guide was a chilled bottle of Hite beer and a tall glass.

"How's Halmoni?" he began conventionally.

As we exchanged pleasantries, pretending this was a casual encounter between old friends, I was thinking that after almost a year, I knew almost nothing about him except the brief sketch of his life I had extracted from him. He was an extremely complicated man with many layers beneath the surface. I guess it really didn't matter now that our mission was accomplished, but for my own peace of mind I wanted to know the real reason why he had done what he did. The question crowded my head, and I had to ask. "Why did you do all this for us?"

"You mean besides you?" He smiled affectionately.

I could feel myself blushing. "Do you do this sort of dangerous work often?"

"Do you always ask so many questions?" he came back at me, still smiling, then began again in a softer, more serious voice, to bring me closer. "At the end of your book, you asked Halmoni, 'Is there anything in your life you would change if you could?' She answered, 'If I could change one thing, it would be the fate of my firstborn. That is my one regret.' I understand that." He stopped, hesitated for a few seconds, and then asked, "Did I ever tell you my father's name?"

"No, what's his name?" I answered just as softly, brushing back a lock of hair that had fallen over my eye.

"His name . . . my father's name was Lee Yong Woon," he said with a long sigh of memory, "and when I finally found him and my older brother in North Korea, it was too late. My father had passed away. I wasn't able to save him. That is my one regret."

Our eyes melted together. I understood now. That was his role, his personal mission. Also, I sensed it had to do with his love for his country, his people, and his passion for reunification. I had been wrong about him. He wasn't afraid of life. He was an extraordinary man who challenged life and attempted to change the injustices, for which he paid a tremendous price—long years of separation from home and family. I wanted to know more about him, but I was aware that I never would. Too much would have to be said if either of us ever began to try.

So I took his hand where it was resting slackly on the table. It was cold and still. The guide turned his hand up so his and mine were palm to palm, our fingertips exploring the texture. I traced his faint lifeline. Of all the people I'd encountered and known this year, this almost-stranger had seen more of me than anyone else. He read me too well and saw my thorns and scars. I'd endured humiliation and gained courage from him. He made me adventurous and daring and compelled me to think deeply about who I am.

"Thank you," I said at last. "You're very brave."

"Am I?"

"Very, very." I punctuated the confirmation with tiny nods.

There was a tenderness in his gaze that made me catch my breath.

At that moment there was a profound understanding between us. We both knew that we would not see each other again. We would go our separate ways.

"If I were ten years younger," he started to say, and then his words vaporized. He didn't have to say it. It was all in the nerves of his skin, his eyes. As he breathed deeply, I distinctly heard the river. For a long time, I sat there, listening to the river until his breathing became more regular.

"I want you to go back to your life in America, your family, and your future."

"And if I don't?"

"I want you to follow me to China or Mongolia or wherever, and we'll live on rice and love. And if you agreed, I'd be terrified. I'd run so fast. I don't want to be unfair to you."

My lips opened and closed to utter a response, but only air escaped. His words touched me, but I didn't know how to tell him. I couldn't think of what to do.

Seeing my hesitation, the guide pressed a soft kiss in the palm of my hand, then withdrew until only our fingertips touched. He smiled tremulously and sat back into the booth. The contact broke.

He watched me as I gathered my jacket and purse and slid to my feet.

When I turned to leave, I could feel his eyes following me, willing me to keep walking.

I walked out of the café, the hotel, onto the dark street, my breath scrolling out a signature before me. The wind whipped the hemline of my jacket and the dress underneath. Its layers of red chiffon flirted with the air. I didn't bother to tuck my skirt around my legs like the other women. I walked on, uninhibited. It felt good to feel the sensation of the soft material rubbing against my thighs with each step I took. My whole body was flashing hotly and freezing cold, all senses were unbelievably aware of the life around me. I noticed and savored everything. I saw the orange moon and stars in the deepening blue sky. I saw each neon light, each winter leaf, each pebble, and each fluttering skirt.

I was alive.

Author's Hope

My family was given a great gift. Sometimes my hands and legs twitch with disbelief that we actually accomplished something that I'd never thought possible. Today, five years later, I am grateful to say that my relatives are living happily in South Korea. Yong Woon Uncle and his wife are retired and living comfortably in an apartment in Seoul, enjoying their grandchildren, attending church, and getting to know our extended family. Ae Ran and her son live in the same apartment building, one floor up from her parents. Ae Ran worked at an insurance company and was honored as top salesperson but then went into business for herself and opened a small restaurant that serves traditional North Korean health food, including her specialty, herb rabbit stew. Hak Churl is employed by the city's environmental department, and his wife, Jung Soon, teaches math at a junior high school. In 1998, they rejoiced in the birth of their second son. Mun Churl works for Pohang Steel Company in the city of Pohang, where he lives with his new bride. And Mi Ran got everything she dreamed. She married a sergeant in the ROK army and had a healthy son on August 17, 2001.

Being in South Korea, my relatives are living without fear or hunger, just with thankfulness. But there are still so many war-torn families agonizing. There are still so many people trapped in North Korea struggling to survive famine and oppression. Those fortunate enough to escape are forced into hiding. There are thousands of refugees hiding out in China, Russia, and Mongolia in absolute terror of being repatriated, because the United States and other nations deny them protection. Without finances and connections, there is no telling how long the refugees will be able to survive.

Who will come to their rescue?

On January 1 and 2, 1998, the Seoul Broadcasting System (SBS) aired our family's dramatic escape in a four-hour documentary to boost unity in the face of economic disaster. Afterward the station was so overwhelmed by responses that they aired the documentary again a month later, on the lunar new year.

Sometimes as I sit at home in America and remember back, I can't believe that the woman on the videotape running around China with Halmoni and my father is me. There were many times when I wanted to throw in the towel because I was going mad with fear and exhaustion, and then in my darkest moment, when I thought I couldn't go on any longer, a message had come to me. It said that once I got through the darkness I would be able to see something I was supposed to see. It wasn't until I reread my journal a year later that the message suddenly made sense to me. I realized that the mission was as much a journey of self-discovery as a rescue attempt. I needed to go through the experience to find out not simply who I am, but what and why. I understand now that I have a role, a responsibility, as an American, a Korean, a woman, and as a writer. I owe it to those who were left behind to take a stand. I haven't forgotten about them and will never forget them. By sharing my family's story with you, I hope to shine a bright light on North Korea's obscene dictatorship and what happens to people's humanity under such a regime.

I believe one family, one person, one action can make a difference, because we are all connected. When we realize this connection, peace is possible.

If you would like to contact the author, you can e-mail her at the following address: helie@helielee.com.

Made in the USA
Lexington, KY
03 April 2011